EDWARD GARNETT
A Life in Literature

EDWARD GARNETT
A Life in Literature

George Jefferson

JONATHAN CAPE
THIRTY BEDFORD SQUARE LONDON

To Sylvia

First published 1982
Copyright © George Jefferson 1982

Jonathan Cape Ltd, 30 Bedford Square, London WC1

British Library Cataloguing in Publication Data

Jefferson, George
Edward Garnett: a life in literature.
1. Garnett, Edward   2. Authors, English – 20th
century – Biography
I. Title
828'.91209   PR6013.A67Z/

ISBN 0 224 01488 9

Printed in Great Britain by
Butler & Tanner Ltd, Frome and London

Contents

	Acknowledgments	vii
	Introduction	1
1	A Touch of the B.M.	5
2	The Young Garnetts	15
3	The Cearne	31
4	Reader's Task	39
5	Conrad	55
6	Leaving Unwin	71
7	Reader as Critic	85
8	Reader as Reviewer	96
9	Galsworthy	109
10	Playwright	118
11	The Mont Blanc	128
12	The Young Lorenzo	143
13	Dostoevsky Corner	160
14	Pond Place	174
15	Cape	192
16	Literary Conscience of the Firm	206
17	'Miss Bates'	225
18	New Generation	239
19	Familiar Faces	261
20	Dew on the Garlic Leaf	275
	Abbreviations	291
	Notes	293
	Index	341

Acknowledgments

I wish to express my profound appreciation of the help and kindness of the late David Garnett and of his son, Richard Garnett. Their generosity in making available so much material essential to the writing of the book, with permission to use this and other documents without restriction, was accompanied by hospitality at Hilton Hall and by conversations and correspondence which added much to the finished manuscript.

I am also very grateful to Mrs Anne Lee Michell who allowed me to read, and gave me permission to quote passages from, the diaries of Olive Garnett 1890–1906, and to Mrs Caroline White for permission to use her notes of the reminiscences of Nellie Heath.

My thanks are also due to Sir Rupert Hart-Davis and to the late Henry Green who spoke to me of Edward Garnett and gave me permission to quote from their recollections. I also acknowledge with gratitude permission to quote from letters to me about Edward Garnett from the late Richard Church, the late Malcolm Elwin, Lady Naomi Mitchison and Frank Swinnerton. Permission to quote from a letter to me from the late William Plomer was kindly granted by Sir Rupert Hart-Davis. I am also grateful to Admiral Sir Angus Cunninghame Graham for the loan of letters exchanged between his uncle and Edward Garnett.

I wish to thank the following for their generosity in granting me permission to quote from unpublished letters and copyright material: Mrs Rhoda Goodwin (letters written by her husband, Geraint Goodwin), Mr H. A. Manhood, Lady Naomi Mitchison, Mr Sean

O'Faolain, Mr Liam O'Flaherty, Mrs Myfanwy Thomas (letters written by her father, Edward Thomas, and her mother, Helen Thomas).

For permission to quote from copyright material I acknowledge with thanks the following: the Estate of the late H. E. Bates for extracts from unpublished letters, and Max Parrish Ltd for extracts from *Edward Garnett*, and Michael Joseph Ltd for extracts from *Blossoming World;* Teresa Campbell (daughter of Roy Campbell) for extracts from letters written by Roy Campbell to Edward Garnett; the Trustees of the Jessie Conrad Estate for letters written by Jessie Conrad; the Trustees of the Joseph Conrad Estate for extracts from the writings of Joseph Conrad; the Trustees of the Literary Estate of R. B. Cunninghame Graham for extracts from his letters; J. Robert Haines for extracts from letters written by W. H. Davies to Edward Garnett; the Estate of Walter de la Mare for extracts from unpublished letters to Edward Garnett ©1982; David Higham Associates Ltd for extracts from the writings of Ford Madox Ford; the Provost and Scholars of King's College, Cambridge for extracts from unpublished letters written by E. M. Forster to Edward Garnett, E. M. Forster texts © 1982; the Trustees of the Galsworthy Estate for extracts from the writings of John and Ada Galsworthy; Sebastian Yorke for extracts from letters written by Henry Green; William Heinemann Ltd for extracts from unpublished letters written by William Heinemann to Edward Garnett; the letters written by B. W. Huebsch to Edward Garnett are used by permission of Viking Penguin Inc., copyright © 1982 by Viking Penguin Inc.; Laurence Pollinger Ltd and the Estate of the late Mrs Frieda Lawrence Ravagli and William Heinemann Ltd for extracts from *Collected Letters of D. H. Lawrence, D. H. Lawrence: Letters, D. H. Lawrence, Phoenix II*, and the University of Nottingham Press for extracts from *Lawrence in Love: letters* (written to Louie Burrows), and University of Wisconsin Press for extracts from *D. H. Lawrence: A Composite Biography*, and for extracts from unpublished letters by Lettice Lawrence (Mrs Ada Clarke) and Frieda Lawrence; the Trustees of the T. E. Lawrence Trust for extracts from letters written by T. E. Lawrence; the Estate of the late Henry Lawson for extracts from letters written by Henry Lawson to Edward Garnett; the two extracts from *Fanfare for a Tin Hat* by Eric Linklater and extracts from two unpublished letters are reprinted by permission of A. D. Peters & Co. Ltd; the Society of Authors as the literary representative of the Estate of John Middleton Murry, new John Middleton Murry texts © 1982

the Estate of John Middleton Murry; the Estate of Eric Partridge for
an extract from a letter written by Eric Partridge to Edward Garnett;
the Estate of the late John Cowper Powys for extracts from unpublished letters, and University of Wales Press for an extract from *Essays
of John Cowper Powys;* V. S. Pritchett for an extract from his article in
Saturday Review; Sheena Odle, Literary Executrix, Dorothy M.
Richardson Estate, for extracts from letters written by Dorothy
Richardson to Edward Garnett; the Society of Authors on behalf of
the Bernard Shaw Estate for extracts from unpublished letters written
by G. B. Shaw to Edward Garnett, Henry Salt and T. E. Lawrence,
©1982 The Trustees of the British Museum, The Governors and
Guardians of The National Gallery of Ireland and Royal Academy of
Art; the Executors of the Estate of the late H. G. Wells for extracts
from letters written by H. G. Wells to Edward Garnett; Richard
Williamson, the Literary Executor of the Henry Williamson Estate,
for quotations from Henry Williamson's writings; Mrs M. T. Parsons
for extracts from two letters written by Leonard Woolf to Edward
Garnett; David Higham Associates Ltd for extracts from unpublished
letters by Francis Brett Young to Edward Garnett.

I am greatly indebted to the staff of the following libraries for their
kindness and help to me during my researches into their collections and wish to acknowledge with gratitude their permission as
owners of the documents to quote from material by and relating to
Edward Garnett: Henry W. and Albert A. Berg Collection, the
New York Public Library, Astor, Lenox and Tilden Foundations
and the Humanities Research Center, the University of Texas at
Austin.

I would like to thank the following libraries for their help and
permission to quote from material in their possession: Colby College;
Columbia University Libraries; Cornell University Library; Uni-
versity Library, University of Illinois at Urbana-Champaign; the
Trustees of the National Library of Scotland; Collections of American
Literature, Beinecke Rare Book and Manuscript Library, Yale
University.

The original spelling of the documents quoted has been retained
throughout.

I am greatly indebted to the British Academy for the award of an
Overseas Visiting Fellowship which allowed me to conduct research
in America.

I am very grateful to Deborah Shepherd of Cape for her detailed scrutiny of the manuscript and for the many suggestions for improvement.

My final and special expression of thanks is to my wife for her encouragement and patience as research assistant in America. In some token of this the book is dedicated to her.

1982   G.J.

Introduction

THE road to Edenbridge, by Limpsfield Chart, winds its way by the church to enter the woodland where trees grow high on either side. About three hundred yards along an unmade track that joins the road on the right, a house stands looking over the wide sweep of country where Surrey joins with Kent.

Built in the closing years of the last century, it became a familiar sight to authors as various in their work as Ford Madox Ford, Joseph Conrad, W. H. Hudson, John Galsworthy, W. H. Davies, Edward Thomas, D. H. Lawrence, H. E. Bates, Liam O'Flaherty and Sean O'Faolain. The house, which he named 'The Cearne', was the country home of Edward Garnett.

Elusive and ubiquitous, his name appears in footnotes to literary histories and to studies of many writers now seen as important to an understanding of twentieth-century literature. When he died in 1937, obituary notices, though rarely repositories of literal truth, were consistent in their homage to a man who 'for about 30 years ... occupied himself in telling authors what to write, how, and how not to write ... and who ... by some curious semi-hypnotic process ... generally got his suggestions accepted, with the result that the Garnett mind left its impress on much of the important creative literature of his time.'[1]

There are many examples in literary history of those whose own contributions to creative writing have been negligible but whose activities as critics, editors or reviewers have had a formative influence on the literature of a period. In some cases this influence has been inextricable from the force of personality and from a reputation earned over the years in the exercise of literary judgment. Johnson, for example, is remembered more as the figure depicted by the feckless Boswell than for *Rasselas*: his mannerisms, utterances and critical faculties rather than his original work give him a legendary position in literary history. Though a much lesser figure, Garnett was as single-minded in his devotion to literature. He was also, as a younger colleague wrote, 'a unique personality in the literary life of England during at least two generations, and [had] an exacting but singularly charming and amazing faculty for friendship'. 'It was paradoxical', he continued, 'that Garnett should know so much about the art of writing and himself write so little and with such difficulty. It was paradoxical that he should be so little known to the general public while the men he discovered and fostered and advised should become accepted, and even popular, masters. It was paradoxical that, under a cumbrous and even crabbed exterior, he should have such grace of mind and sly kindliness, and such a store of self-effacing patience.'[2]

He is remembered with affection by all who knew him, but as these diminish in number with the passing years, the distinction of Edward Garnett needs to be recorded. His contribution to literature was vicarious by nature. It was made by personal association with successive generations of aspiring authors and by a literary acumen deployed as a publisher's reader in the twilight world that lies between literature as a creative art and literature as an article of commerce. It was made by the reviews he wrote which attempted to single out the work of the then unrecognised, but now accepted, authors of worth from the ruck of the popular and now forgotten. It was made by the advocacy of foreign exemplars such as Turgenev and Dostoevsky at a time when insular attitudes tended to stifle literary development.

In appreciations and in criticisms, either published or in unwearying correspondence with the authors he advised, Garnett had a care for the novel as a form of literary art that anticipated in some ways the approaches developed later by critics such as Leavis. Yet he remained, as E. M. Forster called him, a shadowy figure behind the scenes. To bring Garnett out of the shadows is to view him, like a character created by his friend Conrad, from the shifting viewpoints of the surviving correspondence of those with whom he worked or had some acquaintance. To H. E. Bates he was the last of the great Victorian eccentrics, and for Henry Green, 'at first sight, he appeared a pale-faced, menacing, wordless object, immeasurably tall'.[3] This formidable façade, however, masked a kindliness that soon established a rapport with an author and his work. An understanding of the writer's predicament coloured his association with aspiring authors from his earliest days as a publisher's reader. To this perception of the author's difficulties in creation he brought a firm belief in the rightness of his judgment and an equally firm conviction that literature and life were synonymous. These characteristics were undoubtedly encouraged by his upbringing in an environment of family and friends who were influential on the cultural outlook of the day. The story of Edward Garnett, archetypal 'outsider', begins at one of the cultural pillars of the Establishment – the British Museum in Great Russell Street.

ONE

A Touch of the B.M.

ONE of the commonplace observations on the Victorian Age is that it had produced by the turn of the century a few families who, through inherited ability, intermarriage and friendships, had become predominant in intellectual and cultural life – the Darwins, the Huxleys, the Stracheys, the Stephens. Referring to modern times, regret seems to tinge Richard Hoggart's rhetorical question: 'What of the opinion formers and their channel of influence? ... the guardians, the elite, clerisy (If there is such a body?). Where do they come from? Who, if anyone, has succeeded the Stephens and the Garnetts.'[1]

The cultural and intellectual foundation of the Garnetts was laid in the north of England. In the latter part of the eighteenth century, William Garnett – Edward's great-grandfather – carried on his business as a paper manufacturer at Otley in Yorkshire. The firm still operates under the name of Garnett, which is painted in large letters along the side of the mill that stands by the river Wharfe and faces the Chevin, the hill that dominates the grey market town. William Garnett had three sons – Richard, Jeremiah and Thomas.

Thomas, the youngest, was born in 1799. He became head of his uncle's manufacturing concern at Clitheroe and had a lively and speculative interest in science and its application. Jeremiah, who was born in 1793, worked in the office of Wheeler's *Manchester Chronicle* before joining J. E. Taylor in launching the *Manchester Guardian*. During the early and difficult years of the paper he acted as printer, business manager and sole re-porter. On the death of Taylor in 1844 he became editor until his retirement in 1861. His connection with the paper influenced the growth of its readership throughout the North-West, among 'tories and leaguers' as well as those in sympathy with its liberal politics. A reader with a catholic taste, to the end of his life he kept up with most of the important books of travel, history, biography and fiction.

The eldest son, Edward's grandfather Richard, who was born in 1789, attended Otley Grammar School. After school he learned French and Italian in preparation for a career in a mercantile house but decided instead to help in the family firm. He continued to develop a natural talent for languages by teaching himself German. Realising that his vocation lay in more scholarly fields he took up the post of assistant master at the school of the Rev. Falkner at Southwell in Nottinghamshire in 1811. Within two years he had taught himself divinity and a standard of Latin and Greek sufficient for ordination by the Archbishop of York. As curate at Blackburn and assistant mas-ter at its grammar school, he continued to study and research the European languages. When his first wife, whom he had married in 1822, died in 1828, he moved to the post of priest-vicar at Lichfield Cathedral. Here he absorbed himself in the study of the new science of comparative philology. In 1834 he married his second wife, Rayne, daughter of John Wreaks of Sheffield, and accepted the living of Chebsey, near Stafford, in 1836.

Two years later he relinquished his living to become assistant-keeper of printed books at the British Museum, at a time when Panizzi was embarking upon its transformation from a series of miscellaneous collections towards his conception of a coherent national library. Richard Garnett proved to be a loyal and hard-working second-in-command and they got on well together. Garnett combined conscientious attention to his duties with active interest in the new Philological Society, contributing extensively to its transactions. By the time of his death in 1850 he was recognised as an outstanding scholar and philologist.

He had two sons, Richard (Edward's father) and William John, and a daughter, Ellen Rayne. Richard, born at Lichfield in 1835, inherited his facility in languages. Educated at home with little formal schooling, he was intellectually precocious and firm in his distrust of the educational efficacy of the universities, so much so that on his father's death he declined the proposal of relatives to prepare him for entry to Oxford or Cambridge.

Instead he preferred to accept an assistantship in the British Museum which Panizzi, in tribute to the self-effacing scholar whose comparatively early death had been such a bitter blow, persuaded the Trustees to make available to one so young. It was an act of kindness that drew a warm letter of thanks from the widow and which the biographer of Panizzi has called a wise move, for: 'Richard Garnett was to dominate, in his own way, the next generation at the Museum, as Panizzi had done his, and was always grateful to his old keeper for giving him his first chance.'[2]

For nearly fifty years Richard Garnett worked in the Museum; his ability was soon recognised by Panizzi and in turn his admiration for his mentor made him determined to carry out those reforms and innovations that Panizzi had initiated.

His first task as copier of titles for the catalogue was soon followed by that of placer, which involved classifying and shelving new acquisitions. By 1875 he had been promoted to assistant-keeper of printed books and superintendent of the Reading Room. In 1881 he was also made responsible for resuming the compilation of the printed general catalogue which Panizzi had inaugurated, and however long and tiring the day he never went to bed without doing some work on it. Editorial work occupied more and more of his time until his appointment in 1890 as Keeper of Printed Books.

Wide experience was matched by such a tenacious memory that anecdotes, apocryphal or otherwise, circulated on the phenomenon of Garnett's bookmanship. He had an uncanny knowledge of even the most unlikely parts of the library, derived no doubt from his days as a placer. This was accompanied by a polyglot learning that came from a lifelong study of the classics and of the literatures of France, Germany, Italy and Spain. He was especially interested in the Popes of Rome, the Byzantine Empire, the poetry of Shelley and his contemporaries, South America – and cats. (A love and understanding of cats characterised all the Garnetts and his son Edward edited a family periodical entitled *The Cats Newspaper*. In this he recorded the liaisons, births and deaths of the cats at his home in St Edmunds Terrace.) Altogether Richard Garnett spoke seven languages and wrote many more. He edited numerous poets, and contributed voluminously to nearly every literary periodical and to literary histories and biographical series. In his *Twilight of the Gods* he revealed in semi-classical tales a vein of pleasant scepticism and irony that has worn well and was in tune with his personality.

His character was marked by a civilised, rational approach to life with that dash of eccentricity common to many Victorian scholars. In Richard's case it took the form of a firm belief that astrology was as much a physical science as geology. This 'secret life in occult affairs' he kept strictly to himself and he published papers under the assumed name of A. G. Trent. His discretion attracted confidence and 'enwraps Richard like a veil'.[3] Legions of ladies sought and obtained his friendship as a kind of father-figure. Lady Shelley for instance placed her trust in him. In their long association while preparing the *Relics of Shelley* for publication, she knew she could rely on him not to tarnish the poetic idyll. In his professional life Richard was adviser to countless enquirers who relied on his knowledge and kindliness, and this brought about a vast correspondence with scholars in every part of the world. Ford Madox Ford remembered him as 'one of the quaintest, most picturesque and most loveable figures of English literary life', and 'surely the most erudite man as far as books were concerned'.[4]

Richard was courteous and absent of mind. His home life was that of the Victorian paterfamilias. In 1863 he had married Olivia Narney Singleton who came from County Clare in Ireland. With her brother Edward she had spent her early life at Kilmaedan Castle until her mother took a house in Camden Square in London. Warm-hearted, witty, vivacious and with the Irish gift as a raconteur, Narney (as she was called) was well suited to Richard. A typically philoprogenitive couple, their children were produced at regular intervals: May (1864), Robert (1866), Edward (1868), Olive (1872), Lucy (1875), Richard (1877, who died in infancy), and Arthur (1881). The character of the family life in which Edward grew up has been described by his son David Garnett as an 'odd blend of Victorian respectability with complete liberality of opinion. The children were undisciplined and extremely untidy; only when they exhibited anything like worldliness or self-seeking were their parents surprised or shocked.'[5]

The nursery of these unruly children was supervised by 'Chapple', Narney's diminutive maid, who had begun service in the Singleton family at the age of fifteen. A romantic by nature, Chapple was a confidante in the clandestine romances of the children's friends, such as Ford Madox Hueffer and Elsie Martindale. As the children grew older Chapple connived at their waywardness, abetting Edward in raiding the larder on his visits home and in helping himself to the clean shirts of his father and brother Robert. They regarded her with affection and she was cared for by the Garnetts in sickness and old age until her death in 1902.

Liberal values, intellectual commitment and altruistic attitudes characterised the family living at No. 3 St Edmunds Terrace, a row of tall houses on Primrose Hill. Three doors away at No. 1 was a special friend, the artist Ford Madox Brown. In childhood and adolescence, the lives of the young Garnetts were bound up with those of the children of Madox Brown's two daughters: Lucy, who married W. M. Rossetti, and Catherine, who married the German music critic Hueffer.

Edward grew up in a world peopled by Victorian littérateurs, scholars and critics who called on his father either in the ordinary course of his work or from friendship, and by those who attended the 'At Home' evenings held by Narney on Thursdays. Frequent visitors were George Meredith, Coventry Patmore, the Rossettis, and Dr Furnivall, who held that the family were well known as 'The fighting Garnetts' with the exception of 'Papa, as genial and suave a man as ever existed'. Samuel Butler expressed similar sentiments in an anecdote on 'Mr Garnett' who, he wrote, 'as all who know him must admit, is one of the most amiable and benign of men; he is also very tall'. 'One day', Butler recalled, 'I saw him stretching himself to his utmost to reach one of the top shelves of the Reading Room reference library, so I said, "Why Mr Garnett, you are the very embodiment of Milton's line 'Of linked sweetness long drawn out'." He was much pleased.'[6]

On his appointment as Keeper of Printed Books, Richard Garnett took up residence in the Librarian's House which formed part of the right wing of the British Museum; a move which the family regarded as 'into Town'. Legend has it that the Garnett children disported themselves on the roofs of the Museum; perhaps after Ford Madox Hueffer suggested to Olive Garnett that a torchlight procession on the Museum roofs would be 'an ordinary and equable amusement'.[7] It is certain that on one occasion Olive and Lucy were seen by a Museum official climbing out of Olive's bedroom window to sit sunning themselves under parasols on the roof leads. Richard was formally requested not to allow his family to make such use of the residence, nor was it, it was hinted, quite proper for the children of the Keeper of Printed Books to play ball on the grass forecourt of the Museum. This hint was disregarded.

Edward attended the City of London School where Ford Madox Hueffer remembered him as a bowler of 'twisters' so puzzling as to make him unpopular with opposing school teams. He was tall and lanky, quick-tempered and with a deadly tongue. C. E. Montagu, a contemporary scholar, thought him 'the greatest teaze in the school'. He acquired early in life an authority on literary matters which he inherited directly from his father, and indirectly from the day-to-day world of letters in which he had been cradled; in a family which V. S. Pritchett succinctly but in no way disparagingly thought had 'a touch of the B.M. about all of them'.[8] An omnivorous reader, Edward reacted against the academic certainty of his father's acquaintances, believing that in their concern for the departed they paid little attention to the living. On leaving school at the age of sixteen (from the Fourth Form), he followed an individualistic and presumably idle existence. He spent his time lying on the hearth-rug reading, haunting bookshops and the bookstalls of Farringdon Road. His father regarded it as improper to use his influence to help his children make their way in the world and was so devoid of social ambition for them that this desultory life of Edward's would have continued but for Constance Black.

Constance was one of eight children. Her father, David Black, was a coroner in Brighton. She had gone up to Cambridge at the age of seventeen from Brighton High School, with a scholarship to Newnham College, and she had a distinguished academic record, being placed in the second class of part i and first class of part ii of the classical tripos. Her four years at Cambridge were a revelation to her; she was overwhelmed by its beauty and enjoyed her studies greatly and also the social life of Newnham; but 'most precious was the revelation of the aesthetic side of life' which hitherto she had associated only with the beauty of the countryside. At Cambridge she was almost always 'in an excessing emotional state – thrilled and almost weeping with delight, or downcast and despondent to the point of despair'.⁹

After coming down from university in 1884 she began teaching the two girls of a well-to-do family, the Whites, and went to live in their house in Cromwell Road. Later she took other pupils, among them Antonia Booth, a daughter of Charles Booth, who was then engaged on the social surveys that were to become famous as *The Life and Labour of the People of London*. She became friendly with the Booth family, spending the summer with them in Leicestershire and coaching the eldest boy in Latin.

Like her two sisters, Clementina and Grace, she was small, deceptively fragile in appearance, and shortsighted, so she used pince-nez on a long chain; the combination of good looks and intellect was impressive. Constance had two sides to her nature; on occasion frivolous and light-hearted, at other times almost puritanical. It was through Clementina, who was to be the novelist of the trio, that Constance met the Garnetts.

Richard Garnett had been kind to Clementina when she used to read at the British Museum and she had become a frequent visitor at his home in St Edmunds Terrace. One Sunday in 1885 Constance was taken there for tea. She had seen the two elder children, May and Robert, and had heard about the youngest, Arthur, who was about four years old and bore the nickname Bishop. She remembered her surprise when 'a very tall, very thin boy of eighteen walked in, looking as though he had outgrown his clothes and his strength. With his very bright eyes, curly head, dimples and roguish expression, he was very charming. "A kitten on the top of a maypole" was a happy description of him. He was at once shy and bold, very amusing. I have never seen a face so full of mischief.' Edward stayed in the drawing room throughout Constance's visit; a fact at once commented on, for 'Edward hates visitors', they said, 'and always has tea in Chapple's room.'

Edward was attracted to Constance but she, who was

decidedly sober-minded in her beliefs and in her work, did not take him seriously. Constance was then living with her sister and an old school friend Katie Phillips, in lodgings on Campden Hill, which they were to leave shortly afterwards on account of bugs. One evening Edward turned up ostensibly with a message from his sister May and stayed on for some hours. When he departed Grace commented to Constance, 'You say nobody looks at you when I am by, but there is someone with no eyes for anybody but you.' Edward began to spend more and more of his time with her and she found in him 'the most charming companion, amusing, fresh and original'. In the summer Edward and Constance with a family party of May, Robert, Grace and Clementina went on a walking tour, sleeping and eating at inns as they explored the Sussex countryside. At the end of the five days' walk Edward and Constance were great friends.

Very soon she was as much in love with him as he was with her. They went for long rides on the top of omnibuses and in the evening she took him to meetings of the early Fabians and the Kelmscott House socialists. Edward, however, refused to treat them seriously. To the earnest Constance his 'terrible lack of faith in my eyes' in matters such as Land Nationalisation was 'a real grief'. When George Bernard Shaw, with whom she had often gone to such meetings before, asked her who was 'the pretty young man he has seen with me' she replied that 'he was a boy whose education I was undertaking'.

When Constance and her sisters moved to 27 Fitzroy Street early in 1887 to set up house on their own account, Edward was always at their disposal to help paint, varnish and move furniture. To Constance 'the fact that he was spending the most precious years from 16 to 19 with absolutely no duties or regular studies' was as astonishing as the lack of concern shown by his father whom she found 'in other respects a sensible and prudent man'. Richard Garnett at one time suggested Edward should learn shorthand on the vague premise that this might be of use if he joined the staff of a newspaper. When Edward scotched the idea of working on the *Manchester Guardian* by announcing he did not want to go to Manchester as this would mean leaving Constance, his father bestirred himself sufficiently to arrange with T. Fisher Unwin for Edward to enter his office, 'as a wrapper of parcels'.

Edward's casual attitude to taking up employment and the way in which he drifted into the vocation he was to practise all his life was well put by his future wife:

It happened that I was ill and my sisters being away, Edward was staying at the flat looking after me when the day came on w^h he was to make his first appearance at the office in Paternoster Row. He was to be there at nine – but to my consternation though I called him repeatedly, took him coffee in bed, and did all I could, it was impossible to get him off till long after that time. Finally I had to fetch a hansom – w^h seemed to me in those days a terrible extravagance and with a sinking heart sent him off. It is quite possible that this reckless unpunctuality – was more diplomatic than a humble eagerness to please would have been. It probably gave Unwin the impression that Edward – though so young – was a person of consequence and this idea must have been confirmed by his studious inability to pack books, tie up parcels etc. He had quite soon slipped into the position of 'publisher's reader', w^h was of all callings the one he was fitted for by character, tastes and habits.

Constance and Edward's liaison received the approval of Edward's father. Dr Garnett had taken a great fancy to Constance from the first and had told her on one occasion that 'he had dreaded Grace's attractiveness because she was fanatical'. The sensible Constance thought 'any sensible father desires nothing better for a young son than a connection with an intelligent woman a little older.'

Sisterly doubts over the match appeared in both families, however. Clementina was worred at the couple's increasing absorption in each other and thought it her duty to try to check it. Edward's older sister May was more direct. She called on Constance and came to the point at once:

'Of course, you would not dream of taking Edward's feeling for you seriously' – she began – 'Of course not' – , I responded forcibly. She proceeded to tell me that he was a hopeless character, 'he never says a prayer', and also 'he takes after Uncle William John, and he'll never earn his living'. I was disinclined to look into the future; sure (as I thought) of the permanence of my own feeling, I could not think it possible that Edward's passion for me could last very long – and had at that time no thought of legal marriage – It seemed as though that w^d be 'taking advantage of him'. But May's words put rather a different face on it – If it were true that he would never be self-supporting, obviously somebody would have to look after him – and so why not I?

The opportunity to break away from family surroundings came when Constance was recommended by Charles Booth for the post of co-librarian at the People's Palace in the Mile End Road. A friend, Richard Heath, who knew something of social work in the East End found Constance two tiny rooms in College Buildings, Wentworth Street, just behind Toynbee Hall. It was a highly convenient situation, near to Constance's work and also to Unwin in Paternoster Row so that Edward could meet her there for lunch and spend his week-ends with her. Constance now thought her salary of £100 a year 'quite ample' and they married in 1889. Edward was twenty-one years of age and Constance twenty-seven.

TWO

The Young Garnetts

EDWARD and Constance were attracted by the cosmopolitan nature of the East End. Constance thought 'Whitechapel with its numerous Jews and other foreigners, its broad picturesque highway and lively working class manners unlike all other parts of London.' To them it was 'full of charm'.

They had a busy and carefree social life. At Unwin, Edward made many friends in literary circles. Constance, with her sister Clementina, was active in the affairs of the Fabian Society until the kind of socialism espoused by the Webbs, whom they detested, began to predominate. Constance remained active enough to be elected a member of the Executive Committee for 1894–5. Their interest in early socialism brought lasting friendships with, among others, Graham Wallas, Edward Pease who was secretary of the Fabian Society, Sidney Olivier and Ramsay MacDonald. Edward's irrepressible and mischievous spirit, according to his son David, often put Constance to shame at public meetings. Olive Garnett noted with disapproval that her brother, Graham Wallas and David Rice, a colleague at Unwin, during a Theosophical Society debate between Mrs Besant and Mrs Ramsay MacDonald, stood at the back and clapped furiously, sometimes doubling themselves up with laughter.

Life in the East End and the people he met in the socialist and other 'advanced' movements of the time provided the background and the characters to Edward's attempts as a novelist. The first, *The Paradox Club* (1888), was full of the very faults which his later devotion to the novel was dedicated to eradicate. Self-conscious and clever epigrams imitative of Wilde, embarrassingly stagy dialect, the antediluvian practice of the 'gentle reader' and the practice of interposing author between novel and reader, accompanied his efforts to explore contemporary issues – female emancipation, socialism and Home Rule for Ireland. The *Academy* reviewer shrewdly detected that 'The author of *The Paradox Club* is obviously a very young man, who has skimmed the surface of most of the leading controversies of the time. But his first effort supplies no data for judging whether he will or will not do anything important in literature.'[1]

A kinder assessment was made by George Meredith, reader for Chapman & Hall, whose curiosity prompted him to write to his friend Richard Garnett on 30 April 1889: 'This reminds me of a book *The Paradox Club* written by one, said to be a very young man, who bears your name, and has just a touch of the close epigram and large irony, as shown in your "Twilight of the Gods" (The Episcopal Uncle of Peacocks Parsons). Is he a descendant of yours? I meant to do my best to encourage him, but time slipped.'[2] It seems hardly likely that encouragement from such a quarter would have made any difference to Edward's future as a novelist, for his next and only other novel illustrates again his inability to breathe life into his words. *Light and Shadow* (1889) is a barren wilderness of despair where Hardyesque pessimism, without the Hardy genius, imbues the doom-laden life of Maurice Driscoll, the central character. The *Athenaeum*'s reviewer wrote encouragingly that 'Mr Garnett is rather a haunting than a powerful writer, one who studies to make his effects really effective, and succeeds.' However, he went on, the book 'hardly answers the description of a "novel"' and it 'grows rather into the likeness of the fantastic and almost subjective nightmare of a single mind than a story of action and incident'.[3]

G. E. Woodberry used stronger terms in a letter to his friend Richard Garnett. The novel, he wrote, gave 'a view of life as hopeless as the field of hell [and] the sorrow in it, the ugliness, moral and physical, do not tend to any end.'[4] Its archaic English, 'purple patches', set scenes and description of character with little relevance to the story compounded the unreality of the narrative.

Edward persisted for a while longer in his desire to be a novelist and Constance remarked to his father, 'Edward is absorbed in his novel of which I have seen nothing as yet. He has told me the main idea but I am afraid that (as with Light and Shadow) he is trying something so difficult that he can hardly be even moderately successful. However I have not said this to him for after all he must write after his own impulse and it would be foolish to discourage him.'[5] Her prediction was correct for the novel was never finished.

Life for Edward and Constance in the East End came to a close in March 1891 when, as Edward put it to his father, they effected 'a household removal from College Buildings to 24 John Street where we have taken two very nice rooms'. The move coincided with a rise in Edward's salary. He told his father, 'I am now getting 4£ a week from Mr Unwin – a sum which I am quite content with. I pointed out that 2£ 6/– a week was inadequate payment for the headwork I have been doing for sometime for him and I offered at the same time to take a further quantity and he accordingly met my wishes in a kind and liberal spirit.' Edward added: 'I have given the money you sent to Connie to put by for "The Thatched House" a house to be created. Your gift inaugurates the fund.' Under the new arrangement with Unwin the extra work could be carried out at home and would remove what Edward termed 'the very probable annoyance of having to write to order'.[6]

The increase in salary was especially welcome, for as Constance announced to Dr Garnett in a letter of 28 September, 'I am hoping to bring you a little grandchild early in the Spring. It is a great happiness to us.'[7] She resigned from her post at the People's Palace and they took a cottage belonging to some Garnett connections called Pennington at Henhurst Cross in Surrey. Though she had been a cripple until the age of six and was looked upon as delicate, Constance felt better in health than ever before, and energetically dug over the heavy clay soil of the garden. (This passion for gardening was to remain with her and form a common bond with the young authors befriended by Edward later, such as D. H. Lawrence and H. E. Bates.) The pattern of life in the cottage was described by Constance to her father-in-law, who no doubt appreciated the reference to cats: 'Edward of course is in London – he leaves

me every Wednesday morning and comes back on Friday night.
I am not lonely though for my noble Puss, Sir Pertinax, gives
me all the society and protection I need.'[8]

A description of Edward at this time is given indirectly by
W. B. Yeats in a letter to Olivia Shakespear about her *Journey
of High Honour*: commenting on the characters in her book
he found that they took on the appearance of various familiar friends and acquaintances and 'Christopher, as soon as I
discovered his approximate age, put on the form of a certain
ungainly, long-suffering and freckled publisher's reader'.[9]
Though they were to quarrel later over the rival merits of Lady
Gregory's version of the Cuchullain Saga and the more scholarly work of Eleanor Hull, Yeats was then a frequent visitor to
the Garnett home in the East End. Sean O'Faolain recalled
Edward telling him that, 'When he was very young, and they
were both poor, in the days when W.B. used to have to black-
up his heels so as to cover up the holes in his stockings, they'd
walk from his digs to Edward's digs and back again, all night
long, absolutely forgetting everything in the most natural
way.'[10] When the Garnetts moved from Whitechapel, the poet
of Innisfree found visits to the country cottage a relief: as he
wrote to Katharine Tynan, 'I have not been out of London for
longer than a few days at Oxford and two days with Edward
Garnett in Surrey since I came here from Ireland and feel my
imagination rather overpowered by central London din.'[11] Edward remarked to his father of Yeats at this period: 'I am
thinking of my friend Yeats whose genius seems opposed to the
building up of anything whatsoever, or to anything but the utter-
ance of vague dreaming words or songs which ripen naturally
and drop from his mouth like nuts. And anything constructive
materially seems beyond the Irish.'[12]

Edward was accepted as the 'permanent' guest of the Rhymers Club which Yeats with Ernest Rhys and F. W. Rolleston
had begun some time before 1891 and which met at the Cheshire
Cheese.[13] An anecdote by Ernest Rhys illustrates the growing
number of acquaintances Edward had made in literary circles:
'It was at the room in Gray's Inn of Edward Garnett, already
known as the author of *The Paradox Club*, that one evening I met
a man he described as "an original East End bookbinder called
Dent, with an ambition, a rosy face and a long black beard."'

When he brought his new acquaintance over to me, his own overtopping, lanky boyish figure rather dwarfed the other by contrast ... He told me that his unconventional bookbinder publisher had printed two or three books experimentally in a loft in Great Eastern Street, and before the evening was over we had arranged a visit there.'[14] From this visit emerged the Everyman Series.

Edward's social connections reflected an involvement in the youthful revolt against what were seen to be Victorian bonds limiting human freedom and fulfilment. At the Rhymers Club, 'The rousing revolutionary influences of Wagner, Ibsen, Whitman, William Morris and Tolstoi were considered, and above all Nietzsche.' As Ernest Rhys wrote, 'We did not necessarily accept his ideas, but we felt their powerfully stimulating, challenging effect.'[15] The Club promoted the ideas of Nietzsche in England. One of its members, John Gray, a Catholic priest and poet, translated his poetry and Edard pressed Fisher Unwin to take over the prose translations of Nietzsche which were being published by a firm going out of business.

Edward also followed a family tradition in making friends with and offering hospitality to European refugees. One day on his return from London he declared to Constance, 'I have met a man after your own heart, a Russian exile, and I have asked him down for the week-end.'[16] Felix Volkhovsky, and other Russian exiles whom they met through him – Prince Peter Kropotkin and Sergei Stepniak – were to influence both their lives, and perhaps indirectly the course of English literature.

Volkhovsky, a Ukrainian; Kropotkin, a Muscovite; and Stepniak, a Tartar, were involved in the anarchist and nihilist movements that were achieving prominence in European newspapers. *The Times* reserved a column twice a week for anarchist outrages. The acts of violence were deplored by public opinion, but the liberal-minded had sympathy for exiles who were victims of an oppressive regime. These exiles were regarded as heralds of a revolt against the old order of society which liberals viewed as riddled with prejudice, insincerity and hypocritical conventions. Volkhovsky had escaped from Siberia and suffered from deafness, the consequence of seven years in the Peter and Paul Fortress. He had no home and the Garnett cottage became his headquarters but, being very independent, he insisted on paying his board. He became a great friend and earned the lasting gratitude of Constance by suggesting she should learn Russian. He gave her a grammar, a dictionary and the first story she attempted to read in Russian. Moreover it was through Volkhovsky that she came to know Stepniak.

During the evenings in the cosy cottage, Constance, Edward and his sister Olive endlessly discussed false ideas of morality, oppression in Ireland, the *Friends of Russian Freedom* founded by Seton-Watson and the periodical *Free Russia* which Volkhovsky edited with Stepniak. In her enforced idleness the practical Constance set herself seriously to the task of learning Russian from Volkhovsky and began translating as an exercise Goncharov's 'A Common Story'. The first sentence took her hours to puzzle out but she advanced to translating a page a day, writing it out as she deciphered it. This was the training which led to her prodigious programme of translation of Russian literature.

As there was no competent doctor at Henhurst Cross, Constance went to her parents at Brighton for her confinement – which was fortunate, for on 9 March 1892 David, long and fat, gave her a bad time in arriving. Because the cottage, which had been a gamekeeper's, seemed likely to prove too cold and draughty in the winter for the baby, the anxious parents contemplated a move to a warmer house in Cobham, where they would be near friends such as William Archer, dramatic critic and translator of Ibsen. They remained at Henhurst, however, where in idyllic countryside the wild life was rampageous. On one occasion a mouse was found preserved in a jar of treacle and rabbits burrowing under the parlour window were in danger of coming up through the floor.

In May, Edward and Constance decided to go to Paris for a month's holiday: Edward's eldest sister May and Chapple agreed to look after David at the cottage. They had been away only a short while when Constance's father, David Black, died and they had to return to Brighton. Constance had not enjoyed Paris very much; the food did not agree with her, the cynical nature and indecency of the people sickened her, the immorality and absence of idealism among the students shocked her. Edward on the contrary was delighted and thought she was behaving like a British matron. He even considered taking a flat in Paris and going over for the occasional visit. Constance remarked tartly to Olive: 'He doesn't see what he doesn't want to, but he has changed so much, he used to be so idealistic and now he surprises me by the hardness of his views, and by imputing low motives to people.'[17]

Temperamental differences seemed to be developing between them. When Olive remarked that the worst of us must have at least one good quality, Constance replied thinking of Edward: 'Yes but suppose the person does not happen to care about that quality,' and subsequently commented, 'Edward was a bundle of paradoxes whom no one can possibly understand.'[18]

Constance resumed her study of Russian and busied herself in the affairs of the Russian émigrés. With Volkhovsky she compiled a list of 'respectable addresses' to whom letters could be sent for safe communication between England and the Continent. But the central figure in the Russian connection for Constance, for Edward and for Olive, was Sergei Stepniak. On a visit to London, Volkhovsky had taken Constance to see the Stepniaks, who were then living in Blandford Road, Turnham Green. Constance counted this as one of the important events of her life. Stepniak asked to see her translation of Goncharov, undertook to go through it with her and urged her to finish it.

Stepniak had fled Russia in 1880 after knifing a general who had ordered two girls associated with the revolutionary movement to be arrested and flogged. He confessed to the assassination in 1893 when a man arrested for the crime was under sentence of death. Despite this seemingly violent background Constance was immensely attracted to him. She thought 'he possessed an intellectual honesty so rare in the English. At the same time he was undisciplined, incapable of living by rule. His "softness" made me despair, he was shamelessly exploited by the other Russian exiles, and often did injudicious things ... To my horror I found that he habitually carried books out of the British Museum at the lunch-hour and I could not make him feel that it was a crime, since, he said, he always took them back.' He was, in her opinion, 'The most aesthetically sensitive and appreciative man I have known and had a gift for divining the best others could do and for inspiring them to do better still.'[19] Indeed Constance and Stepniak were very much in love and Edward found this hard to bear. He began to lose the carefree outlook he had retained from boyhood as the strain of rising above hurt feelings mingled with his own regard and affection for Stepniak.

Stepniak became closely involved in the Russian translations that Constance began to prepare and encouraged her to visit Russia. On one occasion he told her she ought to go to St Petersburg and enter society where 'she would be all the rage'.[20]

By June 1893 Constance had made up her mind to visit Russia and stay with a friend, Zina Vengerov. Constance had met Zina when she had visited England and introduced her to George Meredith, whose novel *The Egoist* she was translating. By this time Constance could sustain a conversation in Russian to such an extent that at a party organised by Stepniak for Vladimir Korolenko, the Russian story writer, she was able to communicate with Korolenko who had no English and only imperfect French. When Zina returned home she promised to invite Constance to Russia. While she waited impatiently for the letter, Constance on the advice of Stepniak worked at what became her customary rapid pace on the translations. Prompted by Stepniak she sent her Goncharov to William Heinemann, who accepted it. To her intense joy he gave her £40 and a commission to translate Tolstoy's *The Kingdom of God is within us* and then the stories of Turgenev. Increasingly she found herself attracted to Stepniak, though to Olive, who had also fallen deeply for the charismatic Russian, she remarked bitterly, 'Stepniak doesn't think anything of me now. You are just in the heyday; wait a bit and you will be in my position.'[21] She also felt fretfully that Zina had forgotten about her invitation. No letter had come, though Fanny Stepniak had received one saying how disgusted Zina was with Petersburg; the literary people all got drunk and she dreaded Constance's visit for she was afraid she would be disappointed. Constance said to Olive, 'I am very angry with her. Russians are all alike; all capricious and all vulgar.' Olive thought Constance had changed, recording that, 'She is bent body and soul upon getting and making money and owns that at present she feels uncomfortable and unsettled. She wants to be independent of everyone, and to be that of course she must be financially free.'[22]

She was also discontented with Heinemann over the prefaces

to her proposed translations of Turgenev. He didn't want Stepniak to write the critical introductions for he was afraid of his politics. Edward made the overture to Heinemann that Stepniak's name should merely appear at the end of the introductions and not be advertised at all. But Constance commented to Olive that 'she would not have half of the pleasure in translating if he has no share, the idea was his, and no one else can give the facts about these epoch-making novels as he can.'[23]

At last Zina's letter arrived saying that everything was satisfactory and Constance set off for St Petersburg. Olive confided in her diary: 'On Sunday, the last day of December Connie dined with us. Connie wore her money and keys around her neck, and was a little, not much excited. She hurried back to John Street to correct proofs with Stepniak, after bidding us an affectionate farewell. How admirable she is in many, many ways.'[24]

Edward's sister May stayed at Henhurst Cross to look after David, now known as Bunny. Looking back on this period Constance was to write, 'How I could have had the heart to leave him at that age I can't understand.'[25] David used to take her photograph out of the dresser drawer and almost obliterate it with kisses, saying, 'Mum gone Russ.' But she had a passionate longing for adventure and everything Russian seemed romantic and interesting.

More practical reasons also lay behind her journey. Following the failure of the Russian harvest, money for famine relief had been collected in England, but it was thought that this might be stolen if it was sent by official channels. Constance volunteered to take some of it to Russia. She took it in ten-pound notes and with it letters to social revolutionaries as part of a scheme to arrange means of communication between exiles such as Stepniak and secret revolutionary organisations in Russia.[26]

She set off in a new fur-lined coat which Stepniak had helped her to choose and her father-in-law had paid for. Among her travelling companions, 'Two awful Rumanian merchants, perfect mountains of fat, kept fingering her coat and skirt saying they could see it was English – it was such good material.'[27] Whenever she opened a window or ventilator in their absence they closed it on their return. Nevertheless it was an exciting journey, via Queensburgh to Flushing, through Holland to

Berlin and the frontier, travelling day and night to reach Petersburg on Wednesday morning. She was met by Zina Vengerov and went with her to a room Zina had booked for her for the night. It turned out to be a cupboard in the landlady's kitchen!

In Russia Constance enjoyed a varied itinerary and wrote to tell Olive about the insurrection taking place and the danger of going to and from the bank. St Petersburg customs and late hours were making her ill, however, and she set out on 21 January to stay for a month in the country with her friend Sasha Yershov. She had to travel via Moscow, Nijhi Novgorod and Tver, and by sleigh for 100 versts to reach the estate.

The letters she received were all opened and read before they reached her. Her letters to Edward were a mixture of news of her activities, concern for his health, disappointment at his negligence in writing to her and reflections over the growing gulf between them. Writing from St Petersburg on 7 January, she cried:

> Dearest I wish I could get a letter from you. It is just a week ago this evening since I parted from you at Holborn Viaduct but of course it seems infinitely longer to me. I got a card from Jane posted on Jan 2 and a letter from your father on the 4th reached me today. I think you must have got my first letter by now. Please write to me how you are and what you are doing. I keep going back to what you said that evening at the cottage that something told you we should get nearer together and not drift any further apart. And that other evening when you told me that I must not be an egoist. Whenever I think of all you said to me then I am filled with inexpressible tenderness for you. Dear one, we know each other so well; we have been so close in the past that we never ought to lose what is precious to both of us. Only let us be honest and give freely what we still can give each other. There can be no reason for coldness for neither of us asks more than that, you think me colder than I am, because I am timid with you and increasingly timid and the first condition for all happy relations is absolute freedom to be oneself.[28]

Their differences and the anxiety these caused, together with concern about his changing disposition, came to the fore in another long letter. It gives an insight into their troubled

partnership and into Edward's physical and emotional constitution. She was alarmed that he 'would become a pessimist and
slave to moods and dependent on stimulants for sleep and work'.
Her letter has a note of desperation:

> I could not bear you to become to Bunny what our father
> was to us, poor man, when we were children, through his
> nervous irritability. You know anyone who cannot be freely
> approached because of the possibility of throwing him into a
> bad temper or nervous agitation, becomes more and more
> isolated. Everyone had a tendency to avoid treating him
> openly and to try to get around him. If you are not careful
> that will happen to you. Already I am afraid it begins to be
> so – Darling don't be angry for writing like this. You must
> look at yourself dispassionately without egoism – and you
> must see that it is simply love for you that makes me. It seems
> to me that for the last year – though you have gained so
> much – that you have become far more variable in nerves
> and temper. It is really all physical I am sure – but no doubt
> self-control would check it. If it were only with me, I should
> not think anything of it – but I see it more in your relations
> with others. We must try in all the arrangements of life to
> secure the best possible conditions for nervous health for you,
> just as we do for Bunny. Of course it is of the utmost impor-
> tance for him – but it is far more important for you than for
> me, I am sure and I have been horribly selfish in not having
> done more to persuade you of the necessity for care before.
> Of course your work must always be a strain on your nerves
> and so you must do your utmost to balance that with fresh
> air, regularity and long nights when you are not working.
> You want a good wife, poor boy like Oscara, to take care of
> your physical well being. I will be better in that way when I
> come home.
>
> Well I expect you are saying I am just like Gracie and all
> my family (only not so nice) instead of taking what I say to
> heart. Dearest, there is no one else to tell you the truth, and
> no one else who cares as I do for your happiness. Nothing
> makes you dearer to me than when you show me you care
> what becomes of me, that I should not be egoistic, or cow-
> ardly, but should care for what is beautiful and worth

caring, I want you to make the best possible of your life. You are something very rare and you have something worth prizing and perfecting. It is terrible to think of your sinking into something inferior to what you have been, getting less and less self-control, weaker, more moody. You have a strong will and could exercise self control, but you will not recognise the necessity that is the danger. Forgive me for this lecture. I want so much to hear from you, I am awfully homesick, though I am enjoying myself too. I long so dreadfully to hear 'Mum, Mum!' One week gone. Dear me, my heart is full of tenderness for you, of fine and unselfish love for you. Forgive me for all I said and did that last week to vex you. Kiss my little Twee for his loving Mum.[29]

Alarmed at his silence she wrote again, bitterly and with maternal concern:

Dear Edward I have been away ten days and not a single letter from you. And only one card from Jane written on Jan 2. What does it mean? Can Bunny be ill and you are afraid to tell me? I know that if you were in my place, I would have behaved differently. When you are only in London – an hour's distance – I let you hear every day how Bunny is. If you would use your imagination a little, you would see that neglect in that way is cruel . . . [30]

At last a letter arrived from Edward on 15 January. Relieved, Constance replied, 'My dearest one I can't tell you how glad I was to get your letter yesterday,' and turned to the negotiations Edward was conducting with Heinemann over her Turgenev translations: 'If Heinemann', she wrote, 'is willing to let the vols. come out one every *three* months that is what I should prefer, and if so, fix it and I can feel perfectly safe adhering to it.'[31] In Moscow a letter to Edward gives an opinion on the Tolstoy entourage: 'I have just come back from a fruitless expedition to Tolstoi. These prophets are dreadful people to deal with. He has gone into the country with his whole family and will not be back for a week so it is impossible to talk things over in regard to his book. But I shall see the Countess on Tuesday. She is a Philistine, admirably qualified to be the wife of the Mayor of Brighton.' When she eventually managed to see Tolstoy he told her that he was very anxious to see her translations and that he liked the English translations of his works much more than the French. Tolstoy had a formidable presence. She remarked: 'He made a great impression on everybody who saw him for the first time. His piercing eyes seemed to look right through one and to make anything but perfect candour out of the question, at the same time there was an extraordinary warmth of affection in them.'[32]

Her visit to Russia, a tremendous undertaking for a frail young woman on her own and at such a time, came to an end and after a telegram telling Edward she was being detained at the frontier, she arrived home on Saturday 24 March. Next day she went with Edward to his father's for dinner where Olive recorded that 'Connie looks very well and absurdly young for thirty-two'.[33]

She resumed her translations, finishing *On the Eve* by October and beginning *Father and Son*. The prefaces, however, remained a vexed question; Stepniak, who had written the first five, would not go on with them because, he told Olive, 'Heinemann has treated me badly.' To Edward, who had volunteered a new plan to overcome this impasse, Constance wrote:

... I feel very strongly that you must not undertake them. It is just like you to suggest it to get Stepniak out of a hole and to help me – but I can't consent to it. You know very well you can't do that sort of criticism easily in a slipshod fluent way – and to write on the *same author – four times in succession –* even though you only write half a dozen pages each time would be an awful grind. To write something good on Turgenev – you must either put the accepted views of him more beautifully and aptly than they have been put, or else take a new line about him. You could perhaps do either of these if you gave time and trouble but you feel no impulse to do it from either, and I won't have you take time and trouble on it. You want to keep all your energies for work you care for and feel really drawn to. I know if you did the work ever so slightly and quickly I should like it a great deal better than a preface by a fool like Gosse and his tribe. But I would rather have a foolish preface by Gosse than a slipshod one by you or a good one that cost you time and trouble. The money would

be nice but we don't want it and you must not write potboilers. Then Stepniak's position in retiring after the *second* preface is ludicrous, to retire after the first is comparatively
sensible and dignified.[34]

Shortly afterwards Constance wrote that she had informed
Heinemann that Stepniak refused to write more prefaces under
present conditions. If Heinemann insisted on having prefaces
they would revert to Edward's plan. When Edward said he was
not angry at her action she was relieved. Her relief was no doubt
due to the fact that over the last year Edward had suffered
increasingly from nervous tension and his touchiness had been
more and more evident. This became so acute that Edward was
ordered to take a complete rest from work and Fisher Unwin
gave him two months' holiday. Constance, very much agitated,
appealed to Olive Garnett to come down to the cottage with
Lucy to help him recover. Edward thought that they would be
'nice quiet companions'. Olive observed in her diary with sisterly affection that Edward was 'all for spontaneity, natural
impulse and change'. With familial bias she contrasted 'the
Garnett plainness of speech overlying good essential qualities,
the Black narrowness and provincialism – the Black independence and non-perception of mind in other people'.[35]

During his illness Edward walked the fields and from this
mood of bucolic introspection he wrote a prose poem, *The
Imaged World*. He persuaded his friend William Hyde to provide
illustrations: an artist whom E. V. Lucas described as 'a strange
man of genius who was one of the many gifted persons first
brought to light by Edward Garnett . . . Hyde was an unhappy
man with a large family, small means and a tyrannical conscience. He was not fitted for the mercenary world and became
embittered and remote.'[36]

Edward dedicated his book to his mother: – 'Olivia Narney
who loves the open air'. The prose poem attempted to express
an empathy with the earth and sky forming a background to a
never clearly expressed tragedy between lovers. It was a gauche
and artificial composition characterised by a convoluted style,
pseudo-archaisms and a conscious desire to write beautiful prose
full of cryptic meaning. Edward's friend Yeats asked encouragingly, 'How does the *Imaged World* thrive? Please let me know

before any work of yours comes out as I am now reviewing on the Bookman and may be of use.'[37]

J. M. Dent, who published it, had been attracted by Hyde's drawings as much as by Edward's words. In his letter of acceptance he said, ' ... I would, however, like to say that I am entertaining the proposal firstly, because I am very much in sympathy with the book, and next, because I am very desirous to have in Mr. Hyde's drawings the interpretations of your beautiful word pictures; it is not with the hope of making any money out of this book that I undertake the enterprise ... '[38] In the words of Yeats when he did review it in the *Bookman*: 'There is enough poetry in this remarkable book for many poems and yet it seldom perfectly satisfies the artistic ensemble ... Mr. Garnett's own thoughts and methods struggle for mastery with a mannerism from Walt Whitman, or Richard Jefferies, or the peasant poets of Romance.'[39]

On his return to work Edward came to a new arrangement with Fisher Unwin whereby he was guaranteed not less than £350 a year and, according to Olive, '5% for something or other and Connie feels quite rich and anxious to build a house'.[40] This ambition had been with them from the beginning of their marriage. Now, with £1,000 which Constance had inherited from her father, they decided to find a suitable plot on which to build a small house within easy commuting distance of London.

Edward thought the neighbourhood of Limpsfield Chart in Surrey would be suitable. Their friends Sydney Olivier (a civil servant in the Colonial Office) and his wife Margaret had just converted two cottages into a house there. Edward, taking his paternal responsibilities seriously, wanted David to grow up in the company of other children such as those of the Oliviers – Margery, Brynhild, Daphne and Noel. In their search for a site Edward and Constance separately but coincidentally hit on the same place. Unaware of this, at first they argued fiercely on the merits of their choice.[41] It was an isolated field which belonged to the Leveson Gower Estate. With the purchase of the land and arrangements for the design of the house in the hands of Harrison Cowlishaw, a brother-in-law of Edward, they left Henhurst Cross at the end of March 1895 and moved into a cottage nearby while the house was built. Cowlishaw's original plans bore the influence of his admiration for William Morris and the medieval, and featured a great hall open to the roof and a central fireplace with no chimney but louvres in the roof. Mercifully, as Olive remarked, good sense prevailed and the plans were much modified, to an L-shaped design characterised by thick walls, great stone fireplaces with inglenooks and low oak beams. There was a bathroom with a cistern in the roof to which water had to be pumped, and an earth closet for sanitation.

The temporary home, at Froghole near Crockham Hill, was a tiny old cottage with worn doorstep, worn floors, low ceilings and a warm chimney corner. It was, however, rat-infested. Constance wrote to Dr Garnett in November of the 'raids of devastating rats and we seem to be especially favoured by their attentions. I suppose they are clever enough to see we are poor spirited innocent creatures who cannot defend ourselves. On Saturday we had three in the house and lively scenes followed. We have entered upon a vigorous campaign fearing to be driven out by their invading hosts and six of the enemy have perished in three days.'[42]

When the new house neared completion, they thought of giving a housewarming party. This plan was abandoned when news came of the tragic death of Stepniak. The Stepniaks had rented a cottage on Limpsfield Chart to be near to the Garnetts but, while returning to London on 23 December 1895, Sergei was run over by a train at the level crossing near Shepherd's Bush. This bizarre demise was occasioned by his facility to shut out noise which he had developed during a sojourn in a Turkish prison. Deaf to the outside world, he hadn't heard the warning whistle of the train. When Olive Garnett had remarked upon this habit of retiring within himself he had replied, 'How else could I survive English dinner parties?'[43]

His death affected Constance and Olive very deeply. Olive cut off her hair in mourning and David Garnett recalled that it 'was a blow from which it took my mother long to recover'.[44] In February 1896 Edward, Constance and David moved into the new house.

THREE

The Cearne

THE new house derived its name from its situation. The Cearne was built in a 'buttercup meadow on a slope', encircled by a beechwood copse, with a magnificent view to the south and west. Olive gave a romantic description of its interior: 'A deep porch, unstained oak, bare floors and deep window seats, all gave off a delicious aroma of wood smoke, apples and country sweetness.'[1] A later visitor, D. H. Lawrence, who no doubt found that it contrasted greatly with his home in Eastwood, called it 'one of those new, ancient cottages', expanding his description for the benefit of Louie Burrows: 'It is a house thirteen years old, but exactly, exactly like the 15th century; brick floored hall, bare wooden staircase, deep ingle nook with a great log fire, and two tiny windows one on either side of the chimney: and beautiful old furniture – all in perfect taste. You would be moved to rhapsodies, I think. The house stands on the last drop of the north downs, sheer, overlooking the weald of Kent. The wood in which the cottage is lost ends with the scarp slope.'[2]

Edward and Constance had just moved into this idyllic setting when he contracted an illness diagnosed eventually as typhoid. During the nine weeks he lay ill Edward was reduced almost to a skeleton by the starvation treatment then prescribed, barely kept alive by cups of milk and water. The treatment, as much as the disease, Constance was convinced caused an impoverishment of the blood which was responsible for the varicose troubles in his legs in later years. He was, however, a

wonderfully good patient. Constance found that, though irritable and impatient when in health, only in convalescence did he
begin to be like himself and 'threw a tapioca pudding at Mary
Belcher who had come in to help us – (It stuck in her hair!).'[3]
She also reported to her father-in-law that 'he seems to fret a
good deal about money and to be constantly calculating ways
and means and what must be paid for and what need not. This
is so unlike his usual happy-go-lucky way in such matters.'[4]

Edward's irascibility and impulsiveness, too often accompanied by a tendency to force his views, led his son to think his
grandfather was a much more civilised being than his father.
But 'no-one', David Garnett wrote, 'could have less sense of
property than Edward. He was always generous and as a young
man would press books and anything else that was handy upon
the parting guests. Nor was this generosity confined to what was
strictly his own.'[5] In Constance, however, the new house awoke
proprietary instincts. For a brief euphoric period they employed
a domestic help called Alice Martin and a handyman, Bert
Hedgecock.

But both Constance and Edward opposed the conservative
elements in Edwardian society. It was a period when diverse
groups although united in opposition to the old order of things
followed many different paths in their rebellion – socialist,
Fabian, Nietzschean, Bergsonian, Theosophist and others.
Edward, however, was sceptical of organised movements. When
Wells tried to recruit his support in his machinations regarding
the Fabian Society, Edward replied: 'Dear Wells, My signature
will discredit you. I have only been once to the Society, since I
joined, and it is known by Pease and others that I am not a
serious person – re socialism at least. My own strong belief is
that "Socialism" is now the scape-goat for a much wider movement which let us call "Collectivism". The word *Socialist* is now
being used by the Public as the word "Atheist" was used
throughout the last half of the 19th century . . . '[6]

Perhaps the choice of site for The Cearne, away from the
village and lost in woodland, was an expression of opposition to
the rigid social order and ethical system. The villagers looked
askance at their isolation, and the fact that as atheists Constance
and Edward did not attend church added to their distrust.
During the Boer War, when predictably Edward and Constance

sympathised with the Boers, the local people became openly hostile and David was stoned and booed by the village children. The war aroused strong passions on both sides; Edward and Constance were fiercely anti-imperialistic and Edward always regretted the surprisingly fervent patriotism of his father, who went so far as to write a sonnet against President Kruger which appeared in *The Times*. Edward, who throughout his life took pride in a combined inheritance of Yorkshire obstinacy and Irish rebelliousness, joined a voluntary force of militant pro-Boers armed with sticks to protect their public speakers. If Ford Madox Ford is to be believed this pugnacious avowal of support for the minority also characterised Edward's support of the Salvation Army. 'The Salvation Army', Ford wrote, 'was then young and marked out for persecution. I remember Mr. Edward Garnett, then too, young and gallant. He constituted an anti-Skeleton Army and purchasing an enormous cudgel went down to protect the Salvationist lasses at Brighton.'[7]

Edward's mettle was also evident in an incident at The Cearne which he reported to his friend Cunninghame Graham. 'I would have written before,' Edward wrote on 9 February 1901, 'only your letter arrived when I found myself living in a Dostoevsky novel. An interesting character, a young horse stealer, labourer, poacher and ne'er-do-well, whom I was providing with food, work and shelter in a shed here, suddenly turned into a raving maniac and after wandering to and fro with him in search of the Authorities, after twelve hours excitement was finally landed by me in the District's Infirmary. The poor fellow is now in an Asylum. I have been living inside the man's mind for days and the final phase of deep sanity and insanity – though unforeseen – has left me more in sympathy with him than with any of the kind neighbours, friends, officials, doctors and police etc. etc. whom I have been forced to interview.' Edward added that Constance 'had been so upset by the madman episode – axes and pitchforks and knives were "properties" on the scene of action – that I have had to take her away for a week or so, and have had less time than usual.'[8]

The 'poor fellow' was Bill Hedgecock, brother of Bert first employed at The Cearne. David Garnett, remembering Edward's 'courage, patience and humanity' in dealing with him, depicted the incident years later in his novel *Beany-eye* (1935).

Though fiction, the book he wrote was as 'true as I could make it'[9] and the reviewer of *The Times Literary Supplement* observed: 'But Mr. Butler is the triumph of the book: Mr. Garnett has never surpassed this memory, if it be such, of his father, whom he exhibits, in this particular episode, as a man of a lovable yet wilful temperament, patient at one moment, irascible at the next, almost irrationally fearless and when frightened absolutely courageous . . . '[10]

As typical of Edward was the interest he continued to show in the unfortunate Bill; his sympathy and helpfulness are reflected in a brief correspondence. From No. 2 Male Ward of Brookwood Asylum near Woking, William Hedgecock, as he signed himself, wrote to Edward on 13 June 1903 about his wish to work, saying, 'I have asked to go out but can get no decided answer so I made up my mind up to ask your help once more you being the last gentleman I was under before I was put away I should be glad of a situation of any sort and be glad of it under any one you may know. Please remember me to the little boy. Obeidently William Hedgecock.' Eventually with Edward's help he did 'go out' and wrote finally to Edward on 25 April 1904 from Canada, 'c/o Curran, Youville, Quebec', to say he was now working and wanted to be remembered to Bunny and 'respects to Mrs Garnett'.[11]

With Edward's predilection for the maverick came a view of life in which the uncomprehending majority oppressed the sensitive and gifted minority and thus 'the finest talent was unrecognised and the ruthless and stupid suppressed the compassionate and intelligent'.[12] It was a cast of mind accompanied by idiosyncratic habits. He was unable to sleep well and David Garnett recalled the silence necessary in the morning so that Edward could rest after working through the night. His habit of unselfconsciously walking about in the nude after washing made Constance concerned lest he alarm some unsuspecting caller.[13] In the 1920s on medical advice he took to smoking a brand of herbal tobacco which he rolled expertly into cigarettes with one hand.[14] His belief in its efficacy led him to advise Richard Curle, who suffered from heart trouble, that 'as for smoking invent for yourself a Herbal Tobacco you'll soon get fond of it'.[15]

As he grew older, youthful lankiness gave way to ungainly bulk and an impression of clumsiness was reinforced by the thick lenses he had to wear as his eyesight deteriorated – yet he retained an ability to juggle with surprising dexterity. Customarily dressed in a brown Jaeger shirt, loosely cut jacket and shapeless trousers, Edward had an air of eccentricity naturally carried: the outward manifestation of attitudes and beliefs that relied more on intuition and instinct than theory or logic.

When the isolation of The Cearne diminished before the influx of other residents attracted to the wooded High Chart and its proximity to London, so did the social insularity which stemmed from Constance's innate shyness and Edward's pronounced antipathy to bourgeois respectability and its values. The Cearne came to be part of a community of literary figures and intellectuals who settled or visited the vicinity of Limpsfield. E. V. Lucas, publisher's reader and essayist and friend of Edward's, took over the cottage they had left at Froghole. Edward Pease, secretary of the Fabians, was a neighbour. Fanny Stepniak came to live at Crockham Hill to be near to them. Indeed Fanny had become more attached to Constance after Sergei's death and his loss deepened the Garnetts' friendship with the Russian exiles who had been his close friends. Constance wrote to Dr Garnett about 'the delightful evenings they had with the Kropotkins who were staying with Fanny for a few days'.[16] Prince Peter, a man of immense charm and intellectual vivacity, asked Edward to become his intermediary in dealing with publishers.[17]

Edward approached Charles Longman with Kropotkin's *Autobiography*, but Longman replied cautiously: 'Before making any definite proposal on the subject, I should be glad to have your views on one matter which seems to me important.' Longman was very concerned about Kropotkin's adoption and advocacy of anarchism, writing: 'Anarchism has a very ugly sound in English ears and it is difficult to understand how an intellectual and cultivated person, such as Prince Kropotkin, can be identified with such a creed.'[18] He wished to know if the Prince had denounced the means used by the Nihilists. In the end, however, negotiations apparently foundered on the question of payment. Edward wrote:

I have seen and talked your proposal over with Kropotkin. I find that from the many encouraging letters he instantly received from all quarters on his 'Memoirs' that he thinks it to his advantage not to sell the book outright but to adhere to this plan of a certain sum paid on publication on account of a royalty – and this sum he thinks ought not to be less than 500£. On my pointing out to him the publisher would have a serious sum to pay for advertising and producing the book he suggests that you pay him 500£ for an edition, an edition of so many copies – but that should the sale of the book *exceed* this agreed edition or editions, you then begin paying him royalties on all further sale of copies.[19]

Two other publishers, Heinemann and Smith Elder, were both expressing interest. Kropotkin decided to leave the decision entirely in Edward's hands, and declared, 'Dear friend I cannot tell you how grateful I am to you about having it settled so far.' He also commented, 'I learned lately *for sure* that there is here in London an agency, at the embassy, to buy out of the trade the books hostile to the Russian government.'[20] Smith Elder eventually published the book and Kropotkin in gratitude sent a copy to Edward with a letter: 'Accept it as a token of affection from a friend. There is something of yours in it. I never forgot our conversation about Memoirs writing, and your kind words of encouragement – which I was much in need of – and your friendly hints. And I cannot but repeat how thankful I am to you, dear friend, for your good interference, and all the trouble you took with it. It appears now, as you see, not only from a good publisher, but also in a nice form.'[21]

As well as with the Russian exiles, other past acquaintanceships were renewed through the tenancy of Gracie's Cottage. This had been built by Harry Cowlishaw about half a mile away in one of the meadows on Scearn Bank for Constance's younger sister. Grace and her husband Hugh Human had departed for Colombo where he was to take up a teaching appointment and the first tenant, Ford Madox Hueffer, arrived on 4 March 1898. Ford took on a Walter Mitty existence as a farmer. With the gravity of an expert he gave the boy David Garnett inimitable misinformation on agriculture in England, and Constance and her sisters were much amused, but with a hint of outrage, by his drawling comments on the eating propensities of the three ducks which he had named after them and which constituted the entire livestock of his farm.[22] More realistically, Ford had taken the cottage to be within the orbit of Edward's circle of literary friends and visitors, Hudson, Stephen Crane and Conrad among them. It was here that Edward introduced him to Conrad, who was to be so important to his future development as a writer.

Harold Frederic, the American novelist, gave the reason for the increasing number of visitors who trod the path to The Cearne in a letter to his friend Stephen Crane in 1898: 'Mr Edward Garnett would be an El Dorado to an American publisher of the superior class. He seems to be able to scent a new talent in fiction from a thousand writers and as a critic he possesses both sincerity and distinction of manner.'[23] When Stephen and Cora Crane came to England it was such a sentiment that perhaps prompted them to settle nearby. Edward was instrumental in providing them with information on Brede Place, which became their home, though he warned Cora, '*Don't go with expectations*. For it is a miracle if something has not happened to it since the days when I saw that farm bailiff encamped in those ancient walls.'[24] Cora replied: 'Stephen suddenly made up his mind to go to Brede, so off we went to Hastings. We drove out and of course it was very dark – Stephen was mad over the place. We tramped, later, after a supper of ham and eggs beside the kitchen fire – to a cottage in the village and put up for the night there. Then we spent the day at Brede. We are going to move Heaven and Earth to get there. Stephen said that a solemn feeling of work came to him there so I am delighted. Come and see us soon.'[25]

Edward 'disapproved of the offensive crew of journalists'[26] who surrounded Stephen Crane and was disturbed by the distractions this caused a writer whom he so much admired but whose intuitive mastery of language he thought suffered from too careless and casual an approach. Cora put his concern in another way: 'I hope that the perfect quiet of Brede Place and the freedom from a lot of dear good people, who take his mind from his work, will let him show the world a book that will live.'[27]

To Edward creative writing required dedication as much as talent; a goal which he himself desired but which escaped him. In a letter to Wells in 1903 he wrote:

I have not yet thanked you for your letter about my youthful
novel. I was very pleased to see that it affected you by its
mixture of strength and weakness exactly as I thought it
would. Only your criticisms were too indulgent. I felt that I
knew too little about life to write any more at that time, and
I went in for living. Now I feel I've accumulated experience,
and I may set to work and write another – tragic – if I can hit
the style necessary.[28]

He never did. An inner discontent over his own lack of
creative power can be detected in Edward's letter to his father
shortly after the publication of the youthful novel, *Light and
Shadow*. It also gave early expression to an idea which he was
to follow all his life, that criticism could be creative and was a
duty to be carried out for the sake of others. 'You are far too
kind to my critical power,' he wrote to Richard Garnett on 19
July 1890:

Unless criticism be creative I am not drawn to it, and most
critics are created, not creative. Great works are like the
earth, ever fresh and fertile; and they are ever producing the
flowers (and the weeds) of criticism, which, however beautiful, must die like all flowers, and be forgotten. This simile
shows I am a discontented flower who would be the earth,
and so am fit for nothing. But I have had an idea in the back
of my brain for a long time that it is not impossible to put
criticism into living form, or rather that it is one's duty to try
and do so ... Anyway I am convinced that genius with many
is like a smouldering fire. Generally it gets choked up, or dies
out – but a chance wind, another's hand, or even its own
decoherence (answering to a man's mental or physical disease) may cause a burst of beautiful flame. I came across a
sentence of La Rochefoucauld today which I wish I had
remembered to put on the title page of *Light and Shadow* as it
answers criticism by anticipation: 'Nous avons tous assez de
force pour supporter les maux d'autrui.'[29]

It was in this spirit that the idealistic and eager young Edward
approached his work at Unwin.

FOUR
Reader's Task

EDWARD entered the world of publishing when the stability, yet restrictiveness, that stemmed from the economic relationship between the three-decker novel and the circulating library was coming to an end. This relationship had been regarded by both authors and publishers as necessary to profit margins and also as the most effective way of bringing the novelist's name to the public. The subscribers to Mudie's formed a guaranteed market and this stable and uniform readership influenced the way in which fiction was written. The three-volume novel, with a spaciousness that allowed for incident and multiplicity of plots, had a prestige that Gissing features in *New Grub Street*. In publishing, the dominance of the circulating library had caused publishers' readers such as Geraldine Jewsbury of Bentleys 'to keep the figure of Mudie constantly in mind'[1] as she read manuscripts. But by the 1890s the three-volume novel had come to an end. George Moore, angered by Mudie's exclusion of his novels, launched his famous attack on *Literature at nurse*; criticism grew over the illogical pricing of novels; Mudie became discontented with the increasing number of novels and the steadily shrinking market for used copies as cheap reprints were made available before these could be off-loaded on the secondhand market. Accordingly, on 27 June 1894 Mudie announced a drastic change of policy: 'The three volume novel does not suit us *at any price* so well as the *One* vol. and upon the old terms it is *no longer possible*.'[2]

The literary market-place was transformed virtually over-night and confusion followed as to the value of copyrights, the payment to authors and the number of copies to be printed. Among the old established firms 'it resulted in a kind of be-wilderment and paralysis'[3] and their inability to adjust to new circumstances ripened opportunities for new entrants to the trade. The 1890s saw the formation of firms such as T. Fisher Unwin, Hutchinson, Heinemann, Duckworth, Edward Arnold and Methuen. More competitive and with a greater onus on enterprise, the new kind of publishing structure stressed the importance of the publisher's reader.

The three-decker novel and the circulating library axis had placed a heavy handicap upon the 'budding novelist' with the tradition that 'first books had to present exceptional promise of popular success to justify the risk of publication'.[4] When new concepts of fiction began to grow towards the end of the century, the circulating library 'was more keenly felt as a great im-movable block to all new work'.[5] As these considerations ceased to be decisive and the needs of a better-educated public were being voiced in the bookshops, greater discernment in what to publish and in seeking new ventures to secure the survival of the firm became of paramount importance. T. Fisher Unwin was among the first publishers to 'tickle the public's literary palate with unaccustomed fare'.[6] Ford Madox Hueffer, looking back on this period, viewed as a 'heaven sent combination for publisher and young writer' that which existed in the 'house of T. F. Unwin in the nineties of a chief reader of determined tastes and a salesman of second sight – Edward Garnett and David Rice'.[7]

Edward began work at Unwin on a salary of 10 shillings per week. His companions were W. H. Chesson and for a time G. K. Chesterton who, after leaving the Slade School, came to the firm in the same haphazard way as Edward. An incorrigible versifier, Chesterton composed a long poem entitled 'Lines to Waterloo Station' which began:

> An overflowing of feeling
> Come hither, Fisher Unwin
> And leave your work awhile,
> Uplooking in my face a span

With bright a day smile
All happy leaping publishers
Round Paternoster Row . . .[8]

The ebullient Chesterton found Fisher Unwin's cold and hu-
mourless personality an apt subject for his satirical doggerel,
but the head of the firm was a shrewd judge of how to use his
employees. The redoubtable Stanley Unwin, describing the
state of the firm when he joined it in 1904, wrote that it had
'already acquired a considerable reputation for discovering
promising authors. This was due in part to an interesting venture, the "Pseudonym Library", a series which introduced a
number of brilliant new writers such as "Lance Falconer",
author of *Madamoiselle Ixe* [*sic*] (praised by Gladstone) and John
Oliver Hobbes, W. B. Yeats, Vernon Lee, "Ralph Iron" (Olive
Schreiner) and "Ouida". The discoveries were Edward Garnett's and W. H. Chesson's but to Fisher Unwin must be given
the credit both for employing them and acting upon their
advice.'[9]

The importance of the publisher's reader in such matters had
not always received such recognition. An early historian of the
press, R. H. Horne, had looked upon this obscure office as a
'Skeleton in every house', declaring that 'invisible behind his
employer's arras, the author's unknown, unsuspected enemy,
works to the sure discomfiture of all original ability. This fool in
the dark who knows not what he mars.'[10] It was a view denied
by Fisher Unwin's nephew, who believed that 'publishers'
readers seldom, if ever, get the praise they deserve. The public
knows nothing about their conscientious and exhausting work,
and few are the authors who are prepared to recognise publicly
the benefits they have derived from their friendly suggestions
and criticisms.'[11]

The reading of innumerable manuscripts in a variety of literary genres, of wildly differing merit and without any previous
judgment having been made upon them, was a task which
rarely had its highlights: much was of a mundane nature on
which both literary and commercial assessments had to be
made. But Edward, as he grew more into the role of reader and
adviser to Unwin, retained 'a penetrating eye for character and
a quick sympathy'[12] and never lost his hope that among the

manuscripts he read there might be a work of promise. His reports to Unwin, couched in the royal 'we', had the authority of close analysis, confidence in his own judgment and realistic reference to commercial possibilities. Individuality and originality were two characteristics he particularly sought in a manuscript, whatever the source. Of *The Babe Unborn*, submitted by his erstwhile colleague G. K. Chesterton, he reported: 'We certainly advise you to publish these poems, or rather a selection of the poems. Mr. Chesterton has temperament, he has individuality and a new point of view. It is the new *point of view* that counts in poetry. If the attitude to life is *derived* from older authors, the result is *not* poetry, however cleverly it is fashioned e.g. Mr. Gosse's poetry is all inspired by other people's poetry, borrowed, *derived*. That of Mr. Chesterton has original thought, original inspirations, a temperament of his own.'[13]

Insistence on the writer's individual rather than derived qualities became a regular feature of his reports to Unwin whatever the form of literature. *The Confessions of a Gamekeeper* was 'what is rarely met with, the genuine article ... The author shows a distinct individuality.'[14] That this sprang from a knowledge of the life depicted was a *sine qua non* for Edward. His report on *The Sate of Life* [*sic*] by N. Mayne was one of the many during the 1890s on this theme: 'Miss Mayne can do one thing. In the future she must place her heroine in a social milieu she herself has lived in, and *knows*. She must write of the people she knows, and *then* she may do good work. Her analysis of a woman's feelings is very good, very good but all the *imagined* people and surroundings are untrue to life.'[15]

The 'true to life' quality was a characteristic that graced the best work of a greater writer, Olive Schreiner, though Edward in his report on *The Boer* made clear the faults she should avoid:

> In this series of articles, at least, there is practically none of that *posing*, *exaggeration*, and *cheap sentimentality* which has spoiled Mrs Schreiner's later writings ... Her solution of vexed questions is probably no solution at all – founded as it is on the simple precept of 'Love one another' – but her book should certainly succeed through the fact that her *old charm of style* returns to it, and it really brings *S. Africa and its people*

before us and is written in a free and lofty spirit. The author's good opinion of herself is of course apparent, but if in the later chapters she does not pose too much as the S. African Prophetess and if she does not over-do her attack on Rhodes we think it ought to be a success in every way and one that will give her superior class of readers hope that the old Olive Schreiner will get rid of her latter day posing and cheap sensationalism . . .[16]

His reports on the work of another established Unwin author, John Oliver Hobbes alias Pearl Craigie, were interlarded with strictures on the way her cynicism and flippancy distorted reality. 'The old faults', Edward wrote of *The Sinner's Comedy*, 're-appear in perhaps more marked a degree . . . She sacrifices again and again reality for wit and flippancy . . . The fact is, as we said, in criticizing *Some Emotions* for T.F.U., Mrs Craigie is a clever woman with decided limitations. She knows a good deal of life on one side but little on the other and she is too bent on being cynical to write anything great in any way.'[17] Of her next work, *A Study in Temptation*, he said: 'Mrs Craigie will always write smart and witty and rather superficial work. All her characters talk epigrams!' However, he found her later book, *A Bundle of Life*, better 'than we thought possible' because it had 'less improbability, less of that smart and utterly wearisome cheap cynicism, less of artificial *narrative* than in her other books'. Approvingly this report concluded it to be 'more artistic in that it *leaves out* things, the other books *put in*'.[18]

Comments on construction and the management of characterisation recur in his reports and correspondence with S. R. Crockett, another standard Unwin author. In a long nine-page report on *The Raiders* Garnett thought the

. . . language and the whole style . . . extremely well managed, many chapters are considered as word-painting quite as good as Stevenson could do, the plot is a good one and though Crockett's fault is to hang back in the tale when he should go forward and vice-versa and though he is a better hand at detail than at massing the proportions of the whole, still as a piece of workmanship the story is satisfactory indeed and marks an advance in no slight degree . . . The danger of most novelists is the desire to get *more out of their human material* than nature and surroundings warrant.

Edward concluded that 'of course all these adventure books, Stevensons, Q's etc. etc. it must be remembered want active and vigorous publishing. There is a large public, but it wants getting at . . . '[19]

His observations on the market for romance and adventure acknowledged one of the distinctive reading publics of the time. Reporting on John Buchan's *Don Quixote*, Edward began: 'This is a romance à la Stanley Weyman and is not badly done' but some rewriting was required to rectify characterisation and the seventeenth-century flavour.[20] Buchan evidently complied for the second report comments that it had 'been amended to its benefit and though we think that the phrasing generally might be made a little more old fashioned, still the book makes a very presentable appearance'.[21] Edward's recognition of the public's taste for this kind of story is well put in a report on *The Temple of Folly*. The author, 'Paul Creswick', he began, 'is a wise young man, he has piled *Anthony Hope* on *Stanley Weyman*, put in a dash of *Q* and invented some brave mannerisms à la *Crockett*, and lo and behold we have a very typical story of adventure for the general public, (and the City clerk in particular) to pronounce damned good.' Though the 'story has certainly merits of its own', he added, it 'is *not* literature – it is *an adventure story simply cooked up* to the taste of the "Stanley Weyman" public'.[22]

The vagaries of public taste and its re-education were an evident preoccupation for Edward at the close of the century. Of *A Winning Hazard* by 'Mrs Alexander', he wrote that ' . . . the time for this "Early Victorian" style of MS is past. It is no longer even popular. It never deserved to be popular, but the British public wanted educating to a sense of better things' and concluded that 'it would be a mistake of policy for T.F.U. to have anything to do with this style of cast off and dying work'.[23] More favourably he wrote of *Through Fire* that 'this seems to be suited to popular taste' and 'we think that *her old public* will thoroughly understand the book and that she may by it, perhaps, gain more readers . . . '[24]

The reputation and progress of the Unwin firm, however, could not depend solely on unsolicited manuscripts and as a

reader Edward promulgated series which would capitalise on
probable demand and also introduce authors of distinction to
the general public. The Pseudonym Library which he inaugurated was one of the most successful of the many which Unwin
launched – Adventure Series, Cameo Series, First Novel Library, Story of the Nations Library, Mermaid Series, Overseas
Library. At Edward's instigation several of Yeats's earlier books
were published in such series. Writing to Katharine Tynan on
6 October 1890, Yeats confided that he had retouched his story
'John Sherman' and 'Edward Garnett, author of *The Paradox
Club* is going to read it and see if it will suit the publisher he
reads for'.[25] Due to Edward's enthusiastic support this autobiographical novel appeared in the Pseudonym Library in March
1891 under the name of 'Ganconagh'. At Edward's prompting
Unwin followed this by publishing Yeats's second collection of
poetry in the Cameo Series as *The Countess Cathleen and Various
Legends and Lyrics* in September 1892. They also discussed a
proposed contribution by Yeats to the Adventure Series which
Edward had participated in launching, and to which he had
contributed an introduction to an edition of the rascally Trelaw-
ney's *Adventures of a Younger Son* in 1891. Yeats's book never
appeared though evidently he had assembled the greater part
of the material and had sent the introduction. During late
October 1892 he wrote: 'My dear Garnett, I shall finish my
introduction to the "Irish Adventurers" tomorrow and post it
to you. I hope the thing will do ... Please let me know about
the "adventurer" introduction as soon as possible as I shall be
in suspense until I hear.'[26] The following year Yeats wrote that
he had sent from Dublin part of the contents of the 'Adventurer
volume'.[27]

At the time Yeats was preoccupied with his grandiose scheme
for an Irish Literary Society movement. He turned to Edward
for support in persuading Unwin to bring out a series connected
with this, The Library of Ireland, which came into conflict with
a venture independently put to Unwin by Yeats's rival Sir
Charles Gavan Duffy. Yeats wrote a succession of letters in
October and November 1892 to warn Edward of Duffy's machinations. Edward used his friendship with the poet to make
peace between them: 'Now, my dear fellow,' he wrote to Yeats,
'I'm not going to preach at all but I do ask you to examine what

the differences are between your view and the rival and see whether it is for the good of the idea *you* are working for that you and your party should be irreconcilable ... Why not drop personal feeling, quieten the hornet's nest in your side, come over here first and see whether you cannot make a practical agreement?'[28] Eventually the dispute ended in compromise, but the series had only a short life as it 'was killed after a couple of years by the books chosen by the editors'.[29]

On a more pedestrian level, in a memorandum to Unwin, Edward outlined the specification of a Builders of Great Britain series which would be concerned with the 'doings of those who have built up the fabric of the British Empire such as Walter Raleigh, Cabot, Clive, Rajah Brooke etc.'[30] Each volume would be written by a specialist under the general editorship of Sir Henry Wilson, Private Secretary to Joseph Chamberlain.

Later he persuaded Unwin to launch another series on this theme, partly with the intention to challenge, while exploiting, Kipling's readership. It was tentatively entitled the 'colonial series' and later the Overseas Library. Edward's prospectus envisaged a scheme with 'no pretence at Imperial drum beating', which would depict 'the actual life of the English immigrants, travellers, traders, officers, overseas away among foreign and native races, black or white'.[31] Among the eight writers to launch the series he particularly recommended R. B. Cunninghame Graham, to whom he wrote:

I have asked Conrad to forward you this letter about your sketches, as I prefer writing to you direct to writing through a business house. I read your Sketches as they appeared in *The Saturday Review* and was very much taken with them – the paper on Morris's funeral appearing to me the best thing of its kind I have met with. I am asking Mr. Fisher Unwin to get hold of your Sketches if possible, my idea was that they might be used as the opening and model volume of a new projected series – 'The Overseas Library' which would contain Tales and Sketches about Colonial Life and English Colonial Settlers, Emigrants, Travellers' life all the world over. The note of this series would be *not* Imperialism but the inclusion of any work sufficiently artistic to give to local life atmosphere and point of view of the new countries. Such a

series would be experimental and probably its volumes would
be rather suggestive than be finished artistic work ... [32]

To Unwin he reported that Cunninghame Graham 'has written a capital series of sketches of roving life (chiefly in the
Argentine Republic) ... This *style* of writing is exactly what we
want ... The Publisher should certainly secure Mr. Graham
who is a most brilliant writer ... '[33] Going through Graham's
Sketches Edward wrote to the author in complimentary terms:
'Your Hotel courtyard scene is worth thousands of careful "articles on the situation" ... you have the magic touch ...' He
returned the *Sketches* with 'a few pencil marks in the margins of
Bloody Nigger and a few others' for Graham to consider.[34] Cunninghame Graham for his part was thankful for the comments,
remarking to Edward that 'you could not take a better way if
you wanted to get out of me the utmost of my capabilities – if
they are there to begin with... And when I thought that
wretched stuff I sent to you was a book! Why I had simply
sketched out the Scenery and placed two lay figures in it of
inconceivable rigidity. I work with your notes beside me. I have
found them of utmost service. You have been my guide not to
say "Vade Retro Satanas" to me from the first when I ventured
to approach you with my rubbish.'[35] It was the beginning of a
lifelong friendship.

Edward recommended for the Overseas Series another writer
of whom he had great expectations. Henry Lawson, then unknown in England, Edward described as 'the *best* native Australian writer which we have come across. His work is original
and brilliant and we can see that he voices Australian life and
sentiment in a way that will make him a great favourite with
the Australian public.' He urged Unwin 'to bespeak any further
work Lawson does and commission him'.[36] The series, however,
ran into only six volumes. Good manuscripts were few and far
between.

A more successful project was the Children's Library which
attracted authors and titles of value. Outlining to Unwin the
shape of the series, which Edward thought would yield a fair
profit, he drew into the proposal the work of two of his friends.
'If T.F.U.', Edward began, 'will take my advice he will start
with *The Brown Owl* making Volkhovsky No. II. Both volumes

are of exceptional merit, *much above the average in fact*, and would be appreciated by intelligent children of ten upwards. We can then have time to look about for an old favourite (such as Grimm) to make No. III.'[37]

The Brown Owl was by Edward's boyhood friend, Ford Madox Hueffer. It was a highly successful fairy story for which his grandfather, the pre-Raphaelite painter Ford Madox Brown, promised to supply two illustrations. Madox Brown wrote with evident pride to Watts Dunton, 'By the same post I send you and I think you will like to see and have my grandson's first book, *The Brown Owl*. Fisher Unwin and young Edward Garnett have between them thought it worth publication.'[38]

Volkhovsky's contribution to the Children's Library varied in quality. Edward thought his first stories too sentimental but, reporting on a collection entitled *A Court Story*, he was of the opinion that these were 'full of sly humour and all very well adapted to be read aloud to children'.[39] Perhaps of all the manuscripts he read in 1898 and 1899 a collection by a Mrs E. Nesbit aroused his most enthusiastic admiration and received his wholehearted encouragement. He reported:

> Yes these stories are good. They are written on a rather original idea, on a line off the common run. Here we have the life of a Family of Children *told by themselves*, in a candid ingenuous and very amusing style. Of course no children would write as E. Nesbit writes, but the *result is* that we have drawn for us a very charming picture of *English Family* life. We do not remember to have read any book for a long time that so cleverly brings out the fine points in the English outlook and ideal of life since the days of Mrs Ewing and Aunt Judy. We think that the stories are worth taking up and worth publishing, for the stories are *individual*. They will please every grown-up who reads them. At present there are only 7 stories. Is this amount sufficient to write a book, or will E. Nesbit write more?[40]

Mrs E. Nesbit did, of course, write more and the collection which became the successful *Treasure Seekers* was the subject of a second report in which Edward confirmed his first impressions. 'Yes,' he wrote, 'a re-reading of these stories makes us of the opinion that T.F.U. must make a special effort over the book for Xmas sales. The whole *idea* of the book is fresh and bright, the conception of the children of the household trying to aid the Father in impecunious straits is *great, the sort of thing to please* the British mind. We will say that the authoress has worked out the idea very well and gracefully, the stories are all humorous and original, quite modern in tone ... '[41] His conviction that her ability should be backed by good salesmanship was reiterated in his report on *The Seven Dragons*:

> Yes these are also good. Mrs. Nesbit has a delightful touch. She makes things go – the four tales she now submits, are not part of the series (i.e. tales of the special Family of Children) – but this matters little. The tales will form a kind of afterpiece, a little series by themselves. *We* find these stories about dragons distinctly amusing, full of unexpected turns and we think children of 9 or so will be much taken with them. Altogether Mrs. Nesbit's book *ought to go*: it must be pushed and advertised of course, but it really is a notable Child's book and helped by the illustrations (which are all good) it should be brought boldly before a bookseller as *the* best child's gift book.[42]

The various series developed by Unwin had their relative order of merit in so far as literary style was concerned, and were destined for different elements of the reading public. Of *Husband of No Importance* by 'Rita' (Eliza Margaret J. Humphreys) Edward asked:

> Will this do for the Antonym? It won't do for the Pseudonym. It is too vulgar and cheap and altogether on a different level to what has now come to be expected as a sine qua non in the Pseudonym, good distinctive art. Rita's story is a potboiler, but a potboiler about 'The New Woman' and not unlikely to be fairly popular. It therefore seems to us to be the sort of thing that will help to pull the Antonym up, and make it talked about. What we want in that series is up to date fiction, fiction essentially of the hour, with now and then an extra good thing thrown in. Rita's sketch of a modern go-ahead strong minded woman, with the slapdash vulgarity of style,

and semi-taking off of different types of society will commend itself to the great railway bookstall public who like some sensation and cheapness for their money.[43]

The potboiling nature of many of the manuscripts he read and his assessment of public taste in this regard were themes common to many of his reports. Edward's opinion in such matters featured particularly in his report on *Margaret Forster* by Sala:

> Mr Sala has always the *grand manner* at his command, even in writing pot boilers to general order. *Margaret Forster* is a pot boiler, a pot boiler of the most flagrant description – but Mr Sala is the king of cheap and glittering journalism and he shows that he has mastered his craft once and for all. Mr Sala is of course old-fashioned – that is to say he has caught the mannerisms of his two favourite authors *Dickens and Balzac* and he has written their story of *modern* up-to-date life on the illustrious lines of these two great men. For ourselves we prefer, frankly, a glittering imitation of Thackeray and Dickens when the author is Sala, and an atmosphere of vulgar luxury and ostentatious splendour is conveyed in the florid Italian manner. We prefer Mr Sala in fact to any number of Coulson Kenahans and Francis Hames of the day. The novel is one that must be treated probably as *a bookseller's volume* i.e. in a gaudy coloured binding it will be worth so much at the Railway bookstall and cheap booksellers. It is just a pot boiler, showy, meretricious, and written on lines popular in 1870 ... [44]

Among the ruck of manuscripts, however, there would come one which satisfied criteria of literary style and commercial possibility sufficiently to nurture hope for the author's future. In such cases Edward would combine analysis of the manuscript and the likely manipulation of public appreciation. In his first report of 20 July 1896 on the literary attempts of a young medical practitioner, Edward wrote rather doubtfully of a story entitled 'A Bad Example': 'There is some ability in this but not *very* much. Mr. Maugham has imagination, and he can write prettily but his satire against society is not deep enough and humorous enough, and his fairy tale is *not* striking enough to command attention. He should be advised to try the humbler magazines for a time, and, if he tries anything more important to send it in to us.'[45]

Six months later he gave much more detailed and complimentary consideration to a novel by the same author: '*A Lambeth Idyll* may be compared to *The Jago* by Arthur Morrison. *The Jago* was a very clever study of the semi-criminal class, done more or less from life, not always artistic, but going deep in places. Mr. Morrison's book has been rather well received by the intelligent section of the public. It, probably, has *to be forced* on the public and on the booksellers and we understand that *Tales of Mean Streets* sold 1200 copies in response to £300 advertisement, but still Messrs. Methuen know well that their own payment comes in reputation.'

Though in his estimation the young author 'has not produced so powerful a study as *The Jago*', Edward went on, 'but when all is said and done *A Lambeth Idyll* is *a very clever realistic study of factory girl and coster life.* The women; their roughness, intemperance, fits of violence, kind-heartedness, slang – all are done truthfully, Liza and her mother Mrs. Kemp are drawn with no little humour and insight. The story is a dismal one in its ending, but the temper and tone of this book is wholesome and by no means morbid. The work is *objective*, and both the atmosphere and the environment of the mean district are unexaggerated.'

In assessing the market for the book Garnett concluded, 'The question for T.F.U. to decide is this – The Arthur Morrison public – a steady growing one will understand and appreciate the book – though of course it was through Mr. Henley's backing that "Mean Streets" and "The Jago" found publisher and public and Mr. Maugham has not got Mr. Henley on his back.' Nevertheless, Edward wrote, 'If T.F.U. does not publish "A Lambeth Idyll" somebody else certainly will. Of course half the critics will call the book "brutal". Now it is no good trying half measures – we mean there is a definite public for and against the "study of realism". We should say *Publish* but of course nobody can guarantee a very favourable reception. All we say is that the book is a *clever*, a *humorous*, study of rather low life, and that its *tone* is quite wholesome and the reverse of morbid. Mr.

Maugham has insight and humour, and will probably be heard of again.'

Critically he remarked: 'We suggest, if the book is taken, that one chapter, that which describes the *outing at Chingford* is too long and has too much the effect of a *piece of clever reporting*. The physical details concerning the dinner and its digestion by A and B are too much insisted upon. In other places some of the bad words might be softened down or Henleyised a bit – à la "Mean Streets". Indubitably', Edward declared, ' . . . the conversation is remarkably well done.'[46] Edward's report overcame Fisher Unwin's hesitation and the book, published as *Liza of Lambeth*, brought its author into the public eye.

Edward was as complimentary of Maugham's next manuscript, *The Making of a Saint*, emphasising the talent of the author and his realistic characterisation. In his first report he commented: 'So far as we can see Mr. Maugham is going *strong*. Nothing is more difficult than for an Englishman to deal with Latin character and temperament and make them move and act in their own environment . . . but Mr. Maugham does make his people real living Italians (at least comes near to the Italian nature). The novel promises to be a strong unusual piece of work, full of vigour [and] it is decidedly interesting and shows Mr. Maugham has plenty of talent left in him to start on so new a tack.'[47] In a second report he concerned himself with its presentation to the public: 'This novel *ought to be* a success. Much depends on the advertising. It must be put forward as a *Romance of Italian History* – a Historical Novel by the author of *Liza of Lambeth*. As we have said it is very strong, fresh and good. The idea must be implanted into the Public's mind that it is a *new thing*, as indeed it is, quite new in its way . . . We will give T.F.U. in the afternoon one or two suggestions about the finish.'[48]

Though he found Maugham's next book, *Daisy*, deficient in some ways, Edward reported favourably on his talents as a story-teller:

In some respects the story is not very artistic. The points Mr Maugham makes are *too broadly* touched in – i.e. – the art is not subtle enough. The conversations of the characters are true enough to life, but we miss this fine touch, we miss the *delicate* hand of this man of great insight. Nevertheless the

story is very *effective*. It is strong and able, and the end undoubtedly has emotional force. In fact the story *hits* one –
there is no denying that: we believe this story will *hit* nearly
every reader. One strong point in its favour is that it is
realistically true. It deals directly with life: it is not the *make-
believe* life that most authors go in for describing. Mr
Maugham is really writing of *life*: and that goes a long way.
We believe this story will meet with a good reception, and
will increase Mr Maugham's reputation. And we should call
it a publisher's mistake for you to lose an opportunity of
missing a volume of such stories.[49]

Edward was doubtful about the prospects of a fantasy novel
sent in by another young author entitled *The Time Machine*. He
wrote: 'This is at all events an ingenious idea. Unlike most
writers of impossible romances of future times the author starts
with the ingenious idea of a Time machine which transports
people backwards and forwards in *time* and not in *space*. The
goodness ends here however and the story drifts into an allegory
of the world divided between Rich and Poor.' In Edward's
opinion, 'The author breaks down and his story becomes commonplace. If it were a little better written and published in a
magazine like *The Tatler* it might be read by uneducated people
with great pleasure and become a favourite à la Bellamy. It is
however a poor performance and we do not advise you to touch
it.'[50] *The Time Machine* was subsequently published by Heinemann.

There were writers, however, whom he regarded as consummate artists within their limited range and these he recommended Unwin to publish whatever the market considerations.
Sarah Orne Jewett fell into this category and he summed up his
opinion of her to Unwin with:

Miss Jewett has a vein of her own. Exquisite, simple, grey
and quiet in her literary touch. She succeeds in bringing
before us the *exact* shades of a countryside and country people
as they appeared in the mind of an observant and cultivated
woman. But the public will not understand the *deftness*, the
restraint, the *dignity* of Miss Jewett's simple and sober style. No
doubt Mrs Meynell and a hundred picked people would

delight in the book, and T.F.U. for auld acquaintance sake, with Houghton Mifflin & Co can no doubt take 250 copies. The story *is* good in its way – simple, delicate, restrained – but we don't expect any but Bostonians to recognise this.[51]

Edward was especially concerned that Unwin should also 'retain at any cost' the work of W. Hale White (Mark Rutherford) whom he regarded as 'a consummate master of a certain range of art – the art of presenting a quiet absolutely true picture of the spiritual life of the middle of the nineteenth century'. Indeed his report on *Clara Hopgood* ended with the conviction that 'to cast away such an exquisite piece of work would stamp any publisher whatsoever, as a barbarian'.[52]

But his conception of the task of the publisher's reader was not confined solely to writing reports that gave assiduous attention to literary worth and to the commercial possibilities of manuscripts. He brought to it a personal involvement combined with critical advice which had consequences for the author that went beyond the mere recognition of quality in a new writer or editorial supervision. Ford Madox Hueffer in his fantastic fashion gave his version of the beginning of such a relationship. He described the day that 'Mr. Edward Garnett came down to the village, bringing with him a great basket of manuscripts that had been submitted to his firm'. According to Fordie, 'We were all dressed more or less medievally, after the manner of true socialism of the William Morris school, drinking, I think, mead out of cups made of bullock's horn.' Edward, he wrote, threw one of the manuscripts across to him: '"Look at that" he said. I think that then I had the rarest literary pleasure of my existence for this MS was that of *Almayers Folly*, the first book of Mr. Joseph Conrad, which he had sent up for judgment – so was Joseph Conrad discovered.'[53]

FIVE

Conrad

Following the daily routine of the Unwin publishing house, on 5 July 1894 the reader who took charge of incoming manuscripts, W. H. Chesson, entered in MS Book 4 (which recorded the receipt of typescripts) the details of a romance that had arrived the previous day.[1] Written under the curious name of 'Kamudi' with the hope that it might be suitable for inclusion in the well-known Unwin series the Pseudonym Library, the manuscript was accompanied by twelve penny stamps. The author wrote to his aunt, Marguerite Poradowska: 'I sent my manuscript to Fisher Unwin & Co who publish a series of anonymous novels. No reply yet. It will doubtless come in the form of a return of that masterpiece, in anticipation of which I enclosed the necessary stamps. To tell the truth I feel no interest in it. And in any case its fate could be no more than an inconsequential episode in my life.'[2] Despite such uncaring sentiments he wrote to her later, in August: ' ... let's speak of that silly Almayer. I have written asking the return of my MS and as soon as I get back to England it will wait your disposition.'[3] On 8 September and back in his lodgings in Gillingham Street he remarked in another letter to her that 'I have just written Fisher Unwin about "Almayer". I am demanding a reply or the return of the MS.'[4]

Pressed for a decision, W. H. Chesson read the novel. He decided instantaneously that it was too good to be surrendered to the author and, as Unwin was away on the Continent, 'It must be submitted to Mr. Garnett.' Chesson's reaction was confirmed by Edward who promptly wrote: 'Hold on to this.'[5] Later Chesson remarked that as receiver and weeder of manuscripts he remembered 'how the magical melancholy of the masterpiece submerged me ... ' The favourable reception of *Almayer's Folly* was a turning point in the life of its creator, who hid his identity behind the Malayan word for rudder – the Polish sea captain Josef Teodor Konrad Korzeniowski. He reported its acceptance to his aunt, saying that 'Fisher Unwin offers me only £20 for the copyright' but he had taken it 'for really the mere fact of publication is very important. Every week dozens of novels come out, and it is terribly difficult to get one's work printed – Now I need only a ship to be almost happy.'[6]

Joseph Conrad was poised at that moment between following the sea or a literary career. As he was to confide to his friend Richard Curle, if *Almayer's Folly* had been rejected he would never have written another book.[7] Despite this statement Conrad's literary aspirations had even then been sufficient for him, whilst waiting for a verdict on *Almayer's Folly*, to begin a story tentatively entitled 'Two Vagabonds'. When Unwin had offered him £20 for *Almayer* he had asked if the author had anything shorter. This, Conrad wrote to Mme Poradowska, was 'quite flattering' but 'I have nothing. The two vagabonds are idle. I am too busy running after ships.'[8] Reporting his discussion with Unwin in more detail Conrad quoted the arguments put to him to justify the terms of publication: 'We are paying you very little,' Unwin had said, 'but consider, my dear Sir, that you are unknown and that your book appeals to a very limited public. Then there is the question of taste. Will the public like it? We too are running something of a risk. We shall bring you out in a handsome volume at six shillings, and you know what we publish always gets serious attention in the literary journals. You may be sure of a long notice in the *Saturday Review* and *The Athenaeum*, not to mention the general press. Write something shorter, of the same kind, for our Pseudonym Library and if it suits us we shall be very happy to give you a much better cheque.' Conrad concluded ironically to his aunt: 'There you are. I am proceeding very gingerly with a vagabond under each arm in the hope of selling them to Fisher Unwin. Slave traffic, on my word of honour.'[9]

Although he had remarked in this same letter that on his visit to the Unwin firm, 'the two "readers" had received me and complimented me effusively (were they by any chance making fun of me?)', he later dramatised his first meeting with Edward in a reminiscence recorded by a mutual friend of Conrad and the Garnetts, Gertrude Bone. In appropriately romantic terms, the wife of Muirhead Bone set the scene:

It was Christmas Day at Conrad's house and his last Christmas Day, it transpired, though the shadow was not then upon us. Muirhead, the boys, Jean Aubry & Jessie & I sat around the fire, a soft wet mist drawing the curtain from outside the windows of the salon. Conrad, less than anyone I have ever met, had the home-making faculty. He, the voyager, sought his home here and there in the mind of a friend. No furniture contained him for long. Seated on the other side of the fireplace from myself, he addressed me across it, his face winning and sweet.

She transcribed their conversation:

'*You* admire Edward do you not?'
'Exceedingly,' I replied.
'The first time I saw Edward,' Conrad recollected, 'I dared not open my mouth. I had gone to meet him to hear what he thought of *Almayer's Folly*. I saw a young man enter the room. "That cannot be Edward so young as that," I thought. He began to talk. Oh yes! It was Edward. I had no longer doubt. But I was too frightened to speak. But that is what I want to tell you, how he made me go on writing. If he had said to me "Why not go on writing?" I should have been paralysed. I could not have done it. But he said to me, "You have written one book. It is very good. Why not *write another*?" Do you see what a difference that made? Another? Yes, I could do that. I *could* do that. Many others I could not. Another I could. That is how Edward made me go on writing. That is what made me an author.'[10]

The meeting between the small dark foreigner with an aristocratic air and the tall angular Garnett took place at the National

Liberal Club, where with Unwin they came together to discuss the novel. Conrad took Garnett to his lodgings for further discussion. Here their mutual feeling of isolation from society helped to cement a friendship between an author uncertain of his literary development and a reader committed to the advance of literature. The association which was to last until Conrad's death was woven over the years into that circle of acquaintances 'with which Conrad protected himself from public indifference – Wells, Sanderson, Symons, Colvin, Cunninghame Graham, Swinnerton, and Curle'. In a passage that revealed his awareness of both the ideals and the practicalities of literary life, Conrad explained: 'When writing one thinks of half a dozen (at least I do) men or so – and if these are satisfied and take the trouble to say it in so many words, then no writer deserves a more splendid recompense. On the other hand there is the problem of the daily bread which cannot be solved by praise, public or private ... ' In J. D. Gordan's estimation, 'Of these [half a dozen men] incomparably the most important, perhaps the only one with direct influence, was Edward Garnett'.[11]

The importance of Edward to Conrad's development was accentuated by four interrelated factors: Conrad's personal circumstances, his ideas about the novel as an art form, his psychological make-up and his expectations (and disappointments) from the reading public. His uncertainty in his own powers and his reliance on Edward were constants in the early years . Their correspondence is punctuated by Conradian sentiments: 'I am getting so used to your interest in my work that it has become like a necessity – like a condition of existence.' [12] Later, apologising for 'interminably worrying you with my affairs', he wrote, 'you are my father in letters and must bear the brunt of that position'.[13] In 'that position' Edward was simultaneously the confidant of Conrad's ideals of the literary art and his personal predicament. Above all he was the critic in whom the author could have confidence because of his unerring sense of what was right and as one who would reveal any faults in the artistic standard. This, by prompting self-scrutiny in Conrad, further affected his work.

In practical terms Edward threaded his views into the approach of a writer whom Gordan has summed up as 'one of the most conscious and conscientious artists who ever lived. The technique, the manner, the fundamentals of writing, were an obsession with him.'[14] While *Almayer's Folly* was going through the press under the supervision of Chesson, the work which Conrad had begun as 'Two Vagabonds' received Edward's chapter by chapter criticism during 1895 to emerge as *The Outcast of the Islands*. The tenor of his criticism, urging Conrad to shift the psychological invention in the novel from the subjective to the objective, is most apparent in the characterisation and motivation of Willems at crucial stages of the story.

Intrusive paragraphs presenting Willems's state of mind and thoughts were deleted on Garnett's advice. Conrad responded to Edward's strictures with convoluted flattery and self-abuse. 'All you say is true. All, absolutely, and the only thing that I can think of is to administer to myself a moral bastinado'[15] – so Conrad wrote to Garnett when he expunged from the manuscript a passage that sought to render Willems's thoughts in the act of betraying Lingard's secrets to the Malays. In the narrative of the four following chapters he asked Edward to look at stylistic experiments in tense changes: 'In chapter XII beginning with the words: "And now they are ... " are the two paragraphs in the new style. Please say in the margin what you think. One word will do. I am very much in doubt myself about it; but where is the thing, institution or principle which I do not doubt.'[16] He dropped the new style on Edward's advice.

Both style and characterisation, which had been affected by Conrad's attempt to interlace irony on human illusions with the psychology of Willems's motives and behaviour just before his death at Aissa's hand and the arrival of his wife, took a different tack before Garnett's adverse comments. 'I shall try,' Conrad wrote, 'without faith, because all my work is produced unconsciously (so to speak) and I cannot meddle to any purpose with that which is in myself. I am sure that you understand what I mean. Still with your help I may try. All the paragraphs marked by you to that effect shall be cut out. For Willems to want to escape from *both* women *is* the very idea ... '[17]

By September 1895 *The Outcast of the Islands* was finished and soon Conrad began 'to write another'. *The Sisters* had as its central character a young Russian artist searching for his soul in Paris. According to Ford Madox Hueffer it would have analysed a complex of incestuous relationships and the same source commented: 'judging from Mr. Garnett's profuse annotations of the actual handwritten copy' he criticised *The Sisters* with a 'minuteness that must have cost him infinite pains'. [18] Confronted by Edward's condemnation of its stilted and insistently adjectival manner Conrad wrote: 'As to that other kind of foolishness: my work [*The Sisters*], there you have driven home the conviction and I *shall* write the sea story at once (12 months). It will be on the lines indicated by you.'[19] But *The Rescuer: A Tales of Narrow Waters* did not see the light of publication until 1920; its spasmodic production was accompanied by exasperated hysteria. Edward greeted the draft Part I with the enthusiastic salutation: 'Excellent, Oh Conrad. Excellent. I have read every word of *The Rescuer* and I think you have struck a new note.' He enclosed in return 'some hasty criticism, mere whims of mine, on only *minute* points'. The closeness of his reading of the text is shown in such notes:

(L15) 'awakened lyrism of his heart ... dangerous' ? too far fetched for Lingard's case *also lyrism* not good in the associations the word awakens

p17 'Contemplating a shabby little home' charming & admirable touch!

page (2) *Omit* 'with the whisper of its hopes and fears' ... stronger without it

page (2) *omit* 'fathomless serenity'

p4. Very good description – admirable & novel & strong

p.9–20 'This man ... This description, though very clear seems to me a little out of proportion *in length*.[20]

Edward's mixture of approbation and suggested emendation was sent from the sick bed where he was recuperating from the bout of typhoid that had so alarmed Constance. The crisis had passed by the end of April, but it was June before he had recovered in health, and in deference to Constance's wishes Conrad did not bother Edward with his work on the novel. He had reached an impasse and for the sake of his own health went to Brittany in May for a holiday. On the 24th, however, he wrote to Edward with characteristic despair over his literary efforts and of his constant battle against the debilitating illness that was to dog him the rest of his life. 'I have been rather ill, lots of pain, fever etc. etc. The left hand is useless still' prefaced his comment that, 'This month I have done nothing to *The Rescuer* – but I have about 70 pages of the most rotten twaddle.'[21]

During his sojourn in Brittany, 'in the intervals of squirming' under the load of *The Rescuer*, he had derived material for a story of peasant life and wanted to know what Edward thought of the idea. Conrad's relationship with his publisher was uneasy: 'The worst of it is that The Patron knows of it. I don't know why I told him about it. I never know what to write to that man. He numbs me like an electric eel.'[22] On the other hand a letter from Conrad to Unwin at this time made plain his faith in Edward's judgment: 'I would consider it very friendly of you to have a look at it yourself and let Mr Garnett have also a try. He has a wonderful sense of what "will do" and spares me not in his criticism which I consider most valuable.'[23]

Later, on 2 June, excusing the fact that The Patron had got hold of his short story with the jocular remark, 'It's a most damnable occurrence – but you should not indulge in typhoid fevers discomposing your friends,' Conrad continued, 'I wrote to him instructions to forward it to you. *I would not* have it published unless you see and pass it fit for the twilight of a popular magazine, I want to know what you think of it with an absurd intensity of longing that is ridiculous and painful.'[24] A further letter a few days later with self-dramatic anxiety for Edward's opinion declares: 'I wrote to Fisher Unwin urging him to forward "Idiots" to you. Have you got it? What do you think? Oh my friend speak the truth if you do tear my entrails through my palpitating flank! from you even torture is sweet. It seems to me I am intruding too much on your life.'[25]

In this letter he also pleaded for Edward's reassurance regarding *The Rescuer*, revealing his trials with the book and his faith in his friend's advice. In reply to Edward's points of criticism welcoming the first draft, Conrad wrote: 'I have read your criticism of the first chapter with profound thankfulness and I surrender without the slighest demur to *all* your remarks. It is easy to do so because they express my own thoughts. Yes! The first page *is* bad.' In considering Edward's comment over the use of 'lyrism' he cried: 'But I don't want the word. I want the idea. Could you help me shape it in an unobjectionable form.'[26] Pleas for Edward's aid were accompanied by confessional passages which a reviewer of Conrad's letters to Edward thought betrayed the writer's 'central deep-seated disenchantment with life itself' and that in his 'appeals for guidance in his work he appears to be ever in a torment of dissatisfaction with his creations. The causes were deeper ... never to him came the artist's satisfaction in regarding the thing accomplished.'[27]

Conrad's attitude to his work was reflected in the letter he wrote to Edward on 19 June, announcing that, 'If I don't believe in the book (and I don't somehow) I believe in you – in you as a last refuge, somewhat as an unintelligent and hope-less sinner believes in the infinite mercy on high.' His search for the artistic satisfaction that eluded him underlay the self-doubt he expressed to Edward in the same letter: 'And I am frightened when I remember that I have to drag it all out of myself. Other writers have some starting point ... my task appears to me as sensible as lifting the world without a fulcrum ...'[28]

The labours of Conrad in 1896, however, were bearing fruit in a burst of creativity, the short stories 'Outpost of Progress' and 'The Lagoon' followed by *The Nigger of the Narcissus*. During this formative period Conrad tested the intention, theme and construction of his work against the judgment of Edward. Des-patching 'Outpost' to his friend he added that it had been written specially for him and wrote to Unwin on the same day to say that he had 'sent it to Garnett for the reason that if refers (in its execution) to a certain discussion we had on matters of art and I should like to know whether I have succeeded in achieving my purpose – my artistic purpose. The effect on him will tell me that.' [29]

Garnett's role as the true standard-bearer of artistic integrity was borne out by Conrad's agreement with Edward's reaction.

> You are right in your criticism of the *Outpost*. The construc-tion is bad. It is bad because it was a matter of conscious decision, and I have no discrimination – in artistic sense. Things get themselves into shape – and they are tolerable. But when I want to write – when I do consciously write or try to construct then my ignorance has full play and ... is disclosed to the scandalised gaze of my literary father ... Let me assure you that your remarks were a complete disclosure

to me ... It's very evident that the first 3 pages kill all the interest. And I wrote them of set purpose!! I thought I was achieving artistic simplicity!!!!! Am I totally lost? Or do the last few pages save the thing from being utterly contemptible? You seem to think so – if I read your most kind and friendly letter aright.

In the same letter he took himself to task, describing 'The Lagoon' as 'a tricky thing with the usual forests, river – stars – wind, sunrise, and so on – and lots of secondhand Conradese in it'. It was a revealing disparagement showing an awareness of his failings before the authority of Garnett and rhetorically asks: 'Don't you think I am a lost soul? – Upon my word I hate every line I write.'[30]

The tone of self-denunciation and doubt ended in September when he turned from the abortive *Rescuer* and embarked on *The Nigger of the Narcissus*. From a book whose characters and conflict he had little equipment to portray, romantic love between urban upper-class Europeans, he returned to familiar territory – the country and the inhabitants of the sea. This engendered a note of confidence and optimism in his letters to Edward. By 21 November he was saying, 'I shall make sail with the Narcissus to expect to make a quick passage. Weather fine – and wind fair.'[31] Conceived as a story of 30,000 words, it blossomed into a novel of twice that length and of all Conrad's writing was the work for which he had most affection. With this novel he felt that he had become a professional and had achieved to a large extent that artistic perfection which he craved: 'Candidly I think it has certain qualities of art that make it a thing apart. I tried to get through the details at the essence of life.' He told the purchaser of the manuscript, John Quinn, that, 'It is the story by which, as a creative artist, I stand or fall ... '[32]

Conrad took infinite pains over the text and sent it piece by piece to Edward for his comments, meeting him frequently to talk over problems in its construction. Typically, and showing affection for the book, he asked: 'I send you seventeen pages more – 65–82 – of my Beloved Nigger. Send them on to Mr. Pawling, but first look at them yourself. I am ashamed to think how much of my work you have not seen. It is as if I had broken with my conscience, quarrelled with the inward voice. I do not feel very safe.' He added, 'Tell me what you think of what you see,' and declared, 'I am going on. Another 20 pages of type – or even less – will see the end, such as it is.' [33] But shortly afterwards in a letter of 2 December, anxious for Edward's counsel, he invited him to lunch to discuss 'a handful of paper in my pocket. Some of that must be in MS for I won't let my wife sit up to type. There will be enough to see the last headland anyhow.'[34]

Garnett, however, turned Conrad away from his usual hurried finish, towards the inclusion of the mutiny scene and episodes designed to add force to the central character and to the dramatic intention of the book. 'Ever since I left you in the mud of Oxford Street I have been back at work,' Conrad wrote after their meeting. 'I think the pages just written won't dishonour the book. Your book which you try to coax into bloom with such devotion and care. And the thing is dramatic enough. It will be done by 7th Jan. Not before.' [35]

The textual changes made at the suggestion of Garnett on a work of which Conrad had said 'Of course nothing can alter the course of the Nigger,' have been studied in manuscript to reveal that some 'thirty pages of the mss. bear Garnett's marginal comments'. Gordan, comparing a passage in the manuscript with that in the printed version, commented that it was 'especially significant for its illustration of Edward Garnett's influence'. In depicting Donkin's sensations after he had done Wait to death, Conrad wrote in the manuscript:

And the immortal sea stretched away, immense and hazy, like the image of life, with a glittering surface and lightless depths; the sea restless . . .
fei unforgiving fateful ? , cruel, entrancing and
terrible ever changing and always the same
                                         at the sea but
Donkin shivered slightly. He gave a defiant look around and
                    slinked slunk noiselessly he had felt himself
suddenly starting off slinking away forward as if if condemned
and cast out by its by the anguished silence of the waters, the
    exacting
sea wringing tears and toil; promising, empty, inspiring and terrible – ever changing and always the same. Donkin *stoo* it

a judges defiant glance and slunk noiselessly as if *condemned* and cast out by the august silence of its might.

In Gordan's view Conrad wished to contrast the contemptible Donkin with the indefinable majesty of the sea. He indulged in excessive use of adjectives against which Garnett wrote 'Cut?' in the margin. Ultimately Conrad carried out Edward's suggested moderation to the letter. The passage read: 'And the immortal sea stretched away, immense and hazy, like the image of life, with a glittering surface and lightless depths; promising, empty, inspiring – terrible. Donkin gave it a defiant glance, and slunk off noiselessly, as if judged and cast out by the august silence of its might.'[36]

When Conrad wrote his preface to *The Nigger of the Narcissus*, important as a statement of his principles as a writer, he sent it to Edward with a letter saying: 'I don't want you to be impatient with it and if you think it at all possible to give it a chance to get printed. That rests entirely with you – the *Nigger* is *your* book and besides you know very well I daren't make any move without your leave ... '[37] Fittingly Conrad dedicated the book to Edward in gratitude for their close association during its writing and Edward's guidance towards the objective realism that raised it above the melodrama of a boys' sea story. He turned to Edward for reassurance when it had been published and had met with an unfavourable reception. Symons compared Conrad's 'beloved Nigger' to its disadvantage with Kipling's *Captains Courageous*. He wrote: 'Look only at the last year and take only two books. Mr. Kipling's *Captains Courageous* and Mr. Conrad's *Nigger*. In one of these what an admirable mastery of a single bit of objective reality, of the adventure of trade, of what is external in the figures who are active about it! In the other there is almost endless description of the whole movement, noise, order and distraction of a ship and ship's company during a storm, which brings to one's memory a sense of every discomfort one has endured upon the sea.'[38] Conrad asked Edward for his opinion of Symons's charge: 'I am sending you here a bit of the *Sat. Rev.* Symons mentions Kipling and myself as you can see. Frankly is the remark true?'[39]

Although *The Nigger of the Narcissus* gave Conrad the deepest personal satisfaction, shortly after it was finished he regressed into other works which were to give him little comfort and which brought from him again frequent complaints to Edward on the arduous nature of his writing. He began a short story in early February 1897 with the typically pessimistic declaration: 'My heart is in my boots when I look at the white sheets. Offer up a short prayer for me.'[40] He delivered part of 'Karain' to Edward at the end of the month with the self-dramatic cry: 'Ecco la! I deliver my misguided soul into your hands. Be merciful. I want you, besides as much criticism as you have time and inclination for, to tell me whether the thing is printable. And understand well this: If you say "Burn!" I will burn – and won't hate you. But if you say: "Correct–Alter!" I won't do it – but shall hate you henceforth and forever!'[41]

Edward ignored the familiar extravagance, and his firmness in criticising its construction produced from Conrad appreciation of his insight: 'I have been at *Karain* and have rewritten all you had seen. A painful task. Strangely though I always recognised the justness of your criticism it is only this evening after I had finished the horrid job that the full comprehension of what you objected to came to me like a flash of light in a dark cavern.' Interpolated into his letter was an expression of admiration for Garnett's dedication to literary excellence. 'I think your mission is to work for *art* – and I know you will work artistically *for* art – for the very essence of it.'[42] He voiced his gratitude in this respect on the completion of 'Karain' on 14 April: 'Karain has gone to Unwin today. In the letter I ask *U* to give the story to you before sending it out among the editors. I ask you to read it specially because it is your advice that has reshaped it and made it what it is – in good. I have not got rid of *all* the bad (in the first 15 pages) but I am nevertheless grateful to you for putting me on the right track.'[43]

'Karain' can be seen as an approach to chronological dislocations in unfolding a tale which foreshadowed the technique used in *Lord Jim*. It may be that Conrad was acknowledging that its construction was the product of discussion and criticisms between them. As he said to Edward apropos the revised version: 'Where do you think the illumination – the short and vivid flash of which I have been boasting to you came from? Why! From your words, words, words. They exploded like stored powder barrels. An explosion is the most lasting thing in the universe. It leaves disorder, remembrance, room to move, a clear space ... '[44] In the use of time-shifts it was the beginning of an approach to fiction that was to reach its zenith in work such as *Nostromo*, and in which inevitability resulting from moral choice raised Conrad above the mere teller of a tale.

In his next book, *The Return*, Conrad was again enmeshed in difficulties of composition and asked Edward for the usual comfort and discussion: 'The Return being accomplished in about 23,000 steps it is natural that I should ask you to come and kick it back again whence it came. The fact is my dear fellow your criticism, even when destructive, is so shamelessly adulatory that I simply *can't live* without it. As a matter of fact it's all I have to live upon. Please consider! Seriously. Am I to send it to you? Are you at leisure and have you the disposition: How much nicer if you could come. Say – on Thursday – or rather any day after Monday.'[45]

But Conrad developed a distaste for the story and his further correspondence with Edward over its completion is punctuated by histrionic refusals to alter it: 'But I swear to you that I won't alter a line – not a comma – for you. There! And this for the reason that I have physical horror of that story. I simply won't look at it any more. It has embittered five months of my life. I hate it.'[46] On 29 September a letter to Edward shows the difficulties he had over the effects he wished to achieve coupled with an implicit acknowledgment of Edward as the arbiter of its achievement:

I don't know whether to weep or to laugh at your letter ... I am hoist with my own petard. My dear fellow what I aimed at was just to produce the effect of cold water in every one of my man's speeches. I swear to you that was my intention. I wanted to produce the effect of insincerity, of artificiality ... But if I have to explain that to you – to you! – then I've egregiously failed. I've tried with all my might to avoid just these trivialities of rage and distraction which you judge necessary to the truth of the picture. I counted it a virtue, and lo and behold! You say it is sin. Well! Never more! It is evident that my fate is to be descriptive and descriptive only. There are things I *must* leave alone.[47]

Later in exasperation he wrote to Edward: 'But the more I think of that story the more I feel (I don't see yet) the justice of your pronouncement as to the unreality of the dialogue ... I felt all the time there was something wrong with that story. I feel it more than ever.'[48] What Conrad was to call his 'left-handed production' cost him much in 'sheer toil, in temper, and in disillusion'.[49] Disillusionment also came from his difficulties over the financial rewards that his work received. As he had remarked to Edward, 'his first view of New Grub Street was as inviting as a peep into a brigand's cave and a good deal less reassuring.'[50] At their first meeting he had reacted vehemently to Edward's view of the necessity for a writer to follow his path and disregard the public's taste: 'But I *won't* live in an attic. I'm past that, you understand. I *won't* live in an attic!'[51]

To their literary association Edward brought the practical advantages of his knowledge of the book world. When Conrad's usual chronic financial state led to a breakdown in his relations with Unwin in 1896, Edward steered him and *The Nigger of the Narcissus* to Pawling of Heinemann's at more advantageous terms. Conrad expressed his appreciation with the usual super-latives in a succession of letters: '... I am as you imagine exceedingly pleased with what Pawling has written. My dear fellow you are the making of me ... '[52] and later, ' ... [Pawling] is an excellent fellow and you are a super-excellent one to have introduced me to him.'[53] It was the 'selling business' that caused Conrad so much anguish and to be relieved of it lessened his anxiety, as he said to Edward: ' ... I had this morning a letter from Pawling so utterly satisfactory that there can be no question of even thinking about anyone else as long he wants me ... I hope I've done with the *selling* business for life.'[54]

Conrad, whose stature is now so assured and so fixed by influential academic critics as a great 'modern', was entering uncharted seas when he began as a writer. He depended on publication for survival yet strove to maintain his artistic ideals. It was through Edward's exertions that Conrad achieved both to some degree at the outset of his career. One of the most fruitful connections followed from Edward's comments that '*Karain* was destined by providence for Blackwood's Magazine.'[55] Years later Conrad wrote that 'it was you who turned *Karain* on to the Maga. with inspired judgment'.[56] The happy relationship Conrad had with *Blackwood's* derived from the fact that in 'this journal of Empire and the outposts of civilisation, Conrad, a middle class writer, had found an audience congenial to his talents, a public that he had discovered nowhere else';[57] in Conrad's words, 'the one to catch on best to my stuff'.[58] He said to Edward, 'All the good moments I owe to you. You sent me to Pawling – you sent me to Blackwoods. '[59] At the outset of his career the 'forty-five shillings per thousand words' which he received from *Blackwood's* for 'Karain' had to be set against the 'protracted tension and anxiety as to the saleability of his work which Conrad suffered from in 1897'.[60]

By this time Conrad was committed to his future in literature. Though their friendship continued, as Edward put it, 'My advice as his literary friend and critic, was in fact becoming unnecessary. Apart from the *Rescuer* which he continued to send to me, chapter by chapter, he had confidence in himself and was receiving encouragement from various quarters.'[61] Indeed this was to be the regular pattern of Edward's association with aspiring authors – to encourage them, then to leave them when they had developed their own distinctive capability. Conrad by his origins and by his genius was one of the first and the most complex of the writers he dealt with in this way.

A letter from Constance to Conrad reflects her accurate estimation of Conrad's linguistic characteristics.

I have been reading the 'Nigger' ... I feel as I have always told Edward that your brain does not think English thoughts – as Turgenev's own – it is more delicate, more subtle, richer and more varied than ours. Your use of adjectives, so chosen – fastidious – often ironical, reminds me again and again of Tourgenev's manner. It gives me greater pleasure that you should have dedicated your book to Edward, and I am sure that in sympathy you are never divided.[62]

When Constance wished to express her admiration for Conrad as a writer and as a friend of the family by dedicating to him her translation of Turgenev's *A Desperate Character*, Conrad wrote to Edward on 26 October 1899 in praise of her translations. 'She is in that work', he wrote, 'what a great musician is to a great composer – with something more, something greater.'

The same letter revealed that a change in the fortunes of Edward and Constance was imminent for it ended, 'The news about the Patron is grave. Is it grave? Surely you – you! are wanted in too many places to bother much about the placing of your wits. I keep mum but let me know the finality of this thusness.'[63]

SIX

Leaving Unwin

JOSEPH CONRAD with his collaborator, Ford Madox Hueffer, fictionalised his dependence on Edward during his formative years in a passage in *The Inheritors*: 'Lea's opinion formed, to some extent, the background of my life. For many years I had been writing quite as much to satisfy him as to satisfy myself.'[1] Of this portrayal, J. A. Meixner commented that 'Lea, who is modelled on Edward Garnett, is particularly fine; though he appears in one brief chapter he leaves a trace of his pre-occupied and dry-witted rectitude trailing after him through the book.'[2]

The opposing character to Lea, the publisher's reader, is Polehampton – an avaricious publisher drawn from T. Fisher Unwin. For Conrad, 'The Patron' soon became the 'odious' Unwin and Cunninghame Graham shared his dislike, remarking sarcastically to Edward in a letter of 8 July 1898: 'Yes, I have seen Mr. Unwin, thank you. It appears Mr. F. Unwin has published once a most curious book for Hudson "The Chrystal Age" [*sic*]. He regrets that it was a "pecuniary" loss to him and he pursed his lips as he spoke.'[3]

Differences in temperament and outlook overshadowed the relationship between Edward and Fisher Unwin. The manner and character of Unwin, as described by his great-nephew Philip, irritated many people. To cover a basic anxiety he posed as 'the great and omniscient publisher, the patron of authors, who were exceptionally fortunate to be published by him'.[4] With little sense of humour he had an apparent coldness of manner which made personal relationships difficult. Though he had a genuine flair for publishing, a sense of the market drawn from a long apprenticeship in the trade and a knowledge of where to seek advice, he found it difficult to come to a decision. In addition, perhaps unjustifiably in view of the economics and custom of the book trade at that time, he had a closeness in financial matters which unfortunately was not backed by good accountancy.

Edward, however, was self-willed and impatient. Impulsive in his early years, he had a concern for the advancement of the author he believed in that transcended mere allegiance to his employer. This became generalised into references to the 'ignorant and degenerate race of publishers'[5] as he wrote on one occasion to W. H. Hudson; or with more heavy irony in a letter to Cunninghame Graham:

Ten days ago I told him (T.F.U.) that the *Sketches* (of about 31,000 words) was practically ready and I suggested a royalty on X copies – to which he demurred. For many publishers hold the queer view that an author's royalty is an unearned increment and to these men (respected) the word *publisher* spells the trouble, the labour, the responsibility of doing the perilous work of the middleman! Some publishers see horrible pictures of capital sweating its uphill way drawing faint behind it the triumphal car of the proletariat author ... [6]

The deterioration in the relationship between Edward and Unwin and views upon Edward's future were put in a letter by Constance to Dr Garnett on Boxing Day 1899:

I fear you must be feeling some anxiety on our account. I have felt for such a long while that it was impossible Edward should remain at Fisher Unwins – his business seems to be going downhill in more ways than one – And it is so much better that such a crisis in our fortunes should come now when Edward is thirty than that he should have had to seek fresh openings a few years later, when he will be older ... I do not myself feel apprehensive as to our future – I have complete confidence in Edward's energies and good sense –

the only anxiety which troubles me is on the grounds of his health. I doubt whether he is strong enough to stand a long strain of very hard work. His health is good as long as he leads a quiet life free from worry – but if he should be forced to depend on journalistic work to any great degree I am afraid the necessity of working against time and the uncertainty of the work would tell upon him.[7]

More cheerfully Constance viewed the fact that ' ... meanwhile it is fortunate that 3 volumes of Turgenev should appear in such rapid succession bringing each its cheque, so that we shall have a nice little sum to replace for a few months our regular income and to tide over a period of transition. We are hoping to arrange some more work – probably Tolstoi – for me and I shall set upon it with great zest after this holiday ... ' On a more personal note indicative of a lifelong susceptibility she concluded happily: 'I have been so extraordinarily free from headaches during the last four or five months and I have never been in my life before and can hardly believe in my good fortune.'

Her fears for Edward and her financial forecast proved to be well founded in the next two difficult years. 'Mr. Fisher Unwin', Edward wrote, 'dispensed with my services as his literary adviser at the end of 1899.'[8]

Now that he had finally broken with Unwin, finding sufficient sources of income was a problem which Edward, writing to his father on 15 February 1900, hoped could be solved by a combination of literary tasks:

You will be pleased to learn that I have begun this week to read some manuscripts for Mr. Pawling. At present the arrangement is a tentative one, and I do not quite know what it will lead to – probably to my advice being asked with reference to those manuscripts as to which it is not easy for Mr. Heinemann to make up his mind. In any case the work is valuable to me and may develop in the future. Heinemann also wishes Connie to translate a French novel for him – to form one of a series of 12 translations. I have thought over your idea of telling Dr. Robertson Nicoll that I am free to do any reviewing and should be writing to him, you might put it casually. I have met him once. I shall probably be writing more for The Academy and I hope to meet Mr. Massingham by and by with reference to possible work on his new Daily Paper in prospect.[9]

In reply the sagacious Dr Garnett was 'very glad to hear of the work with Mr. Pawling. It is not entirely new to me for he had himself told me of it, showing the best inclination to be of service to you.' He hoped that Mr Massingham's design 'will come to something' but thought 'he must be discreet if he is to remain at the head of it. It is quite possible to take the unpopular side without being un-English and unpatriotic.'[10] The uncertainty of continuous employment with Heinemann and their precarious financial position, which was of so much concern to Dr Garnett, is reflected in a letter to him from Constance on 2 March 1900: 'Edward goes up once or twice a week to Heinemann's though so far nothing definite is arranged and we are not speaking of it to anyone till things are more certain ... about our financial position you need feel no anxiety for a good while to come. At least we can stand a siege, or rather I should say I suppose a lock out. Even if we were so unfortunate as to be without work for a year I fancy we should manage to meet our liabilities.'[11]

The arduous nature of Edward's work at Heinemann, however, and the effect it had upon his health was the subject of a letter to Constance's father-in-law on 2 August: 'Edward was unwell with toothache and hardly fit for work at the time. He has been altogether much too busy this summer and looks tired and overworked. Heinemann has a most unfortunate system of giving translation work to quite incompetent persons who don't know English – and then giving their unintelligible translations to be revised to Edward, who does not know the original languages. I feel for the poor authors almost as much as for the unhappy reviser!' Drawing comparisons with Edward's erstwhile employer she continued, 'Mr. Heinemann and Mr. Unwin suggest the fable of the sun and the wind and the traveller's cloak. Mr. Heinemann's amiability succeeds in getting an amount of work out of his employees that Mr. Unwin's chilly and repellent manners never managed to do. I hope Edward will go to the Huts on Wednesday for a night or so.'[12]

The days at Heinemann were coming to an end. Edward disclosed his feelings about this in a brief, spirited letter written with customary affection to his mother on 5 July 1901:

> You will like to know that I slept decently well last night, without the taking of suphonal. There is nothing the matter with my health or spirits beyond my being worried just lately by business matters. I am leaving Heinemann in two or three months time and I have written the details to Papa – but don't mention this to anybody for the present. I daresay I shall do better in the long run by leaving Heinemann as for a very responsible position he holds out practically a clerk's pay. Your son has plenty of wit and ingenuity with which to fight his little battles, till he is sympathized with by his Irish mother when he becomes suddenly soft for a minute. At any rate his Irish mother's sympathy is very dear to him.[13]

To his father Edward wrote that he was of the view that 'as Pawling's protégé I have, from the first, been looked upon by Heinemann with some jealousy, and he has now taken an opportunity of putting his own man in my place'. Edward assured his father that the 'dismissal is certainly not due to lack of care on my side I can most certainly avow. I have worked extremely carefully and diligently at Heinemann's in the hope of building up a position, and I have worked too for the extremely small sum of 3£ to 3£ 10/- a week.' For this 'the amount of reading, editing and correction that Heinemann required' was exacting and continuous. Bad publishing seasons, he told his father, made 'the position of anyone as Reader however efficient, original and devoted in the service of good literature' very precarious. Edward doubted if he would be able to 'get another situation as Reader' and for the future he hoped to 'do more journalistic and literary work' and wondered if his father could suggest avenues for this amongst his correspondents and friends.[14] To absolve himself from any charge of waywardness Edward enclosed Heinemann's letter and in this, dated 2 July 1901, Heinemann explained:

> I am more than fully alive to the fact that the salary we are paying you now is hardly adequate to your qualifications

and your work, and I am also aware that I require soon – and shall require even more in the future – a certain editorial assistance which is somewhat outside your lines. Under these circumstances I cannot afford further to burden any 'reading budget' by offering you a salary such as I should like to offer you. This consideration has led us to revise the whole question of reading, paragraphing, editing, etc. and we have come to the conclusion that it will suit our purposes best to remould our arrangements entirely. Under our new arrangement we could I fear even less than in the past offer you what is so unquestionably your due, and we think therefore that it will be best if you at your own convenience and in your own time dispose of your work elsewhere. In depriving ourselves of your services we are more than conscious of their great value, and we beg to thank you very cordially for the efficient, original, and devoted manner in which you have conducted our affairs. Your relations with our authors have certainly been entirely satisfactory to ourselves.[15]

The close-knit family relationship and an insight into the kind of working relationship congenial to Edward is apparent in the letter that Constance addressed to Dr Garnett on 15 July:

I am afraid you must be feeling anxious and troubled about Edward. I am very sorry indeed that he is leaving Heinemanns – much more so than when he left Fisher Unwins. The work he has done for Heinemann though it has required and received more time and care than the reading for Fisher Unwin did, has been more congenial and the atmosphere of the office has been so much pleasanter and more friendly I had quite hoped that it would prove a permanent haven. The income of course was very small, but there were many compensations. I fear it would be difficult to find in any other publisher's house a man to whom Edward could feel as warmly as he does towards Mr Pawling. It gave a special zest and interest for him to be working for someone he liked so much. However the loss of this position is certainly in no way due to any act or omission of Edward's and so one can but accept it and trust something else turns up before long ... Your kind sympathetic offer to Edward touched me very much, especially your offer to undertake the cost of David's education . . .[16]

Edward and Constance were in difficult financial straits that summer. Without employment of any kind Edward used his knowledge of fungi to enable the family to subsist throughout the wet summer days of 1901 and his son David recalled later that they had mushrooms for every meal. Relief from such a monotonous diet came when Edward finally found settled employment with Gerald Duckworth. 'You'll be glad to know', he told his anxious father, 'that I have now concluded an arrangement with Duckworth by which I shall "read" for them on the same terms as I had at Heinemann. I have also settled with them to start a certain series, which, if successful will bring the same money and also give literary work to several friends. At present don't mention that I am at Duckworths.'[17] In *her* letter to Dr Garnett which was written on the same day, 4 October, Constance expressed her gratitude for this fortuitous arrangement and the effect the past few months had had on Edward:

> I know you will rejoice to hear that Edward has got what promises to be permanent work as reader to Duckworth. He saw Duckworth on Tuesday and this morning received a decisive reply from him. He has been in Town seeing him today and everything is satisfactorily settled. I am very thankful for Edward has been exerting himself in all sorts of ways to a point when there seemed to me a great danger of his breaking down. And of course it is a great piece of luck. There are so few houses in which Edward could possibly be employed that one could hardly expect him to find a vacancy at once.[18]

Edward, Constance reported later on 12 November 1901, became very busy working at all sorts of schemes for Duckworth's benefit and his own.[19] 'Everything', she remarked later to Edward's father, 'depends on whether he can turn out saleable books and that one cannot reckon upon with any degree of certainty.'[20] He transferred to Duckworth the energy in the promotion of series which had characterised his time at Unwin. He brought into the series the authors he had befriended. One of these, who was to be a firm friend and an author he greatly admired, was W. H. Hudson. While with Unwin, Edward had reported on Hudson's *Mr. Abel: A Romance of Guyana* in doubtful terms regarding its saleability. 'Mr. Hudson has written a very readable book,' he began. 'It is exciting, it deals with a comparatively unknown country and it is, in short, a good adventurous novel. It is not, however, the sort of book that we should advise T.F.U. to speculate on. If he had a cheap series at 3/6 or 5/- of adventurous romance such as Cassell has, he might hook it on to Q's works and his followers but issued in the ordinary 6/- style we fear it will not attract sufficient attention to sell well . . . '21

At Heinemann, however, another manuscript from Hudson aroused his enthusiastic support and he arranged to meet him in his last days with that firm. As Edward wrote later: 'I first met Hudson over the publication of *El Ombu*. It was my last day as Heinemann's reader and I was clearing up my work when a lad announced "Mr. Hudson." . . . Some weeks before I had impressed on Mr. William Heinemann that *El Ombu* was a work of genius and that he must publish it. "But we shan't sell it," objected Mr. Heinemann in his nervous, excitable fashion. He had temporised, afraid either to return the manuscript or to accept.'22 He had expressed his admiration for Hudson's work in a letter to his friend Cunninghame Graham:

I would have sent you *El Ombu* before, but it is being 'read' by American firms, with a view to halving the expense and safeguarding the interests (!) of Mr. W.H. [Heinemann] I have tried to induce the partners (there) to make Hudson a fair offer of some cash down – but they do not seem to see the necessity. Will you therefore tell him from me that I advise him, if they decline to give him an advance to print *El Ombu* first in some Magazine – such as *Macmillan's Magazine*. He may thus get *something* for his labour without waiting two or three years for a miserable sum. I speak freely as one poor man to another. I have an excessive admiration for *El Ombu*. It remains in my memory as a masterpiece. It is indeed a great literary 'Ombu' which casts a deep shadow, while all around are the horrible manufactured little Christmas Trees, in penny pots – acres and acres of the popular 'stuff' reared to sell in their publishing 'seasons'. By the way my capitalist

at 21 Bedford St. finds he can 'dispense' with my services. No
doubt he is quite right. It is ironical that one cannot 'dispense'
either with one's soul or one's employer ... [23]

Hudson's *El Ombu*, one of the first titles in the Greenback
Series Edward launched at Duckworth, was followed closely by
a collection of sketches and stories by his friend Cunninghame
Graham. Edward wrote to Graham: 'Duckworth will be delighted to publish your "Success" in the "Greenback Series" –
paying you 15 per cent royalty on the published price of all
copies sold. And should he sell an Edition or copies to America
he will give you 15% on what he gets ... '[24] Edward's energetic
promotion of the series is shown in the garrulous replies which
May Sinclair wrote to his typical analyses of her work:

> My best thanks for your kind and valuable criticism. I will
> say at once that I agree to most of it. My hero is very Henry
> Jamesy: Frieda ought not to have had a Russian mother, and
> the story does not confuse ... I have no business to go on
> hitting the nails after they were driven in – into a coffin too!
> Pointing the moral doesn't adorn the tale ...
>
> I believe, if I asked you what my special literary vice was,
> you would say 'a love for too much neatness and completeness
> of idea'. And you would tell me that nature abhors ideas as
> much as she abhors a vacuum. And you would be right. I
> shall be most interested to know what you think of 'Mr. &
> Mrs. Neville Tyson' ... Many thanks for the Green-back
> prospectus it is a very tempting one, and I should very much
> like to try to write something for it ... Again thanking you
> for your criticism – which is exactly the sort I want most and
> has, I believe, helped me already.[25]

Shortly afterwards she wrote:

> Your last letter gave me a great deal of matter for reflection
> which is why I did not write immediately to thank you. And
> I *do* thank you most sincerely for your criticism, which I think
> is most excellent and just in theory. I don't in the least resent
> its application, only if I've failed to make you share in my
> own simple faith in the reality of Mr Neville Tyson, I think

that is due to my clumsiness in the portraiture and not to my idea of the man ... Please don't think that I want to dispute every point – it would be a very poor return for your having written to me so carefully and fully. I only wanted you to believe that I care for nature and reality as much as you do and that it was the 'art' that was lacking if I have failed to prove it ... But to prove how much I value the principles of your criticism I am going carefully over my long novel, and wherever I find anything that seems to me like 'romancing' – out it goes ... I have already yielded to the temptation you threw in my way in your first letter: I have begun a story which I should like to send you for the Green-Back Library if it is any good when it's done. I defy you to find any romance in it whatever.[26]

For another series which he started for Duckworth, the Popular Library of Art, he interested and encouraged Ford Madox Hueffer to write monographs on Holbein and Rossetti. Ford, with the enthusiasm and concern for the craft of writing appropriate to the founder of the *English Review*, suggested to Edward a parallel series to be devoted to literature: '... The idea keeps booming in my head: Why shouldn't there be a popular Library of Literature on the lines of yr. Library of Art? – conceived on the broad general idea of making manifest, to the most unintelligent, how great writers *get their effects* ... '[27]

Whatever their later differences, in their friendly early years it would seem that Ford turned to Edward for advice and that Edward was sympathetic to Ford's aspirations. Edward acted as adviser and agent to Ford when Ford's uncle commissioned him to write the life of Ford Madox Brown. He responded to Ford's plea for advice on the style and construction of the book and Ford thanked Edward 'for all you've done – I don't know why you do it'.[28] Edward's sister Olive noted in her diary the occasion 'after dinner' when 'Edward talked brilliantly about the Life showing Ford what a valuable literary property it was'. But she remarked on another occasion, 'Edward criticised Ford's M.S.S. severely. "German, ambitious, slovenly, vague; he will generalise about things of which he knows nothing." Edward took trouble in trying to make it better, underlining bad English, crossing out useless things and so on. But I can't

help feeling for Ford. Of course it is kind of Edward, and good
for Ford, but when one thinks of the immense labour he has
taken, one feels sorry for the further necessity of ruthless amend-
ing.'[29] Ford also sent the manuscript of *Rossetti* to Edward for
his opinion and though he trusted his judgment found Edward's
suggestions 'almost shocking'.[30] It would appear, however, that
Ford continued to submit his work to Edward for advice and
correction. In the opinion of Professor A. Mizener, it was with
The Benefactor that Ford found his own true voice and though
published in 1905 it had been completed two years earlier and
seen in manuscript by Edward Garnett.[31] Certainly Ford wrote
in 1903 to Edward: 'Herewith the end of the *Altruist* [i.e. *The
Benefactor*]. Let me have the whole rotten bunch back when
you've done with it. I mean don't send it back in detachments
to draw out the agony of re-corr[ns]. I'm sick of it.' Ford ended
his letter with the information: 'I see the Art Books are advertised largely in a Pub. Circular that Robert [i.e. Edward's
brother] has sent me. I hope they'll go.'[32]

In his efforts to make the series more attractive, Edward tried
to interest his friend May Morris, daughter of William Morris,
in contributing to the Popular Library of Art, but she replied:
'Your suggestion that I should write a book for Messrs Duckworth's charming little series is flattering, but I assure you I
have no specialized knowledge of painters ... I have always
avoided writing anything on my Father, having felt it was
perhaps not judicious to attack a subject so intimate. I may be
mistaken in this, but I am sure you will understand the feeling.'[33]
Edward himself made his own contribution to the series with a
monograph on Hogarth. It was a particularly apposite choice,
for Hogarth exhibited those traits of realism and truthfulness
which Edward sought in literature. Moreover the 'neglect' of
these Hogarthian qualities was, as Edward put it, 'during the
Victorian era ... but a reflex of the general movement towards
"elegance" and genteel refinement.'[34]

His work at Duckworth continued on the same lines as at
Unwin and his reports were larded with the usual pithy observations on the writer's style and on public taste. An early manuscript, *Bristles*, by E. M. Dell, who was to be a best seller of the
period, and whom he mistook for a male author, received the
comment:

The Tales have a certain amount of ability. They are a deification of the qualities of modesty, sincerity – love of duty – loyalty, that the English middle-class conceives it has more or less a monopoly of – and there is a certain amount of that *unreal* picture of fancy soldiering that the British public adore – but of course these artistic defects are what make for this author's popularity – so far as *stage effects* goes however the tales are just what the public requires and we should have thought a magazine such as Pall Mall Magazine would have printed them with eagerness. Personally we dislike the style and find the picture of military life *sentimental and overdone* but it is only right to say that E. M. Dell might gain the public's *ear with a novel*. There is an utterly unreal 'Russian woman' in tale No. 1. – but the public would like her immensely.[35]

Ironically E. M. Dell was to be attracted to Edward's old firm, T. Fisher Unwin. She submitted a manuscript to Unwin's First Novel Library and her subsequent books for him ensured bumper profits during the following seven or eight years. As her popularity declined after the Great War so did his firm.

Edward also dismissed *The Real Way* by Frank Swinnerton as:

Not up to Duckworth's standard for a novel. The author means well and his effort is laudable. We should like to help him – because there is something pathetic in the tone revealed (between the lines) of a clerk's aspirations towards the richer mental life beyond his power of attaining. But the story fails. It is too *unreal*: there is too much pseudo-romance in the presentation of the scenes. Mr. Swinnerton should be advised to analyze unsparingly – to tell the real truth about the people he knows, not to idealize life but to probe it. Decline with thanks.[36]

Edward counted as his greatest discovery the work of C. M. Doughty. His enthusiasm for Doughty was expressed in his report on *Adam and Eve*, submitted as *Hawwa*:

We look on this as a piece of the highest genius. Of genius that can only be matched by Milton. We have read and studied every line with the greatest attention and we can only say that in *atmosphere* and simple severe sublimity it is a *masterpiece of the highest order*. It is a great conception – executed with a stern and unfaltering hand. We find no difficulty whatsoever in the language, which though mannered – the manner of a genius – is *comparatively* simple compared with The Dawn of Britain. We think that this is just the poem that *Duckworth required in order to bring Doughty to the knowledge of the better-class public* ... In publishing 'Hawwa' Duckworth will not eventually lose money. It should sell on its merits an edition of 500 copies – and we pledge ourselves to write twenty personal letters to people selected. We can only report that 'Hawwa' is great literature and that Doughty is a great poet.[37]

Edward always remained obstinate in his conviction that Doughty's *Dawn of Britain* was a great unknown poem, an opinion that was not shared by his contemporaries or later readers. He was to strike up a lifelong friendship with the author and such was his firm belief in Doughty's work that Richard Church called him 'Doughty's John the Baptist'.[38] When he had first read *Dawn of Britain*, Edward 'felt confounded by the strange style. But reading the MS. for the second time all the difficulties vanished and I became enthusiastic. It seemed to me, alike in conception, imagination and language, to be the work of a titan. I told Mr. Duckworth that Doughty was a genius, and, like a good sportsman, Mr. Duckworth rose to the occasion and agreed to publish the Epic.'[39]

A more fruitful outcome of his belief in Doughty's ability came with an abridgment he prepared of *Arabia Deserta*. Edward had read it after Sydney Cockerell had told him that it was one of William Morris's favourite books. His combative spirit was aroused when he found that 'nobody I know had heard of it' and he persuaded Duckworth to publish the abridgment under the title of *Wanderings in Arabia Deserta*. As D. H. Hogarth, Doughty's biographer, put it on its issue in 1908: 'Reviewers to a man greeted it with enthusiasm – some of them also with surprise that for so long they should have known so little of the classic from which it derived ... Inevitably, moreover (though of few abridgments in literary history could the same be said), it created a demand for *Arabia Deserta*.'[40] This remark was corroborated by Edward Thomas in a letter to

Gordon Bottomley of 30 March 1908: 'You won't get the old
Arabia Deserta for a very long time. The London Library is full
of demands for it.'[41]

On more commercial lines Edward made an acute assessment
of the manuscripts submitted to Duckworth by Arnold Bennett.
He read and recommended for publication *Anna of the Five
Towns*, though he criticised the suicide of Willie Price in the last
chapter as 'irrelevant and out of focus'. The novel, however,
went to Chatto & Windus because Duckworth would not meet
Bennett's request for a higher royalty.[42] In considering *The
Truth about an Author*, Edward called Bennett 'a shrewd young
man from the North of England with a great faculty for "getting
on" and producing marketable copy. He has in addition a very
fair "literary instinct" and has raised himself from the position
of a solicitor's clerk to that of "a successful author and dramatist".' Bennett, he went on, 'takes literature seriously, but also
takes successful journalism seriously and the most interesting
thing about him is the strange amalgam he presents of *commercial*
man pure and simple, and author'. There was 'no literature' in
the manuscript submitted, but in *Anna of the Five Towns* Bennett
had written 'a real fine novel, that *is* literature, and is on quite
a different plane to his catalogue of potboilers'.

Edward concluded that Duckworth would have to weigh up
the advantages of publishing a book which might add to his
reputation as an enterprising publisher willing to seek out light,
amusing literature. On the other hand the 'grave literary men –
real and serious – Leslie Stephen, Sydney Lee, Colvin, Gosse,
the Macmillan Olympians – might and would say "What could
induce you to take this preposterous book of this journalistic
and literary 'tupper'?" '[43]

Edward, however, was at odds with these 'grave literary men'
on a number of issues, upon which he commented not only in
his role as a publisher's reader but also as a literary critic. It
was the critical Establishment which, he felt, had stifled literature and stunted the development of new forms of writing in
England.

SEVEN

Reader as Critic

I T was during that anxious time between leaving Unwin and joining Duckworth that Edward turned his mind to the possibility of published criticism as a source of income. His ambitions in this direction received the support of Conrad, who wrote to D. S. Meldrum of *Blackwood's Magazine*:

> E. Garnett thinks of publishing (in due time) a vol. of criticism. It will be something fresh and intelligent too – and it is about time intelligence had its say in these matters. What he would like to do would be to publish very soon what is intended [to] form a sort of introduction to such a volume, as a paper in some magazine. This would be illustrated by examples (from Lyolf Tolstoi to Joseph Conrad I believe) giving his idea of the relation between literature and life in their modern conditions. A large order for 6000 words. Still the man is quite capable of it; and I am sure there will be no platitudes in it whatever amount of sound truth there may be. Do you think he would have any chance of being given room in the Maga.
>
> For myself I don't see why not. Whatever his political and social opinions may be (and he is not one to obtrude them in questions of art) his attitude towards literature is, one may say aristocratic. This obviously is not the same thing as conservative – still. And, at any rate, it would be a fresh utterance. If the idea commended itself to you and you were

to drop him a friendly line he would call and explain exactly
what it is he wishes to say – and thus you could judge better
whether he would be acceptable to Mr. Blackwood.[1]

Once established within the haven of the *Maga.*, Conrad tried
to draw in his friends,[2] and pursued his efforts to interest Blackwood in Garnett:

> Some time ago Edward Garnett telling me he was about
> to terminate his connection with Mr. Heinemann spoke of his
> intention of doing some work in the sphere of criticism ... I
> have always been anxious to see him do something off his
> own bat instead of judging in obscurity the more or less
> deplorable play of countless others. His unaffected desire to
> appeal to that part of the public which the Editors of *Maga*
> had known to group around their magazine – the *only*
> magazine – my great belief in his talent and abilities, our
> general agreement upon the subject in hand – have induced
> me to promise that I would forward his introductory study
> to you ...[3]

Shortly afterwards Conrad wrote again to say that: 'I own that
I am anxious he should find a way to your convictions; for this
man too is very genuine, capable under encouragement of
achieving even brilliance and at any rate solidity of not an
obscure sort ... '[4] Despite Conrad's recommendation and efforts, Blackwood replied, 'I am sorry but I must disappoint you
and Mr. Garnett about the "Contemporary Critic" papers. I
have little sympathy with articles of this kind, which to my mind
are somewhat futile as nobody reads them.'[5]

This rejection did not surprise Edward's father who wrote:

> I heard that your essay had been declined by Blackwood, for
> which I was not unprepared though I had hoped otherwise.
> Olive thinks that this might be partly owing to some reflection
> upon Mr Andrew Lang contained in it. I do not know if this
> is right, but I hope that if you send the essay for another trial
> you will be most particular to clear it of anything at which
> anybody could take personal offence. You have quite diffi-
> culties enough without needlessly adding to them, and of all

persons in the world Mr Lang is the last with which it is
judicious to quarrel. It is of course impossible to illustrate
principles without reference to persons, but by the exercise of
a little tact it is generally possible to do so without giving any
grievance.[6]

The essay, however, was accepted shortly afterwards, as
Constance commented to her father-in-law on 12 November
that the proof of Edward's 'Critic article has come. I am so glad
it is to appear in the *Monthly Review*. It is strange that they
should have taken it.'[7] Dr Garnett had good reason for his
rather reproving letter to his son as the article, remarkable for
the sentiments it expressed in the context of the state of criticism
at that time, insistently attacked *the* representative of current
literary criticism – Andrew Lang. Edward pointedly criticised
Lang's passion for what is 'old and seasoned' and of 'waving
various manifestations of contemporary literature aside'. He
particularly challenged Lang's assertion that 1860 marked the
degeneracy of literature and he listed fifty authors who had
produced their main work since that date – among them Meredith, Tolstoy, Turgenev, Zola, Hardy, Mark Twain and many
others whose inclusion added to the absurdity of Lang's remark.[8] The adroit Lang, Malcolm Elwin remembered,
'gracefully recognised Garnett as "a writer of weight and ear-
nestness", reminded him that Stevenson, Kipling, Robert
Bridges and others "were new and unseasoned in my time" and
coolly entered into reasoned argument, as with an equal, to
prove his view that "better novels were produced between 1814
and 1860 than between 1860 and 1901".'[9]

Lang symbolised the dominance of the 'public bookmen'
during the late Victorian and Edwardian decades. One of the
most consciously literary of periods, newspaper and periodical
publishing flourished and a wide range of London and provincial newspapers, and innumerable periodicals catering for
'things of the mind', regarded books as important and gave
generous space to reviewing. Particularly esteemed were dailies
such as the *Standard, Daily Telegraph, Morning Post* and *Daily
Chronicle*; evening papers such as the *Echo, Star, Pall Mall Gazette*
and *Westminster Gazette*; periodicals such as the *Athenaeum, Academy, Speaker* and *Spectator*.[10] Literary clubs and coteries, often

centred around some dominant literary figure, were numerous at the turn of the century and included once famous but now largely forgotten groups such as the Fitzroy Settlement, the Odd Volume Club, the Omar Khayyám Club, the Rhymers Club and the Henley Regatta.[11] Curiosity about authors and the literary world (analogous to interest at a later date in radio celebrities and television personalities) produced a market for those adept in literary gossip such as E. Robertson Nicoll and Clemence Shorter. The kind of reviews put out became judgments in tune with the wide middle-brow audience – 'bland, stuffy precepts for "Mudiesque" readership'.

Though the wider market provided opportunities for competent journalists and writers, it aggravated the growing estrangement of the serious writer, especially the novelists, which Gissing so graphically depicted in *New Grub Street*. It led to the idea, unusual earlier in the nineteenth century, that restricted appeal was a necessary indication of intellectual integrity. This notion was promoted by figures such as Lang who pontificated for about twenty years in Longman's magazine, *At the Sign of the Ship*. Lang's polymathic and prolific work, written with effortless style, had so great a following that it was said, ' A puff from Lang usually meant that a publisher's troubles were over, and provided it had its quota of swashbuckling and high adventure he was willing to condone the trashiest melodrama.'[12] The Stevenson of the romantic novel, Rider Haggard, Anthony Hope and Stanley Weyman were the kind of novelists whom Lang boosted. Worse, in so far as a person of such prestige and scholarship could influence public taste his 'one consistent policy as a reviewer ... was to ridicule or disparage practically every truly important novel which came his way'.[13] Criticism therefore as it existed in the press when Garnett wrote 'The Contemporary Critic' had little to do with serious writing and much to do with the cultural divisions which in more recent times have received attention from writers such as Richard Hoggart and Raymond Williams.

In the academic arena criticism also set its face against innovation and concerned itself with the past. The scholarly pundits, Saintsbury and Gosse, in their different ways kept to 'well-trodden paths of criticism, where the pitfalls had been explored and mapped by sundry predecessors'.[14] Saintsbury, who became by far the 'most influential academic literary historian and critic', argued against naturalism and welcomed the revival of romance in late nineteenth-century literature; he excluded realism, condemned Ibsen and the Russians and 'helped to bring about the situation that reached its nadir before the advent of T. S. Eliot: the loss of standards, coherence, penetration, and critical tools'.[15] Saintsbury, who had begun in journalism, was successful in gaining the Regius Chair in English at Edinburgh in 1895. Over the years his prodigious reading and innumerable publications, written in meandering, parenthetical prose, made him the doyen of academic critics.

Gosse, who lived long enough to become the archetypal fashionable critic, was elected to the post of Clark lecturer at Cambridge in 1880. His self-esteem and reputation were rudely shattered shortly afterwards by John Churton Collins who exposed the inaccuracy and shoddy scholarship of his published lectures, *From Shakespeare to Pope*, and ten years later of his *History of Modern English Literature*. This exposure was part of the campaign which Collins was conducting against the state of English studies in the two old universities.

Emerging from the academic world came a 'mandarin' type of criticism. This, and 'gossiping, often highly metaphorical description and unspecified praise',[16] formed the orthodoxy of literary analysis before the work of I. A. Richards, the avant-garde of Eliot and Pound, and 'the Golden Age of the Little Magazines'[17] ushered in new critical approaches.

Garnett's essay 'The Contemporary Critic' foreshadowed such approaches, taking as fundamental the view that 'all literature is documentary evidence on mind and life'.

The spirit that urged Garnett the critic was akin to that expressed in Eliot's pronouncement that criticism must always 'profess an end in view, the elucidation of works of art and the correction of taste ... to promote the understanding and enjoyment of literature'.[18] Edward's devotion to these objectives was in keeping with his personality; at odds with conventional views, and with a strong belief in his own judgment. He also had that particular qualification for criticism which another influential critic put in the aphorism – 'the ideal reader is the ideal critic'.[19]

Edward's work as a publisher's reader was not inimical to a belief that criticism should foster fresh talent, initiate its appreciation and by correspondence help the as yet unrecognised writer. In a series of articles in the *Academy* entitled 'Books Too Little Known', shortly after he had joined Duckworth, Edward concerned himself with books which, as he declared in his article on Hudson, formed 'a peculiar class of independent and unconventional works of art which are destined to have but the scantiest audience for many years after their first appearance, for they neither ride on the wave of the tendency of their day nor do they carry within them the seed of any coming fashion'.

This article on Hudson contained characteristics that were to be familiar in all his published criticism – a belief in the honesty of the work, a pugnacious comparison with that of another more popularly received and a contempt for public opinion in literary matters. 'Never', Edward wrote, 'give the public what it wants is a maxim we would gravely impress on every serious writer.' In his appreciation of Hudson, he said of *The Purple Land* that it 'does precisely succeed in preserving for us a feeling of life's spontaneous character, its complex texture, and so, apparently artless and casual, it is on a far higher plane than some of the carefully arranged and brilliant novels of Stevenson – to take one example among many'.[20]

The energy which marked Edward's approach to the articles is acknowledged in Hudson's letter of 19 June 1902: 'Your geese are all swans, we know, but this individual goose must be simply grateful to you for your splendid advocacy. As a person, or goose, with the old fighting Adam pretty strong in him, I must be specially grateful to you because you seem ready and even anxious to knock somebody down. In one way your article has already hit the mark. I didn't know it was in the *Academy* until this morning, first post, when I got a letter from Ch. Longman asking for the loan of a copy of the book.'[21]

Edward also began his lifelong championship of C. M. Doughty with an article in the *Academy* series. After sardonic asides addressed to the 'indifferent public', Edward directed the reader to Doughty's *Arabia Deserta* with an enthusiasm that grasps what Eliot has termed the entelechy of the text. 'The book is a masterpiece,' Edward wrote, 'but whether more than three hundred copies have been put into circulation in fifteen years – the publisher's ledger – it knows, it knows. It would seem a point of honour with certain literary masterpieces to hide themselves soon after birth from the eyes of the unconscious world.'[22]

He was equally convinced that Richard Jefferies had not received his due recognition and in the *Academy* series gave a critique of *Amaryllis at the Fair* and *After London*. In this he answered those critics who exclaimed, 'What a pity Jefferies tried to write novels!' 'We do not judge every novel by the same test,' Edward wrote and argued that *Amaryllis* 'as an artistic revelation of human life and character . . . is a living picture of life, a creative work of imagination of a high order'.[23] He repeated the gist of his sentiments in his introduction to the New Readers Library edition of *Amaryllis at the Fair* a year later. Edward had no illusions about the effect of this critical introduction. Writing to his friend Cunninghame Graham who had congratulated him on it, he said: 'I don't expect that this edition will receive any attention, but will fail as the original edition did.' In the same letter he expressed his admiration for Jefferies and his contempt for contemporary critics: 'He was a wonderful man and had a desperate struggle at the end. Absolutely isolated and dying by inches. That stupid old fool Walter Besant tried to do his memory and his family a good turn and wrote a humbugging and sentimental eulogy, with the tone of a kindly chandler of means addressing a guardian of genius.'[24]

Personal involvement as well as critical appreciation came together in his advocacy of the work of Henry Lawson, an Australian writer whom he thought scandalously neglected. Edward and his friend and neighbour E. V. Lucas, who was publisher's reader to Methuen, helped Lawson to get his work published and promoted its appreciation.

Lawson, who had travelled to England, carried on a correspondence with Edward on the progress of his work. At the beginning of 1901 he reported that he 'was grafting hard at a new book – present title, "As Far as I'm concerned". A lot of it was written but it was too strong and bitter for Blackwood.'[25] Later he confided: 'Have been decidedly "off" the last few days, but I post you a bundle of stuff which will enable you to decide whether I go on with proposed "sarcastic" book or shelve it for the present. I think it would go. Have an idea of a series of "Doc Wild" stories which would suit Ward Lock & Co. "Doc Wild" a sort of medical Capt. Kettle yet true to life. Have first sketch

drafted. You might decide with Lucas for Tuesday night next
and tell me where to meet you.'[26]

Later letters reveal that Lawson relied upon Edward's judgment and advice, discussing his plans with him and sending him
manuscripts for comment. Edward certainly helped to shape
the collection published as *The Children of the Bush* and also *Joe
Wilson and His Mates*.[27] In a letter of 29 January 1902 Lawson
said:

> Just finishing putting a new book together 'The Bush
> Philosophers', abt 300 pages. I've got a lot too much matter
> and it's the old trouble 'what to leave out'. I intended to
> publish another new book of mixed sketches before the novel,
> but since my last chat with you I run 'Mitchell' through the
> stories and he linked them together. I feel much more com-
> fortable about the new book than I did about Joe Wilson and
> Mates but am getting excellent reviews for that. 'Steelman'
> also shows up in the new book, and 'Joe Wilson' in the end,
> but all the other characters are new. Have sundowners, bush
> missionaries etc. When could you come out here and see me.
> Anytime will do, only drop a note. Mrs. Lawson and children
> blooming. Kind regards to Mrs. Garnett . . .[28]

In June 1902 Lawson wrote: 'Am sending proofs from here –
up to page 224 – and will send the rest if they reach me here
. . . I don't think the proofs will need much correction. But *do
just what you like with them* and alter and cut out where ever you
think fit. You have a free hand.'[29]

Edward took up the cudgels for Lawson in his *Academy* series,
heading his article 'An Appreciation'. 'Lawson's special value
to us', he wrote, was due to the fact that he was 'the representative writer of a definite environment, as the portrayer of life
on the Australian soil, and that he brings together before our
eyes more fully and vividly than any other man the way the
Australian settlers' life had been going.' Lawson 'as an artist',
he thought, 'is often crude and disappointing, often sketchy and
rough, but many of his slightest sketches show he has the faculty
of bringing life to a focus, of making it typical'.[30] Henry Lawson expressed to Edward his satisfaction with this article,
which appeared in March 1902. 'Thank you many times for

"appreciation" whether it goes through or not. I want you to understand that I *fully* realise how much I owe you and Lucas. Will post first part of book in a day or two – or the whole in rough – I think it will be alright – no complaints or grievances against publishers. It is as true to England as Australia – But when you've read it you will be able to tell me what to do with it ...'[31]

The article appeared when Lawson's stay in England was coming to a close. It was a period marked by financial difficulties which are depicted in a homely anecdote recorded by Lawson's biographer: 'One day, without warning Bertha [his wife], Henry brought Garnett back to their rooms for a meal. Bertha was in a flutter. Although finances had improved, they were still very poor. But she did the best she could. She hashed up a meal of corned beef, fried potatoes, and cabbage, with bread, and jam, and tea. Garnett accepted it with good grace. Indeed it only confirmed his belief, in the genuineness of Lawson's democratic outlook.'[32] Lawson himself described his period in England as a mixture of success and ruin; his domestic and financial circumstances figured largely in the unhappy environment in which he had to work.[33]

Edward's critical opinion, in which he 'unerringly detected the "Australianism" of Lawson', is still regarded as being the most perceptive.[34] He brought as acute an assessment to the work of Sarah Orne Jewett, whose talent, he wrote in his *Academy* series, 'had far too scanty and transitory attention paid to it'. She fulfilled for Edward that true criterion of excellence in a novelist – 'unerring perception of her country people's native outlook and instinctive attitude to life'. Of all her work he singled out *The Country of Pointed Firs* as the novel which would permanently assure her a position in American literature. 'So delicate is the artistic lesson of this little masterpiece', he wrote, 'that it will probably be left for generations of readers less hurried than ours to assimilate.'[35]

His appreciation brought a letter from the author and in subsequent correspondence Edward expressed surprise that her book *Deephaven* did not seem to have appeared in an English edition. He suggested publishing arrangements for this and for a new selection of her stories. In correspondence they exchanged opinions on her work. Edward with his usual candour thought

that none of 'your sketches of Irish-American life seem to reach
the level of your best work' and as a 'half-Irishman himself'
thought she dealt with 'the Irish as a stranger people'. Many of
the earlier stories also had 'touches of moralising which as it
were weigh down and destroy their clarity'. Nevertheless, he
wrote, 'I cannot tell you how deeply your best work penetrates
me, and how exquisite certain chapters in "The Country of
Pointed Firs" appear to me.'[36]

For her part Sarah Orne Jewett expressed her gratitude for
Edward's interest and criticism, remarking in a letter dated
10 March 1904: 'I have so long wished to write to you. Your
review of The Ambassadors was wonderfully good. I delight in
Mr. James's work. You shall not find me wanting in sympathy
when you write such an appreciation – or failing now to read
everything you write of books and men with eager interest ... I
had all Mrs. Garnett's edition of Turgeniev ready to my hand
with the delightful looking Prefaces ... and I am looking forward to getting back to them. This is to say that I have not
forgotten your kindness or the pleasure of reading what you
write.'[37]

Edward had confessed to her his preoccupation with fiction
above all forms of literature, declaring that: 'My own work is
very spasmodic and perfunctory but I have written some few
Introductions to my wife's complete translations of Turgenev's
Novels and Tales in which I have perhaps expressed better than
elsewhere the few things I have to say about the art of fiction.
Fiction! What a ridiculously inadequate word it is ... '[38] To
Edward, as with D. H. Lawrence, the novel was the 'one bright
book of life': so much so that his advocacy brought the irritable
rejoinder from his friend W. H. Hudson: 'The novel is not
everything, whatever you and Wells may say, especially for
those who are not made to write it.'[39]

E. C. Bentley, of 'Clerihew' fame, gives a brief picture of
Edward's devotion to the novel as a serious literary form when
he asked Garnett of the chances of his entry, *Philip Gaskell's Last
Case*, in the Duckworth first novel competition of 1912. An
American publisher, Douglas Z. Daly, had been impressed by
Bentley's manuscript and had suggested he withdrew it from
the competition so that he could be free to accept an offer.
Bentley asked Garnett as a friend what he would advise. In

Bentley's words Edward's reply, 'written, like other letters I had from him, in a tiny and untidy script on a small scrap of paper, was to the effect that my book was not in running for the prize. I gathered that he did not think much of the psychology; with which judgment I fully agreed. He added that, for all he could say it might do well as a detective story. It is quite possible that he never read one; his taste, which was faultless within its chosen range, was not for the kind of books that are popular.'[40] Retitled *Trent's Last Case*, the book was published in 1913, promptly became a best seller and was widely regarded as a classic detective story.

Frank Swinnerton, describing Edward as 'incorrigibly serious as a member of the intellectual left must be', went on to say that 'his taste was fine, and he was the only critic of quality and standing known to me [who] throughout his life made the novel as a form of art his particular theme and his particular care'. In correspondence, in reviews and articles, Edward Garnett 'forever drew attention to new work by English and Continental novelists who otherwise might have whistled for praise',[41] and in a graphic passage Swinnerton judged him 'along with Conrad, Galsworthy, Ford Madox Ford and others who wrought their fictions as strong men twist iron bars', to be one who 'had much to do with the new seriousness of the novel'.[42]

EIGHT

Reader as Reviewer

Two principles guided Edward's criticisms and appreciations: firstly that the novel *was* an art form and ultimately
had to be judged by the arrangement of words; secondly that
the novel had to have 'veracity' – to be true to life and have its
own truth. As reviewer to the *Academy*, and later to the *Speaker*
and the *Nation*, he campaigned for a conception of the novel in
which these principles were realised.

Edward believed Conrad to be the apotheosis of his definition
of the novelist. He attempted to explain the nature of Conrad's
achievement in a contribution to the *Academy* in October 1898
which, in its understanding and percipient criticisms, foreshadowed critical approaches to Conrad's work. In this, the first
ever general article on Conrad, Edward answered his own
rhetorical question: 'What is the quality of his art?' The quality,
he suggested, 'is seen in his faculty of making us perceive men's
lives in their natural relation to the seen universe around them
... This faculty ... gives Mr. Conrad's art its extreme delicacy
and its great breadth of vision. It is pre-eminently the poet's gift
and is very rarely conjoined with insight into human nature
and a power of conceiving character. When the two gifts come
together we have the poetic realism of the great Russian novels.
Mr. Conrad's art is truly realism of that high order.'[1]

This prescient article was followed by reviews in which he
detected what others were to repeat with academic hindsight.
Reviewing *Youth*, *End of the Tether* and *Heart of Darkness* in the

Academy in 1902, Edward wrote that the 'first two will be more popular than the third, *Heart of Darkness*, a study of the white man in Africa which is most amazing, a consummate piece of artistic diablerie'. Such a consummation could only occur, Edward went on, if 'the artist takes his method of presentation more seriously still. For the art of the *Heart of Darkness* – as in every psychological masterpiece – lies in the relation of the things of the flesh, of the visible life to the invisible, of the subconscious life within us, our obscure motives and instincts, feelings and outlook.'[2] Edward's insistence that the novel of genius needed to be read for its artistic arrangement as much as its content seems to anticipate Leavis;[3] in his review Edward wrote: 'The weirdness, the brilliance, the psychological truth of this masterly analysis of two Continents in conflict, of the abysmal gulf between the white man's system and the black man's comprehension of its results, is conveyed in a rapidly rushing narrative which calls for close attention on the reader's part . . . and the artist is but intent on presenting his sensations in that sequence and arrangement whereby the meaning or the meaninglessness of the white man in civilised Africa can be felt in its really significant aspects.'[4] Conrad himself responded to what has been called 'the most intelligent appreciation of "Heart of Darkness" '[5] with a letter to Edward on 22 December 1902: 'My dear fellow, you quite overcome me. And your brave attempt to grapple with the foggishness of H. of D. to explain what I myself tried to shape blindfold, as it were, touched me profoundly.'[6]

Indicative of Edward's critical perception are the faults he notes in Conrad. Apropos *Nostromo* he criticised the 'somewhat lengthy handling of the early history of the San Tome mine',[7] and the abrupt and hurried chapters describing Nostromo's death he thought artistically too violent. In a letter to Cunninghame Graham,[8] Edward remarked on facets which he later put in his review in the *Speaker* in 1904. 'The psychology of certain characters,' he wrote, 'Charles Gould, Decoud, and Nostromo himself, is indeed not always clear and convincing . . . We regret the last two chapters . . . Their touch of melodrama does violence to the evening stillness of the close. The narrative should have ended with the monologue of Captain Mitchell and the ironic commentary of Dr. Monyghan on the fresh disillusionment in store for the *regime* of "Civilisation" planted by European hands on the bloodstained soil of the Republic of Costaguana.'

Years later Edward gave another view of *Nostromo* and of Conrad as a novelist in a letter of 5 June 1934 to Richard Curle: 'Yes, I think that your paper on *Nostromo* is excellent. It makes one want to read the book again – it is so full of rare, buried treasure. At the same time Conrad undertook more than an artist of his quality should do. There are two or three books buried in one – and he was always at his best in a recital such as Heart of Darkness when *you* can see the wood for the trees.'[9]

As a critic of the novel, Edward had attracted attention with his first piece of published criticism, an appreciation of Stephen Crane in the *Academy* in 1898. In the article he defined Crane as the perfect artist and interpreter of the surfaces of life, the chief impressionist of the day and, within limits, the master of form.[10] According to Edward, the faults in Crane came from having to write under the duress of time and money. When Edward sent Cora Crane a copy of the 'few words I wrote on Stephen' he apologetically qualified them by saying that they had been asked for in a hurry and 'there are things you will like in it, and things perhaps you won't. But I meant to add in it that I looked forward to seeing Stephen do the novel of the American journalistic world, someday, a thing great, and in a larger scope than he has yet done.'[11] Though Cora Crane liked it very much indeed she disagreed with Edward when he said that Crane might fail when the picturesque phases of the environment that nurtured him gave out. 'The beautiful thoughts in Stephen's mind', she replied, 'are simply endless.'[12]

'The uncanny insight',[13] as Conrad described Edward's assessment, became a point of reference for later critics. J. B. Calvert in 'Style and Meaning in Stephen Crane' (1958) remarked: ' . . . And to get at his meaning – to search out not only the structure of his art but also the nature of the world view which it expresses – is to remove his best writing from the stigma of a naive and ingenuous philosophical naturalism and find in it, as Edward Garnett did years ago, something of the "perfect tension of the forces of passion and irony." '[14]

When Edward came to review Crane's posthumous novel *The O'Ruddy* in the *Speaker* in 1904 he used the device of reviewing

two writers so that he could support his propositions about the
merits of an author not fully appreciated and about the novel in
general. He contrasted Crane's work with that of a popular
American novelist, Winston Churchill. 'What American literature', he wrote, 'has gained by [Crane's] appearance and what
has been lost to it by his death is apparent indeed when we turn
to the unnatural and carefully staged picturesqueness of works
such as Winston Churchill's. Crane's best work is always a
strange, subtle and deep revelation of the odd workings of the
passions within us, but works of the calibre of *The Crossing* really
add to our knowledge of human nature as much as can a horse
grazing in a field.'[15]

For Garnett the touchstones of significance in fiction followed
from a 'very simple test', that 'every fresh native talent emerges
by virtue of its revelation of fresh aspects and original points of
view, which create fresh valuations in our comprehension of life
and human nature'.[16] In his reviews he disparaged novels and
novelists where lack of sincerity distorted the depiction of life.
Reviewing *The Marriage of William Ashe* he took Mrs Humphry
Ward to task, stating that she 'skilfully doctored and patched
up her situation, twisting human nature here and there to suit
her moral purpose . . . so that, however vivid and interesting the
novel may be, however full of clever and penetrating passages,
it is as a work of art full of falsification and is second rate'.[17] His
friend W. H. Hudson appreciated Edward's manner in reviewing novels of this kind, saying: 'I've read you always in the
Nation and being a sportsman of sorts myself I always admire
your neat way of taking your captured rabbits from the net and
often tickling them with a little caress or two before snapping
their necks and putting them in your bag. How many do you
slay each year?'[18]

Edward was contemptuous of the 'brooding swarms of sugary
sentimental erotics, artificial in feeling' and in various reviews
referred to the 'harmful effects of material progress' and of the
'scholarly aestheticism of drawing room culture'.[19] Such viewpoints found most cogent expression in a review article in the
Speaker of 1904, 'Mark Rutherford and Others'. This began with
an acknowledgment that 'the Victorian age had produced a
"string of talents" who showed by their example that the novel
is of all literary forms the most adequately flexible for the serious

analysis of modern life.' Comparing Rutherford's *Revolution in Tanner's Lane* with E. F. Benson's *The Challoners*, he wrote that Rutherford 'creates, with unswerving verisimilitude, the veritable bodily environment and atmosphere, physical and spiritual, of these people [i.e. the English lower middle class of 1814–40] with an artistic sureness that is positively astonishing'. By contrast Benson's work typified modern fashions in fiction and the 'childishly crude artistic standards set up in practice today by most of our "popular" novelists. Yet such a book with its sham drawing room aestheticism and artificial "art" raptures will be probably hailed by unblushing reviewers and will sell ten thousand copies and be read by fifty thousand people ... though it is ... the very type of those innumerable pieces of false art which are cried up with the beat of drums in the market place and then pass away as utterly as the smoke of a snuffed candle.'[20]

Edward warned novelists of the fatal effect of departing from the springs of their creative power. Reviewing Bennett's *The Grim Smile of the Five Towns* in the *Nation* in 1907 he attacked the market forces affecting literature and authorship. He wrote:

> Consider that from modern fiction we can gather more knowledge about the life of the Kaffirs, the Malays, the Hindus, than about the life of the Yorkshire miners, the Lancashire millhands, or the Staffordshire 'black country'. And why is this? Mr. Bennett's case is a very good illustration of the middle-class system today in silently discouraging the artist – which means that drama and the novel can only offer us perfunctory pictures, and practically no criticism of national life. The method is automatic, and simplicity itself. Young men of literary ability find no market in the provinces, and, forced to migrate to London to pick up a livelihood in the shoals and shallows of Metropolitan journalism, their artistic talent is used up to satisfy the fourth-rate tastes of Philistia. The Provincial loses touch with the local types and local atmosphere that should be and is the real fount of his inspiration ... [21]

A year later, reviewing *The Old Wives' Tale*, Edward recalled his advice to the author to go back to the matter and

method of *Anna of the Five Towns* and praised the success of
Bennett's return to this territory. Edward thought that, both as
a human document and as a novel, *The Old Wives' Tale* would
have delighted the great French naturalists. 'Most novelists', he
wrote, 'are rarely quite at one with their subject, they enrich,
romanticise or impoverish it. But Mr. Bennett is really his
subject, the breath of it, intellectually in a remarkable way.' In
his view this was due to the fact that 'the tone of our author's
judgments, standards, and tastes seems to be the spiritual legacy
of generations of hard headed, commercial Midlanders'.[22]

Arnold Bennett wrote to Edward to thank him for his
'masterly review'. He wondered, however, if Edward was of the
opinion that he had frittered himself away 'in pleasing the
fourth-rate tastes of Philistia' in *A Great Man* and *Buried Alive*.
Though these novels did not deal with the Five Towns, Bennett
thought them 'just about as fine in the ironic vein as we are
likely to meet with'. He also confessed that he had no intention
of sticking exclusively to the Five Towns as he often felt 'short
of room' there.[23] In reply Edward admitted overdoing 'the
"Philistia" business' because in his opinion Bennett's energy
and development had been absorbed by *The Great Babylon Hotel*
series which he classed as 'potboiling stuff'; *A Great Man* with
all its justness and clever satire had 'an element lacking in it and
the detailed atmosphere is generalised instead of being parti-
cularised'.[24] When Edward commented on *Hilda Lessways*, Bennett wrote: 'It is a relief to me that you are satisfied with "Hilda"
as there are just a few critics who could intimidate me, and you
are one.'[25]

In this fight against the Philistine, Edward showed an early
appreciation of E. M. Forster. In an unsigned review in the
Spectator in 1905 he perceived that in *Where Angels Fear to Tread*,
'Mr. Forster has succeeded with a cleverness that is almost
uncanny, in illustrating the tragic possibilities that reside in
insignificant characters when they seek to emancipate themselves from the bondage of convention, or to control those who
are dominated by a wholly different set of traditions.'[26] E. M.
Forster observed later that only two critics had noticed the
publication of his first novel, and of Edward he said: 'I like to
think it was his flair. I know it was his generosity. He picked up
a book by an unknown writer, which, in his opinion, was

promising, he forced an enthusiastic review into a magazine, and so gave me a chance of reaching a public.'²⁷

In the year in which that first novel was to appear, Edward had submitted a report on a collection of short stories which Forster had sent to his employer, Gerald Duckworth. In his report dated 8 October 1905, he suggested that the best order for the stories would be '1. The Eternal Order, 2. Allegro Empedocle, 3. The Road from Colonus, 4. The Purple Envelope, 5. The Story of a Panic, 6. The Helping Hand, 7. The Other Side of the Hedge'. Of these he commented that:

> No 1 is extremely fresh in conception and style. It has a distinction of its own. Nos 2, 3, 4 and 5 are all variations on the same motive – the supernatural world coming into collision with the normal world. The chief character on each occasion suddenly receives some illumination, some eye-opener and he becomes a changed personality. Mr Forster uses very cleverly the contrast between the two worlds of prosaic fussy English tourists, and of supernatural forces, to give a slight thrill of horror. And his neat satirical touches drive home the uncanny feeling that our everyday world is only the surface world of appearances.

He went on, 'After reading Mr Forster's new novel – just published by Blackwood, we shall be in a better position to advise D. as to the feasibility of publishing the Tales.'²⁸

Duckworth did not take up the short stories but Edward's interest in Forster's work continued. When his second novel, *The Longest Journey*, appeared in 1907, Edward featured it in the *Nation* as 'The Novel of the Week'. He began his review with a passage in which Agnes, the hero's wife, asks: 'Couldn't you make your stories more obvious? I don't see any harm in that. Uncle Willie floundered helplessly. I had to explain, and then he was delighted.' Edward concluded that, 'In truth it is not easy to explain the subtle quality of Mr Forster's brilliant novel to Uncle Willie and his kinsfolk.' In his opinion, 'A quiet hatred of shams has inspired Mr Forster to one of the subtlest exposures of the modern Pharisee that we can recall in fiction. Bit by bit he gently peels off the respectable casings that enwrap his Philistine soul.' The style and method of Forster was, he thought, as original as his outlook on life. 'All lies in the telling,' Edward wrote, 'but how can the art of telling, this network woven of a succession of tiny touches be brought home to Uncle Willie?'[29] Forster wrote to Edward on 5 May 1907: 'I thought', he said, 'the *Nation* review was yours; it gave me tremendous pleasure for the Uncle Willies are encompassing me sorely. I'm not sure whether what I try to do is worth doing, but it's a great encouragement that you think I've done it well.'[30]

When Forster began his next novel he asked Edward a favour: 'I thought I would venture to write to you about my book [*A Room with a View*], I doubt it interesting you personally but if you could cause it to be reviewed by the *Nation* I should be extremely grateful.'[31] When Edward surveyed the novel in England for American readers in the American periodical the *Nation* in 1909, he referred specifically to 'a younger novelist who has taken the British Philistine in flank so to speak ... E. M. Forster, whose two books *Where Angels Fear to Tread* and *The Longest Journey* would have excited the admiration of Matthew Arnold.'[32]

Their correspondence continued over the emergence of *Howards End*. On 10 November 1910 Forster enquired: 'Are you usually or ever in town on Wednesday? I am and would call on you for a talk. Do you dislike the Savile? If not, would you come to lunch there ... I am interested to see what you will write about *Howards End* and even more interested to hear what you say privately. Plenty is wrong with the book, but I have not yet treated the evil to my satisfaction though I fancy it suffers from paralysis in its hindquarters. Is that what you mean?'[33]

The review which Edward composed for the *Nation* was laudatory. Under the heading 'Villadom', he referred to the book's far-sighted criticism of middle class ideas and said that it conveyed 'most effectively those very things that the intelligent minority feel, but rarely arrive at formulating'. In his opinion the 'novel's original value, which is great, rests primarily on an acute analysis of the middle class British code of ideas and standards, typified by the rise and progress of the Wilcoxes. Mr Forster understands the outlook of Villadom perhaps better than fourscore of writers ... '[34]

Forster wrote to Edward on 12 November appreciatively: 'With the possible exception of *The Times* which avowedly omitted bad points, your criticism is the only one that strikes me as just. I only hope I may profit by it in the future, and a writer can't say more. Though whether I can profit is another matter. It is devilish difficult to criticize society and also create human beings ... P.S. Do you remember some short stories of mine? I have at last entrapped a publisher into taking them. I am very glad, for I think them better than my long books – the only point of criticism on which I have ever disagreed with you.'[35]

They continued to meet and discuss Forster's work though filial responsibilities took precedence, as Forster wrote on 11 December 1910: 'I am much disappointed but since seeing you I find that my mother intends coming to town next Wednesday, a rare event, and I want to be with her, and help her through the shopping. I shall write in the New Year, and hope that you will be good enough to come to the Savile then. I am more disappointed because the novel will then be fading in both our minds, but we can still discuss character drawing and criticism of civilisation if you will.'[36]

Though Edward never reviewed any of the works of H. G. Wells, the considerations which guided him in reviewing – the 'artistry' of the novelist and how he interprets 'life' – characterise their correspondence. Wells had sent *Love and Mr Lewisham* for his opinion; Edward's letter of 21 June 1900 shows a close reading of the book and his usual combination of critical comment and praise. 'The first half' he thought 'very inferior to the second'. In general 'the author *as artist* has not so completely absorbed and assimilated the author's philosophy as to make the lines of structure and the colour of the whole sufficiently *beautiful* ... Love and Mr. Lewisham is a very interesting document of life because its scientific spirit is secretly at war with its artistic emotional force.' Edward criticised the intrusiveness of 'explanation, analysis and demonstration' in the book but congratulated Wells on the creation of Chaffery: 'No novelist has ever so identified himself with a Chaffery as to really let us feel his world a reality ... and the beauty of your Chaffery is you comment so little on him.'

In conclusion Edward wrote that 'I should like to have reviewed Love and Mr. Lewisham at some length somewhere, but Editors are not fond of books being criticised and so things rarely come my way ... Perhaps this letter only hints my meaning – that there is a contradiction in the novel; that the scientific and artistic spirits meet and clash, that the whole work is a good criticism of the English mind which seeks outlet and yet cannot abandon itself freely to life, and that in this respect Love and Mr. Lewisham recalls Gissing ... ' In a tailpiece Edward said that Wells had 'very adequately hit off' the typical young Englishman's attitude to women – 'perhaps better than you know ... '[37]

In reply Wells was 'really obliged to you for reading then telling me what you think of what is practically my first novel. I did indeed want you very much to do it. And if I may criticise a critic I would like to say how much I appreciate the acute distinction you draw between the two methods of treatment that interweave in my work. I had no idea how strong the touch of "demonstration" came in at times ... It is the sort of thing that a man is almost unable to discover himself – it is a matter of habit – and in making it suddenly clear to me you have done me a service for which I can scarcely thank you enough.' Wells ended with the 'hope I may meet you soon. Intelligent talk about the work which is practically the substance of our grey existence now does not come in my way ... '[38]

Thereafter he made a custom of sending Edward a copy of his books for criticism and they shared views on his progress. Thanking Wells 'for your *Utopia* book', Edward remarked, 'I took it up with great prejudice, as I much dislike other people constructing *their* Utopias for *me*. But (beginning in the middle and reading to the end despite your express command) I was delighted to find that the whole atmosphere (of that half) is one of spiritual freedom ... '[39] Wells replied in mock anger, 'Fancy reading my Utopia from the middle onward in order to see if your totally inadequate views of things are denied or confirmed. Wait till I've got you here. Then I'll talk to you ... '[40]

On 22 September 1906 Edward congratulated Wells on another book (presumably *Ann Veronica*) and praised his iconoclastic approach to contemporary ethics. 'Many thanks for your new book. You seem to me to stand on firm ground and to be doing the work of educating people by methods nobody else has attempted,' began a letter which referred to the 'contemptible line' taken by the *Daily Express* in attacking Wells. Edward believed that Wells had opened up 'a deliciously rich subject in the last chapters. It's inexpressibly funny the public's alarm at the idea of "free love". A free heaven or hell is more realisable for the British public than "free love", which acts as a red rag to the bull.'[41]

Edward's wish to review Wells was frustrated by his editor, Massingham. As he explained in a letter: 'I had hoped to have shown by reviewing "Tono-Bungay" my intense appreciation of your achievement; but as I hear Masterman is to do it for "The Nation" I write a line to say that the value of your criticism of the social muddle beats the criticism of all your contemporaries put together.' He had, as he told Wells, 'been lending the "E.R." [*English Review*] instalments to friends and everybody is enthusiastic', though he added that he had had a 'long talk with our London traveller, Cape, who declares that only one man in 300 in the suburban classes is unconventional enough to realize his daily life is a "fraud" '.[42] Again, when *The New Machiavelli* came out, Edward wrote to thank Wells saying: 'I wanted to review it for the *Nation* but Massingham, I understand, is doing it himself. I'll let you know my view of it when we meet ... My best regards to your wife, for whom, as you know, I have a great admiration.'[43]

As a reviewer Edward's convictions often clashed with those of the editor of the *Nation*. Massingham sometimes found Edward's reviews too messianic and disputatious and their correspondence reveals differences between his and Edward's standpoints in criticism. In some respects Massingham supported Edward: ' ... I don't at all object to an occasional slating of a bad book by a writer who ought to do better works, or who has a swollen reputation for working well when he is really working ill. Also I think a *general* stand should be made against the new "article of commerce".'[44] But on another occasion Massingham wrote to his reviewer: 'I think we must aim at a *little* more tolerance for the better kind of conventional art in fiction, or we shall be regarded as too [?] altogether, too impossibly critical of anything that does not reach the highest, or nearly the highest standards.' He also took this occasion to warn Edward of another aspect of his reviews: 'Also we have to be a little careful on sexual problems, as I hinted earlier I don't want to cut your wording, perhaps you can [?] on a less severe line by exclusion.'[45]

This concern evidently continued, for Massingham referred to it again in another note on 'views of the sex question', asking Edward to 'please be more careful in future, as good as your work is, just a little more care in form might I am sure be useful. We write for serious people – mere flippancy disconcerts us.'[46]

Massingham's caution was in keeping with the times. Due to cheap editions and the growth of public libraries, the wider circulation of books which might challenge accepted conventions on religion, politics and sex was viewed as a threat to a conservative social order now aware that the late Victorian introduction of state education was promoting a higher rate of literacy. When a self-regulating censorship by price or illiteracy was no longer present, resort had to be made to legal or extra-legal means.

The irony which Edward used to expose the irrational application of censorship and his contempt for an undiscriminating public was combined with an aside at male chauvinism in his review in 1905 of *A Dark Lantern* by Elizabeth Robins. The author was a beautiful American actress applauded for her role as Hedda Gabler and admired by leading writers such as Shaw and Henry James. She was an advocate of female suffrage and her play, *Votes for Women*, which dealt with the fundamental injustice of sexual relations, was a brilliant success when it was produced at the Court Theatre.[47] In reviewing her novel Edward pronounced that 'the irregular relations of the heroine with the man she loves will probably be met by Mrs. Grundy with a strong eye ... It is amusing to see how writers of established reputation, who dare to write frankly, cow the public into uneasy acceptance ... which from writers less well known would elicit a general chorus of exacerbated disapproval. *A Dark Lantern* will probably draw forth in protest merely the puzzled density of mannish prejudice.'[48]

He took the opportunity to put forward his views on these matters in a preface to *Downward: A Slice of Life* by M. C. Braby entitled 'The Sex Novel'. He challenged the 'modest claim of the Circulating Libraries to sit in judgment' on new books and 'their scheme of placing on the reserved list books of "doubtful" or seemingly unorthodox tendencies'. Such practices pandered to fashion and suppressed the original writer, he declared: 'The spirit of censorship never alters: it is always orthodox, and it is always to be seen energetically defending the big battalions. For this reason alone any publisher's reader who is worth his salt takes a kindly interest in the fate of books that are on the side of the minority.'[49]

Massingham often took Edward to task for his outspokenness when reviewing novels. On one occasion he wrote: 'I had rather a difficulty over your novel review which I only saw just before the time for going to press. You are, I think, rather militant as an anti-puritan. I also am not a puritan, but was brought up exclusively by Puritans, am more friendly to them and certainly think that we ought not to class them altogether ... I lean to the view that puritanism is a thing to be examined and criticised not always unsympathetically – rather than attacked ... '[50]

For Edward reviewing was another avenue whereby, in his total commitment to literature, he could follow his basic tenet that it was the author and his development which was of para-mount importance. It was a belief that was matched by an equally strong conviction that the public had neither the discri-mination nor the taste to detect quality or appreciate it. The encouragement and development of the unrecognised writer in the face of the 'Philistine' drew Edward and the author together against the unknowing public. The everyday task of the pub-lisher's reader and the formal practices of critic and reviewer took second place to a closer advisory relationship which was fostered as acquaintance with a writer developed into friend-ship. In this his conversational criticisms in 'the writer's work-shop' affected the evolution of an author's manuscript before its submission to a publisher. Conrad was the first of many and it was Conrad who introduced him to another – Galsworthy.

NINE

Galsworthy

W HEN Galsworthy met Conrad on the ship *Torrens* it was the fortuitous meeting of two literary aspirants from very different national and social backgrounds. As great a gulf existed in the kind of reception given by Garnett to their first literary endeavours. In contrast to his spontaneous enthusiasm for *Almayer's Folly*, Edward at Unwin on 27 February 1897 reported on *From the Four Corners*:

> We understand that this is the MS mentioned to us by Mr. Conrad, as being by a friend of his, a man who has travelled a good deal and is now anxious to publish this collection of stories à la Rudyard Kipling in some shape or other if necessary on commission terms. The stories undoubtedly show the influence of Kipling, although very likely Mr. Galsworthy would not welcome the remark. All are fair, some good examples of narrative of a typical man of action, a good fellow and a gentleman who has seen a good deal of life in familiar highways and out of the way quarters of the globe. The stories are all readable and two or three of them show the author has a faculty of observation.

In his estimation, however, with a sidelong glance at the address on the manuscript (Junior Carlton Club) Edward went on: 'All are up to a good level of literary technique, but none of them shows any *strong or particular talent*. The fact is the author is a man of action *and he is not artist enough* to score a high success in literature, we should judge. If however he wishes to appear as author and is willing to take all the risks, and we suppose as a Junior Carlton man he is pretty well off, we see no reason why he should not appeal to the public and get respectable press notices – on commission terms.'[1]

In January 1898 he was even less enamoured of the young man's work, disparaging the inner capacity of Galsworthy to express the realities of life. This report on *Jocelyn* said bluntly:

> Mr. Galsworthy will never be an artist in his writings, but he has improved on his first volume of stories. Many of his short stories were trivial or melodramatic in tone: whereas the novel before us is written with considerable care, the subject is worth treatment, and there is *more of genuine life* displayed than we expected. Truth to say Mr. Galsworthy is an excellent fellow, a good Briton and one neither stiff nor prejudiced. He visits foreign countries diligently and examines foreign manners intelligently, but he is always hopelessly *bored* and sees things always through the eyes of a Clubman who carries England with him wherever he goes.

After giving a synopsis of the book Edward concluded: 'Certainly it might sell to a certain extent; but T.F.U. had better quote modified terms on commission *as the book has no vitality in it* and unless the Press is absurdly eulogistic, we should expect it to go with the ruck.'[2]

Such inauspicious 'reader' assessments nevertheless were precursors to a series of advisory criticisms and to an acquaintance that ripened into friendship. When Conrad introduced Edward to Galsworthy their discussions and correspondence over his writings engendered a mutual regard. Until Galsworthy set up house with Ada he became a frequent visitor to The Cearne. He had in any case already introduced himself to Constance in a letter about Turgenev, a writer he admired and sought to emulate in his early years.[3]

Edward made a detailed analysis on 25 September 1900 of Galsworthy's next manuscript, *Man of Devon*, and his incisive criticisms suggested improvements in construction and characterisation. He made the general point that 'There was a feeling given one early that the writer was rather overpleased with the picturesque ... the writer is placing himself outside the characters, yet all the time is telling us about their secret history ... ' This was followed by a commentary that fixed faults to pages of the manuscript with observations on the techniques employed: 'One is left asking oneself whether the story would take higher rank if the objective method had suddenly vanished on pages 124, 125 and 126, and if the hints and token of a fierce, unexplored subjectivity had expanded into a few pages of those flashes by which human nature suddenly goes off into tracks of intense individuality ... '[4]

Shortly afterwards in August 1901, Galsworthy began a book he called *The Pagan*, later *The Island Pharisees*. By February the following year he had a first draft which he sent nervously to Edward with a disarming letter: 'I am not sure that I am doing wisely in sending you the MS so early [but] will do it all the same, and trust to you not to crush it altogether until I have finished it.'[5] Edward allayed any fears by a reply in which he remarked that 'quite independently of all criticism, let me simply say that your MS makes one like you as a *man*, and that a MS may have great value to a writer and to a reader together, as tending to remove both distance, diffidence and misunderstanding'.[6] By now they had the habit of meeting regularly to discuss his work and their correspondence reflects the comprehensiveness of Edward's advice. He urged Galsworthy to 'seize the *one* idea, or salient thought, that each chapter offers and to work it through the presentation – and to throw overboard everything else'. The detailed manner with which he criticised each chapter and the observations he made are exemplified by his comment on Chapter IV: 'Pages 45–50. You really *must* cut out this episode. The machinery is all wrong; and will destroy all the illusion. Don't you see your plan is to develop the argument, or thought, of pages 45–50 – through the play and *in* the play.'[7]

Galsworthy acknowledged the value of Edward's suggestions,[8] and an examination of *The Island Pharisees* shows that he revised with 'careful attention to Garnett's advice'.[9] The main target of Edward's criticism was Galsworthy's falseness in characterisation. Galsworthy used this episode in his early career to illustrate that he owed his transformation from amateur to professional author to Garnett. He recalled the arduous nature of this transformation:

> I began a book ... which became the Island Pharisees. The first draft was called *A Pagan* and was a string of episodes recounted by Ferrand in the first person. When it was nearly finished I showed it to Edward Garnett. 'No, my dear fellow', he said, 'it's all very well but you shouldn't have done that fellow subjectively. You can't possibly know the real inside of a vagabond like that; you ought to give him to us objectively, through a personality like your own.' I gnashed my teeth, set them, conceived Shelton and rewrote the book. 'Better' said Edward Garnett, 'but do it again!' I re-gnashed my teeth, re-set them, and wrote it a third time. So in 1904 it was published – first of my own books under my own name.[10]

Meanwhile Edward had, as reader, reported to Duckworth on Galsworthy's 'Novel' in favourable terms. He wrote:

> This we think is the best piece of work Galsworthy has done. It is clever, really a clever criticism of modern society – a criticism that nobody has yet made so ably. Of course the reader may feel that the novel is one sided. So it is. It only pretends to exhibit types of modern people in a certain light – a light that is clearly keen, a little hard, a little extra-ironical. The various shades of modern life are etched in with much brilliancy – especially the scenes in the last half of the book. The hero is a *medium*, through which the society represented is criticised ... On its literary merits alone, Duckworth might publish it because it is original and really does present and analyse aspects of modern life and modern types of man with considerable skill and force ... Our own view is that it has such *real literary merit* that it would be a pity to pass it over. Duckworth must however see how it affects him *as a whole*. One thing is however certain – that the book is decidedly *original*.[11]

In a letter to Galsworthy of 20 May complimenting him on a novel that 'is good criticism of life, and brilliantly written', he recounted, 'I have reported this to Duckworth yesterday; and have told him I advised you to try people like Heinemann and Methuen and come back to him later on your half profit system if necessary.'[12] This change in his opinion of Galsworthy as a writer was confirmed when he received the first chapter of another book sent to him in June 1904. He wrote back to the author with delight: 'Chapter 1 is splendid, perfect in phrasing and conception ... those Jameses and Soameses etc. you have really *got* in the most uncanny fashion.'[13]

In *The Man of Property*, Galsworthy found a subject and a way of writing in accord with his own nature. During the gestation of the book he turned to Edward to discuss both theme and characterisation; sending drafts for his comment and arguing with him over the progress of the book in a series of letters. At the time the two friends had planned a walking tour of South Wales and years later Galsworthy would recall to Edward 'our long walk in Wales, and the morning we went up the Carmarthen Van in dense fog and talked of *The Man of Property* (then on the stocks) on the way down'.[14] In two years the final draft of the book was ready; by now Galsworthy, visiting Italy with Ada, hoped to persuade Edward to join them, for as he wrote in March: 'It would be so much more satisfactory if you cast your eye over the MS once more, and it would be so awfully jolly if you could do so in Italy with us, that I want you to spare the inside of a fortnight at least, the last fortnight in March, and come to us at Amalfi. I *of course* providing the wherewithal.'[15]

Edward, however, stayed in England and Galsworthy sent him the complete manuscript and waited anxiously for his verdict. This when it came in a long letter of 27 May began approvingly enough. 'Briefly', Edward wrote, 'I regard it as containing splendid stuff, all on a high level, and containing two or three passages *near to genius* ... ' To Galsworthy's chagrin, Edward went on: '*But*, and I emphasize this in every way, I consider Bosinney's suicide *an artistic blot* of a very grave order, psychologically false, and seriously shaking the illusion of the whole story.' After a detailed list of reasons for this view, Edward suggested two alternatives, one of which would be ' ... to make Bosinney meet with an accident in the fog – so that you can preserve your psychological analysis of the Forsytes' attitude.'[16]

Following a series of letters between them Galsworthy came

round to Edward's view, writing: 'I have been working in advance on Part III and I think I am meeting your point as to B's suicide, the technique was grievously at fault.'[17] Later he admitted, 'Bosinney's death I think will gain in strength and credibility *as an accident* by judicious use of a suspicion of suicide which the reader by inferior knowledge is enabled to reject.'[18] Galsworthy paid homage to the many aspects of Edward's help in the construction and characterisation of *The Man of Property* with: 'Yes, it is more appropriate, I have been re-reading your letters of criticism in the bulk and cold blood, and I am humbled and astonished at their clear justice. You have too good an eye.'[19] Ironically, in view of their dispute, Galsworthy had modelled Bosinney upon Edward.

Though Edward still had reservations about the 'uninspired and tame' workmanship of the last chapters, he wrote to Galsworthy on 26 July that Pawling of Heinemann had accepted *The Man of Property* 'on your terms'.[20] Duckworth had rejected *The Island Pharisees* in spite of Edward's recommendation, having had little success with *Jocelyn* and *Villa Rubein*. When Edward took the book to Heinemann it was accepted with the proviso that Galsworthy should offer his next book to the firm; and the next book was *The Man of Property*. Galsworthy in gratitude wrote early in the new year: 'Dear Edward, I forgot to say would you mind if I dedicated *The Man of Property* to you? Don't hesitate to say so ... '[21]

He soon embarked on another novel of a 'social' kind which, finished with speed and confidence, was sent to Edward in November 1906. Edward gave it his unmitigated approval, enthusing: 'It's splendid. Congratulations. I think *The Country House* is a great advance artistically. I feel this chiefly because the author is so much more in sympathy with his characters, so much fairer to them than to the people in *The Man of Property*. Then the writing is brilliant. You've quite surpassed yourself in many pages ... You've worked out your own style, your own peculiar outlook, in a remarkably complete and perfect manner.'

To a degree Galsworthy was motivated by a persistent wish to gain Edward's approval; to a degree Edward began with doubts of Galsworthy's ability and surprise tinges his warm approval: 'From the specimens I saw months ago, I never suspected so strong and fine and rounded off a piece of work.'[22] Edward's congratulatory letter shows what he had aimed for in his literary association with Galsworthy, to encourage the individuality of the writer, to enable him to demonstrate his own distinctive ability. Edward recalled how he had said on their first meeting: 'Write about the English, for you've got it all inside you – all the keys that nobody turns in locks.'[23]

When Galsworthy departed from this in his next novel, Edward unhesitatingly wrote to him on receipt of the manuscript in September 1910: 'I'm not complimentary to *The Patrician*. I'm not going to be. I send you the notes I took as I read the pages ... I'm afraid this book will, in the public mind, draw a line around your talent and will circumscribe it definitely – and will let the light in on – not chiefly your strength, but a good deal on the blanks at the back of the strength.'[24] In a lengthy correspondence Edward returned to the theme of fidelity of characterisation. He argued that Galsworthy didn't know the people he depicted well enough to produce an original and really convincing picture. Galsworthy resented Edward's forthrightness and wrote rather sharply: 'As to knowledge of the people. Well, how can you tell? In the first place, you don't know them yourself; in the second place, after all, half my set at Oxford belonged to them ... Thirdly, G. Murray, who is married into them, and knows some of them intimately and is not likely to be too favourable, finds no fault, quite the contrary ... '[25] He also resurrected Edward's comments when he first encountered Galsworthy's work as anonymous reader for Unwin: 'I have always suffered a little from a sense of injustice at your hands – ever since I read an extract from your report on *Jocelyn* (which should never have been sent to me) to the effect that I should never be an artist but always look at life as from the windows of a Club. Well, book by book, I've always a little felt, that you *unconsciously* grudge having to recede from that position.'[26]

Galsworthy elaborated on this, saying that he thought Edward with his 'strong, and in those days, still more set belief' in his own insight had summed him up and 'could not be wrong' and that Edward perhaps had categorised him 'as something, special, definite, narrow'. He still resisted Edward's accusation of implausible characterisation in his new book and, in order to

convince Garnett of his knowledge, took the trouble to send him
a list of those whom he knew of that kind – 'they come to about
130, see the list enclosed for your unbelieving eyes'.[27] Eventually, though he maintained that he had not altered the essence
of the book, he admitted: 'I am approaching the end of this
revision. I have added some fifty pages and re-written practically all those passages which you queried; besides eyeing the
book closely for the soft touch.'[28]

Galsworthy had now established himself in his own eyes and
in those of the public, not only as a novelist but as a dramatist.
The social conscience which had informed his novels was also
the mainspring of his plays. These attacked the smug conven-
tionality and self-righteous hypocrisy of the middle classes and
championed the underdog. The first of these, *The Silver Box*,
originated from a suggestion by Edward that he should write a
play for the newly formed Vedrenne–Barker management at
the Court Theatre. In its writing he asked Edward as usual for
criticism and received on 8 March 1906 a detailed analysis.

Edward thought it would 'act very well *as it stands* – but much
better if you remodel certain things' and he gave a scene by
scene commentary for suggested improvements, 'chiefly on verbal matters'. He did not like Galsworthy's 'general contention,
. . . that there is one law for the rich and another for the poor'.[29]
Galsworthy in his reply said that he would adopt Edward's
verbal hints 'practically wholesale' but 'as to the thesis – this I
must keep, or start a fresh play . . . '[30] Indeed it was the whole
raison d'être of the play. When he submitted *The Silver Box* it was
accepted immediately by Barker and Shaw. It was produced at
a matinée performance on 21 September 1906 and was an instant
success, receiving 'splendid reviews'.[31]

The play arrived at a fortuitous time; it was just what the
Vedrenne–Barker management were looking for in their commitment to an 'uncommercial theatre of ideas'. Galsworthy went
on to write more didactic plays – *Joy*, *Strife*, *Justice* and *The
Skin Game* – and to become an acknowledged member of the
group of new dramatists of ideas pioneered by Shaw, which
was changing the English theatre. He still asked Edward for his
opinion, however, writing to him for instance on 3 May 1907
to say: 'I'm sending my Strike play . . . Could you read it and
let me have it back in haste? I want to give next week to its *very*

serious alteration, and would like your verdict before I begin.'[32] But as Edward said in reply on 6 May: 'I seem to have lost my critical certainty of instinct in reading Plays and speak with less and less confidence. I think that the Play as it stands is very dramatic and strong and cleverly managed . . . *But I don't presume to judge.* Your instinct as to how it will work out, on the stage is far more to be trusted.'[33] Indeed Galsworthy had a sense of theatre which Edward lacked. The roles of adviser and advised were being reversed as Edward, attracted by the Repertory theatre movement, attempted to find a creative outlet in drama.

TEN

Playwright

IN his introduction to his collected plays published in 1931, Edward gave as the reason for his dramatic attempts between 1906 to 1911 the fact that the Repertory movement, then new, promised to find audiences for plays that had no chance of being staged in commercial theatres.[1] No doubt an interest in drama as a vehicle for ideas inspired his attempts; it was as certain that this was unaccompanied by any real talent for dramatic composition or characterisation.

His first play to be accepted for the stage, *The Breaking Point*, is of interest not for itself but for the part it played as a focus for agitation against the way censorship was being conducted. The play dealt with an unmarried girl's fear of the consequences of her pregnancy; torn between her father and her married lover she kills herself. Frederick Harrison, manager of the Haymarket, accepted the play though he realised 'There is no money in *The Breaking Point* because the general public sets its face stubbornly against sad plays. And yours is more than sad. It is tragic.' Nevertheless he told Edward: 'I should be proud to introduce your dramatic work to the public, or that section of the public which is alive to what the theatre might be.'[2]

Harrison, however, was refused a licence for its production by the Lord Chamberlain. The Lord Chamberlain, who had absolute power over the public stage, in practice delegated the approval of plays before performance to an assistant, the Examiner of Plays. G. A. Redford, who held this office, not only held archetypal censorial views but predicated them in the actions he took at a time when the theatre was trying to break free from its Victorian straitjacket. His tactic was to approach theatre managers to request revisions, sometimes even after a licence was granted, and often in response to secondhand opinion or newspaper comment rather than from his own examination of the play in question. His capricious application of his duties he considered a private and confidential matter to be arranged with managers of theatres and not with the playwright.

Redford wrote to Harrison to suggest that he withdraw *The Breaking Point* before submitting it for a licence to avoid publicity and friction. It was an action bound to infuriate Edward and he refused to witness such surreptitious suppression. He wrote to Redford asking the reasons for the refusal of a licence and Redford's reply with its circuitous but implicitly insulting courtesy angered him further. 'I trust', Redford wrote, 'you will absolve me from any discourtesy if I point out that my official relations are only concerned with the Managers of Theatre. It is always painful to me to decline or recommend a License, and in this case I hoped to avoid any possible appearance of censure on anyone by suggesting privately to Mr. Harrison the desirability of withdrawing this piece. I cannot suppose that he has any doubt as to the reason.'[3]

Edward sparked off a fierce renewal of anti-censorship agitation. He refused to conform to Redford's conception of censorship by gentlemanly arrangements and published the book of the play together with an account of their correspondence and a long letter, signed by him but written by William Archer, which had been sent to the Censor on 10 August 1907. With indignation and a wealth of historical instances of the absurdities of censorship, the letter queried the illogical practice which restricted serious work yet was always ready to license 'plays (with or without music) which glorify and idolise vulgar and flashy lewdness'.[4]

Together with the censorship of Granville-Barker's *Waste* this incident caused leading writers to come together to protest against the operations of the Censor. As John Galsworthy recalled: 'Garnett stirred me up, and I went to Barrie, and with Gilbert Murray we induced all the leading authors to sign a protest written by myself.'[5]

William Archer in a letter of 1 November 1907 to Lady Mary Murray described the elaborate arrangements made for a demonstration organised to accompany a deputation to the Prime Minister, Campbell-Bannerman. These now sound faintly ludicrous but indicated the strength of feeling among leading writers, not only dramatists. Archer wrote:

> This Censorship fight is taking up all my time ... You will be glad to hear that all arrangements are now completed for the deputation to C.B. The Dramatic authors of England are to assemble in Trafalgar Square. Barrie will address them from the base of Nelson's column, and the Savoy Orchestra will play 'Britons will never be slaves'. The procession will then form, and will be headed by Pinero and Shaw walking arm in arm. Immediately behind them will come Garnett and Galsworthy, each bearing the pole of a red banner with the inscription 'Down with the Censor'. An effigy of Redford, which is being prepared by the Savoy property-man, will be carried by Frederick Harrison and W. B. Yeats, and over its head will wave a banner, carried by Gilbert Murray, with the inscription 'Ecrasez l'Infame!'. Arriving in Downing Street, Swinburne will declaim an 'Ode to C.B.'[6]

Fortunately or unfortunately, the procession with such a unique assemblage of literary *personae* did not take place. The Prime Minister was ill. A deputation was received by the Home Secretary, Herbert Gladstone, on his behalf on 27 February 1908 and as a result a committee to examine the question of stage censorship was appointed.

Frank Vernon commented on this furore and also on Edward's theatrical ability in his book *The Twentieth Century Theatre*:

> Much pother was made at the time about Mr. Edward Garnett's *The Breaking Point* but *The Feud* ... and *Lords and Masters* seem to prove him one of those men of letters who were attracted to the theatre without the gift of writing stage dialogue. It is not of course the office of the Censorship to quarrel with a play because it is not stage-worthy, but it was the affair of the agitators to have made their concentration

on a play better worth their efforts than *The Breaking Point*. They were lucky in that instance only because Mr. Garnett's records proved him the author – not his play – one of those distinguished outsiders may or may not turn out to be playwrights, but one wouldn't have them scared away from making the effort by the bogey of Censorship.[7]

Vernon had been the producer of Edward's play at the Haymarket Theatre on 5 and 6 April 1908 for the Stage Society – as a private performance this was not subject to action by the Lord Chamberlain. His opinion of Edward's stagecraft is corroborated in the letter which Shaw, a leading figure in the Stage Society, sent to Edward on 14 March 1908. 'Unluckily', Shaw began, 'I was unable to attend the Producing Committee of the Stage Society when your play was cast.' He proceeded to give expert and kindly advice to Edward, declaring the role of the heroine to be 'not by any means an easy part to cast. It is one of those off-the-stage parts that actresses do not appreciate ... ' In addition Shaw remarked on the fact that:

The second scene of the first act is an exceeding dangerous one, because the slightest slip on the part of the actress, or even the chance east wind putting the audience into a perverse humour, might make the lady's allusion to her condition provoke roars of laughter. To tell you the truth, if I were you I should be strongly tempted to cut out that scene; to get rid of every scrap of small talk that does not refer to the actual persons of the play and help the action along (you have been simply devilish in one or two places in your offences against this rule of thumb) ... [8]

He gave Edward some direct advice regarding the acting profession, explaining that he himself 'was pretty careful as to who I begin rehearsing with but once I begin I go through with it and never allow the actor or actress to feel that I am not thoroughly interested and hopeful about the performance. If you are dissatisfied with Miss McDougall put down your foot at once and say that you must have somebody else, because at the end of the week you will not be able to get rid of her ... But it is very important, if you are to do this with effect, that you should be ready to name her successor... '

Despite Shaw's warning letter, in the event the miscasting of the heroine, on whom so much depended, made a travesty of a play whose dramatic attributes Conrad had summed up in a letter to Edward. 'My point is this, that I don't think, my dear fellow, you have realised the firmness of mind necessary to an audience who would face your play ... the play is too concentrated. It hits one exactly like a bullet. You can see it coming, I admit, but that doesn't make it easier in the least. On the contrary, it prolongs the agony and brings on the feeling of *helplessness* which I think is fatal to the effect of the play... '[9]

Prior to *The Breaking Point*, Edward, who was interested in the Icelandic Sagas and their dramatic possibilities, had written a play entitled *The Feud* on the theme of 'a savage blood feud between two aristocratic families in thirteenth-century Iceland. The drama is heightened by the passionate sexual attraction of the son of one family and the daughter of the other ... '[10] Edward sent the play to Johnston Forbes-Robertson, who, in a letter of refusal, accurately predicted its lack of popular appeal: 'I am deeply impressed by *The Feud*, it has great drama and strength and should be taken up by one of the Societies in London which exploit such plays as have great merit but are not likely to please the crowd. I have "to please to live"; were it otherwise I would produce your Play with the greatest enthusiasm... '[11]

The play was eventually produced at the Gaiety Theatre, Manchester, in April 1909 by Iden Payne and Miss Horniman's Co. Edward Thomas was favourably impressed by its construction and dramatic possibilities. Writing to Bottomley, he said: 'Garnett's play I ought also to tell you is out and I have read it. It's a very fine heroic shape to hang many good voices and dresses on. In fact Helen and I came up chiefly to see it played and a good deal of it was excellent ... I had read the play of course and I thought nearly all of it carried well... '[12]

Galsworthy, who in a series of letters had commented on the construction of the play and had suggested improvements, predicted that it could not fail to be a dramatic success, and, after amendments had been made, he was 'more than ever confirmed in the certainty that it is a fine, simple, strong and dramatic work. It stands perfectly firm and square. It inspires one. That is the test.'[13]

David Garnett, whose emotion during the Stage Society performance of *The Breaking Point* at the Haymarket in 1908 was compounded from 'an agony of sympathy for Edward' and the play as 'an agony which I had to sit through', suspected that Conrad's comment on that play was also true of *The Feud*. Though excellent acting at the Coronet Theatre in Notting Hill, where he saw it played, obscured its faults, these arose from the same basic flaw – 'it was too concentrated without any secondary interest'.[14]

Garnett enjoyed some success with *Lords and Masters*, which portrayed the entangled relationships and conflicts between a wife, husband and lover. Unhappily married to a husband who wishes for appearances to keep up a semblance of marriage, the wife leaves him for her lover only to find that her lover has a mistress. The lover argues that this mistress – 'one of the lower classes' – does not affect his love for the heroine. The play ends with the wife walking out on both husband and lover. Galsworthy, who read it under its original title of *Jealousy*, thought that it contained 'fine psychological insight all through, especially in the women's parts'[15] and that Garnett had 'got over the technical difficulties very well on the whole'. Published under the pseudonym of James Byrne (in case the principal character was identified by mutual friends), it pleased Conrad whose criticism of *The Breaking Point* had so stung Garnett. In a letter of December 1911 he wrote: 'Frankly I never suspected in Mr. Byrne that power of "haut comique" ... And the wit: not the wit of repartee ... but the whole conception of the play being so witty! I have had there a most delightful surprise going on from page to page from act to act ... '[16]

Garnett's next play, *The Spanish Lovers*, had a much less favourable reception when Mr Iden Payne produced it at the Little Theatre on 22 May 1912. What the critic of the *Athenaeum* called 'an audacious venture' was an adaptation of Fernando de Rojas's drama of 1499, *La Celestina*. Garnett worked from a French version of the 'enormously long Spanish work which had twenty-one scenes' and which was 'more like a novel in dialogue than a play'.[17] The critic of the *Athenaeum* wrote:

'Unfortunately, Mr. Garnett seems to have been too ruthless in his modernisation. He has lopped and pruned the rank, prime blossoms of the roughshod but effective contrasts ... Its strength and actuality were eviscerated.'[18]

In performance the same fatal flaw of over-concentration caused David Garnett to remark that he longed for a break in the play, with a sub-plot and a change in mood. For some time Edward's friends had urged him to turn from unrelieved tragic themes and exploit his natural wit and powers of conversation. Conrad suggested to him, 'Why should you not execute a change of front and take up a subject where your irony could find its opportunity, your wit an aim for its shafts? Why not write a play about the literary world ... You have heard so many confidences, observed so many illusions, weaknesses and struggles by that particular world. You have a sense of the comic which would be governed by complete comprehension and sympathy.'[19]

Edward did attempt two comedies, *Mischief* and *The Political Sex*, but neither was published or produced. His inability to translate what seemed a natural talent puzzled contemporaries. As Galsworthy wrote: 'Barker has read *The Political Sex* – he said he was "bothered about you". He felt that you were too good not to come through but that all your work that he had seen so far failed in one respect or another. *The Political Sex* struck him as clever, but somehow removed from public interest...'[20]

Edward's last and major dramatic effort came with *The Trial of Jeanne d'Arc* which he feared 'judging by the rotten reception given to the Spanish play ... won't be acted till I'm dead'.[21]

Galsworthy did his utmost to help him in dramatic construction and stagecraft, scrutinising the manuscript and suggesting changes that reveal his own dramatic ability and Edward's inability. In a long letter in September 1910, he wrote that he had read the play 'very carefully ... making a lot of pencil notes and cuts purely on the "acting" side of the business ... ' and advised Edward to consider the 'hopeless length of the play as it stands, with all its changes of scene – and cut out every word that you can spare'. In another letter he suggested: ' ... abandon the notion of an historical document ... give us instead ... a purely emotional play.'[22]

Galsworthy's observations were confirmed in a letter which Herbert Trench of the Haymarket Theatre wrote to Garnett refusing the play:

> I have read your play on the Trial of Joan of Arc, with great admiration.
>
> Its defect, from the point of view of putting it on here, is the extremely rare one of too great concentration, and too close unity. Admirable of course as a piece of literature, its structure is that of a close series of scenes of torture in one form or another. I am afraid that this would produce a sense of over-monotony in the minds of the audience, superb as the handling is in its sincerity and directness.
>
> I therefore have to return the play to you with regret.[23]

William Archer, who had submitted a report on the play, covered the same ground. With an experienced eye, Archer asked: 'Have you produced a play that will hold people's attention in the theatre? & my answer would be: you are on your way to it, but have not by any means got there. It seems to me that you have not clarified or really dramatized your subject...' Succinctly Archer criticised Garnett's technical equipment as a playwright with:

> In the earlier acts you have all the materials for a fine drama, but they are not arranged in such a way as to bring out their dramatic quality. You lack two things, it seems to me: (1) exposition, (2) progression ... As to exposition, we ought to see clearly from the first, what we never see clearly at all: namely, what are the forces that are really contending for Jeanne. You rely far too much on the previous knowledge of the audience...

As far as progression was concerned, in Archer's opinion there was 'no expectation to carry us forward from one scene to the next' and episodes followed each other 'like beads on a string'. 'In short', Archer wrote, 'your play is unconstructed' and 'Of one thing I am pretty sure: namely that you should try to reduce the number of your changes of scene. I say this not from any consideration of convenience in mounting but because you seem to be always dropping your curtain without any particular reason.'[24]

Parts of the play, however, were performed on 26 October 1913 after Edward's friend William Poel approached him for permission to stage them at the Ethical Church in Bayswater.[25] Edith Evans, most surprisingly, played the part of the Bishop of Beauvais. The first stage performance was delayed twice because of Shaw's play on the same subject. On the first occasion, in 1923, Edward was sending *The Trial of Jeanne d'Arc* to theatre managers 'when Shaw announced to the press that he had completed *St. Joan*. This made it impossible for any management to risk putting on Garnett's Joan play.'[26] On the second occasion, in 1931, Shaw and Edward chose the same actress for the principal role – Jean Forbes-Robertson. The situation is explained in a letter from Shaw to T. E. Lawrence:

> What I make of Garnett's letter is that Jean F.R. does not want to play his Joan and has cast me for the part of Mr. Jorkins. Fortunately I am able to play it quite effectively. I have sent an epistolary wink to Jean and written to Garnett to explain that she would certainly give mortal offence to the highly influential Council of The Royal Academy of Dramatic Art if she anticipated her first appearance as Joan as fixed for the great Gala performance which is to rescue the R.A.D.A. from the desperate financial straits into which it has been plunged ... If I were to die tomorrow it would make no difference, she dare not disappoint the rest, who include her father, Ainley, Du Maurier, Barry Jackson etc. So Edward must wait. I cannot alter the situation ...[27]

Edward did wait; and though Jean Forbes-Robertson acted the main part with her usual accomplishment in a performance at the Arts Theatre in Great Newport Street, Shavian competition swamped what merit existed in the different approach Edward made to his theme. Edward had conceived his play as one which would follow the exact course of the trial of St Joan for heresy, believing that it was 'one of the greatest, perhaps the greatest trial recorded in history'.[28] His son David recalled the performance at the Arts Theatre as a moving and historically accurate reproduction of the trial. Nevertheless he felt as he had done at the performance of *The Spanish Lovers* that compression and the lack of a counterplot made it emotionally exhausting.[29]

Faced once again with evidence of his want of creative talent, Edward came in time to accept his limitations with a magnanimity which characterised the role in which he succeeded – that of literary adviser. As Edward Thomas said to Gordon Bottomley: 'I dare say you are right about *The Feud* ... In any case I should never have thought of saying it proved Garnett's powers. You have to see and hear him to know them and I am convinced he can never write anything worthy of them. He knows himself this weakness in literary expression and though he must feel my inferiority to him as a nature and as a mind he says quite honestly with a smiling admiration that I have a natural talent for writing which he has not.'[30]

The conversational powers of Edward, and respect for his literary judgment, despite his own creative failure, attracted over the years a widening circle of friends and acquaintances, many of whom made it a practice to meet regularly for lunch. Their venue was an upstairs room at the Mont Blanc Restaurant in Gerrard Street, Soho.

ELEVEN

The Mont Blanc

R. H. MOTTRAM described the occasion he accompanied John Galsworthy to 'the upper room of the Mont Blanc Restaurant'. There he found 'in queer semi-clerical clothes at the top of the table Edward Garnett, who might have been called "Maître", or the leader, if this tenuous association had ever the rigidity of a French school. Garnett ate with his fork while reading for review a book propped against a cruet, and tried to calm Belloc, who rather dominated the conversation.'[1]

The lunch-time meetings began when Edward became Duckworth's reader, and literary acquaintances that he made about this time would also come to the Mont Blanc: 'In this way a small circle of habitués was formed, among them Thomas Seccombe, R. A. Scott-James, Stephen Reynolds, Edward Thomas, W. H. Davies, Hilaire Belloc, Muirhead Bone, Ford Hueffer, Perceval Gibbon, occasionally Galsworthy and rarely Joseph Conrad.'[2] They took place, as Edward said to Wells, 'on Tuesdays (and Wednesdays also) when some nondescript "literary persons" forgather in a more-or-less protesting sort of manner, over their pot-au-feu and navarin de mouton at 1.30.'[3]

Such gatherings are a commonplace in literary history and have antecedents in the eighteenth-century coffee houses and Edinburgh literary clubs. What Hudson, who was an occasional visitor, termed 'the free and cordial interchange between authors'[4] provided opportunities for the discussion of forthcoming work and the criticism of current publications. The habitués of the Mont Blanc also passed on to Edward the work of aspiring authors for his opinion. Out of respect for his judgment the Galsworthys had encouraged Mottram to refer his work to Edward. John Galsworthy wrote to Mottram in 1904 to say, 'Those of us who want to do good work generally come to him sooner or later, why not sooner?'[5] More specifically Ada said, 'I like *The Old Book Room* so much that I should be glad to pass it on to be read by Edward Garnett, whom some of us think the finest of English critics.' Galsworthy on 28 April 1904 followed this with a letter on the outcome: 'The trouble you speak of over *The Old Book Room* was a real pleasure to me. In Garnett's criticism, and he is always sincere, you have the dictum of the most penetrating critic we have.'[6]

That Edward held to rigorous standards unswayed by personal considerations was a characteristic which Conrad had noted earlier. In his letter to Edward Noble he declared: 'I shall see Garnett and mention your manuscript and name to him. He is young and very artistic. He is also a very severe critic. Of course your work will be judged strictly on its merits.'[7]

In conjunction with his critical judgment also came a patience and willingness to listen, together with suggestions that would help to clear the author's path to what he wished to achieve. Stephen Reynolds wondered: 'Have I been overwhelming you with letters lately. Tisn't to be helped. I'm collecting ideas – or rather impressions to grow into ideas – at such a rate, that I must spout them out and share them with somebody; and no one but you that I know is likely to see what I am getting at. Indeed one or two of your remarks, and various political considerations have had more than summat to do with it.'[8] In the same vein Reynolds wrote later: 'Can you think of a better form into which to throw such splendid material ... Please let me know what you think ... Other people can't be expected to comprehend my private thought dialect as you do ... '[9] In an appreciative letter that shows the origin of *Poor Man's House* and Edward's part in it, Reynolds said, 'Most of the things came to you in letters, and but for you I shouldn't probably have started on the thing; and but for disagreeing with you I should have no clear idea of what I was getting at ... Anyhow *Poor Man's House* has the best of me in it ... Believe me I'm genuinely grateful to you ... '[10] When Edward eventually persuaded a publisher to take the book, Reynolds wrote: 'I do believe if we haven't been and gone and done it. Lane's accepted *Poor Man's House* ... And you'll let me dedicate the PMH to you and Tony jointly? ... '[11]

While Edward was reading for Duckworth the weekly meetings at the Mont Blanc were a sounding board to current literary activity, and provided an acquaintance with literature in process which was an invaluable asset to his employer – for it was expected of the reader that he would actively seek out 'publishable' work or have an early option on writers with potential. Edward was particularly taken with the work of Perceval Gibbon, who became a regular at the Mont Blanc. He made an emphatic recommendation to Duckworth: '*Salvation*', he wrote, 'is a very clever piece of work by a man who is a born writer and has led a varied life. We should like to see Duckworth become Mr. Gibbon's English publisher – *as this author may go far*. As the latter's sales are much better, we understand, in America than in England, now is the time for Duckworth to get him on reasonable terms. We suggest that Duckworth should see Pinker and ask for details of Gibbon's next two books – in prospect.'[12]

Edward expressed an equally strong belief in the future of H. M. Tomlinson, who was also drawn into the Mont Blanc fold. Reporting to Duckworth on *London Clay* on 25 May 1903, he announced: 'There is one decidedly striking story in this collection of sketches – "Mrs Penrose". The author *knows* what he is writing about and *feels* the whole situation: he shows considerable literary restraint and that is why "Mrs Penrose" makes a strong impression on the reader.' Though he wrote, ' ... we can't urge Duckworth to publish unpopular stuff by unknown authors at the same time Mr. Tomlinson has the right stuff in him. If he could add three or four as good, in the same vein and the book were called "Mrs Penrose" – in bold black letters – we think it would be *discovered*. The fact is it touches the English conscience in a very weak place and its truth is unmistakable ... Anyway we propose to write a sympathetic letter to the author.'[13]

He reiterated his conviction of Tomlinson's ability in a report of 1907 on *A City on the Sea*: 'This man can write very well. He has mastered the difficult art of *description* and many of his impressionistic sketches of the life and atmosphere of the London docks are worthy of many a writer of wider reputation. Occasionally he is a little misty in style, but only occasionally. The sketches are quite worth publication and they fill a gap. Mr. Tomlinson loves his subject – Thamesside life and he writes with original feeling.' Edward thought him a writer 'worth keeping an eye on' and in a further laudatory report praising Tomlinson's 'unusual gift of delicate description' he voiced the belief that 'probably Dent could put the thing through if Duckworth does not see his way'.[14]

Altruistic interest rather than mercenary commitment to a single publisher marked Edward's consideration of promising work and the Mont Blanc provided a meeting point where he could encourage authors and promote the publication of their writing. Of all the Mont Blanc habitués Edward developed a particular friendship with Edward Thomas. They had met in 1905 following an attack by Edward on Thomas's disparagement of Walt Whitman. From this exchange a close friendship followed and Thomas's regard for Edward as a critic and adviser occurs frequently in his letters to Gordon Bottomley. 'Garnett tells me he likes the *Jefferies* very much', he said to Bottomley, 'and his praise means a great deal as I feel his ideas have ramified through me until there is little else when I am writing books.'[15] Typically Edward, who was a great admirer of Jefferies and who knew his wife, had secured an introduction to her for Thomas and encouraged him in compiling the writer's biography. On 10 November, Thomas wrote: ' . . . you have a paternal right to criticize my book since very little but the impression is mine. I held the pen, but since you contradicted me about Whitman (it seems a long time ago) you have done the rest and I value your opinions more than anybody's because they are great ideas or the ramifications of them . . . I shall look out for your review. Is it to be in "The Nation" or the "D.N."?'[16]

The rapport between them enabled Thomas to discuss and to correspond with Edward from their first meeting about his various projects and literary aspirations. In 1909 he wrote: 'I have written about a score of tales and sketches, real and imaginary, such as I have never attempted before; and though I feel a little more confidence than I used to, I am not at all sure that I am on a wise path – far less a profitable one – and

you are the only man I can turn to for an opinion.'[17] Some
Edward thought 'intolerably affected'[18] and Thomas defended
himself from other strictures with 'you are unjust in your view
of what you call "literary phrases" that "smell of the lamp".
Such phrases however bad, came to me without thinking or
sinking. It is your "simple and direct" phrases that I have to
seek for.'[19] Thomas revised and pruned the sketches 'under
Garnett's expert guidance'; some were published in the
Nation and the *English Review* and by Edward's influence at
Duckworth nine appeared in book form in 1910 entitled *Rest
and Unrest*.[20]

This advisory relationship between them was made more
significant by the fact that Thomas looked with suspicion upon
critics, most of whom he thought dealt in misunderstanding
rather than perception. In the *Daily Chronicle* he was making his
own reputation as a critic with exacting standards and becoming known for his advocacy of poetry in the lyrical tradition.[21]
It was in this capacity that Thomas encountered the remarkable
W. H. Davies and introduced him to Edward and to the rest of
the Mont Blanc circle.

Thomas had been attracted by the natural poetic gift of
Davies and his review of *The Soul's Destroyer* and other poems in
the *Daily Chronicle* no doubt helped 'a great deal towards making
Davies's budding reputation secure'.[22] Despite his own financial
difficulties Thomas helped Davies in more practical ways. When
he discovered that the poet was having trouble over accommo-
dation he found him a small cottage near his own at Sevenoaks
and paid the rent; he introduced Davies to Edward, who helped
to pay for the coal and light. Hudson was also inveigled into
providing funds and Davies became a regular visitor to the
Mont Blanc. Davies had begun a book of prose in response to
prompting from his new literary acquaintances, 'to put together
a record of his fabulous adventures in America and England
while the events were still fresh in his memory'.[23] The manuscript which he prepared was given by Thomas to Edward who
submitted a report to Duckworth in 1907. Under the title of *A
Poet Tramp's Life*, Edward wrote: 'We advise Duckworth to
accept this. It is an extremely interesting narrative of the unusual experiences of a wandering life, chiefly as a professional
tramp roving through America. Every page is interesting and

fairly vivid and the picture is varied and full of human feeling. The narrative is written in a clear modest and highly condensed style. Its defect is the *detail* is generalised and not fine or subtle in colour and atmosphere. Considering the writer is practically uneducated it is, however, a clever and solid piece of work.' On the practical side, Edward stated: 'We think that the book may very likely *sell*. Some interest has already been evoked by the author's poems and we think the reviews will be undoubtedly good.' He also reminded his employer that 'Thomas says the MS will be revised and additions will be made, if Duckworth makes the author a modest offer. We are decidedly in favour of Duckworth taking up the book.'[24]

The MS was in need of revision because Davies had passed over tramping experiences in America and England in favour of 'more garish adventures in low places'.[25] Through inexperience he did not take kindly to revision but complied, with the encouragement of Thomas. By 29 August Thomas wrote to Edward: 'I am sorry about the Poet's life. But I think I have succeeded in setting him to work to increase it as far as possible in the way you suggest. I agree about the details and I think he can do them pretty well ... Davies says you shall have the MS when it is ready and he is grateful to you for troubling on his behalf ... '[26]

To bring the book more forcibly to the notice of the public, Thomas and Edward had suggested that it should have a preface by some well-known figure. Shaw, who had been one of the recipients of *The Soul's Destroyer* accompanied by its begging letter and had asked for eight more copies,[27] agreed to do this. Mrs Shaw, who had taken to the incorrigible Davies (to the extent of contributing £60 to his publishing expenses) also pressed her husband to write it and on 14 June Davies was able to tell Edward: 'I wrote to Mrs. Shaw and have received her answer which is that Shaw has begun a Preface for my Autobiography and that it will be ready soon. I don't think there will be much more delay and that it will soon be in your hands.'[28]

The terms which Duckworth offered for *The Autobiography of a Super-Tramp* were the subject of dispute. Because the Preface would be part of the book, Shaw took an interest in the contract and questioned the exclusive rights Duckworth demanded over the manuscript and subsequent editions and also the clause indemnifying Duckworth from libel. When Duckworth refused to alter these conditions, it was placed with Fifield and published in 1908.

Although the *Autobiography* was a success it did little to further Davies's financial security, nor did another volume of poems published by Fifield – *Nature Poems* – though these confirmed his poetic reputation. Again Thomas did his best to help and attempted to place some articles for Davies in periodicals, lamenting his failure to do so to Edward with the generous comment: 'I don't consider myself unlucky, because I can't hope to attract attention; but a man with a wooden leg in one hand and a preface by Shaw in the other – ! But luckily Davies does not know how good his work is . . . '[29]

In the ingenuous hope that a sensational novel might both bring him money and help his reputation, Davies began to write *The Weak Woman*. He had little knowledge of novel writing and, in spite of help from Thomas and Edward, the book when published was not successful in either of its objectives.

Edward and Thomas decided that a Civil List pension would help to bring about the financial security which Davies deserved and after approval from the Prime Minister, Asquith, they organised a petition. In February 1911 they composed a circular letter which read: 'It is proposed by various admirers of the poetry of Mr. W. H. Davies to petition the Government to grant him a pension on the civil list. Your name has been given us as one willing to aid in this matter . . . '[30] It was signed by the two sponsors and drew replies predictably from the Mont Blanc circle and Edward's acquaintances in the book trade. Hudson wrote of Davies as 'an original genius of a rare and delightful quality';[31] Conrad of 'a poetical gift enriching our literature'.[32] Davies wrote to Edward on 26 February of his delight that the petition 'was getting signed all right', hoped that it did not interfere too much with his own work and thanked him for his kindness.[33]

The Civil List pension was awarded to the value of £50 a year. For good measure Edward had also applied to the Royal Literary Fund for a grant for Davies. News of its award came through quickly and the view of its committee on Davies and his ability to handle money is implicit in the letter Edmund

Gosse wrote to Edward on 12 March: 'I am happy to tell you that we made a grant of £50 to Mr. Davies this afternoon ... and I hope you and Mr. Thomas will not be disinclined to act as paymasters. We thought – as Mr. Roberts will explain that it wouldn't be really kind to pour out the whole sum upon the poet at once ... '34 Llewellyn Roberts, the Secretary, more specifically requested Edward to act 'with Mr. Thomas and disburse the moneys'; adding that they thought 'it will be well not to let Mr. Davies know the actual amount ... '35 Davies wrote appreciatively: 'Dear Garnett, Thank you very much for your good news. I am delighted to hear that there are to be trustees. You and Thomas are the two ... We *are* to be congratulated ... '36

Davies thought that another book of prose pieces might help him to capture the public's attention; the motive, as with *The Weak Woman*, derived from his belief that a writer's reputation depended on notoriety as much as talent. Edward took up the prospective book with Duckworth and it appeared in 1912 under the title of *The True Traveller*. It was a collection of omissions from the *Autobiography* and during its writing Davies met Edward at the Mont Blanc to discuss it. As he said in his letter of 11 November 1911: 'Many thanks for the £4 for November. I will bring up the stuff I have discarded on Tuesday and will meet you at the Mont Blanc at the usual time. You will then see that the book is more direct as it now stands, and that the things left out are digressions and of very little interest. However, we will talk the matter over ... '37 Later, sending Edward a copy of his *Songs of Joy*, he went on to write: 'I can now see my way clear to do that you suggest and will bring the MS with me the Tuesday after next, when I expect to meet you at the usual hour ... '38

He became a regular and welcome visitor at the Mont Blanc, finding in its members congenial company. Muirhead Bone, recalling the 'innocent and impish' character of Davies, compared his appearance with Hudson: ' ... if Hudson was like a hawk or an eagle, Davies was by comparison the picture of a robin.'39 Davies for his part, with a shrewdness in summing up people necessary to his colourful past, gave a view of Edward at the head of the table at the Mont Blanc: he had 'a natural wit, and it had to come out, whether people liked it or not; but being a kind hearted man, he was very quick in smoothing matters over if he saw his words taken too seriously.'[40] Edward had, he said, 'a most destructive mental punch to which there was no answer' but was 'a man who sometimes said hard things to your face, but always soft things to your back'.[41]

Ford Hueffer, who came regularly to the restaurant at first, often found Edward's 'teasing' hard to bear. When it touched upon a project dear to his heart he took umbrage and wrote afterwards:

> Dear Edward – I think I ought to tell you that I resent – and resent intensely – yr telling people that I can't write. It does not matter before intimates but when it comes to a table of comparative strangers I really think it is in distinctly bad taste. I don't use a stronger word. After all I am a writer as serious, as conscientious, & earnest as yourself &, if our views of the functions of literature do not tally, that is not a reason for the denial of one's right to express one's views ... I don't say anything about the review of the Apollo I know that that was intended to tease ... but when it comes to an – I hope unconscious crying down of the magazine wh. I am doing absolutely for the love of literature & without an idea of advancement or any profit at all for myself – a project wh. is intended to help so many people & causes wh. you desire yourself to help – I think that it goes too far.[42]

The magazine that Ford was so concerned to defend was the *English Review*, now recognised as one of the most brilliantly edited of literary periodicals. He had discussed such a periodical with Edward, among others including Conrad and Wells, during 1908. Edward had warned him about the dangers inherent in the profit-sharing financial basis he envisaged, but Ford, though he realised that 'inevitably there will be quarrels and recriminations', remained optimistic.[43]

Inevitably there *were* quarrels and these arose partly because Ford's concept of the truth was a highly personal one, based on impressions rather than fact; partly because 'highly serious critics like Edward Garnett were inclined to think him a dilettante – a fanciful egotistical person who turned his back on "real" life and moved from one unreality to another';[44] and partly because Ford by demanding impossibly high standards from contributors offended those who could have helped him. In the words of his friend and contemporary, Edgar Jepson, 'Ford demanded a quality of writing in that review such as no review had demanded before, or has since, and it was by that demand that he so hindered the recognition and advancement of his novels. As editor he rejected the work of so many critics. For the life of me I do not see what else he could have done, that was his standard of writing, and they could not reach it.'[45]

R. A. Scott-James, answering a 'sharp letter' he had received from Ford, referred jocularly to his notorious quarrelsomeness to which Ford replied: 'I wonder if it is true that I am troublesome and quarrelsome to such a degree. I dare say it is ... '[46] He became more and more estranged from the literary 'establishment' and from those who attended the meetings at the Mont Blanc. He described the restaurant sardonically as a place where ' ... the elect of the city's intelligentsia lunched and discussed with grave sobriety the social problems of the day ... under the presidency of Mr. Edward Garnett who has for so long been London's literary – if Nonconformist – Pope ... '[47] Writing to Jepson he scathingly remarked, 'I am so glad too that you have been writing on the *Future of Love*. It sounds a promising subject for your pen which is so unlike that of Aretino, Edmund (sic) Garnett or Sir Something Robertson Nicholl (sic) and Mr. John Galsworthy. (These are, are they not, the principal ornaments of the Royal British Academy of Letters).'[48]

In *The Simple Life Limited*, published in 1911 under the pseudonym of Daniel Chaucer, Ford satirised the Mont Blanc circle and the Fabians who lived on Limpsfield Chart. Edward is portrayed as Mr Parmount, the tired old critic who, with others, forms 'a group of silly fanatics with ideas borrowed from Tolstoy, Edward Carpenter, William Morris and H. G. Wells ... ' In depicting a group preoccupied with theoretical discussions on the way life should be lived, Ford attempted to 'expose their foolishness and self-deception'.[49]

Douglas Goldring, who was Ford's young assistant on the *English Review*, made a fierce defence of Ford and a personal attack on Edward in his book *South Lodge*. He repeated Jepson's view on Ford's editorship and specifically cited Edward 'as one of those whose writings certainly did not reach *English Review* standards and this may account for his subsequent venom against the editor'. In Goldring's opinion Garnett had an 'animus against Ford' and a 'jealousy of Ford's superior critical acumen'. Describing one of the 'celebrity parties, given by Ford, Goldring wrote:

> ... Edward Garnett, who might quite well have ignored my existence, seemed to go out of his way to be offensive to the 'office boy', I noticed also that his manner to all the 'rising' authors present was so heavily patronising as to suggest that they had no business to 'rise' without his consent and approval. Ford always treated him with exaggerated consideration – their parents had been intimate friends and they had known each other all their lives – but it often struck me that he would have liked to patronise even Ford.

The impression of Edward, so much in contrast to that given by the writers whom he had helped, continued with:

> Of his personal qualities, apart from his boorish manners and quite remarkable ugliness, I know nothing. I can well believe that he has a heart of gold, was a model of domestic virtue and fully deserved the appreciation of members of his circle. It was merely as a Literary Pontiff that he seemed to me then, and seems to me still, largely a fake. It is claimed that he 'discovered' Conrad, D. H. Lawrence and other geniuses, but actually he got Lawrence from Ford and Conrad from Galsworthy. His personal judgement may have been fairly sound, but it is doubtful if he would have achieved his reputation as a publisher's reader had he not been in a position to pick the brains of his betters.[50]

This wholesale (and inaccurate) condemnation of Edward by the former sub-editor of the *English Review* appears to have been provoked by dislike and by excessive zeal to do battle on Ford's behalf. As Edward Crankshaw, who was a close friend of Ford and one of the three people present at his funeral, wrote in his review of *The Last Pre-Raphaelite*, Goldring 'gives us a picture of a man who so bewildered his contemporaries that they rejected him', and 'discusses Ford's contemporaries as an act of piety to Ford'.[51]

Even so Ford himself wrote of Edward during the period that saw the inception of the *English Review* that:

> As a critic – and above all as a discoverer of talents ... Mr. Garnett has habitually shown a preference in the books that he published or praised for either the irresponsibly joyous or the genuinely tragic ... there are very few writers of any real worth that do not owe something to his support ... His odd eruditions, his singular belief that the business of a critic is to evolve standards, his, as if inverted, Puritanism he owes no doubt to his Yorkshire ancestry and to his descent from distinguished scholars. His Irish blood accounts, no doubt, for his love for the emotional and the genuine in literature.[52]

For his part Edward, whatever their later differences, had a friendly interest in the fortunes of Ford, writing to Galsworthy on 8 May 1905 with the news that: 'Hueffer has at last been *boomed*, boomed furiously and has come into his own. I'm so very, very glad.' The reception given to Ford's *Soul of London*, Edward thought well deserved: 'It is very good you know; the best thing he's done. And I hope and trust it will definitely pick him up, for if ever a man wanted recognition, poor Ford does.'[53]

In fact both had in common an obsessive interest in encouraging literary talent. Ford like Edward became involved with writers of promise at varying stages of their development. Conrad, who had met Norman Douglas during a visit to Capri in 1905 to recuperate, forwarded Douglas's essays, then entitled 'Nelson' and 'Sentimental Love', to Edward for his observations.[54] He also 'enlisted the interest of other literary men in Douglas's work'.[55] Of these Ford, delighted with 'The Isle of Typhöeus', accepted it for the *English Review*, and it appeared in its third issue in 1909. Other articles – 'Brigand Forest', 'Sirens', and 'Tiberius' – were published subsequently and thus Douglas was launched into publication in company with the array of talent that graced the early issues of that periodical. Douglas, who later became Assistant Editor of the *Review*, began to 'drop in to the informal literary luncheons at the Mont Blanc'.[56] He formed a friendship with Edward, who on occasion invited him to The Cearne. David Garnett, then aged fourteen, recounts how he wanted to take the guest out exploring but 'my plan of taking him to my favourite haunts in the woods of the High Chart was knocked on the head. My father would not leave me alone with Douglas for one minute.'[57]

Edward admired the special quality of Douglas as a writer – usually referred to as epicurean or sybaritic or hedonistic – and helped Conrad, who was busy on Douglas's behalf, to persuade Dent to publish *Siren Land* in 1911 after the book had been 'hawked around publishers'.[58] Of *London Street Games* (1916), a book that pioneered observations on children's play, Edward wrote to Douglas: 'I hugely enjoyed it. Warm congratulations! It is a fine piece of literature – the work of a scholar & it has all the delightful spontaneity of Rabelais in his list of Medieval Games. I shall want you to annotate my copy with one or two of the improper versions!'[59] When Douglas was correcting the proofs of *South Wind* the value he placed on Edward's opinion caused him to request his publisher to 'send the first copy to the "Punch" man [Arthur Eckersley]', adding that 'the second copy should go to Garnett; between the two of them they should give the book a good start'.[60] The book in which Douglas gave a summation of his particular views and attitudes, *In the Beginning*, aroused Edward's admiration. He wrote, 'I am glad you have nailed our colours to the mast' and delighted the author by describing the supper party of the harlots as 'pure gorgonzola'.[61]

By this time the lifestyle of Douglas had made it necessary for him to leave England. As David Garnett recalled: 'Compton Mackenzie wrote that after Douglas was arrested for picking up a young boy in the Natural History Museum, practically all his friends avoided him. Some did not. After my father's death, I found a letter from Violet Scott-James telling Edward of what had occurred and calling on him to help her get Douglas out of England as soon as possible.'[62]

Generosity of mind to his friends was a feature of Edward's character – he had not deserted Wells during the Amber Reeves affair, and he was one of the few whom Gilbert Cannan continued to regard as a friend during the social difficulties accompanying his tortuous affair and later marriage to the wife of J. M. Barrie. Edward had first noticed Cannan when he reported to Duckworth in 1903 that *Watchman of the Night* was 'a very curious MS – one half good and one half bad. The author has a

certain amount of dramatic instinct, a talent – we might almost
say – for striking situations.' He was, however, 'agin it', feeling
that it was 'written in pieces' and 'the plot broken backed' but
he thought Duckworth might find it worth looking at.[63] In the
end it was Cannan who approached Edward, writing to enlist
his support in a campaign to establish a Society for the Abolition
of Censorship, appropriately enough at the time of his difficulties with the Censor over *The Breaking Point*. A friendship
followed and Cannan began to correspond with him about his
work. On 21 July 1908, he wrote to thank Edward 'for the nice
things you say about the Clara play. Lapage has returned it to
me and I send it to you herewith.' He went on to say: 'I began
a short story about a little slavey the other day which grew and
grew until it is now a portentous length and nowhere near the
end' and that he hoped after a visit to France 'to fish you out to
lunch on Thursday if that suits'.[64] Cannan, whose life was to
take such a tragic turn, began to experience those financial and
literary disappointments that contributed to his eventual breakdown, and confided in Edward on 7 September that Heinemann
hadn't given him much encouragement over his stories: 'It's a
nuisance as I wanted to get something done so as no longer to
be working in the dark. Things have taken a serious turn with
me, as my silly family's affairs have gone bust and I must earn
money.'[65] As he became more and more concerned with his
future he thought Edward would help him to publication: 'If
you can bully some publisher into issuing [the stories] I should
be grateful as I think I had better have some sort of status,
however small. I have one or two other stories lying about
somewhere, and have already sketched out one or two more as
a result of reading those I sent you.'[66] Eventually the affair with
Mary Barrie culminated in the 'rather startling announcement'
which Cannan made to Edward on 24 September: ' ... I'm to
be married next April to Mrs. Barrie. She will be divorced next
month. It has been a mighty thing and she's splendidly happy,
as I am. Wish us well.'[67] Cannan's financial struggle became
more acute and, looking for a regular source of income, he, as
he put it to Edward, 'sold myself to the Star as dramatic critic'.[68]
He also frequented the office of the *English Review* with other
aspiring young authors, where Ford thought him the most
silent man he knew.[69] Before his career was curtailed by mental

instability he was looked upon as a writer for the future, like so many who had connections with the *Review*. Henry James named him in his famous article 'The Younger Generation' in *The Times Literary Supplement* in 1914, putting in the 'dusty rear'[70] another young writer who was already a contributor to Ford's magazine and on the threshold of writing the short stories and novels which marked a new voice in English fiction. D. H. Lawrence was at the point in his career when, feeling rejected by his publisher and abandoned by Ford, he needed advice and encouragement.

TWELVE

The Young Lorenzo

IN his introduction to *A Collier's Friday Night*, Edward recalled the 'loveableness, cheekiness, intensity and pride'[1] of Lawrence when he first knew him and when he came to visit at The Cearne. Lawrence was to write of this period: 'How well I remember the evenings at Garnett's house in Kent by the log fire. And there I wrote the best of the dialect poems. I remember Garnett disliked the old ending to "Whether or not". Now I see he was right, it was the verse of the commonplace me, not the demon. So I have altered it. And then again, those days of Hueffer and Garnett are not past at all, once I recall them. They were good to the demon, and the demon is timeless.'[2]

They came together as a result of Edward's appointment as representative to the American firm The Century Co. Writing on 13 July 1911 to J. B. Pinker, Edward had asked: ' ... The Century Co. of New York has lately appointed me its literary representative on this side. I understand that the *Magazine* is in search of good short stories by English writers of high reputation ... The Century Book Publishing Dept. would also be glad to consider any MS or proof sheet of anything *notable*, that is likely to suit the American market ... '[3] It was in this capacity that Edward contacted Lawrence, who wrote to him on 24 August 1911: 'Many thanks for your letter ... I have several short stories which I shall be pleased to send to you for your approval on behalf of the Century Co ... '[4] On 10 September he asked: 'I beg to send to you the accompanying two stories for your approval on behalf of the Century Co. I am afraid they may not be of the requisite length: as for the kind of thing, would you mind telling me if these are suitable. If not, I must do up something else. I have not very much time for writing. I shall be very glad if you can dispose of a little of me in the *Century*. Certainly my work is not in demand. And if, any time, you would give me a word of criticism on my MSS I should go with surer feet ... '[5]

So began an association which was to be illuminated by Lawrence's combination of confession, exasperation and aspiration. He replied to Edward's assessment of his MSS on 25 September:

> Thanks for the advice concerning *Intimacy*. I myself felt the drag of the tale, and its slowness in accumulating. I send you this, which I think would easily split into three. It is only the first writing, rough, and not sufficiently selective. Bear with me if the first part is tedious – there are, I think, good bits later on. I tried to do something sufficiently emotional, and moral and – oh American! I'm not a great success. If you think this is really any good for the Century, I will revise it, and have it typed. But if it's not fairly hopeful I won't have it typed out. I am badly off. I should also like to – to be seen, if you will have it so. But I teach in school, in Croydon. I will try to get an hour off, and will call on you at Messrs Duckworth's next week – 3rd or 4th October, if you wish. I hardly like foisting this lump of MSS on anybody.[6]

On 2 October Lawrence thanked Edward for the return of *Two Marriages* 'with such good hopes' and arranged to meet him at Duckworth on the 12th in the afternoon.[7] Edward invited Lawrence to The Cearne and Lawrence sent further manuscripts for Edward's perusal. Following this visit a letter from Lawrence indicates their growing rapport over his work and his future publishing arrangements. 'Dear Mr. Garnett,' Lawrence began, 'I have been to Wm. Heinemann's lately, at that gentleman's request. He, and his Satraps, are very much sweeter. It is very remarkable. Last week they were sneering and detestable today they are of the honeycomb. Heinemann wants to publish verses. That will be all right, it will save you the bother. He will publish them in the Spring. Will you send the batch, at your convenience. Do you want to see the others before Heinemann has them? – I know you are not keen on verse. Then he wants me definitely to promise the next novel – the one that is half done – for March, and to withhold the short stories from Martin Secker until autumn. That I suppose is a fairly good arrangement.' Their evident discussion over what was to emerge as *The Trespasser* is mentioned as 'I forgot to ask him about the "erotic" MSS.'[8]

His slighting reference to Heinemann mirrored a dislike shared by Edward which is illustrated in a letter to Louie Burrows on 10 October: ' ... while Garnett and I were having lunch who should come into this place but Atkinson, Heinemann's man. Garnett does not like Heinemann's people, so he was beastly sarky with him ... As for myself', Lawrence added, 'I hate Atkinson – I don't go to Heinemann's because I don't like the sneering, affected little fellow.'[9] He asked Edward's advice on his dealings with Heinemann in a letter of 7 November. 'Shall I ask Wm. Heinemann to allow me an income of £100 a year for one, or two years. He will owe me £50 in February. He shall have another novel before June – not to mention the verses. Shall I ask him?'

This concern over finances was to be a constant anxiety to Lawrence during his writing career as much as the ill-health which was to dog him all his life and which he mentioned to Edward in his letter as: 'This last fortnight I have felt really rotten – it is the dry heat of the pipes in the school, and the strain – and a cold. I must leave school, really.' But buoyantly the letter closed with 'I've got another ripping long short story – shall I send it to you? Don't let me be a bore. I'm sending the last, best verses, the latest and most substantial, to the Cearne tomorrow.'[10] But the onset of illness interrupted his plans and Edward received on 26 November from Lettice Lawrence a sisterly letter with dispiriting news: 'I am writing this in place of my brother who is very ill. He was taken ill the Sunday following his visit to you, and has since developed pneumonia. I came yesterday to nurse him and hope, with care to pull him through. My brother wishes me to tell you that he's afraid the correspondence will not be kept up. Heinimann [*sic*] will not acknowledge the poems, and so the last lot have not been sent. It is best to let this stand, and with this the Secker business.'[11]

Lawrence had contracted a chill watching Edward chopping logs at The Cearne during his visit there, but fortunately, as his sister wrote on 2 December to Edward: 'You will be pleased to know that my brother has now got over the worst stage of his illness, and is on the high road to recovery. The only thing to fear now is a relapse, but I am trusting such a thing will not happen. It has been a fearfully anxious time for me. My brother wishes me to tell you he would very much like you to come and see him, as he is improving nicely. As soon as he is strong he will go down South for a time.'[12] Her letter to Edward on 17 December continued the good news but was prophetic about her brother's constitution: 'My brother is now able to sit up for a short time each day, but is very weak. The doctor says he may be downstairs by Xmas, and, soon afterwards be fit to go to Bournemouth. He has really made wonderful progress the last week. The report concerning the expectoration was very satisfactory. No germs were discovered, and since then both lungs have almost completely cleared up. Of course my brother will be very liable to consumption and as the doctors say will always need great care. He has to give up school too.'[13]

Edward had shown his concern for the young writer in practical ways for as Lawrence wrote appreciatively on 17 December: 'I got the cheque yesterday, and accept it gladly from you. But a little later, when I have some money, you must let me pay it back to you, because that seems to me honester.' They had also resumed their discussions over his work, for Lawrence wrote: 'I shall look for you on Wednesday. Don't bring the novel MSS unless you have read all you want to read. I don't want it a bit. It is a work too chargé, too emotional. It's a sponge dipped too full of vinegar, or wine, or whatever – it wants squeezing out. I shrink from it rather . . . '[14]

The following day Lawrence expressed his growing disillusionment with Heinemann as his publisher and doubts regarding Hueffer as counsellor. Replying to Edward's favourable comment on the manuscript he exclaimed:

Your letter concerning the Siegmund book is very exciting. I will tell you just what Hueffer said, then you will see the

attitude his kind will take up. 'The book,' he said, 'is a rotten
work of genius. It has no construction or form – it is execrably
bad art, being all variations on a theme. Also it is erotic – not
that I, personally, mind that, but an erotic work *must* be good
art, which this is not.' I sent it to our friend with the monocle.
He wrote to me, after three months: 'I have read part of the
book. I don't care for it, but we will publish it.' I wrote back
to him: 'No, I won't have the book published. Return it to
me.' That is about fifteen months ago. I wrote to Hueffer
saying:"The novel called *The Saga of Siegmund* I have determined not to publish.' He replied to me: 'You are quite right
not to publish that book – it would damage your reputation
perhaps permanently' ... Is Hueffer's opinion worth anything, do you think? Is the book *so* erotic? I don't want to be
talked about in an 'Ann Veronica' fashion.

Lawrentian pride in the nature of his work and in self-
sufficiency characterises the conclusion of the letter when he
responds to Edward's decision to take the book to his employer.
'If you offer the thing to Duckworth,' he wrote, 'do not, I beg
you, ask for an advance on royalties. Do not present me as a
beggar. Do not tell him I am poor ... I do not want an advance –
let me be presented to Duckworth as a respectable person ...'[15]
The letter marked the closer literary association between them
that Lawrence was to describe to Ernest Collings as a turning
point in his career: ' ... Ford Madox Ford discovered I was a
genius – don't be alarmed, Hueffer would discover *anything* if he
wanted to – published me some verse and a story or two, sent
me to Wm. Heinemann with *White Peacock* and left me to paddle
my own canoe. I very nearly wrecked it and did for myself.
Edward Garnett, like a good angel, fished me out ... '[16]
Like Conrad, Lawrence found in Edward a friend and critic
with whom he could discuss the nature and progress of his work.
He responded to Edward's advice and had confidence in his
editorial supervision.
As it passed to and fro between them *The Saga*, which
became *The Trespasser*, forged what was to become the familiar
connection linking the mentor and the beginner appealing for
comfort and criticism. On 19 January 1912, Lawrence asked:
'What do you think of the enclosed? Is it merely soft sawder? I

really don't think the Saga was read at Wm. Heinemann's – not by anyone. But they make me feel so uncertain and down about the wretched thing ... I am always ready to believe the worst that is said about my work and reluctant of the best. Father was like that with us children.'[17] Two days later he sent 'herewith the 180 and 190 pages of *The Trespasser* which I have done. It won't take me much longer will it? I hope the thing is knitted firm – I hate those pieces where the stitch is slack and loose. The *Stranger* piece is probably still too literary. I don't feel at all satisfied.'[18]

In the actual manuscript Edward's critical note refers to this episode: 'Something is wanted to carry off this passage with the *Stranger*, i.e. – you must intersect his talk with little realistic touches to make him very (?) *actual*. He must not spring quite out of the blue and disappear into it again. He's too much a *deus ex machina* for your purposes. Make his talk more ordinary and natural. Slip in the pregnant things at moments.'[19] While writing the novel Lawrence was a frequent visitor to The Cearne. Reporting on 29 January that 'The Trespasser goes quite fast ... I am past the 300th page now' he hoped 'I shall finish by the time I come to Edenbridge – or at any rate before I leave you. So, when you can find time to go over the thing, we can decide about the publishing.'[20]

The same pattern of sending manuscripts and receiving advice, encouragement and criticism occurred with *Sons and Lovers* and the early versions of 'The Sisters', destined to become *The Rainbow* and *Women in Love*. As E. W. Tedlock, who produced a descriptive bibliography of Lawrence's manuscripts, remarked apropos *Sons and Lovers*, Lawrence's letters have much to say about 'the personal problems in which the novel is rooted', and were 'a subsidiary part of the process that created the novel'.[21] In this sense Edward entered into the creative process at two crucial periods of Lawrence's career – the initiation of *Sons and Lovers* and the change in direction to *The Rainbow*.

Sons and Lovers bears the urgent mark of Lawrence following the tradition of the nineteenth-century autobiographical novel, but enriched with his own passionate involvement in the characters created. It received from Edward criticism within the framework of that conception of the novel, with its insistence on 'form', and an editorial supervision that had much to do with the final published text. The first is implied in correspondence between them, and the second is there in the comparison between manuscript and published text.

Edward's comments as the novel progressed can only be conjectured from the letters which Lawrence wrote in appreciation of his close scrutiny of the manuscript in its early stages and which reflect the encouragement given to him. 'I got *Paul Morel* this morning', he wrote, 'and the list of notes from Duckworth. The latter are awfully nice and detailed. What a Trojan of energy and conscientiousness you are. I'm going to slave like a Turk at the novel – see if I don't do you credit. I begin in earnest tomorrow.' In a postscript he reiterated his determination: 'I'll do you credit with that novel if I can ... '[22]

More revealing, in anticipation of Edward's insistence on form, Lawrence wrote from Italy on 14 November 1912: ' ... I hasten to tell you I sent the MS. of *Paul Morel* to Duckworth registered, yesterday. And I want to defend it quick. I wrote it again, pruning it and shaping it and filling it in. I tell you it has got form – *form*: haven't I made it patiently, out of sweat as well as blood.' He went on to explain at length the motif, characterisation and psychology of the novel to remove from Edward's mind an apparent doubt that its conception was not matched by its construction. He challenged Edward: 'Now tell me if I haven't worked out my theme, like life, but always my theme. Read my novel. It's a great novel. If *you* can't see the development – which is slow, like growth – I can.' Nevertheless he declared: 'I should like to dedicate the *Paul Morel* to you – may I? But not unless you think it's really a good work. "To Edward Garnett, in Gratitude." But you can put it better.' Later in the same letter he asked: 'Have I made those naked scenes in *Paul Morel* tame enough? You cut them if you like. Yet they are so clean – and I *have* patiently and laboriously constructed the novel.'[23]

Edward's influence on the published text of *Sons and Lovers* is complicated by the distinction which must be made between his advice on the text as literature and his role as publisher's reader. He was at once both literary adviser on a personal level and in theory, as reader, expected to observe 'one of the chief functions ... to guard against excessive frankness on the part of novelists'.[24] Another more practical function was to edit the text in the light of conventions on length in relation to the economics of publishing. In this context Lawrence's query – 'Have I made those naked scenes in *Paul Morel* tame enough?'[25] – is open to various interpretations. Lawrence had expressed his wish earlier that he didn't 'want to be talked about in an "Ann Veronica" fashion'.[26] He also always resisted any alterations to his manuscripts other than those he regarded as minor. The cuts that were made by Edward in the manuscript for the published text would seem to have been made, not as a means of pre-publication censorship, but for practical reasons.

Correspondence between Lawrence and Edward apparently indicates that the cuts were a disagreeable necessity dictated by trade conventions about novel length. Lawrence's letters express his appreciation of the cutting and of the unpleasant and tedious nature of the task which he had imposed on Edward. 'I sit in sadness and grief after your letter. I daren't say anything. All right, take out what you think necessary – suppose I shall see what you've done when the proofs come, at any rate. I'm sorry I've let you in for such a job – but don't scold me too hard, it makes me wither up ... ' and in his postscript remarked 'Tell me anything considerable you are removing (sounds like furniture).'[27] Later Lawrence wrote: 'I'm glad you don't mind cutting the *Sons and Lovers*. By the way is the title satisfactory.'[28] In another letter shortly afterwards he said: 'I'm glad to hear you like the novel better. I don't mind what you squash out. I hope to goodness it'll do my reputation and pockets good ... I'm glad you'll let it be dedicated to you. I feel so deeply in your debt.'[29]

It could be argued that the reason for the cuts was primarily commercial. A seven and sixpenny novel usually ran to 120,000 words, and *Sons and Lovers* in manuscript made 180,000 words. An opinion that the passages deleted by Edward improved the novel by cutting out duplication is corroborated by Lawrence's frequent references to his own 'prolixity'. Tedlock's *Report on the Final Manuscript* states that: 'The cutting in the manuscript is extensive – some 88 passages, varying in length from three or four lines to eighty-nine and occasionally amounting to several pages ... there is little or no cutting of the sexual encounters between Paul and Miriam, and Paul and Clara ... '[30]

Lawrence expressed his impatience with revision in his letter to Edward on 12 January 1913: 'The thought of you pedgilling away at the novel frets me. Why can't I do those things? – I can't. I could do hack work, to a certain amount. But apply my creative self where it doesn't want to be applied, makes me feel I should burst or go cracked. I couldn't have done any more to that novel – at least for six months. I must go on producing, producing, and the stuff must come more and more to shape each year. But trim and garnish my stuff I can't – it must go ... '[31] When he corrected and returned the first batch of proofs he congratulated Edward and criticised himself with: ' ... You did the pruning jolly well, and I am grateful. I hope you'll live a long, long time, to barber up my novels for me before they're published. I wish I weren't so profuse – or prolix, or whatever it is. But I shall get better.'[32]

Conflict, not harmony, characterised all Lawrence's relation-ships. As Lawrence matured and his genius took new directions, shedding old styles and concepts, he increasingly felt he had to be free from any constraints. Throughout his correspondence with Edward over *Sons and Lovers* there was a growing conflict of opinion about presentation and form, which came to a parting of the ways with *The Rainbow*. The letters which document the transition of the Lawrence of *Sons and Lovers* to the Lawrence of *The Rainbow* illustrate how conscious Lawrence was of this tran-sition; they also show how Lawrence's new style and philosophy of writing had to be tested against Garnett as the confessor of Lawrence's artistic aspirations, and the importance Lawrence attached at this time to Edward's criticism. He anticipates antagonism to his new approach to the novel in a letter of 1 February 1913: 'I have done 100 pages of a novel. I think you will hate it, but I think when it is re-written, it might find a good public among the Meredithy public. It is quite different in manner from my other stuff – far less visualised. It is what I *can* write just now, and write with pleasure, so write I must, however you may grumble.'[33] He repeated his twin themes of expected resistance by Edward and belief in his new approach with: 'I have written 180 pages of my newest novel, *The Sisters*. It is a queer novel, which seems to come by itself ... I will send it to you. You may dislike it – it hasn't got hard outlines ... I can only write what I feel pretty strongly about: and that, at present, is the relation between men and women. After all, it is *the* problem of today, the establishment of a new relation, or the readjustment of the old one, between men and women ... '[34]

His preoccupation with *The Sisters* coupled with curiosity about Edward's likely reaction is shown in his query: 'I wonder how you like *The Sisters*. Not much I am afraid, or you would tell me. You are the sort of man who is quick with nice news and slow with nasty. Never mind, you can tell me what fault you find, and I can re-write the book.' This appreciation of Edward as critic is taken further in a postscript to the letter with a declaration that he was embarking on a new phase in his writing: 'The copy of *Sons and Lovers* has just come – I am fearfully proud of it. I reckon it is quite a great book. I shall not write quite in that style any more. It's the end of my youthful period. Thanks a hundred times.'[35] Shortly afterwards a curious letter, the joint composition of Lawrence and Frieda, indicates, vicariously, Edward's opinion of *The Sisters*, his shrewd detection that it originated in Lawrence's relationship with Frieda, and Lawrence's acknowledgment of Edward's strictures on its presentation:

[Frieda] Dear Mr. Garnett: We roared over the 'remarkable females', you just hit them! The worst, it's like his impudence, they are *me*, these superior, beastly, superior arrogant females. Lawrence *hated* me just over the children. I daresay *I* wasn't all I might have been, so he wrote this! ... The book will be all right in the end, you trust me for my own sake, they will have to be woman and not superior flounders. I say the book is worthy of his talent, but not of his genius ... There, I'm 'Ella-ing' again.

[Lawrence] I was glad of your letter about *The Sisters*. Don't *schimpf*. I shall make it all right when I rewrite it. I shall put it into the third person. All along I knew what ailed the book. But it did me good to theorise myself out of it, and to depict Frieda's God Almightiness in all its glory. That was the first crude fermenting of the book. I'll make it art now.[36]

.   By 4 September, Lawrence was writing to Edward that '*The Sisters* has quite a new beginning – a new basis altogether. I hope I can get on with it. It is much more interesting in its new form – not so damned flippant...'[37] A few weeks later he wrote:

'*The Sisters* is going well. I've done a hundred pages. I wonder what you'll think of it. It is queer. It is rather fine ... I shan't do anything but *The Sisters* now. I hope to have it done in a month. I *do* wonder what you will think of it ... '[38]

The firmness of his intention in departing from his old style and his doubts as to whether Edward will find this acceptable are recorded in a letter of 30 December: 'In a few days' time I shall send you the first half of *The Sisters* – which I should rather call *The Wedding Ring* – to Duckworths. It is very different from *Sons and Lovers*: written in another language almost. I shall be very sorry if you don't like it, but am prepared. I shan't write in the same manner as *Sons and Lovers* again, I think – in that hard, violent style full of sensation and presentation. You must see what you think of the new style.'[39]

A letter of 29 January 1914 expressed Lawrence's agreement with Edward's 'two main criticisms, that the Templeman episode is wrong, and that the character of Ella is incoherent', but the writer was 'most troubled' about a criticism of 'the artistic side being in the background'. The letter reflects a turning point in Lawrence's development: 'I have no longer the joy in creating vivid scenes, that I had in *Sons and Lovers*. I don't care much more about accumulating objects in a powerful light of emotion, and making a scene of them. I have to write differently. I am most anxious about your criticism of this.' Would Edward, Lawrence wrote, tell him *very* frankly what he thought of the second half of the novel which he was sending, and also, if he liked the book, whether he thought Ella was now 'possible'. However, Lawrence declared: ' ... if this, the second half, also disappoints you, I will, when I come to the end, leave this book altogether. Then I should propose to write a story with a plot, and to abandon the exhaustive method entirely – write pure object and story.'[40]

In this letter, which gives an early sign of the division of what began as *The Sisters* into what became *The Rainbow* and *Women in Love*, Lawrence reaffirmed that he was 'going through a transition stage' and thanked Edward 'for the trouble you take for me. I shall be all the better in the end.'

The difference of opinion between Lawrence and Edward on Lawrence's new approach and style was becoming more marked. Lawrence was increasingly defensive about what he wished to do as a novelist. He could not ignore the fact that Edward, although his good friend and mentor, remained an associate of Duckworth, who was experiencing difficulties in publishing his work. A long letter dated 22 April 1914 is punctuated with remarks which reveal Lawrence's mixed feelings:

> If a publisher is to lose by me, I would rather it were a rich commercial man such as Heinemann. You told me in your last letter that I was at liberty to go to any other firm with this novel. Do you mean you would perhaps be relieved if I went to another firm? Because if you did not mean that, wasn't it an unnecessary thing to say? You know how willing I am to hear what you have to say, and to take your advice and to act on it when I have taken it. But it is no good unless you will have patience and understand what I *want* to do. I am not after all a child working erratically . . .

Later in the letter Lawrence returns to this theme with:

> I did not like to see that Duckworth had lost on *Sons and Lovers*. And I *must* have money for my novels, to live. And if other publishers definitely offer, they who are only commercial people, whereas you are my friend – well, they may lose as much as they like. For I don't want to feel under any obligation. You see I can't separate you from Duckworth and Co. in this question of novels. And *nobody* can do any good with my novels commercially, unless they believe in them commercially – which you don't very much.

The purpose of Lawrence's letter had been to say that he was sending as much of *The Wedding Ring* as had been typed and that he was 'sure of this now, this novel. It is a big and beautiful work. Before, I could not get my soul into it.' He was glad Edward had sent back the first draft 'because I had not been able to do in it what I wanted to do'. Lawrence, however, was upset over what seems to have been a second letter from Edward 'against' the novel, because he felt it insulted 'rather the thing I wanted to say, not what I had said, but that which I was trying to say, and had failed in'. He ended the letter nevertheless with 'I shall be glad if you like the novel now – but you will tell me'.[41]

Their disagreement on the kind of novel that Lawrence had now developed, and Edward's criticism of it, is evident in Lawrence's explanation of his new approach which he made in a letter of 5 June: ' ... I don't agree with you about *The Wedding Ring*. You will find that in a while you will like the book as a whole. I don't think the psychology is wrong; it is only that I have a different attitude to my characters and that necessitates a different attitude in you, which you are not prepared to give. As for its being my *cleverness* which would pull the thing through – that sounds odd to me, for I don't think I am so clever in that way.' In characterisation, Lawrence wrote, Edward must not look 'for the old stable *ego* of the character' and used an analogy to the allotropic states of carbon to defend his psychology.[42] Prophetically he said: 'You must not say my novel is shaky – it is not perfect because I am not expert in what I want to do. But it is the real thing, say what you like. And I shall get my reception, if not now, then before long. Again I say, don't look for the development of the novel to follow the lines of certain characters ... '[43]

In their meeting and parting there is expression of gratitude, but as Scott-James declared: 'Garnett has been called the "discoverer" of genius. He was more than that. He often evoked it, inspired it and moulded it in its early stages, till the genius ran away and mocked him by becoming a best seller, or stayed by his side and languished.'[44] This assessment is confirmed by Edward's association with Lawrence, and is illustrated by his remark: 'No, my dear Garnett, you are an old critic and I shall always like you, but you are a tiresome old pontiff also and I shan't listen to a word you say, but shall go my own way to the dogs and bitches, just as heretofore. So there.'[45]

Lawrence had long outgrown a tutelage which he had earlier discerned in 1913 as a matter of generations:

I believe that, just as an audience was found in Russia for *Tchekhov* so an audience might be found in England for some of my stuff, if there were a man to whip 'em in. It's the producer that is lacking, not the audience. I am sure we are sick of the rather bony, bloodless drama we get nowadays – it is time for a reaction against Shaw and Galsworthy and Barker and Irishy (except Synge) people – the rule and measure mathematical folk. But you are one of them and your sympathies are with your own generation, not with mine. I think it is inevitable. You are the only man who is willing to let a new generation come in.[46]

Whatever its merits in explaining their eventual difference of opinion over his new work, such a judgment had an element of contradiction, for Edward believed Lawrence was a new voice that had to be heard. With his usual pertinacity he tried to interest 'his own generation' in what his friend Hudson termed 'your favourite author's *Sons and Lovers*'. Writing to Edward on 7 November 1913, Hudson gave his opinion of it as

a very good book indeed except in that portion where he relapses into the old sty – the neck-sucking and wallowing in sweating flesh. It is like an obsession, a madness, and he may outlive it as so many writers have done. Paul and his mother are extraordinarily vivid and alive. Only they seem more real than most of the human beings one meets ... Thanks for letting me read your Lawrence article ... It doesn't alter my opinion ... With your praise of *Sons and Lovers* I agree, but nothing else much, and he remains to my mind a smaller minor poet.[47]

The tenor of his friend Galsworthy's opinion was similar. He wrote: 'I've finished *Sons and Lovers*. I've nothing but praise for all the part that deals with the mother, the father and the sons; but I've a lot besides praise for the love part. Neither of the women, Miriam or Clara, convince me a bit ... ' Bluntly Galsworthy remarked that 'It's no good to spend time and ink in describing the penultimate sensations and physical movements of people getting into a state of rut; we all know them too well ... The body's never worthwhile, and the sooner Lawrence recognises that the better ... '[48] A personal as well as a literary antipathy existed between the two writers. In his diary on 13 November 1917, Galsworthy wrote: 'Lunched with Pinker to meet D. H. Lawrence, that provincial genius. Interesting, but a type I could not get on with. Obsessed with self. Dead eyes, and a red beard, long narrow pale face. A strange bird.'[49]

Walter de la Mare, who had been involved in trying to place the book with Heinemann, told Edward that the MS had gone back to the author. Heinemann had thought the libraries would ban the book in its present form, and de la Mare agreed with him. He went on: 'I don't feel that the book as a whole comes up to Lawrence's real mark. It seems to me to need pulling together; it is not of a piece and the real theme of the story is not arrived at till half way through.'[50]

Robert Lynd was even more comprehensive in a letter to Edward from the *Daily News*. He could not accept Edward's judgment of Lawrence. He had been afraid that the 'badness' of *The Trespasser* might have biased him unfairly against Lawrence and he had attempted, when the new book appeared, to take 'a special interest in finding out if this was so'. Unfortunately reading Lawrence's other work had only confirmed his view that he was 'a plumber of genius – a painter and plumber ... and cannot see that he is more than a middling artist ... I certainly can't see anything in his work to put beside Conrad ... '[51]

It was in this climate of opinion among well-known literary figures that Edward expressed his belief in Lawrence as a writer. When he sent to Pinker on 23 July 1913 'a very fine story "Honour & Arms" by *Mr. D. H. Lawrence* in the hope that you will be able to place it advantageously for him', Edward argued that: 'This study of German soldiers' life in my opinion is as good as Stephen Crane's best. In fact Crane and Conrad are the only two writers to be named in conjunction with this remarkable piece of psychological genius.'[52]

In published criticism Edward attempted to show the particular qualities of Lawrence in his article in the *Dial* in 1916. 'Mr. D. H. Lawrence and the Moralists' was a pioneering study of a question frequently to be raised by Lawrence's work – the right of the artist to go beyond conventional notions of morality. *Sons and Lovers*, Edward wrote, also had the virtue of being the only novel 'of any breadth of vision in contemporary English fiction that lifts working class life out of middle class hands and restores it to its native atmosphere of hard veracity'. Further, Lawrence added to qualities of realism an 'intimate poetic susceptibility' and an 'evident delight in the exuberance of nature' which had none of what Edward scathingly referred to as 'M. Zola's false naturalism or scientific reporting'.[53]

As well as adviser, editor and critic, Edward by his friendship and hospitality fortified Lawrence during his early troubled years as a writer and the difficult period as Frieda Weekley's lover. Lawrence interpolated into his correspondence with Edward his more personal problems and emotions, declaring in April 1912: 'Mrs Weekley will be in town also. She is ripping – she's the finest woman I've ever met – you must above all things meet her ... '[54] He brought Frieda to The Cearne, prefacing his visit with a letter: 'I am most awfully fond of her. Things are getting difficult. Are you *quite* sure you would like her and me to come to your house? ... But don't mind to say "No," if you feel the least hesitating.'[55] Afterwards he confided to Edward: 'Tell me what you think of Mrs Weekley. I am afraid of you suddenly donning the cassock of a monk, and speaking out of the hood. Don't sound wise, and old, and – "When you've lived as long as I have" – sort of thing. It's insulting.'[56] For Edward or Constance such an attitude would have been out of character.

The Cearne became a regular haven for Lawrence and Frieda. As he wrote in July 1913 to Edward: 'I shall be glad to be at The Cearne, where I feel at home – the only place I do feel at home. Perhaps Frieda will come with me. I shall come at any rate on Thursday. If she must go by the night train I shall be a bit late. But if I can I shall come for lunch. Thank Mrs Garnett for her – she's awfully good to us – Auf Wiedersehn.'[57]

Constance, for her part, had a soft spot for Lawrence; they shared a love of flowers and his health aroused her maternal anxiety. Lawrence, writing from Italy in 1914 where 'May is very flowery and abundant now,' wished she could see 'the rose coloured gladioli and lovely monthly roses, all wild'.[58] He also admired the delicate Constance for her diligence in her work. In later years he recalled her 'sitting out in the garden turning out reams of her marvellous translations from the Russians. She would finish a page, and throw it off on a pile on the floor without looking up. That pile would be this high – really almost up to her knees, and all magical.'[59]

Unostentatiously the quiet Constance was sowing the seeds of an influence on English literature more or less single-handed.

THIRTEEN

Dostoevsky Corner

IN the years following the death of Stepniak, Constance continued in her devotion to Russian literature and the chronology of her translations was to pattern more or less the phases of the 'Russian fever'. She translated Turgenev between 1894 and 1899, Tolstoy from 1901 to 1904, Dostoevsky from 1912 to 1920, Chekhov from 1915 to 1926, Gogol from 1922 to 1928, Herzen from 1924 to 1927 as well as individual works by Goncharov (1894), Ostrovsky (1899) and Gorky (1902).

Gilbert Phelps in his study *The Russian Novel in English Fiction* made the point that, 'Of all the foreign influences that have entered into our literary heritage none has been so completely dependent upon translation. Not only the public who read the great Russian novels but also the critics who commented upon them were, for the most part, utterly ignorant of the originals ... and it was not until the advent of Constance Garnett and Aylmer Maude that the public had the opportunity of reading their completed works in really good English.'[1]

The availability of translations was of crucial importance as one of a series of factors which would transform the intellectual and cultural mores of England. At the close of the nineteenth century, Britain, in a 'splendid isolation' bred of imperial expansion, long Victorian peace, the benefits of industrial progress and social order, had an intellectual complacency that severed it from the Continent. Antipathy and moral outrage usually marked the reception given to the few important European works of literature and art which reached England's shores. They were associated with the decadence and depravity conjured up by the term 'fin de siècle' and the social postures of Wilde and Beardsley. The works of writers such as Zola and Ibsen were viewed as symptomatic of European moral degeneration which could be tolerated only at the level of the 'French' novel or play: sufficient to be indulged as an episode of naughtiness in an otherwise decent order of things and as evidence of insular superiority.

But in literature, as Ford Madox Ford proposed with reference to the works of Henry James and Joseph Conrad, an 'alien cloud'[2] was passing over the landscape of the English novel, leaving behind a feeling that the simple story was gone for ever. Both of these writers, by their origin and work, symbolised fittingly this alien influence. These expatriates of the U.S.A. and Poland signified the Continental rather than the insular in their devotion to technique and their attention to the medium, in their preoccupation with the closely constructed novel and with technical innovation, in their dedication to the novel as an art form. In this Constance's translations of Turgenev played a part; as Conrad remarked, 'She has done that marvellous thing of placing the man's work inside English literature, and it is there I see it . . . or rather feel it.'[3]

If most contemporary authors came to read Turgenev through his wife's translations, it was Edward's systematic and comprehensive analysis in the prefaces that pioneered a full appreciation of Turgenev as a novelist. In writing about Turgenev he was also concerned to urge upon writers and the reading public the importance of the novel as a serious literary form. In his preface in 1899 to *The Jew and Other Stories* he wrote: 'Many of the men of letters today look on the novel as a mere story book, as a series of light coloured amusing pictures for their "idle hours" and on memoirs, history, and poetry as the age's serious contribution to literature. Whereas the reverse is the case. The most serious and significant of all literary forms the modern world has evolved is the novel; and brought to the highest development the novel shares with poetry today the honour of being the supreme instrument of the great artist's skill.' He declared the novel to be 'the most complex of all

literary instruments, the chief method of analysing the complex-
ities of modern life'.[4]

Edward pointed to Turgenev as an exemplar for native novelists. *A Lear of the Steppes* was 'of special interest to authors'
because 'the story is so exquisite in its structure, so overwhelming in its effects, that it exposes the artificiality of the great
majority of the clever works of fiction ... '[5]

When the prefaces were issued as a collection in 1917, T. S.
Eliot called them 'perhaps the first serious study of [Turgenev]
in English' with 'both the merits and defects of a pioneer work'.
Eliot, who was to be such a major influence on critical approaches, in his review in the *Egoist,* thought that 'as the first
book on the subject, it contains just the necessary information;
taking up the novels one by one and sketching their genesis and
accounting for the ideas which went into them'. He praised it
especially for the fact that 'it enables the reader of Turgenev to
see the novels in relation to each other, and the relation of the
characters in different novels. It invites us (and its concise
brevity is an added provocation) to consider the work of Turgenev as a single work, the art of Turgenev as steady and
laborious construction, not a series of scattered inspirations.'[6]

Herbert Howarth in his *Notes on Some Figures behind T. S. Eliot*
claims that Eliot's reading of Edward's chapter discussing Turgenev's *On the Eve* led him to write his own version of the story.
Howarth explains how Edward had described ' "the depths of
meaning which at first sight lie veiled under the simple harmonious surface", behind the lightly spun picture of a quiet household he saw the "wavering shadow" of a nation's hopes and
ambitions and its coming changes. Eliot seems to have intended
an equivalent double effect in his story ... '[7]

The subtlety of Edward's critique of Turgenev was widely
and highly regarded by his contemporaries as Frank Swinnerton remembered.[8] It was the introduction to Turgenev's *On the
Eve* that caught the attention of the young Arnold Bennett, who
wrote to Edward to ask if he would

be so good as to give me further particulars of the book
Souvenirs sur Tourgeneff mentioned in your introduction to *On
the Eve* ... My excuse for thus troubling you must be that I
am making a study of Turgenev as a constructive artist in

fiction, and that I fully share your admiration for his work
... Your prefaces to the different novels contain some of the
best criticism of fiction that I have come across. Especially
that to *Smoke*. Strictly technical criticism (particularly on the
point of construction) seems almost a minus quantity in both
England & France. It is one of my ambitions to revive it – if
indeed it was ever alive. I may mention that I have more
than once had the pleasure of appreciating your edition of
Turgenev in the columns of *Woman*, a little paper of which I
am the editor.

Bennett concluded with an apologetic postscript: 'I should tell
you that I cannot read either Russian or German.'[9]

This letter of 1897 with its ingenuous touches provides a
contemporary indication of Edward's reputation both as an
advocate of Turgenev and as an acute critic of the technical
mysteries of fiction. Bennett remarked later, as a contributor to
Orage's *New Age*, that 'Edward Garnett's introductions to the
works of Turgenev constituted something new in English literary criticism; they cast a fresh light on the art of fiction completing the fitful illuminations offered by the essays of George
Moore...'[10] Bennett's dedication to the novel as an art received
rumbustious treatment from his friend H. G. Wells who was at
odds with the whole idea of a theory of literary methods. Edward figured in his mocking letter to Bennett: '... I was very
glad indeed to get your letter, and to find things are less at
variance between us than I supposed. But as far as the Balzac
theory, no! – I don't hold with you any more than I do with
Garnett and the Turgenev theory or the damned old art critics
and the Michelangelo Raphael theory...'[11] Shortly afterwards
in another letter of 19 August 1901, headed 'PRIVATE AND
ABUSIVE', Wells asked, 'Does it not occur to you that when you
and Garnett solemnly set aside Turgenev's own preference
among his books, you may after all do no more than indicate
your personal quality?'[12]

Edward carried out an insistent campaign to bring the genius
of Russian writers to the notice of English novelists and to the
reading public. In 'Tolstoy and Turgenieff' in 1900 he praised
'the Russian school of realism as the highwater mark in the
development of the novel in the last century'.[13] In his reviews in

the *Speaker* he consistently referred to the Russian masters and propose that 'The "fiction" of the great Russian novel is merely a vehicle for fixing permanently the essential meaning of the facts of life.'[14] He joined forces with his old colleague at Unwin, G. K. Chesterton, in a book on Tolstoy in 1903. Dealing specifically with 'Tolstoy's Place in European Literature', he wrote that Tolstoy as a novelist aimed 'to make man more conscious of his acts, to show society its real motives and what it *is* feeling, and not to cry out in admiration at what it pretends to feel'. He concluded that 'the realism of the great Russian's novels is, therefore, more in line with the modern tendency and outlook than is the general tendency of other schools of Continental literature'.[15]

But public taste in England in Edward's opinion was insufficiently developed to appreciate the great Russian writers. Writing on Gorky in the *Academy* in 1901 he declared that there was a fundamental difference between the two reading publics: 'The English speaking world honestly favours those writers whose pictures show the ultimate triumph of the "moral law" over life's ugliness and nature's indifference. The Russian speaking world, however, is quite intolerant of rosy optimism, and finds pleasure largely in gloomy pictures, where the brutal sinister outlines of life throw up the ineffectiveness of the moral law.'[16] He repeated such an argument in his reviews of Gorky later in the *Speaker*,[17] and in his introduction to Gorky's *Twenty-six Men and a Girl* in 1902, he attacked the present state of English fiction in contrast with the Russian approach:

It is too much to expect that Gorky will be popular in England, but still his work may be of some service. He can be of use at least in the sense that every honest analysis of life, spiritually put, is a natural corrective of those melodramatic, pretentious, pseudo presentations which our 'popular' fiction and our popular stage supply *ab libitum* to the undiscerning crowd. Gorky's work is the natural antidote to novels of the inflated type, which are daily hailed as 'masterpieces', to novels of life *de luxe* for the Pullman car ... In Gorky we find no circulating library 'aristocratic' emotions to admire, and no up-to-date Puritanic eroticism to smile at ...[18]

Arnold Bennett in a letter to Edward noted 'with satisfaction'[19] the jibes that Edward made, and the reviewer of Edward's *Introduction* in the *Academy* commented: 'That such stories as Gorky's can readily be utilised (this valuable word is Mr. Garnett's) by the public today is very certain' and considered the introduction as marked no less by 'restraint of valuation than by sympathetic insight'.[20] Edward made his usual swingeing remarks on English insularity when he turned to Dostoevsky in the *Academy* in 1906. Commenting on the impossibility of getting the translations issued by Vizetelly twenty years previously, he made an acute analysis and assessment of Dostoevsky's work. In Edward's view, 'There is little "wholesomeness" in most of Dostoevsky's novels, but his analysis of the workings of the minds of the sick and suffering peoples, and the possessed, show us how the underworld of the suffering or thwarted consciousness yields us an insight into deep, dark ranges of spiritual truth ever denied to healthy, comfortable, normal folk.' Nevertheless the power and underlying sanity of Dostoevsky's mind, Edward considered, were best attested by 'the perfect clarity, calm, penetrating judgment and classic objectivity of the *House of the Dead* ... not a line of exaggeration, not a word of sentimentality'.[21] Edward had a long-standing admiration for Dostoevsky's work; his youthful novel *Light and Shadow* had Dostoevskian overtones.

Interest in this most Russian of authors, in contrast to the 'Parisianised' work of Turgenev, was gradually developing in England, as the country experienced the influx of Russian ballet, art, music and design. Arnold Bennett, the influential 'Jacob Tonson' of the *New Age*'s 'Books and Persons' column, admired *The Brothers Karamazov*, which he had read in a bad, incomplete French translation, as 'one of the marvels of the age'.[22] He took the matter further in his column a year later, in 1911: 'We have several volumes of minor but very interesting Russian writers in the Pseudonym Library. The crying need of the day, in the translation department, is a complete and faithful Dostoevsky, and it is the duty of one of our publishers to get Mrs Constance Garnett to do it.'[23] Six weeks afterwards Heinemann announced that he would publish the novels of Dostovesky translated by Constance Garnett.

The commercial reality of publishing Dostoevsky, on the need for which Bennett placed so much emphasis, is expressed by Heinemann in a letter to Constance on 19 July 1911. It shows the disparity between the meagre financial reward and the magnitude of the task; the hazard of publishing in this field however great the appreciation expressed. In it he pleaded the unprofitability of publishing the Russians:

> I acknowledge Part I of the BROTHER KARAMEV [*sic*]. With regard to your request for royalty after a certain number of copies are sold, I have on principle, nothing against it, but you will realise that I must also take into consideration the frightful failure of the Tolstoy translations, and the horrible loss they have entailed, eating up so far most of the profit on Turgenev. I should rather say that after three years I would see how we stand and pay you a further fee if I find my Russian translations have been sufficiently successful to warrant it. At the present moment, the Tolstoys balance the Turgenev, and I am hoping that Dostoevski will recoup and pay me; but that of course is a gamble.[24]

Whatever the commercial ramifications, the effect of the Dostoevsky translations upon the public and writers was immediate. When the translation of *The Brothers Karamazov* appeared in 1912, Middleton Murry declared it to be one of 'the most epoch-making translations of the past, one to be compared with North's Plutarch'.[25] A new generation of writers viewed Dostoevsky as their idol and Frank Swinnerton wrote: 'We heard on all sides, roars of ecstatic discovery. How pale Turgenev seemed! How material and common in grain our materialistic writers. How drab the life of restrained feelings!'[26] Dostoevsky became a cult figure; the translations sparked off liberation from the restraints of nineteenth-century rationalism and 'over-rigid aesthetic theories'.[27] In Virginia Woolf's opinion, 'Constance Garnett's translations were a crucial influence on the novel for after reading *Crime and Punishment* and *The Idiot*, how could any young novelist believe in characters as the Victorians painted them?'[28] In retrospect John Cowper Powys summed up his estimate of Constance as a translator:

> I was reading Dostoevsky in those days; and with the exception of Dorothy Richardson I felt that I owe a greater debt

to Constance Garnett than to any other woman writer of our time. Her translations of Dostoevsky are superb, just what I feel translations from the Russians should be; that is to say they do *not* attempt the silly and vain task of substituting *our* ways of speech for that of the extraordinary people of these books; but they allow the English words to retain, hovering around them, something that is strange and stiff and queer and *foreign*, so that, even in their English disguise, you can smell the original Russian.[29]

Her prodigious effort had not been without handicaps, however. It had placed a strain upon her already impaired eyesight; from time to time she had to lay aside her work or wear blue spectacles to protect it.[30] Prince Kropotkin wrote to Edward as early as May 1903 to say, 'We are both extremely sorry to hear about the bad condition of the eyes of Mrs Garnett.'[31] In spite of this, Constance planned another visit to Russia. On 11 May 1904 she set off with David, now twelve years old, via Hull, Helsingfors, Petersburg and Moscow for a stay with Madame Yershov.[32]

Many people felt that the contribution to literature made by Constance's translations should be acknowledged, so Ernest Radford organised a petition to grant her a Civil List pension. Unfortunately Edward took exception to the idea. Though he never minded trying to get pensions for others, he was adamantly anti-Establishment as far as he himself or his immediate family were concerned. He became extremely angry. Galsworthy, who had annoyed him by giving the idea his support, wrote to him to explain:

Before I do anything, I wish you would come down here ... and talk it over. What I can't understand is why you should both be so insulted. I've always regarded a pension on the Civil List as an honour only conferred on people who have deserved well of the State for their services to the State; and though I quite understand that you would have refused to initiate a request for it, I don't see why you should be hurt if it were conferred without your knowledge or request. As to the question of whether you are actually in need of it – that's surely beside the point. Surely you don't think any the worse of Hudson because he has one, or a hundred other men of letters, science and general public service. It seems to me (but I daresay you will show me that I am quite wrong) that it cannot be right for you on a pure scruple of personal pride to stop what might be a substantial and deserved benefit to Constance. At all events my views of the nature of marriage don't carry me to the belief that a husband and wife have anything to do with each other in such a matter. I believe in women being independent of men; and if Ada weren't independent of me I would welcome the first event that would make her so. However you may be right. I can't act without hearing. Always your affectionately . . .[33]

He had written to Constance at the same time, saying, 'Edward's very angry with me, but I plead guilty to *nothing* but what seems to have been a gross error of judgment.' It was 'obvious' that had 'the proposition cast any slur on anyone (either Edward or you) I should have spoken'. He was, he wrote, 'absolutely guiltless of any disloyalty to Edward, in not speaking of the petition to him or to you; I have obviously made a fool of myself in signing the petition . . . '[34] Constance smoothed Edward down by explaining that she had found that the culprit was Ernest Radford who thought he had 'sounded' the Garnetts about a pension: 'after all no harm has been done – if any – we don't want to estrange our friends over the business'.[35] Ernest Radford wrote to Edward to give him an assurance that 'All communications have been "confidential" strictly' and that 'it is everywhere understood that neither you nor your wife have known anything about it whatever, and I hope you will see when your wrath has abated, that you cannot do better than leave it to run its course, because you can always decline the honour'. He went on to advise Edward 'not to think of yourself at all, and only, as a second thought, of the value of Grant or Pension. Could you wish to deprive Mrs. Garnett of the Crown of honour which she would wear if the worth of her work were recognised as it should be by the Treasury? Should she be excluded only because she is married?' He ended with references to the care he had taken with the petition, which had 'chances much too good to be lightly wasted – of being able to do your best, of seeing your wife in some measure compensated for failing sight, and of being able to complete your son's education along the lines of his heart's desire ... '[36]

A touching letter from David about the whole matter casts an insight into the different personalities of Edward and of Constance. Writing from their Hampstead flat, David began:

> I feel that mother will be miserable unless she gets it. You must know her character and your own well enough to see that in the long run doing without it – the continual remembrance of the possibility of having had it – will cause her greater misery and more futile regret, than the fact of her having it will cause you. I love both my parents very tenderly but see them full of imperfections. In mother, I see a peasants true valuation of things. She has all the time a sense of what she could do for Auntie Katie etc with it, in her mind. Also a sturdy independance. You on the other hand are quick to anger and quick to form opinions. She does not know what she wants until she has brooded for some days. Your slight feeling for material advantage is not minute but what little you have is the result of experience. Things also affect you very differently. What is to you and me a cause of anger for a few days – some trivial thing – to mother is a cause of lifelong regret– it grows slowly to be a rankling ulcer ... By their sweetness and stupidity the Radfords have caused us a certain amount of misery inevitably – but I have written to you dear Dad because I feel it will not be so lasting to you as to mother. I love you so and you know I am more like you temperamentally ... [37]

The idea of the Civil List pension had touched on Edward's pride, but the lack of adequate recompense to Constance in ordinary publishing terms had always angered him. It was evidence of what he regarded as the usual mean-mindedness of publishers in their dealings. He pursued the royalty question with Heinemann, who replied at length on 23 December 1915 to explain the impossibility of such an arrangement. The letter begins:

> I have not the slightest doubt that you want to be quite quite fair to both parties, but to me it seems extraordinary how

little able you seem to be to realise that there are two sides to the question of my arrangement for the publication of DOS-TOEVSKY. You asked me to reconsider the arrangement some time ago. I promised then that I would do so when the series was complete. Since then you have from time to time repeated the request, and I have always said that I would reconsider the matter when the series was complete and I was able to see how the books sold as a set.

Though it was true, Heinemann went on, that there was no signed agreement, 'I never thought that a signed agreement was necessary between us.' In answer to Garnett's suggestion that the price of translation should be increased plus a royalty, Heinemann argued that his ledger for the series 'shows a cash deficit of £166.14.6' and that 'if I am going on producing these books during the war they are going to cost me considerably more . . . '

In face of this 'bald statement of fact' which 'does not in the least take away from the consideration of Mrs. Garnett's work as worth the highest price', he thought Garnett's demand was 'not quite as fair as I know you wish to be'. Heinemann continued:

I am happy and have always been proud to publish Mrs. Garnett's work and I shall always hope to publish it. At the present moment publishing is of course handicapped far more heavily than ordinaruly [*sic*], and I therefore fear that it would not pay me to concede both points namely to increase the payment for translation and also to pay a royalty. I hope Mrs. Garnett will see her way to accept the increase in the rate of payment from 9/- to 12/- and not ask me to burden the series with a royalty which will break down my whole calculation of some day also making something out of it.[38]

In what appear to be two undated drafts of a letter of reply, Edward takes Heinemann to task in forthright terms. In the first draft Garnett claimed the suggested '12/- per 1000 words & a 5% royalty on the U.K sales of Vols 7–12 of the Dostoevsky Edition were strictly moderate, giving you absolutely free of royalty all those "profits" on Vols 1–6 which you constantly promised to "share" with her, or give her "a share of" in the future ... ' If Heinemann, Garnett concluded, couldn't pay 'this miserable royalty' he suggested he 'must raise the price of the volumes to the public'. The second draft upbraids Heinemann with 'Come! Come! A miserable royalty of 5% ... is not going to "burden" the series ...'[39]

The unsatisfactory financial relationship with Heinemann affected the publication of the next major project contemplated by Constance – Chekhov. Heinemann had referred to it in his letter, saying that if Mrs Garnett would very kindly make out a synopsis of the six volumes he would look for the American support necessary for undertaking such a publishing venture.

Constance had translated some of Chekhov earlier; notably *The Cherry Orchard* for a performance by the Stage Society in 1911. The play had puzzled the audience, half of whom walked out of the first performance. Reviews had been hostile; *The Times* declared that 'Mrs Edward Garnett's *Cherry Orchard* cannot but strike an English audience as something queer, outlandish, even silly'.[40] Predictably it was Arnold Bennett who realised Chekhov's relevance and in the *New Age* scolded the receptivity of an audience unable to comprehend that characters just as 'ridiculous and futile' as those depicted in the play existed in England. Taken as a whole, he found *The Cherry Orchard* 'one of the most savage and convincing satires on a whole society that was ever seen in a theatre'.[41] Shaw also had perceived the relevance of Chekhov to an English Edwardian society with 'the same nice people, the same utter futility',[42] and took *The Cherry Orchard* as a model for *Heartbreak House*.

However, but for the isolated publication by Duckworth, on *Edwards* recommendation, of *The Black Monk* (1903) and *The Kiss* (1908), Chekhov had little recognition in England until the fifteen-volume translation by Constance appeared between 1915 and 1922.[43] Their publication by Chatto & Windus came about as a result of a fortuitous meeting between Edward and Frank Swinnerton. At a party given by Scott-James and his wife for their literary staff and friends, Swinnerton found that in dressing hurriedly he 'had omitted to fasten a single button of my dress trousers'. He was, he recalled, repairing 'the omission, and turned to find the monstrous figure of Edward Garnett leaning over me like Fate itself'. In reporting the dialogue of this chance encounter Swinnerton wrote: 'What he supposed me to be doing, I cannot think; but with creditably swift composure, I spoke, looking up into those fiendish but on this occasion fortunately purblind eyes. "You wrote an article the other day on a Russian edition of Chekhov's letters", said I. "Yes" he said. "We – Chatto & Windus – have just published some letters of Dostoevsky's. Would Chekhov be worth translating?" He hummed staring at me ... "My wife wants to translate some of Chekhov's tales ... Heinemann is considering the idea. He doesn't seem very keen. If he decides against them would your firm ...?"' Heinemann did decline and Swinnerton managed to persuade Chatto & Windus to experiment with two Chekhov volumes and the remainder followed. As Frank Swinnerton put it, 'The credit thereafter was Mrs Garnett's alone; but the admiration for Chekhov which spread among English writers and readers dates from the publication of those experimental volumes in 1916. This was so great, and so inclusive, that I cannot forbear to claim a tiny flash of purely instrumental virtue for myself... but for what I at first thought an embarrassing oversight I should never have had the brief chat with Garnett ... '[44]

Edward provided a preface to the series of volumes, in which he classified Chekhov's 'range of subject, scene and situation'. In his critique he not only attempted to open the eyes of readers to the art of the Russian storyteller but used it as propaganda for his basic philosophy of the art of fiction: 'The one essential is that we should understand and it is the artist's job to show people what they are.'[45] The Chekhov 'craze' superseded the Dostoevsky 'cult' which, unlike that of Turgenev, was a transitory hysterical outburst which died by 1920 as rapidly as it had flared. In Edward's view Chekhov's work could be likened to 'chiaroscuro' and he analysed the way in which he achieved his effects by 'the shifting play of human feeling ... a delicate responsiveness to the spectacle of life's ceaseless intricacy'.

What Sean O'Faolain was to call Edward's adoration of the Russian realists[46] permeated his relationships as adviser to authors, and he urged the Russian example upon them. Indeed Conrad rather testily remarked to him on one occasion ' ... you remember always that I am a Slav (it's your idée fixe) but you seem to forget I am a Pole ... '[47] Conrad took exception to

Edward's criticism of *Under Western Eyes* with: 'You are so russianised my dear that you don't know the truth when you see it – unless it smells of cabbage-soup then it at once secures your profoundest respect. I suppose one must make allowance for your position of Russian Embassador [*sic*] to the Republic of Letters.'[48] Conrad's sarcasm to a friend whom he held in such high esteem and with such affection could be understood in the light of his family background.

Appropriately enough the neighbourhood of Gracie's Cottage, not far from The Cearne, became known as Dostoevsky Corner in mild mockery of the Russian author and of the foreign origin of those who came to live there – Fanny Stepniak, the Russian friend of the Garnetts', Annjuta Cyriax, a Swedish doctor and physiotherapist, and a Professor of Persian.

Ford Madox Ford, who had lived for a while in Gracie's Cottage, gave a typically romanticised impression of this location and the contribution of Constance and Edward to the Russian influence in England. '[Constance Garnett's] circle of friends and admirers', he wrote, 'was enormous and international – the foreign element being mostly Russian and thus a constant transfusion of Russian ideas into English life went on around the Cearne ... What exact part the activities that went on around the Cearne played in Russian history I don't propose to estimate. Certainly it must have been considerable.'[49]

Life for Constance and Edward, however, was much more complex than that of a couple devoted to a common understanding of literature and to a country home near London.

FOURTEEN

Pond Place

Lawrence drew a pen picture for Louie Burrows of the domestic arrangements of the Garnetts after his visit to The Cearne in 1911. 'Garnett was alone,' he wrote, 'he is about 42. He and his wife consent to live together or apart as it pleases them. At present Mrs. Garnett with their son is living in their Hampstead flat. She comes down to The Cearne for week ends sometimes. Garnett generally stays one, or perhaps two days in the week in London. But he prefers to live alone at The Cearne. But he is very fond of his wife also – only they are content to be a great deal apart.'[1] Mutual independence within marriage had become an established pattern of life. Their intellectual partnership and cultural empathy was not paralleled by emotional ties of a conventional kind.

The extremity of estrangement, which occurred some years before Lawrence's visit and before they had come to terms with their temperamental differences, was apparent in a letter from Constance to Edward. Writing from 24 John Street she used, typically, as a point of reference a passage taken from Tolstoy:

I read Tolstoi's Boyhood yesterday. How well he analyzes. Here is a passage which struck me: 'She would sigh as if enjoying her grief and give herself up to the contemplation of her misery. In consequence of this and sundry other instances of her always considering herself a victim, *a kind of intermittent feeling of calm dislike* began to be noticeable in his treatment of his wife – that *restrained dislike for the once-loved being which betrays itself by an unconscious desire to say something disagreeable.*' That is just what I see so clearly in you now – I see so generally a slightly sarcastic and contemptuous attitude to me. You can't help it of course – but it is ridiculous to abuse me for my consequent want of warmth and initiation. I am tired of flogging a dead horse – if I revive any degree of sympathy and love in you, it leads you at once to 'desecrating your ideal' and is all over with that – leaving you more dissatisfied and cool than before. The consequence of your critical attitude is to make me shrivel up and feel I must not stir hand or foot for fear of making things worse. Love certainly makes people better than they are without it, when it is withdrawn it is not only that the character is seen clearer, it also deteriorates generally. At least I feel myself so soiled and spoiled, so degraded in my own eyes and every hour in such a false position. I am constantly courting the love of a man who treats me with obvious contempt; naturally I try to console my pride by thinking it is more for his sake than mine. When you are away I can take interest in outside things and work and regain my self-respect. When you are here I am apt to alternate between trying to excuse your attitude to me by humiliating myself in my own eyes, and then at intervals simply hating you for it, which makes me more miserable. What I want is work and independence – to regain my self respect. If you would manage to let us see little of one another for some time, there might be a hope of getting into a new and better relation to one another. We are both too sore from so much friction to be able to be natural – If we could be more apart and keep at a distance when we meet, we might come to realise what is precious in what is left to us and to forget a little some of the pain and desecration and want of mutual respect which is spoiling everything for us . . . [2]

Constance found the 'work and independence' she sought in Russian translations; the separateness which she mentioned in her letter as a way to bring about a better relationship between them, in the living arrangements which Lawrence had described. But a reconciliation of their conflicting emotional attitudes only evolved when a triangular relationship developed between Constance, Edward and Nellie Heath.

Nellie was the youngest of the four children of Richard Heath, who had helped Edward and Constance in the early days of their marriage to set up home in the East End and who eventually took Gracie's Cottage after Ford Madox Hueffer. Richard Heath was an engraver who also acquired a reputation as an original and unorthodox religious thinker and writer. Nellie was barely nine years old, when, on the death of his wife, he took her and her sisters, Gracie and Maggie, and brother Carl, to live in France. They settled in Paris after a brief stay in a Normandy village not far from the château of some friends, Monsieur and Madame Dumesuil. The family returned to England in 1891 and Nellie, now eighteen, began to study painting under the tutelage of Walter Sickert who on occasion allowed her to use his Chelsea studio while he was abroad.

Sickert fascinated all his young female students and Nellie developed a passion for him which so alarmed her family that, as she put it, 'I think they felt I was in danger of ship-wrecking.' They succeeded in sending her off to Paris with Edward's help but, in her words, 'Edward's help had a far greater consequence than ever the spell of Sickert's personality had.' It was a relationship that grew imperceptibly from their first meeting and she became devoted to him. When first she knew him Edward appeared to her to have suffered; he looked as if irregular hours and sitting up late to read were taking toll of his health. Very tall and thin, good at games and swimming, walking and climbing, he was fond of company, full of charm, gay and light-hearted. She was impressed by his unselfish nature and his detestation of pretentious behaviour. It was at the time when Stepniak loomed large in the life of Constance and Edward,[3] and Edward was trying to reconcile his bitter feelings with his understanding of the love that Constance and Stepniak had for each other.

Constance had no qualms about the closeness developing between Edward and Nellie. Indeed if she did not actually suggest it, she certainly encouraged the liaison. In January 1899 from France where she was staying with David, she wrote to Edward: 'How I wish I was at The Cearne with you today – with Margaret and Pease too. I expect you will have splendid

fires and the house looks delightful ... Why isn't silly little Nellie
with you too? She ought not to stay in London on Sundays.
Bunnie spoke of her as "a sweet little Puss" the other day (tell
her) and said with great tenderness that we must stop in Paris
a few days in March if she is there ... '[4] Her acquiescence to
Edward's relationship with Nellie was not to an unavoidable
arrangement that would exclude her. It was one in which she
shared and in which she continued to regard both with affection.
From Grove Place in March 1909, thanking Edward for 'your
sweet letter', she wrote, 'I will as you suggest meet Nellie and
you at 1.15 – at Eustace Miles (in the upstairs room – if possible
near the window). Goodbye till Tuesday – dearest love to Nellie – I am longing to see her – and hear something of her plans,
Yours ever Connie.'[5] Throughout later years their correspondence was scattered with similar references that reflected a concern for both of them and a reciprocal affection. When Edward
and Nellie spent the weekend away on holiday she wrote:
'Dearest Edward I thought of Nellie and you at the van last
night. It was bitterly cold ... Love to Nellie. I shall be relieved
to hear that you are neither of you worse for the week-end ...'[6]
Often she wrote to Nellie at length expecting the letter to be
shared; one occasion writing to Edward to say ' ... you will
have seen my letter to Nellie I expect, so I won't detail our day
at Hurst ... Love to Nellie and to you ... Yours ever Connie.'[7]

Edward for his part wrote regularly when away with Nellie.
The amicable nature of their *ménage à trois* and his affection for
Connie is shown in his letter of September 1928: 'Dear little
Puss – We have had two fine days, but today is rainy. The coast
is wild and rocky. Nellie is delighted with the views and the
atmosphere. She wants to paint again, poor darling. St. David's
is a quaint little town ... You had better order a paper for
yourself while we are away. Send me any news of David you
have and about yourself and your visitors. We both feel all the
better for the exercise ... Love from Nellie, Your loving Edward.'[8]

The liaison between Edward and Nellie can only be fully
understood when viewed through the lens of Nellie's personality. Gentle, compassionate and selfless, she was religious but
without overt religious affiliations. She had none of the characteristics of 'the other woman' and had a concern for all the

Garnetts and her affection was repaid by them. David regarded her as he did his mother. Edward's brother Robert, who found it hard to accept the situation, preferred his daughter Rayne not to visit her uncle at Pond Place, where, in 1915, as Rayne recorded, 'Edward and Nellie were living together in open defiance of the conventions.' The spirited Rayne, however, thought such advice absurd and she formed a deep and lasting friendship with Nellie. She declared affectionately: 'Nellie was a darling and my love for her has coloured my life as my love for no one else has done. I owe her a great debt for her loving understanding and a general deepening of my spirit.'[9]

The flat in Chelsea, which so upset Robert, had been taken by Edward after the first year of the war, so that David could have a place near to the Imperial College where he was to study botany. It also coincided with the end of Edward's employment at Duckworth. In December he wrote to J. B. Pinker that 'my London address henceforward is 19 Pond Place'[10] and it was from this address that he wrote again to Pinker: 'Mr D. H. Lawrence tells me that you are getting up a petition by the Author against the suppression of "The Rainbow". I shall be glad to sign this, if so. Of course the book ought to have been revised and a few passages cancelled before publication but, even so, the procedure was unjustifiable ... '[11]

The Rainbow had evolved from the manuscript Edward had criticised so much in its early stages – *The Wedding Ring*. He still held to his opinion. It was, he thought, a novel unworthy of Lawrence's remarkable talent: and he took the opportunity in writing a favourable review of *Lost Girl* to refer to *The Rainbow* as 'jumbled, inconclusive, overheated in atmosphere, a réchauffé of old materials and characters that [Lawrence's] fervid imagination could not lay to rest'.[12] But the suppression of *The Rainbow* was more a symptom of wartime hysteria than a conscious action against alleged indecency. Frieda's German origin, the name she bore and the persona of Lawrence aroused an antagonism which the liberal-minded found irrational. To them it reflected the falsity of those social ethics that supported the war, which they considered an outcome of political chicanery, seeing its glorification as a romantic and hypocritical illusion. When the insensate slaughter on the Western Front revealed the meaninglessness of the battlefield, Edward contributed a series of essays to the *English Review*, the *Nation*, *Labour Leader* and *Cambridge Magazine* in which he turned patriotic values, morals and Christian ethics upside down to give full rein to irony and paradox.

The essays were constructed on the imagined evolution of the war from a simple idea conceived by Papa, the Devil, while he was shaving, and they satirised wartime slogans and sentiments and personified the virtues and vices. The theme is set in the opening essay when the Devil's wife exclaims, 'What an imagination you have, dear, but aren't you dreaming of Barbarism?', and in the conversation that follows: ' "Oh, Mama! it might happen, " said little Luciferina. "Don't people love to kill one another, Papa?" "Yes, my child, from feelings of justice and duty, and even sometimes for gain," said the Devil smiling at his sharp little daughter. "But a Grand War can only thrive through love – love of one's own people and home" he explained to them. "You must always work with love and the Virtues, my pets." ' The essays continue in this vein of heavy satire, the Devil announcing that when the war came each nation 'will know it's done for Humanity's sake ... and ... in that cause all the great armies will gradually exterminate one another. The World War is going to nourish itself on Faith and Hope and Courage and Duty and self-sacrifice ... '[13]

The satires, which have a modern ring to ears used to *Oh! What a Lovely War*, expressed convictions to be expected from one of Edward's temperament and liberal opinions. When they appeared in collected form in 1919 as *Papa's War and Other Satires*, his old school contemporary C. E. Montague, who was author of a telling indictment of the war entitled *Disenchantment*, wrote to him appreciatively: 'I've read it with much gusto. It's terrifically unjust, as all good satires ought to be. What ruin it would have been if Burns had taken 33 per cent of the slashingness off "Holy Willie's Prayer" or the "Holy Fair".'[14] Wilfred Scawen Blunt liked 'the first half dozen especially' but thought 'that not very many of your readers grasped all your satire in some of your later sketches as they take intelligence to understand them ... '[15] Indeed the satire tended to be rather convoluted.

Propaganda characterised Edward's descriptive notes to the folio collection of a hundred cartoons by Louis Raemaekers.

This 'neutral's indictment' of the war, which featured the Kaiser as warlord, was issued by the Fine Art Society in 1916.[16] Edward's detestation of war and the distortions in human value it brings was evident in his foreword to Mary Houghton's *In the Enemy's Country* which was published in 1915. This diary, which he had urged her to complete for publication, covered her experiences in four foreign countries during wartime and, as Edward wrote in his introduction, its value lay 'in the delicate way it brings home to everybody that the civilised European has one enemy to fight and overcome and that enemy is simply the instinct of Aggression . . . '[17]

His satires, however, were written from first-hand experience for in 1915 he enlisted as an orderly with the Friends' Ambulance Unit and served on the Italian Front. In 'The Battle-fronts on the Isonzo' he described the desperate fighting at the siege of Gorizia for the *Manchester Guardian,* which prefaced his report on 10 January 1916 with the remark that 'Mr Edward Garnett, the well-known man of letters [who] ranks amongst our first literary critics, is one of the very few Englishmen who have been privileged to see anything of the terrible fighting on the Austrian frontier.'[18]

Participation in the war was a desperate problem for someone of Edward's opinions and many who shared them became conscientious objectors, including his own son David. The Conrads were aware of his quandary and Jessie wrote to him at that time to say: 'My dear Edward – No doubt you have received a letter from Captain Brett Young by this time. Dr Kenneth Campbell . . . was here on Sunday and he said Captain Young had asked him for your address as he wished to offer you some post in the Military hospital there. I do hope it will be what you feel you care to undertake and that you will be less worried. You know Conrad and I have a very great affection for you and feel intensely anything that happens to you . . . '[19]

Brett Young had a high regard for Edward due to the perceptiveness of Edward's review of his book *The Dark Tower.* On 5 March 1915 he wrote to Edward in appreciation: 'I am very much in your debt. One always looks rather pathetically to one's reviews for help and suggestions but as a rule, whatever else may interest them, they refuse to be concerned with the problems of technique which more than anything else intrigue a young author. Of course I was well aware of the risks which I was running when the story rushed me into the "indirect" method of narration ... ' The letter continued with references to methods employed by Conrad and Hardy and an explanation of his own, concluding that he would like Edward, 'if it's not bothering you too much', to give him some indication of the 'obvious mannerisms' which Edward had detected in his writing. Thanking Edward for 'your most stimulating and helpful review' he expressed the hope that his new book *Deep Sea* would not have these faults.[20]

When Edward read *The Deep Sea* he remarked to Brett Young that 'It's a vigorous thing. I like its breezy roughness, and now you've got well past this style of realism – or rather naturalism – you can look at it with affection. The novel contains things in characterisation that I should not have expected of you. Your problem in your next novel will be to assert your own style.'[21] Throughout his early years Brett Young carried on an intermittent correspondence with Edward over his books. Sending Edward *The Iron Age*, he wrote: 'I don't think you'll find in it many of the mannerisms which irritated you in *The Dark Tower*. If I haven't lost them I shall be grateful it you would tell me about them. Also I have deliberately discarded all romantic "properties" – animate or inanimate ... '[22] Of a later book, *Marching on Tanga*, he was 'glad the atmosphere reached you. That, as you know, is my particular line of business ... I hope you will do the book for the *Guardian* ... Thanks too for your attempt to waken a flicker of interest in *Five degrees south* ... '[23] He sent a copy of *The Young Physicians* in 1919 – 'it is a long and perhaps unwieldy book (the chronicle novel is bound to be) but I have an affection for it, not only because it is my latest book but because it contains a great deal that is poignantly personal to me'. He hoped Edward would do him 'the honour of reading it ... you know much I value and respect your judgement'.[24]

The war had disrupted the circle of Edward's acquaintances where his judgment had been a focal point. In a letter of 31 August 1916, W. H. Davies had written: 'I have been wondering for a very long time what has become of you,' adding wistfully, 'Do you ever go to the Mont Blanc now, or any other place in question. There is not much getting together of literary people in these days. Good luck.'[25] Now in more secure circumstances,

Davies had also contacted Edward earlier with concern about
the plight of their mutual friend Edward Thomas. He had
asked: 'I wonder whether you think it possible to get something
for Thomas out of the Royal Literary Fund. At the present
time, he is, I believe in a very tight corner.'[26] As reader to
Duckworth Edward had done his best to help Thomas to publish his work. In his report he said *Four and Twenty Blackbirds*
was 'charming . . . absolutely perfect in style, full of clear, fresh
colouring and most gay and ingenious in the simple twists of the
story . . . The book *ought* to be a little classic with people who
know – and even in these disastrous times it *may* find its audience.'[27]

Thomas had difficulties earning a living from writing and
became more and more disenchanted; a note of bitterness
marked his plea to Edward in 1913 to tell him 'of some cele-
brated monarch, poet, prostitute or other hero that I can write
a book about. My own list includes none that publishers look
at.'[28] The climate of 'daily journalism created by Massingham
and Nevinson'[29] had altered sharply in the years immediately
prior to the First World War and he was unable to adapt himself
to these changes. In desperation he thought of taking to lecturing and asked Edward for a testimonial to support his application to the London County Council for a temporary lectureship
at their non-vocational institutions.[30] The request was followed
immediately afterwards by a letter in which Thomas said he
would probably not use it for 'the fact is that knowing I had to
do something I had stupidly pretended to be brave. When really
lecturing was as impossible as sailoring. Simply fear of standing
up alone looking at a hundred people and being looked at . . .'[31]
Thomas suffered from a tormenting self-consciousness and from
a shyness so inhibiting that it was taken for coldness or superiority by many on first acquaintance. It was a handicap to him
in approaching publishers for commissions or submitting his
work. When Edward tried to make him aware of how his shyness
was misinterpreted, Thomas wrote the moving poem in reply:
'I built Myself a house of glass . . . '[32]

Thomas had been seeking his true literary path in poetry
during his difficult years as a hack writer. He sent his poems to
Edward in 1909, including the first poem he had written, 'Up
the Wind'. In the accompanying letter he said, 'I hope you will

forgive me and survive the swamping. You cannot imagine how eagerly I have run up this by-way and how anxious I am to be sure it is not a cul-de-sac.'[33] He appreciated Edward's criticism 'filled with good things' and his reply continued: 'I had fears lest I got up in the air in this untried medium. So long as I haven't I am satisfied. Of course I must make mistakes and your preferences help me to see where they may lie, tho' I shall risk some of them again – e.g. what you might find petty in incident. Dimness and lack of concreteness I shall certainly do my best against ... ' He would take Edward's advice, he wrote, and shorten 'July' and 'The Patriot'.[34]

With growing assurance he later defended poems which Edward thought needed alteration. He protested: 'But I don't think I could alter *Tears* to make it marketable,' and explicitly defined his own poetic attitudes in answer to Edward's criticism of his poem 'Lob': 'I am doubtful about the chiselling you advise. It would be the easiest thing in the world to clean it all up and thin it and have every line straightforward in sound and sense, but it would not really improve it ... I think you read too much with the eye perhaps. If you *say* a couplet like: If they had mowed their dandelions and sold/Them fairly they could have afforded gold – I believe it no longer awkward ... But I can't tell you how pleased I am that you like the long pieces in the main, and "Pewits" too. I am going to try and be just about the lines you have marked ... '[35]

Throughout the war years Thomas persevered with his poetry, under the pseudonym of Edward Eastaway, but he did not have any success in placing his work in magazines. To help him over his financial hardship Edward discussed with Thomas the possibility of a pension on the Civil List. Hearing of this, Walter de la Mare wrote to Edward on 15 March 1916: 'If you are doing or thinking of doing anything I would like to do more than this ... '[36] De la Mare continued his interest and corresponded with Edward over the progress until early in 1917 when he said: 'I have just heard from E[dward] M[arsh] that the P. M. has approved a grant of £300 for E.T. I wish it could have been a pension but from the beginning E.M. never held out much hope of that.'[37] But by that time it was too late – Thomas had been killed at Arras.

Thomas had joined the Army in July 1915 and Edward, who

had continued his efforts to place the poems, received a letter written on the journey to France. Headed with the address '244 Siege Battery, 15 Camp, Coolford', it began: 'My dear Garnett – Thank you for your letter & good wishes. I don't think we shall come through London ...' He went on with the news that 'Anything you can do about the verses will be useful, but a book is already being prepared. "Selwyn & Blount", if you know who they are, are publishing a fair number with my pseudonym, Edward Eastaway, which I particularly want now to be *kept dark* because I should hate the stupid advertisement some papers might give it, though going to France two years late is nothing to advertise a book of verse ...'[38]

It was a letter in keeping with Thomas's character. Reticent about his own ability, he was quick to advance that of others. During the war years he had formed, as he had with W. H. Davies, a special friendship with the American poet Robert Frost. 'By the way', he asked Edward on 24 October 1914, 'did Hudson ever send you the book of poems I told you about – "North of Boston" by Robert Frost.'[39] Edward's appreciation of the poems can be deduced from a later letter by Thomas which reads: 'I am forwarding your letter to Frost, it will please him very much for I have often spoken of you.'[40]

Edward went on to develop a critical essay which Thomas thought 'Absolutely right ... I don't think you could have scored more than by insisting on his subtlety and truth ...'[41] When Edward sent the essay to the *Atlantic Monthly*, he commented in an accompanying letter: 'Since writing to you last I have learnt that an American edition of "North of Boston" has been issued by Holt & that it has received some attention on your side, but I take it that Mr Frost's poetic quality is too original to penetrate quickly to any but a select audience. Therefore I hope my paper may not only interest your readers, but may receive attention & comment in the wider circle of the Press. Of Mr. Frost I know nothing personally, but a few particulars given me by Mr. Edward Thomas who sent me "North of Boston" ...'[42] Edward's essay and letter arrived when Sedgwick, the editor of *Atlantic Monthly*, was 'deliberating whether to publish any or all of three poems RF had thrust upon him'.[43] By coincidence he was in the 'very act of opening' Edward's letter when Frost came in to see him. He read 'judicious extracts' to Frost who, as Sedgwick wrote to Edward later, was 'enormously keen to have me print your appreciation'.[44] The essay, entitled 'A New American Poet', appeared in the August issue as an accompaniment to the three poems.

In a letter of 12 June 1915 to Edward, Frost declared that the essay was 'bound to have a tremendous effect, I can see the impression you made by the way you came to judgment last winter on the novelists. We are all prepared to envy anyone you think well of . . . '[45] Frost was referring to an article by Edward in the *Atlantic Monthly*[46] in which he had championed American writers he thought insufficiently recognised by the public, critics and publishers. W. D. Howells, who for over ten years used his literary column, 'Editor's Easy Chair' in *Harpers Magazine*, to preach the virtues of realism and the merits of the new European writers,[47] had replied in print to Edward's article – 'the gentle intelligence' of which, he wrote, was 'in pleasing contrast to the temper of the English reviewers who used to deal out a punitive instruction to our infant authorship'.[48]

In his letter to Edward, Frost added a marginal note: 'You seem to have made a friend for me in W. D. Howells. There is the best American if you want to know the truth.' He also remembered his debt to Thomas and said: 'You must know that I am grateful to you – and to Thomas – but I was that to Thomas before . . . '[49] Indeed the depth of his affection and his regard for Edward Thomas was seen most clearly in his letter to Edward after Thomas had been reported killed. 'Edward Thomas was the only brother I ever had,' he began, 'I fail to see how we can have been so much to each other, he an Englishman and I an American and our first meeting put off till we were both in middle life. I hadn't a plan for the future that didn't include him. You must like his poetry as well as I do and do everything you can for it. His last word to me, his "pen ultimate word" as he called it, was that what he cared most for was the name of poet . . . Do what you can for him and never mind me for the present . . . '[50]

It was superfluous advice. Edward never forgot the bond of friendship he had with Thomas nor his admiration for his poetry. Helen Thomas, who found it so hard to reconcile herself to her husband's death, poured out her feelings to Edward, confessing: 'I don't know why I tell you all this except that you

were his great friend and I would like as well as I can to leave
that gap not quite unfilled, and yet how can I even think of such
a thing. I who now that he is dead, am dead too.'[51] Later, in
1927, she was to ask Edward if he would contribute the entry
on Thomas to the *Dictionary of National Biography*. 'There is no
one', she wrote, 'who I feel is better qualified to fill this niche in
this National Institution, and no one who I personally would
better like to do this for Edward's memory. Will you do it? I
should be so grateful and glad if you would.'[52] Edward also took
the opportunity that year in his introduction to an edition of
Selected Poems by Thomas for the Gregynog Press, to make his
usual pointed remarks on the ignorance of those who should
have given Thomas the recognition he posthumously received:

> How unswervingly the editors follow their tradition of reject-
> ing the first rate, original thing. Of the sixty seven poems
> here chosen from double the number in the Collected Edition,
> from a dozen to a score should take a permanent place in
> English Anthologies of the future, and yet not a single poem
> was found by the editors worthy of acceptance. And Poetry
> Societies were still flourishing in 1915–1916 . . . I took 'Home'
> and 'The Owl' . . . to *The Nation* in January 1917 & tried to
> impress on the assistant genii that these poems were indeed
> considerable; but they came back to me at the end of the
> month with the disconcerting, ancient formula – 'Mr. Mas-
> singham much regrets that he cannot use the enclosed
> MSS.'[53]

The 'first rate, original thing' was Edward's constant concern
as a reader and he looked with expectation for it in all the MSS
he read. Near the end of his time with Duckworth, Edward
singled out for special commendation a manuscript sent in by
his employer's half-sister. As Leonard Woolf explained later,
this led indirectly to the foundation of the Hogarth Press so that
the work of his wife could be published without the process of
criticism normal to commercial book publishing. 'As I have said
more than once,' Woolf wrote, 'Virginia suffered abnormally
from the normal occupational disease of writers – indeed of artists – hypersensitiveness to criticism. The publisher of her first
two novels was her own half-brother, Gerald Duckworth . . . His

reader, Edward Garnett, who had a great reputation for spotting masterpieces by unknown authors, wrote an enthusiastic report on *The Voyage Out* when it was submitted ... Yet the idea of having to send her next book to the mild Gerald and the enthusiastic Edward filled her with horror and misery.' Virginia Woolf was delighted with the idea that they should themselves publish the book she had begun to write, *Jacob's Room*, so that she would 'avoid the misery of submitting this highly experimental novel to the criticism of Gerald Duckworth and Edward Garnett'.[54]

The 'enthusiastic' Edward, however, normally followed a practice which he once explained to his friend Hudson of laying 'stress on the strong points of an original piece of work' in contrast to 'nearly all authors he had met who were readier to blame than praise'.[55] With J. D. Beresford he was responsible for the appearance of the work of one of the earliest exponents of the 'stream of consciousness' – Dorothy Richardson. She recalled that after one refusal by a publisher, *Pointed Roofs*, her first book, was put away, but J. D. Beresford 'persisted and sent it to Edward Garnett, then reading for Duckworth, and it eventually appeared in 1915'.[56] The tactfulness required in dealing with Miss Richardson is hinted at in the letter Beresford wrote to Edward on 22 April 1915: 'Our letters crossed – but I passed your letter over to Miss Richardson, who is no longer staying with us. I believe she has written to you. Be patient with her. I know it will be difficult, but think of my patience in having her here for three months and not once quarrelling with her.'[57]

Letters from Dorothy Richardson to Edward indicate why Beresford was at pains to advise Edward in his dealings with her. They also show gratitude for his help and encouragement over a work which many, such as Edward's friend Hudson, sarcastically referred to as the saga of her 'everlasting Miriam'. A letter begins: 'The author of "Pilgrimage" is aghast in discovering that she is thought to have treated one of her best friends in an unfriendly way. She encloses herewith the first and only [sign] (excepting a covering line for the printed memorandum), she had had of the existence of that friend. It is, as you see, a model of the impersonal, the business-like ... She is most grateful to you for your "illuminating" guidance through the

murkier depths of "Pilgrimage" ... '⁵⁸ Feminine archness characterised her later letters. ' "Betty" tells me you are reviewing
The Tunnel. I am so glad you still like your God-child and hope
you will not have to administer much spanking ... '⁵⁹ A week
later on 12 March 1919 she wrote appreciatively of his review
because 'you said so many nice things and picked out two of my
favourite passages. I forgive you asserting when Miriam told
you that the smell of the counterpane and the shape of hands
and face etc must be got rid of before there can be prayer, that
to the feminine consciousness prayer is accompanied by the
dusty smell of the counterpane. I forgive you completely, absolutely ... '⁶⁰ An article by Edward in the *Nation* in 1920 she
confessed 'set me all a glow', and added that with her husband
Alan she 'shouted with joy ... and [we] sunned ourselves in the
blaze of the clarity of your dealings'. She remembered, she said,
that she was writing in 'the neighbourhood of the birthplace of
Pointed Roofs within a stone's throw of the place where I heard
that you had prevailed with Duckworth and I was free to go on.
My gratitude does not decrease ... '⁶¹

But Edward's perspicacity in recognising a new approach to
the novel, which he saw in the expression of feminine sensibility
by Dorothy Richardson, did not extend to the innovative use of
the interior monologue in a manuscript he read for Duckworth
about the same time as he had championed *Pointed Roofs*. He
began his report on *A Portrait of the Artist as a Young Man* by
James Joyce with a reference to the fact that 'Mr. Joyce published some very clever stories (with Maunsel) "Dubliners" in
the summer but the book was probably *not* successful as the
sketches were rather "realistic" studies of unprepossessing
types'. He continued: 'In the MS now submitted he gives us
reminiscences of his schooldays, of his family life in Dublin and
of his adolescence. It is all ably written and the picture is
curious. But the style is too discursive and his point of view will
be called "a little sordid". It isn't a book that would make a
young man's reputation – it is too unconventional for our British
public. And in War time it has less chance than at any other.
Decline with thanks.'⁶²

But that was not the end of the matter. Duckworth were
asked to reconsider the manuscript and Edward wrote another
report in which he made a fuller assessment of the *Portrait*:

A PORTRAIT OF THE ARTIST AS A YOUNG MAN
JAMES JOYCE

Mr. Joyce is to be reckoned with. You may dislike his work but you cannot ignore it. It is real, powerful subjective work, quite un-English. It is comparable more with the Russian writers than anything we know that has been written by any Englishman – or Irishman. He is not as fluent as our friend D. H. Lawrence and possibly he will never be prolific but it is sure, definite, confident writing, scholarly and full of insight and feeling.

He writes of the life of Stephen Dedalus, a sensitive boy at school in Roman Catholic Ireland, incidentally showing the political and religious feeling of the time (the time of Parnell's death) in scraps of adult conversation which are impressed on the boy's memory.

There are words and allusions which will be foreign to English Protestants but the pictures given of Irish school and college life are sympathetic and etch themselves on the memory. Very deep and searching is the analysis of the boy's sexual longings and experiences just after puberty. This part of the MS. is not at all pretty and will not please the literary censors but it is restrained and rings true and is quite in keeping with the boy's nervous nature. Still more effective is the presentation of his remorse and his fear of damnation, until goaded to confession he obtains absolution. His succeeding feeling of relief which approaches ectasy [*sic*] is very effectively realized. Stephen's adolescence is distinguished by deep religious feeling with much ascetic practice to be broken finally by the need for deciding whether he shall enter the priesthood and his realizing that he has no vocation. After this he declines to a lower standard of conduct and we see him with other students at Dublin University undisciplined in habit, slack and gross, while mentally alert, talking religion, ethics, politics; at the same time feeling a gnawing interest in a girl whom he has known from childhood.

The book finishes in-conclusively with his decision to go away from Ireland at the close of his term at College. 'To encounter for the millionth time the reality of experience.'

It will be seen that this is not a pleasant book. There is no beauty, no hint of anything joyous. It is drab and has the same effect on the reader as a short visit to Dublin has on the tourist. It is real, deals with normal people and presents them, even the most minor characters, swiftly and vividly. It produces conversation faithfully, too faithfully, and this latter must be altered. The ordinary conversation of boys and students is well known and need not be phonographed. Mr. Joyce must be made to see this. But for this ultra fidelity, also one blasphemous sentence there is nothing objectionable in the MS.

Pinker tells us that in his opinion Mr. Joyce is one of the big men of the future and he wants a publisher to believe in him too and stand by him, meaning, we take it, paying an advance above what his books are likely to earn and so enable the author to subsist decently while doing other work.

The question to decide is not whether this MS. is worth accepting. Mr. Joyce would do credit to any publishers list. It is rather to what extent D. & Co. care to speculate. Pinker doubtless will refuse anything less than £100 on account. It might be worth offering this with the proviso that the next two books could be had on the same terms. More than this is too big a risk as Mr. Joyce may be some time in coming into his own.[63]

Apparently Jonathan Cape, who was in charge of Duckworth at the time, wrote to J. B. Pinker on 26 January 1916 enclosing a copy of Edward's final report on the manuscipt. In this the novel is considered 'ably written' and 'the picture of life is good; the period well brought to the reader's eye, and the types and characters are well drawn' but it was thought 'too discursive, formless, unrestrained'. A 'good deal of pruning' was needed in the earlier part, and at the end of the book there was 'a complete falling to bits'. The report concluded: 'The author shows he has art, strength and originality, but this MS. wants time and trouble spent on it, to make it a more finished piece of work, to shape it more carefully as the product of craftsmanship, mind and imagination of an artist.'[64]

In his *Time of Apprenticeship: The Fiction of the Young James Joyce*, Marvin Magalaner remarks that the report 'shows sensitive insights along traditional lines but falls down in mistaking the short cuts of impressionism for uncraftsmanlike confusion'.[65] The reaction of Ezra Pound, Joyce's friend and mentor, was not so calm or dispassionate. In a letter which berates vehemently, perhaps paradoxically, someone who had an obsessive devotion to literature and had shown it in practical and not only theoretical ways, Pound wrote: 'I have read the effusion of Mr Duckworth's reader with no inconsiderable disgust. These vermin crawl over and beslime our literature with their pulings.' He continued in a similar spirit with, among other comments: ' "Carelessly written", this of the sole, or almost sole piece of contemporary prose that one can enjoy sentence by sentence and reread with pleasure ... It is with difficulty that I manage to write to you at all on being presented with the Duckworthian muck, the dungminded, dungbeard, penny-a-line, please-the-mediocre-at-all-costs doctrine ... as for altering Joyce to suit Duckworth's reader – it would be like trying to fit the Venus de Milo into a pisspot – a few changes required ... '[66]

After five publishers had refused the manuscript, Miss Harriet Shaw Weaver, who had taken over the editorship of the *Egoist*, offered to publish it and Joyce agreed. In New York B. W. Huebsch, novice publisher who had been struck by the excellence of *Dubliners* when it was published in 1914, read the *Portrait* and wrote to Miss Weaver to say he would like to publish it, offering Joyce £54 advance on royalties. The book appeared in New York in 1916. Later in his career as director of the Viking Press Huebsch appointed Edward as English representative of the firm. Their association was to be marked by friendship and strengthened by Huebsch's respect for Edward's acumen.

It was to be some time before the possibility emerged of a similar relationship with a London publisher. However, with the war over, a new firm was launched in 1921 by Edward's old colleague from Duckworth, Jonathan Cape.

FIFTEEN

Cape

THE end of the war found Edward working rather discon-
tentedly at the Bodley Head. John Lane now took little
interest in the firm and did not respond to Edward's enthusiasm
for publishing books about the war. In the unsettled post-war
years Edward's old friends had either died or were scattered,
with no meeting place to bring them together. Thomas Seccombe, one of the old circle, wrote to him in March 1919: 'It
seems a very long time ago since I saw you, or heard from you
and we have a good deal I think of reminiscences to exchange.
It would be very nice to see you again. The death of Reynolds
rather strangely evoked our old gatherings at the Mont Blanc
... ' In a nostalgic passage he commented, 'I have had "The
Twilight of the Gods" lent me, so that I have many opportunities of remembering your wicked smile! I expect you are still
discovering creatures of genius. How many have been déterré
owing to your endeavours ... The old familiar faces seem
strangely absent .... '[1]

The opportunity for Edward to leave his frustrating post with
Lane came when Jonathan Cape decided to go into publishing
on his own account. He wrote to Edward on 10 January 1921
to say that he hoped if Garnett was 'ever in the neighbourhood'
that he would come in and see him. In his words, as far as his
new firm was concerned, 'I hope to keep to a respectable standard, and will not fight shy of new authors. If you can pass
anybody along to me I should appreciate it, and would like

to come to a business arrangement with you which I think could be arranged satisfactorily ...'[2] Edward replied that though he feared 'the immediate outlook is not very reassuring to publishers, new and old' he would call and talk over Cape's proposition. In his letter Edward wrote: 'Perhaps you know that I am now reader to John Lane; but I see no reason why I should not put things in your way if we can come to some business arrangement. I have some ideas & suggestions which might be interesting to a firm just starting; & I think I had better call and have a talk ... '[3]

At their meeting Cape proposed a commission arrangement but Edward, in a letter shortly afterwards, put forward a different idea. He was

> ready to take as *a basis* your proposal that in the case of all books you may publish – individually or in series – which have been due to my initiative, you shall pay me 5/- on your receipts from the sales; but I should require a guaranteed sum of 39£ a quarter as salary for my services on account of the sales. Six months notice on either side, to terminate the agreement. The books & series of books I have to propose will necessitate interviews and correspondence, or in other cases, consultation & study, & I cannot afford to give up my working time for a problematic return.

As Cape would be asking him for his opinion on manuscripts offered to the firm, for an additional £13 a quarter Edward said he would be ready 'to add to my duties the work of reporting on all MSS & books you may send me'. Such an arrangement Edward thought would be to Cape's advantage, for ' ... to take one aspect alone, you should bring back from America a number of offers of the work of authors whose *future* it is most important for you to gauge correctly. I have myself some definite suggestions to make about American works & I consider it is most important for you to establish contacts & to procure & study very carefully announcements & advance sheets well ahead.'[4]

In his reply Cape wrote that he and his partner, Wren Howard, had carefully considered Edward's letter and as 'we should appreciate having the benefit of your knowledge and advise [*sic*] which we feel would be of great value and impor-

tance to us ... our considered opinion is that the best arrangement between us would be that of a regular salary.' Accordingly
he offered 'an honorarium of £200 a year' and, as he knew
Edward disliked an office routine and preferred freedom of
action, Cape also stated, 'We should not wish to tie you to more
than a weekly conference, which could be so arranged as to
cover the luncheon hour. Wednesday seems the most suitable
day, as we could then talk over what has come in, and then we
have the remainder of the week to take action on the decisions
we have come to ... We would send M.S. to you as it came to
us, and you could report upon it in the usual way ... '5

Edward joined the firm on this basis. The following year a
letter to Cape betrays anxiety over their connection. In it
Edward said he thought the time had come 'to make a slight
readjustment of our working arrangement'. Though he realised
the difficulty an underlying bitterness regarding his predicament is apparent in his statement: 'I don't want to ask for more
money from you as I quite understand a young firm has to look
sharp after its working expenses. But on the other hand you will
agree with me that a "reader" may go on actively building up
a firm and in the end as a return for his insight etc. on which so
much depends he may look back and see that he got scarcely
bread and butter.' Edward suggested that perhaps a small
percentage on the yearly profit – 'say five per cent' – would
be the solution and be of benefit to the firm as well as to
himself.6

To this Cape replied defensively that it was hardly a practic-
able proposition, for 'Last year we managed to pay our way,
but we worked for nothing, and we did not succeed in paying
interest on our capital. This year we hope to pay interest on
capital, and also to get something towards our salaries. Next
year we hope that the results will be better than this, and that
we shall show a profit, if only a small one.' He went on to say,
' ... so long as you are advising us, we are prepared to pay you
ten per cent of the profits, after we have paid interest on capital
and received salaries ourselves.'7 It was a suggestion he withdrew in December and with Edward's agreement substituted a
salary of £300 a year, took over the publication of all Edward's
books and sent him a case of burgundy for Christmas. Perhaps
he hesitated to reveal the accounts necessary to such an

arrangement, yet wished, by some encouraging revision of their relationship, to retain Edward's services.

Jonathan Cape had a reputation for driving a hard bargain and this often brought him into conflict with his reader. During the early months of their association there is at least one example of Edward's defence of the author's financial interests. He wrote to Cape on 14 July 1921: 'Mr. Fridlander, at my request, has sent me the Agreement you forwarded him, & it does not, I see correspond to the note of the terms I left with you, in two particulars: viz. – you have omitted – 1) An advance of 25£ to be paid on day of publication on account of royalties. 2) After the first 2000 copies sold the royalty to be increased to 15% ... ' He added as a postscript: 'I think that the clause about the Remainders as it stands is hardly fair to the author, & that 10% is the least he should get in the event of such remainders. I have therefore deleted the last part of the sentence.'[8]

On another occasion Edward explained in more detail what had been discussed and concluded rather tartly: 'In future it will be well to keep a note of terms suggested in conversation. I made a note of the 15% after two thousand copies sold; & of the 25£ advance. You will remember you had forgotten to insert the 25£ advance in the agreement for "My foolish sex". And I prefer not to offer you books by my friends than to have any dispute about terms.'[9]

Edward, however, in his son's opinion was 'not a good bargainer'. He remembered showing his father the manuscript of *Lady into Fox* which he had written shortly after Edward had joined Cape. 'Not a word needs changing,' Edward told David, but as it would only appeal to a very select public he would suggest that Cape did an edition of 100 copies. David thought his father was 'quite wrong' and after some negotiation it was eventually published by Prentice. David had suggested that his book would do as well as *The Young Visiters*, which had sold 100,000 copies.[10] *Lady into Fox* not only sold well, it won the Hawthornden Prize.

David Garnett has written that his father's chief concern was to help an author to develop. Edward 'felt it his job to cajole and persuade an author to write more and to develop his talent' even though this 'might involve protecting the author from his own employer'.[11]

Despite their differences Edward respected Jonathan's 'acumen and knowledge of the trade', as he explained years later in a conversation recorded by Sean O'Faolain. Edward claimed with little modesty that:

Cape succeeded for various reasons. He started as a book salesman, known to the trade as Herbert J. Cape, Herbert for short, and 'Erb for shorter. When he decided to go into the publishing business he put the J. first and became Jonathan Cape, a fine solid-sounding name – the sort of name that inspires confidence in the English public. His greatest gift was that he knew nothing about books and admitted it. He looked around for the best reader he could find, chose me, and followed me blind. He had about four hundred pounds in cash. I had always been a great admirer of Doughty. I had made Duckworth publish an abridged *Arabia Deserta*. I said, 'Cape, you must publish this book in full. You will lose money on it, but it will make your name.' He decided to trust my judgment, and he did publish it. He spent all his capital on that first book. And it made his name.

Sean O'Faolain, who enjoyed baiting the irascible Edward, had asked 'in mock innocence', 'Surely every publisher's main aim is to publish best-sellers?' Edward growled in reply, 'That, my boy, is the quickest possible way for any publisher to lose money! Good writers like good company. They want to be published by publishers who publish other good writers. If Cape hadn't aimed at a good list he would never have attracted the writers who are both good and sellers. If he hadn't earlier had Doughty he wouldn't have got T. E. Lawrence and *The Seven Pillars*, any more than he'd have got Sinclair Lewis or Hemingway or Louis Bromfield or Elizabeth Madox Roberts or Sherwood Anderson ... ' To O'Faolain he also enlarged on what he considered two other marks of Cape's success. Cape was one of the earliest publishers to go to America in search of books 'and he did it off his own bat', bringing back from his first trip 'an astounding haul compared with the meagre results anybody got after him ... Before his time the traffic had been all the other way.' In addition, Edward claimed, 'The get-up of his books was first-class, and something new for the time. All that led authors of repute and staying power to him. Quality, my Boy! That's what pays off in publishing.'[12]

Such a telescoped version of the establishment and progress of Cape glosses over the part T. E. Lawrence played in the fortunes of the firm and Edward's role in this connection. Wren Howard was to remark of this progress: 'Always from the very beginning Lawrence was the key to our success.'[13] It was the outcome of fortuitous circumstances: Lawrence was looking for a publisher to reprint Doughty's *Arabia Deserta* which he so admired; Cape, who was assistant to Lee Warner at the Medici Society, wished to begin as a publisher on his own account and remembered Edward's obsessive regard for Doughty's work; and Edward, unhappy with Lane, was ready to move to a firm that would take on such a venture.

Lawrence had gone to Doughty's previous publishers, the C.U.P. and Duckworth, in an attempt to interest them in reprinting *Arabia Deserta*, but without success. It was at the Medici Society in July 1920 that his proposal was taken up. Cape persuaded Lee Warner to make the costly production a joint imprint. Published in early 1921 with an introduction by T. E. Lawrence, *Arabia Deserta* was reprinting again by midsummer. Lawrence's name and introduction no doubt helped to bring attention to Doughty's massive work. Middleton Murry referred to the publication in a letter to Edward, saying that 'in a book of lectures on Style wh: I am just correcting, I find that I have spoken of you as the "only begetter" among critics of the fame of "Arabia Deserta". It irked me somewhat, when the new edition came out, to find that there was no mention of you. Without you no-one would have known of the book – I'm perfectly certain I shouldn't and yet now they all talk as though they had read and admired it at school. I'm afraid that a really "discerning" critic like you will have to be content with treasure in heaven.'[14]

Edward's well-known devotion to Doughty and his newly formed connection with Cape brought an invitation from Lawrence to give his opinion on the Oxford version of *Seven Pillars of Wisdom*.[15] Henceforth Edward was inveigled on to the tortuous path followed by Lawrence in achieving publication. After stating his opinion of the Oxford version, Edward prepared an abridgment and, hearing that Shaw was sounding out Constable as a likely publisher for Lawrence's work wrote to Lawrence: 'I think now the abridgment is done it should be put in the agent's hands without delay. There is one thing I wanted to ask. Shall I tell Cape about the abridgment & that it is earmarked for another publisher? The fact that I am his "reader" etc. makes it necessary for me to be clear and definite with him.'[16] Lawrence's letter to Shaw indicates Edward's part in ensuring his future connection with Cape; 'Cape', he wrote on 27 December 1922, 'is first in the running for my thing – It's good of you to have worked up Meredith [Constable's partner] to the point of offering – but Garnett reads for Cape, and liked parts of the book: so that Cape has a special wish for it.'[17] To Edward, Lawrence replied: 'Mention the book to Cape, by all means, but tell him that it will be a costly production and that I am making Curtis Brown my agent in disposing of it. Of course I'd be very glad if he got it: but it seems to me a speculation unjustifiably large for his resources.'[18]

Cape was coming to terms with Lawrence when the *Daily Express* 'splashed' its sensational disclosures of T. E. Lawrence in the R.A.F. on 27 December 1922. Lawrence's ambivalence towards publicity, together with his peculiar position in the Air Force, resulted in Cape's being told that he would not publish anything while he remained in the R.A.F. Nevertheless in a letter to Shaw saying that 'Cape was furious', Lawrence wrote that 'a while later I was sorry to have cancelled it, and I began to think of publishing not an abridgment: but the whole story.'[19] Again Cape rose to this idea but again it was cancelled when Lawrence was dismissed from the R.A.F. Lawrence remembered Edward's abridgment and wrote to Cape: 'Would you give Garnett the cut down copy of the thing? It was his work, and very well done, and he spent much time on it, and I feel guilty in his sight.'[20] In the following years Lawrence havered about publishing Edward's abridgment, and a subscription edition with its profits.[21] He decided to mount a finely printed subscribers' edition but this ran into financial difficulties and he 'went to Cape & offered him 125,000 words (about 43%) of *The Seven Pillars*'.[22]

This abridgment, which Lawrence had himself prepared by the simple expedient of painting out whole passages of the Oxford text, was ready by 1926. It was published as *Revolt in the Desert* and enjoyed huge sales. Lawrence apologised to

Edward with 'I was sorry not to use your text for the *Revolt in the Desert* abridgment. I wrote twice to Cape, and asked for the loan of it: but he was presumably afraid that I meant to destroy it, and so to do him out of his power to produce an abridgment of his own if I made default. At any rate he would not let me have it.'[23] A second edition of *Revolt* was published in March 1927; then Lawrence, who now had enough money to pay for the subscribers' edition, exercised his option to prevent further production. This remained the position until shortly after his fatal accident on 13 May 1935. Cape, with the permission of A. W. Lawrence, the author's brother, published *Seven Pillars* in totality – a limited edition of 750 numbered copies and a 20,000 edition for general sale. Both editions soon sold out for, as Edward had seen, the book was both good *and* a seller.

The publication of Lawrence's work brought a startling leap in the prosperity of the Cape firm; *Revolt* was largely responsible in 1927 for a net profit rising from 'the usual level of around £2,000 to nearly £28,000'.[24] In one of the expansive gestures which Jonathan made as a result of this upturn, Edward's salary was raised to £400 a year and he was allotted 500 notional shares, giving dividends equal to those paid on the ordinary shares.

During the *Alice in Wonderland* quadrille devised by Lawrence over publishing *Seven Pillars*, Edward became the principal confidant of his 'Uxbridge notes'. Lawrence first referred to these on 28 May 1924, as the 'R.A.F. notes'.[25] Mentions of them appeared intermittently in subsequent letters, one of which so alarmed Edward that he sent a note to Shaw. On 18 June 1925 in a mood of depression because Samuel Hoare had blocked his return to the R.A.F., Lawrence had written to Edward: ' ... I'm no bloody good on earth. So I'm going to quit; but in my usual comic fashion I'm going to finish the reprint and square with Cape before I hop it! There is nothing like deliberation, order and regularity in these things ... I shall bequeath you my notes on life in the recruits camp of the R.A.F. They will disappoint you ... ' Prompted by Edward's alarm at this apparent suicide threat, Shaw saw the Prime Minister and informed Edward, '... I have now sent your letter to Downing St with a card to say that some decision should be made, as there is the possibility of an appalling scandal.'[26]

Lawrence returned to the R.A.F. and conducted a typically intricate correspondence over the notes with Edward and with Shaw and E. M. Forster. By 15 March 1928 he had posted them to Edward saying that he wanted the notes, now called *The Mint*, 'offered to Cape, for publication, in extenso, without one word excised or moderated. Can you, as his reader, arrange this? I'd rather no one reads it but you (and David G. who feels rather like your second edition, revised and corrected by the author, but less spontaneous): and I want him to refuse it, so as to free me from the clause in his contract for *Revolt in the Desert*, tying me to offer him another book. I hate being bound by even an imaginary obligation.' [27] He also wrote to Shaw on 17 March to explain how he had 're-met Garnett, whose name you probably know as a critic of genius. Of course he's more than that; but that's only his reputation. I explained to him that the reason had fallen out of my existence – and so there wouldn't be another book. He remained curious. If not a book what of the notes?' Lawrence continued that Edward had hinted at his 'unfulfilled present from time to time' and now he was sending it to him knowing that 'Garnett will not hawk the thing about; only his son will read it . . . ' He had, as he put it in his postscript, 'meant to please Garnett, who has been very good to me. He won't know whether to insure it, or burn it, or poke it in the British Museum.' [28]

Edward's appreciative reception of *The Mint* brought a long letter from Lawrence in which he described how it came to be written and an admission that 'I'd so like something of my creating to be very good: and I bask for the moment in the illusion of your praise'. [29] Though Cape was eager to publish the manuscript, Lawrence told him that he was leaving it to his brother in his will, for publication after his death.

It's not the sort of book to be decently published. Every character in it is real and every incident actually happened! . . . I am the prime stumbling block. All the fellows in the hut are in the book: and they would regard the record of themselves as betrayal of confidence. When that sort of man goes to be photographed he puts on what he calls 'best': – a special suit of clothes: – and they wouldn't relish the birthday suits in which I draw them. Nor would I like them to think

that I've given them away: though I think I'm absolutely
justified in doing so, and have done 'em honour. By 1950
there will be no reality or soreness left: and till then the book
shall remain hidden . . . [30]

The Mint, like everything in the inexplicable Lawrence story,
had a hinted-at existence during his lifetime; a rumoured mys-
tery which only ended with its publication in the promised year
1950, bearing the dedication: 'To Edward Garnett. You
dreamed I came one night with this book crying, "Here's a
masterpiece. Burn it." Well – *as you please.*'

Jonathan Cape during his exasperating yet profitable association with Lawrence had hoped that Lawrence would join the
firm in some kind of editorial capacity for he 'enjoyed the
fascination of unknown manuscripts, and the adventure of discovery . . . '[31] From time to time Lawrence toyed with the idea
of translating for Cape – *Sturly* and *Salammbo* – and also referred
in his letters to Cape to likely publishing speculations. He was
instrumental in introducing Roy Campbell to the firm. Visiting
Augustus John, who was making a drawing of Lawrence at his
studio in Charlotte Street, he saw the transcript of a narrative
poem which so impressed him that he sent a postcard at once to
Jonathan Cape with the terse message: 'Get hold of it – it is
great stuff.'[32] The poet was Roy Campbell and the poem *The
Flaming Terrapin*. Cape acted promptly and Campbell came the
next day with the manuscript. Cape was 'immediately arrested
by the opening sentence'[33] and gave it to Edward, who was
enthusiastic.

Roy Campbell and Edward discussed the various versions of
the poem and in the final form Campbell explained the alterations to the text. 'The point on which I need most advice is in
part 6,' he wrote. 'I would like you to tell me whether it is better
simply to make the Terrapin disappear as in the first version or
to continue with his disintegration as I do in the second. I think
I can cut out a good deal of the preaching at the end without
altering the sequence.'[34] The poem was published by the Dial
Press in New York and by Cape in England under a royalty
arrangement in April/May 1924. Edward reviewed it in the
Nation on 7 June, and though he said it would be easy to pull it
to pieces by quoting passages showing extravagances of manner,

it displayed poetic imagination 'so fresh and triumphant'[35] and imagery strong and often delicate.

Their deliberations over *The Flaming Terrapin* led to a friendship in which the practical Edward helped Campbell to find a country cottage near where Edward Thomas had once lived not far from Sevenoaks. Mary, Campbell's wife, expressed their thanks when they learned that 'the Terrapin seems to be doing well ... How thankful we both are to you for everything you have done about it.'[36] On his return to South Africa, Campbell wrote: 'When I landed in Durban the papers were full of your review of me in the Athenaeum. Thank you very much for being so kind to Mary in my absence ... '[37] Back home in Natal, he found Edward's letters very encouraging – 'I am well launched into my prose-book now. I am keeping a note-book as you suggested and find it a great help. I am studying Hudson very carefully, especially in that book of selections which you so kindly gave to Mary.' He referred warmly to their meeting: 'Mary and I often think about you and wonder how you are getting on. Our short acquaintance with you is one of the pleasantest of our recollections of the old country. I wish you could have been with us during our stay on the Umhlanga river.'[38]

In what he termed 'the longest letter I have ever written in my life', Campbell confided his ambition to establish a magazine to provide a focus for the intellectual resources of the country, to combat the stultifying effects of party politics and race differences; to rouse some sort of national consciousness: 'I would far sooner, even at the risk of ruining any artistic qualities I possess, load my work with moral purpose and direct the knowledge I possess towards counteracting the ends of race hatred and colour hatred that cause so much misery out here ... ' Inviting Edward to stay with them 'whenever you get too restless ... we would look after you', Campbell declared: 'I want Mr. Cape to have all my work to publish, as he was so very good as to take the "Terrapin". But I don't know if I am free to arrange with American publishers. Could you advise me what to do?'[39]

The colour question loomed large in subsequent letters when after discussing the writings of Conrad, Shaw, Lawrence and Joyce, Campbell wrote that on re-reading Olive Schreiner he thought 'her faults are eclipsed by her virtues'. She had, he thought, 'sensible ideas on the native question and the racial question'. Interestingly in the light of his later reputation as a right-wing sympathiser, Campbell gave his own opinions at length on the political future for South Africa, arguing that segregation of the blacks could only be permissible if accompanied by the provision of fertile areas for settlement. To deny the black population voting rights would, he predicted, merely postpone trouble and not settle it; in view of the '7 to 1 ratio it was obvious the population is to be a coloured one [and] we must meet the natives halfway [and] make the process of assimilation as painless as possible'. In conclusion he hoped that 'as soon as I can reduce my prose to equilibrium I shall send you some. It is very kind of you to offer to get it published and we appreciate it very much that you still take an interest in us after our disappearance into these outlandish parts.'[40]

Though their friendship continued this did not influence Edward's professional judgment of the work which Campbell sent in to Cape. The firm published his next work, *The Wayzgoose*, in January 1928 but on the advice of Edward *Adamastor* was declined. As Jonathan Cape remarked over the disappearance of Campbell from his list: 'I prefer to think that Adamastor was just one of those things where the ideas of the poet and the reader didn't coincide, and I was well content to follow Edward Garnett's judgment.'[41] This was the course which Cape always followed, though he was often exasperated by Edward's manner and by his insistence on a semi-independent status and dominance over what was to be published. The conflict came to a head shortly after their association had begun. Cape wrote a letter to Edward on 2 November 1925 in which he expressed his dissatisfaction with their working relationship and his annoyance at the way Edward carried out his responsibilities. It also reveals much about Edward and about what Cape as a publisher expected from his reader.

Written apparently in reply to a letter from Edward, the letter began: 'I have now had an opportunity of talking over with Howard the contents of your letter, also to think out what we would like to do with regard to the reading side of the business. The present arrangement does not suit us and we want either to mend it or end it.' Cape went on:

We realise that your great experience and wide knowledge of books and your critical insight give you a unique value as an adviser, but that value is reduced considerably because of your complete detachment and because you are not close enough and frequently enough at hand to give us the benefit of your advice when we need it most.

If the business grew out of what was submitted to us in the usual way there would be less to be said in criticism of an arrangement which brings you in communication with us for perhaps two hours every week, but it does not. You are not available by means of a telephone, and unless on a Wednesday we have everything cut and dried and we are entirely free from interruptions the weekly meeting is merely a handing over of the MSS you have been reading. You really have very little knowledge of what we are doing; what sort of organisation we have built up or of the volume and nature of the business we are handling. About 90% of the happenings in the office are unknown to you. For instance, the other day when I spoke of the possibility of publishing Gerhardi you doubted if we could do anything more for him than Cobden Sanderson – Cobden Sanderson who has no machinery whatsoever, even less than Martin Secker!

What we have always needed and have failed to obtain is an adviser with whom we should be closely and frequently in touch, so that we could get advice in detail at the time we needed it. Four years ago I invited you to the office for say one day a week at least, and offered to put a room at your disposal. To this you replied that you dislike offices, and repeated efforts on our part to get you to come to the office more often have failed. The most we ever see of you is about two hours a week at luncheon, and perhaps an hour afterwards.

You speak of being the 'literary conscience' of the firm but this literary conscience has been in the keeping of others besides yourself – to a larger extent than you realise. We hoped that as reader and adviser your interest in the firm's activities would increase, and that you would see the necessity of acquainting yourself with what we are doing. We hoped, that as reader and adviser you would, as occasion arose, bring us new authors and new books other than those passed to you for your opinion through the channels of the firm: and that you would suggest books to us that we could commission. We looked for more from you in seeing and meeting authors and prospective authors, and that you would be the active agent and advocate of the firm in preference to all others ...

The letter continues with other complaints; the fact that Garnett had met Graham Wallas a short time ago and had not made any attempt to discover who was to publish the book he was working on; that Edward had wholeheartedly recommended for publication *Many Marriages* by Sherwood Anderson, which would have put the firm in a 'very difficult position'. (This novel contained an incestuous episode which caused consternation in the U.S.A. and brought allegations of obscenity.) There were books, Cape said, which Edward had strongly recommended and which he had declined because 'I considered them highly dangerous and calculated to give us a reputation for publishing erotic books'.[42]

Such a letter may have been occasioned by Cape's resentment that in April 1925 Edward had been asked by the Viking Press to act as its English representative. Combined with Edward's decidedly individualistic habits of time-keeping, this may have made him wonder how far his control as founder of the firm extended over the 'reading side'. The sentiments in the letter were not pursued, and in any event the specific instances mentioned were not detrimental to Cape: the book by Graham Wallas, an old friend of Edward's, was published by Cape in 1926 as *The Art of Thought*, and Sherwood Anderson was one of the contemporary American authors of significance published by Cape. Edward continued in his own way and gave to the Cape firm a loyalty undivided by his other commitment to, as he put it to Pinker, 'a young American firm with a forward enterprising policy'.[43] Jonathan Cape, despite his remonstrances, also knew that his reader was dedicated to fulfilling the responsibility inherent in the phrase Edward had used to describe his role, as 'the literary conscience of the firm'. In this he was doing as he had done with the first publisher for whom he had worked, Unwin: though the author came first, the publisher and his reputation advanced.

SIXTEEN

Literary Conscience
of the Firm

WILLIAM PLOMER, who succeeded Edward as adviser, summarised the relationship that existed between Garnett and Cape in the comment that 'Jonathan Cape, in a way had a respect for writers, particularly if their books sold well. As the founder of a new firm he naturally had to think of what was profitable. With Garnett, one can only conclude, the quality was far more important that its marketability, so the collaboration of the two men may not always have been perfectly smooth. All the same, it must have done much to give the firm Jonathan Cape the status and prestige and success which it acquired both during and after Garnett's lifetime.'[1] Certainly Edward regarded the detection of 'quality' as the prime function of a publisher's reader; the commercial possibilities he considered secondary.

Liam O'Flaherty remembered that when he was interviewed by his publisher for the first time, Cape 'read me a letter from Edward Garnett advising the acceptance of my manuscript, not because it was likely to sell, but because it was the work of a promising young writer'.[2] Edward, who had been impressed by a short story in the *New Leader* of 12 January 1923, entitled 'The Sniper', had taken note of the young author and he urged Cape to accept O'Flaherty's second attempt at a novel, *Thy Neighbour's Wife*.

The nature of Edward's influence was described by O'Flaherty in his autobiographical *Shame the Devil* (1934):

To me his personality and friendship were of incalculable
importance. There I was, like the innocent Huron of Vol-
taire, afloat in a crazy coracle in the sea of London literary
life, surrounded by deadly rocks and yet without a thought
for the dangers that surrounded me. Like a father he took me
under his protection, handling me with a delicacy with which
one handles a highly-strung young colt, which the least mistake might make unfit for racing ... The calmness of his
judgment, the subtlety of his intellect and the extraordinary
nobility of his character were a glorious revelation to me ...
So that I was only too willing that he should fashion the
development of my literary talent in whatever way he
pleased.[3]

This extravagant praise recalled the formative guidance Edward gave to his work during his most prolific period, from 1923
to 1926, when O'Flaherty wrote over 140 letters to his
'dearest friend'. The correspondence reflected a familiar mixture of confessions of literary aspirations, responses to advice
and encouragement, confidences on his personal predicament
and matrimonial entanglements, the early conception of his
works and his soul-searching in their development.

In one of his early letters he referred to the origin of *The Black
Soul*: 'I think I irritated you last Friday', O'Flaherty wrote on
14 May 1923. 'Excuse me. I am very hard to put up with when
I am nervous. By the way I have discovered a good subject for
my next book. Describing the peasant life of Aran. Got the idea
yesterday reading D. H. Lawrence's Fox. I don't like that fellow
Lawrence's way of writing ... '[4] Shortly afterwards he wrote to
Edward: 'Glad that first chapter was right. I was beginning to
be afraid of it. I think the chapter I am doing now is better. I
have got back more completely into the native Aran Island and
swing of the *Neighbour's Wife* ... I am feeling it moving now
without effort.'[5]

Within a few weeks he was expressing his appreciation
of Edward's advice with 'Damn it I am the luckiest curse on
earth, for I would rather have your praise than a five million
circulation, seventeen whacks of the King's sword and a ducal
dinner with knee breeches complete. Another idea has struck
me with reference to the Black Soul. It is a new idea and I must
talk to you about it on Tuesday, and see whether it's too

abnormal ... You are quite right in saying that any detailed account of everyday occurrences would spoil the effect. Since then that has become obvious to me ... '[6]

O'Flaherty's identification with the story as a whole punctuates a series of letters to Edward in June. 'Truly I have a black soul,'[7] he exclaimed in one, and in another, 'It hurts me as much now as the first day I thought of it ... and if there is anything in me it's going into it. So you can see my bare soul and measure its worth when you read.'[8] Eventually one critic was to describe *The Black Soul* as 'the most revealing and therefore the most important novel in the study of O'Flaherty's genius because he put all of himself into it ... Not only does the novel give a detailed study of the kind of spiritual conflict that gnaws at O'Flaherty, but it also shows most of the themes and techniques that will be used in almost all his future work. The most important theme is the turmoil of the soul in a godless world. This will recur in almost every subsequent novel.'[9]

In this seminal work O'Flaherty paid heed in construction and presentation to a familiar pattern of advice from Edward. In July he declared, 'Anyhow I am following instructions and giving free rein to feeling and emotion.'[10] By August he wrote: 'Really I can never thank you sufficiently for all you have done for me. I mean, apart from other things, the material things, in keeping my feet treading the artistic road. I have begun to write *The Black Soul* again ... I will pay attention to your memorandum re "style" and wording of the Stranger ... '[11] On 17 August he wondered: 'Am I to send you the Black Soul bit by bit or will I wait until I have it all rewritten. I intend to go over it a third time in winter before it is submitted to Cape. You never know what ideas a man might get about style and words after a rest of a few months. If you would be so kind as to be merciless with the new copy I would be pleased ... '[12]

On 23 August he was 'working on the Black Soul like a Jew making money'[13] and gave Edward details of the reconstruction of the book and the remodelling of the Stranger.

The ending of the book was particularly difficult to resolve. It was a matter which he referred to when he wrote later about this period of his writing life: 'The Black Soul was begun in Warren Street, London in May 1923, continued in a Bucks village and finished in King's Road, London in August. I wrote it under the direction of Edward Garnett who burned a considerable number of draughts [*sic*] of various parts. When it was finished neither of us was satisfied. He suggested a change in a certain part but I was too exhausted to attempt it.'[14] In appreciation of this stringent supervision, when the proofs were ready, O'Flaherty asked (6 May 1924): 'May I have your formal permission to dedicate the book to you. Would you permit this dedication: "To Edward Garnett, In gratitude for his valuable friendship". Please tell me. You see you are an awful man and I am afraid to irritate you ... '[15]

By then O'Flaherty had been excited by the conception of another novel, referring in April to a Dublin story, 'The Vendetta', which would be a 'shocker and a thriller'.[16] On 28 June he was 'up to my neck in the creation of a monstrous character called Gypo Nolan – an informer ... (I am calling the novel "The Informer" in his honour). He is a wonderful character and quite original, nobody has touched him, not popular though ... '[17] Enthusiastically he remarked shortly afterwards that he was going ahead 'very well with The Informer. Nothing that I have written so far has taken such a hold over me – although the book will be no means as beautiful as The Black Soul. But even in its present state it's far stronger. This fellow Gypo is a regular monster and I love him. Poor fellow I've got to kill him in the end.'[18] In September he was able to outline the whole book in a long letter, explaining his approach to the story, the characters and changes in Gypo, and told Edward: 'I hope to have it ready for your judgment in another three weeks or so. When you get it I want you to judge it not so much for what it is by itself as for what I have set [out] to make and what I have succeeded in making.' It was, he wrote, for 'the mob to judge it for what it is' but 'in your criticism of Fathers and Children I was greatly struck by the clarity with which you probed the very initial dreams of the author and their subsequent materialisation in the finished creation ... '[19]

It was this belief in Edward's divination of an author's individual talent which encouraged O'Flaherty to develop the literary form in which he became pre-eminent. While busy with *The Black Soul* he had listened to Edward's advice. He reported to Edward that he had written 'an animal story on the lines you told me and sent it to The Manchester Guardian. It had an interesting title anyway, "A Cow's suicide" – that alone might make the editor look at it.'[20] In return he received Edward's letter of congratulation and he remarked of it: 'I got your letter this morning and was delighted to hear that you liked the cow. It's not the sketch itself but the fact that at last I know what is wanted to write one that pleases me. Thanks so much for showing me. You see I was always aiming after this damned cleverness in expression without bothering about the bones of the corpse upon which I was operating – probably copying the daily papers, but I imagine the fault is hereditary ... '[21] He followed up this success with another: 'I did that sketch you told me to write; about the fellow addressing the mob. I called it "The Proletariat Unbound".'[22]

In writing his sketches he turned to Edward for his opinion, saying apropos of 'Chaos': 'I am greatly excited to see what you think of it. It's funny but I can't imagine a thing being alright now unless you pass a favourable judgment on it. The Cow's Death always lives fresh in my mind on account of your congratulations when I wrote it. But I rather fancy it made me too conceited at the time.'[23] Such dependence, whether absolutely true or not, was reiterated at intervals later. When O'Flaherty despatched 'The Wave' to Edward he added a note: 'I am sending it to you for your opinion of it, because it took me two days to do it and I don't know whether it's good or bad or middling.'[24] He was relieved at Edward's immediate response. 'I am very glad you liked "The Wave",' he wrote. 'Very glad indeed. It cost such an immense effort to write it.'[25] But he became increasingly discontented with his sketches, admitting on 12 March 1924:

Thanks so very much for your very encouraging letter ... You are very kind, but I am afraid that you are too flattering. That is about my sketches. However flattery is as nourishing as cod liver oil and malt, so the more I receive of it the better I like it. I thrive on it. See I have written half of the enclosed sketch within the hour on the strength of it. I hope you will like the sketch. It's the one we were talking about in your flat the evening I left. I twisted the plot to suit myself. If you remember I think I told you the story as a true one, but in the interest of art, I must state here that there is not an atom

of truth in the whole thing. It's a pure fabrication. What a
scoundrel I am. But then I told you before not to believe
anything I say ... [26]

Of another sketch he had sent to Edward he remarked: 'Thanks
very much for your appreciation of The Blackbird. I felt that it
was right and I am very glad that you think it is also. But
somehow I get no pleasure from writing those short sketches
now. They seem to advance according to a formula and it's like
doing a day's work that you have been doing for a long time
every day.'[27] Busy with another work he added: 'I cannot write
until I hear from you about Peasant Love.'

Edward's comments on this work brought an exasperated
rejoinder from O'Flaherty: ' ... About style I disagree with you.
There will be written on the tomb stones of most of the young
English writers of talent: "Here might hath lain a genius, were
he not cut off in his youth by the mania of style." Damn it man,
I have not style. I don't want any style. I refuse to have style. I
have no time for style. I think style is artificial and vulgar. If a
man is lucky enough to have a natural gift for saying things in
a pretty manner good luck to him. If he has not that natural
gift he is a fool if he sidetracks his creative energy in an attempt
to cultivate it. Them be my sentiments and I suppose they are
quite wrong but because they are mine the divil from hell with
all his jesuitic guile could not persuade me to change them. This
is all rot and I don't know why I wrote it because I wrote it this
morning and now it is night ... ' Apologetically he ended: 'The
fact is that I am irritated'[28] and the source of his irritation was
the suspicion that Cape was not publishing his book, *The Informer*, as quickly as he would have liked.

Nevertheless he continued with stories whose structure and
style he subjected to Edward's judgment. 'I am enclosing a
story', he wrote on 11 April 1924, 'which is a new departure in
method and in style, to a lesser extent. I wonder what you will
think of it ... I would rather like this method if it could be
developed into anything worthwhile ... '[29] He was 'delighted'
with the verdict on *The Doctor's Visit*, announcing, 'I feel so glad
that I was right about it. You know I never believe anybody's
verdict about anything until you have said Yes ... '[30]

A readiness to fall in with Edward's views was reflected in

further letters the following year. In July 1925 he wrote: 'Thanks awfully for your letter of criticism of my two sketches. I have carefully studied all the points you made and I hope that I will be able to correct exactly to your liking ... '³¹ A week later he asked, 'Would you please criticize it (Exactly) as *strictly* as possible for me especially the last fifty words or so, which I imagine have slipped too readily towards a rather mediocre climax ... What do you think? I am very anxious to hear your verdict, because if you pass this method I intend to use it a lot in my new novel ... '³²

But like others who had received Edward's advice in their formative years he was breaking free to follow his own maturity, which found its most vivid rationale in his letter of 31 July 1925:

> Just for your delightful letter I am inclined not to agree with you about the sketch, except on the point that the struggle should have been more evident between his desire to stay with his child and the necessity to go to work. But unfortunately in real life in Aran there is no such struggle. The people accept *necessity* without any resistance and there is only a dull mourning and rebellion of the heart. It's curious. I don't think I exert any judgment whatsoever in my writing at the moment of writing but seem to be impelled by the Aran Islanders themselves who cry out dumbly to me to give expression to them.

But the letter also indicated the particular connection which had developed between them with the cry: 'Why the hell are you not living near me? There's nobody else in this world that cares a damn about my work except you and you are in London.'³³

Edward had become not merely literary adviser but also a father figure to the young writer who had been a victim of shell shock in the war, who had suffered a nervous breakdown, and whose wild approach to life invariably entangled him in disputes – with the Church and with the I.R.A. – and caused difficulties in his domestic arrangements. If Edward inculcated in O'Flaherty an acceptance of self-discipline and persistent endeavour in his writing, he also brought a reassuring understanding of O'Flaherty's turbulent temperament and of his sense of isolation. 'I am eagerly looking forward to having another talk with you, it's so damn lonely in the street – and the landlady calls me a typewriter man,'[34] declared O'Flaherty during the early days of their acquaintance. Back in Dublin, writing from the 'Hell Fire Club' in May 1924, he cried:

> For me life is very lonely here without you. It seems nobody else is in any way deeply interesting. You see one has a devilish hero worship for a man one allows to throw one's manuscript in the fire. During the past month when I was in agonies trying to find the right way out for my novel I said to myself: 'Now if Edward Garnett were here he would tell me in half an hour what I should do and the way would be clear.' But maybe it's good for me to have to begin to do these things for myself. Although I would like very much if you would be so kind as to read the characters for me and give your judgment.[35]

Throughout their association Edward with his usual generosity despatched books and wine to his protégé. He helped him through frequent periods of financial hardship, provided him with the more mundane gift of a bicycle and arranged the payment of his dentist's fees. 'I'm ever so grateful to you', O'Flaherty wrote, 'for sending me to him and getting these teeth for me. I trust that getting them in will restore my vitality so that I may be able to work in order to pay my rather alarming debt to you.'[36] Both Nellie and Edward were drawn into the writer's personal and marital adventures. It appealed to Edward's 'Irishness' when O'Flaherty ran off with the wife of a university professor. 'Topsy' and O'Flaherty became frequent visitors to the flat in Pond Place. 'Allow me', O'Flaherty wrote in his orotund way on 11 October 1927, 'to thank you for the most enjoyable evening that Topsy and myself spent at your house. I can't remember when I enjoyed myself so much. And I don't remember ever seeing you look so well or talk so well. No, my dear father-in-Christ, I don't want anything, not even ten shillings ... '[37] He asked if Edward would be godfather to his daughter and Edward and Nellie visited him in Ireland.

In his usual way Edward persisted in bringing O'Flaherty's work to the notice of editors. His attempts met with little success at first. Middleton Murry considered and re-considered a

manuscript which Edward had sent to the *Adelphi* and though
he said he would like to see more, 'in this instance the MS is too
literary'.[38] He remained unconvinced by another offering:
'Here is Flaherty back again. I think it's pretty good – distinctly
a border line case; but it doesn't seem to me the *real thing*... Still,
I freely acknowledge he interests me. I don't think there's much
doubt he's a writer, though I don't believe he's as good as you
think he is ... '[39]

Leonard Woolf at the *Nation* was of the same mind as Murry:
'Many thanks for sending me O'Flaherty's sketch. I agree with
you that it has considerable merit, and it interested me a good
deal. But to tell the truth, I did not think that it absolutely came
off; and the difficulty with that sort of sketch is, that unless it
really comes off, it lets one down rather badly. So in the end,
though I had considerable hesitation, I sent it back to him
telling him that it interested me very much, and that I hoped
he would let me see some more of his work.'[40]

Liam O'Flaherty thought of trying a different tack and asked
Edward: ' ... By the way do you think it would be a good idea
for me to get an agent or are agents any good? I suppose not. I
guess it would be better to steer on my own, for all the work I
have for the market.'[41] Edward's opinion of agents is implicit in
the letter he received from O'Flaherty when he had acted on
his resolution: 'Why are you so incredulous about literary agents
... I simply must have an agent so one is as good as another.
These damn short stories have been the cause of more worry to
me during the past year than the whole of the great War. Now
I am rid of that worry. I have packed them off to Curtis
Brown ... '[42]

At Cape's Edward pressed for financial support and
O'Flaherty wrote appreciatively in April 1924: ' ... I also
received a letter from Cape saying he would subsidise me until
the end of September. I can see your hand in this as in everything else. How can I thank you my friend?'[43] But his recurringly
troubled finances reached a low ebb in January 1925 and, from
Dublin, O'Flaherty wrote briefly and desperately: 'I am in
a very low condition. Here and absolutely friendless –
everybody has turned against me. I have no money. Would you
ask Cape to purchase the copyrights of my four books – for
whatever he can give.'[44]

Edward promptly despatched £10 and sought further support. J. M. Barrie replied regretfully that 'O'Flaherty's writing
is uncommonly good but at this time am up to the neck with
trying to help good causes' and suggested Edward should ask
E. V. Lucas to get a grant for him from the Royal Literary
Fund.[45] But the Fund Committee was not due to meet for
another month and Lucas advised Edward to write to the
Secretary stating the gravity of the case and expressing his faith
in the writer's gifts and prospects. Lucas promised to support
the request but warned, 'If it gets out O'Flaherty is in trouble
with the Church, there may be some opposition. You must be
prepared for this. The members of the Committee are very staid
people, at any rate when they sit around the table.'[46] Edward
immediately rallied Galsworthy, who sent 'the enclosed' with
best wishes, commenting, 'I think you're a brick to back your
friend so staunchly.'[47] Leonard Woolf also wrote: 'I am very
sorry to hear about O'Flaherty. I have written today supporting
his claim, saying that he has written for The Nation, that I
think his work of high quality ... I hope that this may do some
good.'[48]

From Ireland O'Flaherty wrote emotionally: 'First let me
thank you for the heroic deeds you are performing for me.
Really my dearest friend, I don't know what I would have done
to deserve all this consideration from you. I know I have been
a dreadful worry and nuisance to you since I met you but the
more I worry you and the more trouble I cause you the more
you exert yourself on my behalf instead of growing to hate me
as an ordinary mortal would do. I do verily believe I was done
for this time had you not come to my assistance. I was surrounded by a great wall of enmity that pressed in upon my soul.
I was alone and it seemed that this time I had overreached
myself ... ' The letter continued in this self-dramatising vein:

My exhausted body was not able to succour my sick brain.
And in those circumstances, the consciousness that you were
abroad, working ceaselessly for me came like a great cool
healing draught. And I said 'He is indeed a friend'. And I
pictured you in your typical posture with one leg thrust
forward, making a curious gesture aloft with your right hand,
and looking at the ground musing. But enough. The best way

I can thank you is by getting well quickly and writing some great thing that I can dedicate to you. It need not be great but it must be beautiful ... Just occasionally I notice subconscious suicidal tendencies but they are quite subconscious ... Tell Miss Heath that I think a lot of her and that it does me great good to think of her ... [49]

When Edward's efforts met with success O'Flaherty exclaimed: 'I am writing again to thank you. The R. Lit. Fund sent me this morning a cheque for £200. When the cheque arrived both Margaret and myself were overcome and we immediately said "What a good friend E.G. is" for I clearly understand my dearest friend that I owe this good fortune to you as indeed I owe everything to you since I began to write ... '[50]

But the volatile O'Flaherty became discontented with Cape as a publisher, accusing him of putting off unnecessarily the publication of *The Informer*, and this feeling coloured a later dispute he had with Edward over the collection of short stories he hoped to have published under the title *The Tent*. Edward disliked the title story – as he said to H. E. Bates later, he felt 'it was faked'. O'Flaherty tried to patch over their disagreement in his letter of 18 January 1928: 'Now that the whole business of *The Tent* is settled let us in the name of God resume amicable relations. Not that my feelings towards you have not been all this time those of deepest love but I have felt that you were vexed with me and in fact rather violent and have insisted on *The Tent* being the title story because I *felt* I was right and I *felt* it had a particular significance which I wanted to give to the volume.' As a solution he proposed: ' . . do you agree that the two of us write a foreword to the book? You will denounce *The Tent* and I will defend it ... I think it would be very good and do us both justice. As you are responsible for my art I feel I owe it to you and as I am your pupil I feel you owe it to me. Please approach Cape on the matter if you are agreeable.'[51]

The practical Cape decided to go ahead with publication. 'Under the circumstances', he wrote to Edward enclosing a letter he had received from O'Flaherty, 'the only thing to do is to let [O'Flaherty] have his own way. Evidently he has got to the stage when he is impatient and he is flirting round with various literary agents. I have seen two this week in connection with his work. We shall have him flitting off unless we are very careful and we shall be left with a long over-payment to work out against the slow sales of his early books, while some other publisher reaps the benefit of our labour. I did not think to show you this letter, but as I understand you have seen my letter to O'Flaherty you may think I should have taken a stronger stand. I think it is as well to let you see the sort of mind he is in at the present time.'[52]

O'Flaherty gave another view of the whole affair and of the reason for his discontent in a letter to Edward. 'I was rather relieved by your last letter', he began, 'because I have been so violently oppressed for the past month by your quarrel with me that I felt very sad about the whole thing ... The fact is that I used it as the title story in the hope that it might sell the book and enable me to sell stories to magazines.' He ended with an appeal to Edward: ' ... please don't make any resignation of your position as literary uncle. For no matter if you never read another word of mine, and indeed that would be a relief to you I am sure, I will always write now, as if you were about to read it. Topsy and you. For I always believe that you care for me myself apart from my work and that is what pleases me and makes me feel tender towards you ... '[53]

They resumed their correspondence. He asked Edward: 'For Christ's sake, answer Gould's review of *Gilhooley*. It's full of holes. Sting him if you love me.'[54] O'Flaherty was, however, as Topsy told Edward, 'very gloomy at present and says that he's completely tired and stale'.[55] Nevertheless 1927 ended with the writer beginning a novel he had mentioned to Edward earlier, entitled *The Assassin*. The old connection between them was repeated briefly when, in an answer to Edward's criticism, he wrote on 28 November: 'I don't know how I could have embarked on such a blunder. Now of course I see it plainly, but only after you pointed it out ... I think I am going to try it again ... In any case, I am very grateful to you for having saved me from perpetrating this atrocity ... What I must do here, I see, is to create a definite type of human being, to wit, an assassin, not to give a picture of the forces that led to the assassination of somebody or other, which is merely a matter of very local and very ephemeral interest ... '[56]

By May 1928 he had shaped the book sufficiently to write to

Edward to say that 'It is good to hear you speak so well of the second half of *The Assassin*. Unless you have any serious objection I'm going to dedicate it to you – just for the sake of that second part and also for the considerable responsibility you have for the finished product. Somehow I feel the same about it as about *The Black Soul* which we wrote together and which is the most artistic thing I wrote even though nobody appreciates it ... Please allow me to do so – it would make me feel somehow that you are still fond of me, as of a disciple who did not get *too* vain of his feathers after leaving the nest for his first flight ... '[57]

But the book when it was published was dedicated instead 'To his Creditors', signifying the financial plight of the author. He went out of Edward's life for a while, reappearing in 1932 with a letter of 29 February in which he begins: 'I dare say you have thought me a particularly low fellow for quite a long time – but for me you have remained the finest man I ever met – together with being the kindest and most joy giving.' With Irish eloquence he said, 'I have been wanting to write to you ever since I wrote you last – but I love you very much and I feel you don't think much of me any more so I didn't. In any case, permit me to thank you once again for all you have done for me and for the joy your existence gives me – you are the one person in this dismal age of charlatans that makes literature appear a profession worthy of a gentleman ... Would you tell Miss Heath that I hope to have the honour of kissing her hand ... '[58]

Edward evidently replied, for O'Flaherty wrote again in March, explaining that he was now separated from Topsy and would probably divorce her and that he had vowed to cut himself off from everybody, 'especially women'. He had, he wrote, 'gone through a lot during the last few years so to speak, deliberately undergone a rather stupid cycle of experiences to arrive at a clearer consciousness of what I want to do ... ' This included writing a novel called *Skerrett* which he hoped Edward might look at for 'that would be wonderful as I have had hardly any intellectual relationship since I last saw you ... '[59]

But their old association was not resumed; Edward was at that time busy fostering the work of another Irish writer whom O'Flaherty himself had introduced to him. Sean O'Faolain had written on 15 August 1926: 'My friend Liam O'Flaherty has encouraged me to send you an example of two of my works, and as I wish for nothing more than criticism I am presuming on your patience to the extent of two short stories.'[60] Edward evidently replied favourably, for in 1928, after his return from Harvard University, O'Faolain was writing: 'Almost three years ago I sent you a story which I had just written – The Bomb Shop – and was pleased to get your words of approval ... Since then I have written some other tales of no great importance but one which I take the liberty of sending you thinking that it may please you ... Some day I hope to prove to others that your original criticism was well founded, for the moment it is between ourselves ... '[61]

The story was 'The Fugue'. It had appeared in the *Hound and Horn*, a Harvardian literary monthly popularly known as the 'Beagle and Bitch'. O'Faolain recalled that he sent the September 1928 number containing the story 'to Edward Garnett, the most remarkable and influential publisher's reader of his time in England, then working for Jonathan Cape. He wrote back those joyous words that every young writer dreams wildly of hearing some day from a reader of Garnett's calibre – "You are a writer". He also asked me to send him everything else I wrote and to call on him if ever I came to London.'[62]

He remembered the invitation when he came to England to take up a teaching post at Strawberry Hill, Richmond. The subsequent friendship was characterised by intermittent and stormy disagreements. 'Perhaps when I finish my story you could tell me if it is really good, as good or better than *The Fugue* that is,'[63] O'Faolain wrote on one occasion. The reply he received aroused his anger. 'Your reference to my negative nature gave me a jolt,' O'Faolain began. 'For a day I have debated how to explain to you. It pained me that you should be such a fool. You have talked like an University professor who thinks he knows everything. And though you know much more about men than an University professor you do not know everything. If that's all the help you can give a man on his way through a bitch of a world you should be content to shut up. Do you think you have helped any? If not what was the purpose of such an intrusion? You surely have heard that young men take themselves seriously when their egos are out of order? You will allow me to tell you to go to hell. Consider it said.'[64]

But their association survived such strains and his regard for

Edward's advice was accompanied by amused affection for his forthright opinions. He wondered whether Edward had ever considered the possibility of one day putting 'into one book all you have known about the eggs that hatched and the eggs that don't hatch. It would apart from its own vitally entrancing interest have a value for *us* (that the greater number of such books have *not*) – Your wisdom about the flowering, budding plant of talent and genius. The horticultural side of genius you must know more about than any man alive – or, in all probability dead either. *I wish you would do it.*' In his own case, he wrote, 'I cannot tell you how much it has helped knowing of your interest in me. Where nobody else is interested it is, in fact, priceless knowledge to me.'[65] When in difficulties with construction and technique he found Edward's guidance particularly helpful. 'I am so befuddled by my story', he began, 'that I am sending it unfinished to you to give me advice.' After explaining at length the approach he had made and his dissatisfaction with its construction he ended: 'But I have learnt that I have learnt a good deal and I feel in a few days I can begin again. I am sorry to disappoint you because I promised this story for now, and here I am *beginning* again ... We hope you are well and strong and that Miss Heath has recovered from her bout with 'flu. I didn't go to the Commercio Friday – you are my taskmaster and I haven't my lesson done!'[66]

In another letter he expressed an appreciation of Edward's judgment in terms reminiscent of Conrad: 'You don't know what it means to be able to say – I hope E.G. will like this, to have an audience before one's mind which is discriminating, ready to praise and blame with justice. You are a brick, a Godsend – and I leave it at that ... You are Cape's *soul*. And all the frigid "thoroughly enjoyed etceteras" of the usual reader are not worth a puff or a ram's horn beside one hearty "Good!" from you. I'll spare your blushes ... '[67]

Edward for his part expressed his conviction to Cape that O'Faolain was worth supporting. He wrote:

I think very highly of the quality of O'Faolain's work. *The Viking Press* is ready to subsidise him for two years à la Manhood to obtain the American rights of *Four stories* and a long novel which he has planned to write as his next book ... He is the most talented Irish writer in sight and much more *of an artist* than O'Flaherty. I am going to write a Foreword to the *Four stories* attacking the Irish for not backing their writers. The Viking Press will pay him 200£ for the next two years and I should think if Cape offered him about the same it would be a fair speculation.[68]

Sean O'Faolain, who hoped that he would be able to drop teaching and return to Ireland to devote himself wholly to writing, wrote to Edward on 27 July 1931: 'I am going to be disappointed if it proves impossible for Cape to imitate Huebsch's offer.'[69] Much depended on the success of the *Four Stories*, which were to be published under the title *Midsummer Night's Madness*. Edward contributed an introduction which, as he had promised Cape, he used as a polemic against the Irish who, he said, should be aware 'that a nation that takes so little interest in its own writers and leaves them dependent on English attention and English alms is culturally contemptible and not worth the snuff of a candle. I write this as an Anglo-Irishman and a London Publishers's adviser who has always taken an interest in Irish authors and Irish literature.'[70] He also took issue with Irish 'literary conservatism' and censorship practices and asked rhetorically: 'How ... can literature flourish in such a sterile, apathetic, rigid atmosphere?'

Sean O'Faolain, fearful that passages in the introduction might be detrimental to its public reception, wondered if some references could be toned down – 'although if any principle is sacrificed', he said he would prefer it to stand as it was.[71] *Midsummer Night's Madness* appeared at the end of 1932 and, like so many other books by talented Irishmen, was promptly banned in Ireland. It was, however, a literary success. As the enthusiastic reviews appeared, O'Faolain's wife said to Edward: 'But you have always said about the critics that they don't know a good book when they see it!' to which Edward replied: 'It was too damned good – even for *them*.'[72]

Differences of opinion between Edward and O'Faolain over the form and approach to his work began to emerge when O'Faolain embarked on his first novel. Its title, *A Nest of Simple Folk*, indicated the writer's model – he had already asked Edward if he knew of any book on Turgenev 'dealing with his techniques'.[73] Their opposing views were catalogued in a succession of letters in which O'Faolain was 'afraid now that you will be disappointed. Because I have not succeeded completely in doing what you advised and what I admit was shrewd judgment. I cut and cut as much as I dared . . . '[74] Posting the novel of about 100,000 words, he said he felt it contained some lovely passages but that his garrulousness had run away with it. He commanded Edward 'by all that you hold sacred to send this manuscript back to me with the most brutal instructions in return as to rewriting and excising and cutting and anything you like I shall humbly try to do so. I have worked so hard at it and I do want it to be as good as I can make it.'[75] On its return he thanked Edward 'a thousand times for your so careful reading and advice . . . I believe that you are perfectly right about the "rounded whole" and the city stuff being a bit anaemic.'[76] In revising the book their differences became apparent. O'Faolain felt a need to explain himself: 'Anything which is not logical and inevitable I hesitate to insert because this is such a real, simple, TRUTHFUL book. I don't think you quite realise how much so it is. It is very precious to me . . . I have finished with wild scenes in Midsummer Night Madness . . . This is a bloody great book . . . But you are quite right about country scenes deepening it and your excisions are nearly all most wise and right. Out they go. Heaven bless you.'[77]

Edward expressed exasperation at O'Faolain's work to T. E. Lawrence in the context of what he believed to be an Irish characteristic: 'They won't take enough pains *to be* artists . . . O'Faolain has just written a novel, "A Nest of Simple Folk" which starts off magnificently & then declines into a mere chronicle of family life in Limerick & Cork. It's unusual & real & has much quality but compared with what it ought to be & might have been it's a damned piece of Irish evasiveness.'[78] O'Faolain was now on a new road in his work and their views became more sharply divided on his next book. He sent the first 20,000 words with a warning note that 'it's utterly different from my plan, quiet and recollected'.[79] Edward's reaction was what he expected and O'Faolain argued:

> I was not surprised you thought it small beer . . . I feel it is a subjective novel and you don't like 'em. I also remember you

hate Pater. I can quite see your point. I go back to Hardy and see the old-fashioned way of telling a story and am full of admiration. Character, situation, suspense, invention of incident, all fine. But chacun à son gout. In a sense it is all that is false – fake – made up. In a sense it is true that all fiction is false and fake. You see each generation finds its own idea of what is true and real. Frankly I find it a little odd that you, most Catholic of critics, should dislike my 20,000 words because they are not the 20,000 words of somebody else ... But you are so wrong anyway in thinking I am repeating myself.

He would not, he explained at length, go back to 'the Midsummer Madness kind of high romance'. Unlike so many others, O'Faolain continued, such as 'Bates who will keep on saying the same thing all over again' and the 'sad example' of O'Flaherty, he wanted 'to say something utterly different in this book' and he was determined to 'say it in a different way'. But Edward, he found, wanted him 'to use the same naturalistic technique for some odd reason. Why should I? – My beloved Edward – I can only do what I can do. I am trying to experiment, I think, really, to see if I can do a new thing ... '[80]

Sean O'Faolain diagnosed his disagreement with Edward over the writing of *Bird Alone* as one which was due to Edward's passion for realism. 'He told me I was not realistic enough,' O'Faolain wrote, 'asked me did I actually know the originals ... and told me I was fantasticating my characters, which was true; told me I should see myself as the Balzac of Ireland (no less), and, to shorten many and heated arguments on his side, met obstinately and rather coldly on my side, he demanded that I rewrite the whole story on solid Balzacian lines or scrap it entirely. I refused to alter a line; he washed his hands of me; and we were both wrong.'[81]

Edward's view of this episode is given in reply to an enquiry from Huebsch who, waiting for the proofs of the book, was 'curious to have your comment, for O'Faolain intimated last Autumn that the book didn't suit you, although in a recent letter he said that you thought well of part of it – I forget whether he said the beginning or the end'.[82] Edward said bluntly:

I am very disappointed about O'Faolain's novel, I did my best to set him on another path last year & told him frankly that he seemed to be on a provincial track; and that he should open out either in a novel about the *Priesthood & Church in Ireland* or in a historical novel about *the Famine*. Indeed I had a great set to with him in Ireland about his going back to his early days – but it was of no use, & I was repulsed & metaphorically had to wash my hands of this book. The end, however is very fine. I don't despair that he *will* do something much better later – but you must decide according to your lights – & can't wait I know for the Millenium! for the Irish Millenium! The Irish are the most disappointing of races & individually are like eels & twist through your fingers. They are damned perverse ... '[83]

Though his admiration and fondness for Edward continued, Sean O'Faolain, like so many others, brought their literary relationship to an end. It was in keeping with an order of things which a letter from Galsworthy sought to explain in 1913. 'Let us hear of your doings my dear fellow,' he had written, 'and whether you are likely to be in London before long. I saw Conrad three weeks ago; we agreed that it was natural you should take no real interest in our productions nowadays, because of our beastly success. I don't say this in anything but admiration – if you were not like that Literature would have been a big loser.'[84] For Edward it was a natural consequence of his view that 'the early works of an author are ... much more interesting to study than the later, when he has crystallized his method'[85] and that there were always new writers to help. One of these, who stayed by his side for a long time, was an author whose first manuscript bore in its writing an evident emulation of Conrad.

SEVENTEEN

'Miss Bates'

EDWARD's associations with Conrad, Galsworthy and Lawrence were typical of his style as a literary adviser before the First World War. In later years his role changed almost imperceptibly in tone. He developed a more paternal relationship with authors, in which his advice became more magisterial and its recipients respected him for his knowledge, experience and reputation. His enthusiasm in launching an author remained undiminished. He never lost his pertinacity in bringing the manuscripts of a young writer to the notice of editors and publishers. Richard Church was one who commented: 'He was a kind man, especially to young authors. He had an uncanny gift for spotting promise in an immature beginner, and for knowing with which publisher to place that sapling.'[1]

What Edward had said to Conrad with 'the fervency of youth' he caught himself saying thirty years later 'with much the same accents and convictions'[2] to a young author. In essence 'it was the thing that one could do that mattered' and in its doing the author trod a path 'endlessly difficult'.[3] Authorship was to be measured by the individual manuscript and the words on the page, and to 'every package of manuscripts ... [he brought] an enthusiastic belief that in it there might be the seed of another genius'. Confident in his judgment, he informed a personal relationship with an author with 'a combination of critical insight, profound sympathy and infinite enthusiasm so great that it is not surprising that no one succeeds him today'.[4]

An understanding of the tribulations of creative writing, derived perhaps from his own 'unhappy experiences',[5] was combined with an acute perception of the literary capacity of the individual author. Liam O'Flaherty and Sean O'Faolain were only two of a number of young writers who began in the 1920s and received from him the familiar mixture of practical encouragement and literary advice. In the last analysis Edward recognised that authorship was a solitary task; as he sarcastically remarked to O'Faolain, writing was not done in the literary salons of London or Dublin.[6]

Jonathan Cape, late at night, surveying the mounting pile of manuscripts that testified to the success of the firm, exclaimed in a mood of exasperation that Garnett had also 'just discovered another bloody genius – Miss Bates'.[7] The mistake in gender, after the first letter he had received just before Christmas 1925, was corrected by H. E. Bates when he accepted an invitation to lunch with the Cape partners at the Étoile in Charlotte Street. Here he would also meet 'our reader', who wished to query passages in *The Two Sisters* which showed an intrusive Conradian influence. The reader came late to the lunch and his entry, to the youthful Bates, was dramatic. Into the restaurant came a

> semi-patriarchal figure in a floppy cloak-like overcoat, a grey scarf wound round his neck like a python, and a preposterously small felt hat. He had grey hair, grey jowl-like cheeks that quivered ponderously like the gills of an ancient turkey, and he appeared to have lost himself completely. He appeared also to be an extraordinarily clumsy person; he was something over six feet tall and big-boned in proportion ... His thick-lensed glasses gave him an appearance that was in that moment, and remained for me for a long time afterwards, quite frightening. He staggered about for some moments like a great bear unable to recall the steps of a dance he had just begun, and then hung up his coat, hat, scarf and walking stick on the hat stand. He then smoothed his hair with his hands, gave several painful snorts of breath through his mouth as if the whole procedure had winded him completely, and advanced towards us.

Bates concluded the hyperbole of this first meeting by his recollection that he 'stood up, hypnotised and terrified by this enormous and grizzly figure, and as I shook hands there was in the air a faint smell of herbal cigarettes and a weird glint of myopic eyes. "Mr Edward Garnett", someone said and I could have fainted.'[8] When Cape and his partners left them to return to Bedford Square, their conversation consisted mostly of queries from Edward and 'diffident answers' from Bates: 'How had *The Two Sisters* come to be written? Was it autobiographical? Had I written anything else?'[9] Edward warmed to Bates's admiration of authors whom he had himself acclaimed – Crane, Conrad, the Russian authors, Chekhov, Turgenev, Tolstoy. Before leaving for home Bates listened to the usual pessimistic Garnettian observations on critics and reviewers who 'don't know' and on parting promised to send Edward every single manuscript he had written.

The letter he wrote on the last day of the year was the first of many in which he was to ask for advice and express his gratitude to Edward. He wrote: 'I have made up a little batch of my work as you asked me to do. Most of the short stories I have written are included ... I really think I must do some sketches as you suggested. Whom do you recommend to read in order to get an idea of the type of thing! Tomlinson? Galsworthy? Could you lend me anything, if it is no trouble? Yesterday was a great pleasure to me. I'm afraid I very inadequately expressed my delight when saying good-bye ... '[10] Within twenty-four hours Bates had received a letter from Edward which not only criticised each story, but expertly allocated them to various editors for their consideration. 'I am sending "Once"', wrote Edward, "to Mr Middleton Murry and hope that he will take it for *The Adelphi*. It ought to please. It is beautifully rendered, the woman's absorption in the baby and the man's absorption in both, and the Bank holiday travel – all is beautifully felt ... "The Flame" shows that you have mastered this form of the short sketch ... "The Unbelievers" is a very good idea and has some excellent passages. But you must keep this back and wait till you can use it with more truth to life later on ... ' The letter ended with advice to 'go on reading Tchehov's stories and sketches. You can't have a finer modern master than him.' He added, with usual generosity, that he was posting a couple of volumes of Chekhov for him to read. Four days later, Bates recalled, 'Leonard Woolf, at Garnett's promptest instigation, had accepted *The Flame*.'[11]

Encouraged by its reception Bates wrote on 11 January, 'On your advice I have written 4 sketches in the manner of *The Flame* and in my own opinion they are about as good ... I wonder if you would care to read through them ... '[12] The critical commentary Edward gave them featured the two emphases that were to see-saw through their later correspondence – condemnation of Bates's facile abilities and the stringent requirements of quality. Two sketches, 'In View of the Fact that' and 'A Waddler', had certain 'individual strengths', while the others he found 'slightly cheap in tone'. He went on: 'I don't think that you should write from your *facile* side, but should try and develop what is distinctive of yourself and develop your own manner. None of these sketches you send have this *first-hand* feeling of "Once" and "A Flame" ... you must aim at quality ... '[13]

Edward put the dual nature of Bates as a writer more clearly when, delighted with a story he had just received, he wrote on 15 January: '"The Mother" *Very, very, good indeed.* This was what I was in search of from you, what I hoped and expected to find. There are evidently two selves in you – the one who observes nature intently and records her faithfully and directly, and the other Bates who can knock off imaginary scenes without emotional influence. One is the author of *The Two Sisters*. The other is the author of the "Pink Garter" ... Don't hesitate to send me any more sketches or poems you may write. But don't force the pace of writing. Take your time and think long over it if necessary.'[14] Bates admitted the justice of Edward's insight. 'I'm very glad you like *The Mother* so,' he wrote on 19 January, 'I feel it's some of my sincerest work and that makes it appeal to you. You are quite right – I must not hurry ... But when I do decent work, that is work like *The Mother*, I go very slowly. I think things out. *Once, Encore, The Flame* and things like that took me days and days, while *The Pink Garter* and *The Devil* took me about an hour or two hours each ... '[15]

Edward's concern for Bates, for the kind of writer he could be and for the recognition of his potential, led him to write a preface to *The Two Sisters*. As he said to Bates on 4 February: 'I think it will be best for the English edition to print this preface also, as I am more and more afraid that the *quality* of your work will be overlooked by the hasty reviewers. I shall put it tentatively and modestly and let's hope the reviewers will echo my judgment. They are "kittle-kattle": reviewers and new authors are always between the Scylla of contempt and Charybdis of neglect or patronage.'[16] In the preface Edward declared that *The Two Sisters* was 'a signal example of a rare species ... easy to be overlooked in the yearly cataract of fiction'. It was so because 'the realistic chronicle novel threatens to suffocate us by mere weight ... One sighs for the sparse line, the grace of outline, for the rare gift that extracts the essentials.' After drawing attention to examples of 'admirable, artistic economy', Edward concluded, perhaps prophetically, 'It is best to hazard no conjecture about the author's future work. There is the path of art endlessly difficult and the path of facile achievement and it depends on the youthful writer's star which he shall follow.'[17]

The discipline required to follow the austere dictates put forward in *The Two Sisters* was apparent in the close analysis which Edward made of 'Youth'. In a long letter taking Bates to task he wrote, 'I don't know if I am getting hypercritical but my criticism of *Youth* is that you have taken 14 pages to tell us things which ought to be done in 7 or 8. You are far too leisurely and long winded and repetitive in style here ... You ought to crush and condense your phrases, so as to give in a flash what you spread out in 8 or 10 lines ... ' After he had quoted offending phrases in the manuscript, Edward went on: 'This is tedious. You want to do it in two sentences of two or three lines each *sharp, crisp, concentrated, direct.*' In this story, he wrote, Bates had 'very little *original* substance but a great deal of *manner* and not your own manner.' Edward concluded that, '*Youth* reads like a rapid first draft and first drafts aren't good enough in general. The artistic effect is in the rough ... '[18]

More bluntly he sent a note to Bates on 16 June 1926: 'I don't like the sketch you sent me. I think it's far too facile and slick in its handling ... There's something mechanical in the execution, as though you had turned a handle and the tune flowed out to pattern i.e. without delicate individuality. You certainly can execute things like this very well, but it's this method you ought to avoid. However I take it that you recognise yourself it's of the inferior order.'[19]

Edward had exacting standards even for work which met with his approval for its insight. 'I like *The Fair day* very much', he wrote on 21 July 1926, ' ... but you will have to work at *expression* a great deal more than you're doing ... You've got to *visualise* and express the emotions by sharp *individual* details – as you do here and there. Think how Conrad and Crane would have made this situation sharp and tense ... Nearly everything I have marked is deplorably flat or roundabout in expression – no creative *images* or similes ... ' The letter continued in a like manner referring to the need for Bates to have 'a higher standard in *language* – in phrasing', to look at 'the telling detail' for 'as Tolstoy said "It's the tiny touches that matter in art" ... ' Edward finished his harangue with the estimate that at present 'in this story you're on the level of thousands of magazine writers – ordinary folk – who try to dodge all the artistic difficulties – and remain satisfied with mediocre effects and style ... ' He instructed Bates in a postscript: 'I've annotated the first 9 pages but I want you to consider carefully every paragraph and sentence and see where you can improve and make each touch living.'[20] Such critical commentary was difficult for a young writer to take in his stride, but as Edward insisted in a reply to Bates's evident disconsolation: 'I'm sorry if my last letter and criticism depressed you. It really comes to this – that when you have finished a sketch or story you should look at them again from the point of view of literary phraseology ... '[21]

Implicit in his fierce criticism, however, was a belief in the young writer and a concern for his development. When Bates transgressed the tenets of art in fiction, as he did in 'The Sinners', Edward took great pains in analysing the manuscript and directing the author to the base on which he must build to realise himself. 'I've read "The Sinners",' Edward wrote, 'I'm very glad that you sent it to me for it would harm you to publish it. It is full of psychological falsity. It's really like "a movie" – And from you! *No.*' He castigated the characterisation, concluding, 'everything from first to last is illegitimate and melodramatic. The end is *very* bad.' Though he thought the writing 'of course is good' and the 'emotional feeling and shades of the descriptions are well done', Edward said solemnly, 'but the story makes me anxious about you – *very* anxious, *truth* is first and last. And you have no inner truth to build on ... I fear for you because you are so impressionable that you can fly off the ground you tread on and go up like a balloon.' He thought it dreadful to think of Bates's work appearing in the *Royal Magazine* and advised him to 'remember what Turgenev's advice was to a writer. "You must be remorselessly true to your own sensations" ... put it away: lock it up and years later – not for years – rewrite it – when you *know* ... '[22]

To comfort an evidently contrite Bates, Edward told him: 'I shouldn't worry about the story. You haven't done anything so bad before and you won't do anything so bad again ... *You had nothing to build it on* ... ' and he recalled the example of O'Flaherty. He, Edward said, 'tried to write about London and his sketches were mediocre. He is sometimes a bit coarse or violent in his humorous sketches. "The Tent" itself started well and fizzled out in a fake. When I told him so he was very sulky and out of wounded pique insisted on putting it first! However we are good friends now.' Finally Edward assured Bates, 'I haven't lost any faith in you ... You have a most sensitive imagination and a very nice gift of seeing and exposing shades. Your *facility* is really your danger. But you have quite a good critical sense – *when you use it.*'[23]

It was the unique mixture of severe criticism and congratulatory passages in his letters that fostered a dialogue between them in the sure knowledge that Edward wished Bates to realise the work true to his talent. Commenting on 'The Baker's Wife' shortly after the abortive 'Sinners', Edward wrote: 'Yes *The Baker's Wife* is excellent, strong and vital, full of colour and movement – a very different thing from that first version which [although] real was meagre and thin and hard ... *If you can write like this you need have no fear for the future.* You see your imagination is rich and vital when you have a *definite foundation* to build on. You must always look about you and find that *groundwork* in nature or human nature ... You have quite a remarkable faculty when you start right and take trouble ... '[24] In his reply Bates was 'immensely indebted' to Edward and thought it 'an assuring sign that lately I get the *right* suspicions about my work'. Edward he thought had 'put his finger unerringly on all

the fallacies large and small. It's wonderful how you combine
the virtues of a microscope and a searchlight . . . '[25]

While he was writing his sketches, Bates was hard at work
during the spring and summer of 1927 on another book, *The
Voyagers*. When it was finished he sent it with misgivings to
Edward and received as he put it 'such a blast of fury . . . I mar-
vel that I survived'. The most disconcerting thing, Edward wrote,
was that he had written it 'in the facile, flowing, over-expres-
sive, half-faked style, gliding over difficulties . . . All that I've condemned in your *bad* sketches – the generalities, the vague cynicism,
the washy repetitions and the lack of firm outlines and exact
touches – You've written it, I repeat, in the bad Batesian facile
manner that you can turn on like a tap to cover up deficiencies . . . '
Edward proceeded to dissect the iniquities of the manuscript –
'written like a muffled echo of Conrad, with a lot of clichés'. Nevertheless, he said, 'Don't despair. You have a facile demon in you,
who gets hold of the reins, as well as the real artist who retreats
in the background' and ended his accusatory letter with the words,
'But remember, it's the essentials and artistic economy that
counts – as Turgenev wrote in *Fathers and Children* and as Tchehov
wrote in *The Party*. It should be a story *without* a superfluous
line – it's got to be *true, true, true*. Nothing but the truth . . . '[26]

Resilient before this critical onslaught, Bates continued with
his stories and sketches and received the compliments of Edward. 'I'm delighted', Edward wrote, 'that you returned home
relieved and soothed in spirit. Both *The Dove* and *The Voyage*, I
think are admirable . . . I feel always you have power to develop
much in that genre.'[27] Throughout the late summer and
autumn Edward vetted a succession of stories with inimitable
touches of correction and congratulation: 'The Peach Tree' was
charming but 'it would be stronger if you had worked at the
end more';[28] '*The White Mare* is good – you are getting in the
way of being roundabout, or repeating your phrases, of drawing
out your effects. It's your great danger . . . ';[29] '*The Schoolmistress*
came off quite well – It is sensitively felt – worthy of a pupil of
Tchehov';[30] 'The idea of *Forgiveness* is good and the end excellent
but the technique seems to me poor and clumsy. And the
psychology is *forced* for completion . . . I have marked the passages I think common and weak. You haven't yet gathered the
point of my advice – *quality, quality, quality* . . . '[31]

In preparation for a collection of short stories Edward advised Bates: 'I hope that you will not lose touch with "The Death of the Farmer". You ought to bend all your energies now to production, something *rare in quality* that can stand first in a volume of short stories.'[32] When the collection was published as *Day's End*, Bates sent a copy to Edward who replied: 'I'm really touched and delighted by your inscription in "Day's End". Well you might be proud of the book. There are most beautiful things in it whether the hurried and ignorant reviewers discover them or not – though I think they will. It is a notable volume, notable in its atmosphere, sincerity of feeling, literary craft, beauty of mood and sensitiveness. It is well worth all the labour you have spent on it and will remain as good for the next generation as for your own.'[33]

Edward also had encouraging remarks to make over the novel that Bates had begun, *Catherine Foster* – 'the style is just right, charming and natural . . . '[34] In March he was as complimentary but with reservations on technique: 'a little too much monotony gathering in the book'.[35] In July he made a detailed analysis of the first version in favourable terms: 'Both Miss Heath and I have read "Catherine Foster" and are pretty well agreed as to its strength and weaknesses . . . Looked at as a portrait of the girl's emotional nature the story holds one and the analysis of her feelings is depicted with great sensitiveness and charm . . . But there is a certain vagueness in the portrait and that arises from your having ignored the *practical* side . . . '[36] The final version received as detailed a treatment and both Nellie and Edward were agreed that Bates was 'essentially a poet not a novelist'. Within its 'very definite limits', Edward said, 'the story is an artistic piece of work' and he suggested that perhaps the only way to publish it would be by limited edition but 'I will discuss it with Cape tomorrow'.[37]

Bates in gratitude asked Edward if he could, 'if you haven't any objections', dedicate the novel to him – 'who have been literary father to me'.[38] Edward accepted this 'as a real proof of a continued confidence with one another'.[39] His letter to the bookseller John Wilson of 9 January 1929 illustrates his regard for Bates's work and his concern that it should receive proper recognition by the public. Edward wrote:

I wanted to ask your advice about the following matter. Our young friend Bates is bringing out a short novel 'Catherine Foster' with Cape and the question is: – should Cape issue, besides the ordinary edition, a small signed edition? I am very anxious, as you know that Bates' work should not be a frost and it is a matter of reaching a helping hand to *fine quality* against public indifference. I believe you rendered valuable aid to 'Day's End' and did what you could for it, and now perhaps you will look at the enclosed copy of 'Catherine Foster' and let me know if anything can be done in the way of an extra signed edition from your point of view. 'Catherine Foster' is a very fine thing in its peculiar way, between poetry and prose you may say. 'Day's End' made for itself a select audience of fervent admirers – but of course it was 'caviare to the general' ... How are you? ...[40]

In 1926 Edward had found the impecunious Bates a job with Bumpus, 'then housed in the old Marylebone Court house and presided over by that king of booksellers, John Wilson'.[41] Edward's kindness and the paternal interest which he showed in this arrangement are evident in his letter to Wilson in August of that year: 'I thank you most warmly for what you have done for Bates – encouraging him and selling his book and giving him a taste of London. It was generous of you – and the two or three weeks more will just fill up the cup of his craving for something new. Let me know later, what I shall owe you for his remuneration – for I cannot see that anything he can do at 350 can be more than ornamental ... '[42] In October he sent a note to Wilson saying, 'You might add on the enclosed amount 3£ to the 9£ you are now giving him. But of course this is merely between us ... '[43]

More directly Edward from the beginning of their acquaintance had generously accompanied his literary encouragement of Bates with loans over awkward periods. Soon after their first meeting, Edward had asked his typist 'to see if he can pick up a secondhand typewriting machine for you to use, I should like to make you a present of this – I think that you should learn to type – as you will have your novel later on, it will save trouble and expense'.[44]

At times he had to be diplomatic and guide the wayward Bates in a fatherly way. 'You had better write those extra passages for "The Peach Tree" as soon as possible – if Wilson is "to bite" you must make it as good as possible and forestall criticisms . . . You must improve your relations with Wilson. He thinks that you are ungrateful for his efforts on your behalf. I agree that he is Scotch over remuneration etc but he was under no obligation to do anything at all. And in other ways he behaved very sympathetically. You must *show* him that you appreciate his kindness.'[45]

As adviser to The Viking Press Edward recommended Bates to Huebsch but on one occasion had to smooth over misunderstandings between them. One such dispute developed over the story 'Alexander' which had delighted Edward. 'Yes,' he wrote on 26 July 1929. 'Very good indeed. Admirable in atmosphere. You have a fine succession of country pictures – real country sensations and emotions . . . It is about the best thing you've done . . . It seems to me *you've* mingled the method of Turgenev with Tchehov . . .'[46] Bates was delighted with Edward's reaction but wrote to say that Huebsch had taken offence and asked, 'What must I do. I really don't understand. Please advise me . . . I cannot get a reply from Huebsch about Alexander.'[47] Edward promptly wrote to Huebsch:

I take it that your problem is to sell the book and that Bates' first two books have lost you money. I may say here, however, that I have been agreeably surprised by the extremely good reviews 'Alexander' has received and that this means Bates has been definitely 'placed' as one of the young writers who are in the first flight. One never knows but there may be a public in a year or so, with an increasing taste for Bates' stories . . . 'Alexander' I regard as a perfect piece of work, a minor masterpiece . . . The Times Literary Supplement and The Manchester Guardian have both taken this view . . . It would be a pity, I think if 'Alexander' goes elsewhere than to The Viking Press . . .[48]

The kindness and affection continued between Bates and Edward now that the writer was established. Edward still persevered with his pointed remarks. *The Hessian Prisoner*, to which he contributed a preface, he thought during its writing 'too literary', its language 'too excessive and a bit clichéd',[49] and he made detailed suggestions to remedy the finished manuscript. Of another, 'Beaumont', he thought the beginning 'florid' and the story 'follows a worn route and isn't distinctive in any way' but 'as Mrs Garnett begged me to show it to her when it came I will take it to the Cearne and post it you on Monday.'[50] Bates acknowledged, 'It was obviously bad, as I saw as soon as my eyes had cleared. It has that terrible facility of mine which you so often instructed me to beware.'[51] Later he wrote to say, 'It's curious how you so often *divine* what I shall do. In reshaping *Alas! poor Beaumont* I had made both him and the girl do exactly as you say ... '[52]

Bates, however, often rebelled against such strong criticism and replied in exasperation apropos the novel he had started:

I am certainly not at all ready to throw up my wretched hands and say 'Mr. G. I can't, can't do it!' I am very much more ready to stand on my head and say 'I have *begun* to do it, and damn the world.' In fact I have begun. I did today a chapter in the 1st person – (but I feel somehow you don't *trust* me to do anything nowadays. You are ready to condemn a thing before it's begun) ... Do you believe in my ability to carry it off in this way! Don't please say it *will* be monotonous. Why should it be? ... Don't worry and think I have lost enthusiasm. Your letter spirited and affectionate and has warmed me magnificently, but if you once bully me, Oh! dear God we shall be nowhere. Believe in me, believe, believe. Tell me I *can* do it. I am full of these people – I only need you, the rock, the colonnade, the redeemer etc at my back and I shall win the lady ...[53]

They had argued over Bates as a novel writer. Edward wished Bates to sit down and begin it very soon but Bates had said, 'You know my conviction is (and Mrs Garnett above all shares it) that I am not a novelist at all but a short-story writer, and I'm inclined to think you share that view also ... You induced me first to write stories and I've always been happiest with them.'[54]

Bates had become a frequent visitor to The Cearne, which he

found enchanting for its situation and for the rapport he developed with Constance – to him a legendary figure for her Russian translations, especially of his idol Chekhov. This admiration was accompanied by an affection for the 'frail, white haired, short sighted' woman whose passion for flower gardening he shared. His regard for the range of her literary knowledge and the sureness of her judgment was such that if Constance, he wrote, 'was sometimes moved to praise a story of mine I was not merely greatly flattered; I always, unhesitatingly took it for gospel'.[55]

The Cearne influenced Bates to move to Kent, where he converted a granary. Much to Edward and Constance's consternation, they saw when they visited him that he was putting into it luxuries such as electric light and an indoor lavatory. The move also marked, as Bates recorded, the beginning of 'a decade of country novels, country stories and books of descriptive and discursive comments on country affairs'.[56] He still turned to Edward for his opinion when in doubt. 'Would you care to look at it', he wrote of the story which became 'A German Idyll', 'and tell me if I am right? I should be very grateful.'[57] In planning a new volume of his tales with 'The Black Boxer' as title story, he wondered if Edward would do what he could to influence Wren Howard to take on the book for Cape 'as you have seen and liked most of the stories'.[58]

His abiding respect for the critical perception of Edward and affection for him and Constance marked their correspondence over *The Fallow Land*. In his letter of 31 May 1932 he said, 'Your criticism of Jess's love affair is most apt, because the affair did originally strike a different note and I cut out the chapter – a pub scene and a quarrel between Jess and Alma, thinking they would upset the tone of the book ... ' After expressing delight that Edward had liked the book, Bates wrote: ' ... as for it being popular I don't care a damn, since Mrs. Garnett has also written saying she likes it a good deal.'[59] When it appeared he sent a copy with an inscription to Edward and said of it in a later letter:

As to my inscription there's nothing flattering about it: if I didn't pay some sort of tribute to you on the publication of every single one of my books I should be more than mean. It's due to you that *The Fallow Land* exists at all and this more than any other owes its existence to you. You must see that it's really that old, awful impossible novel of farm life, which you chopped to bits, come up again in a new form. I still remember how sick you made me feel then but not very sick, full of desire to get to the root of my troubles as a writer, which as you know were plenty and complicated at the time If you hadn't done that I couldn't have done *The Fallow Land* and the critics would have been still saying 'This kind of thing won't do at all Mr. B.' No. I have got a monument up to you inside me.[60]

An echo of Conrad can be heard in such a tribute and it was to be repeated in various forms by many of the new generation of writers who came to the Cape firm with their manuscripts and aspirations.

EIGHTEEN

New Generation

T HE range and quality of the books that Jonathan Cape were publishing gave the company a reputation which owed much to Edward's perception. As the years went by, however, this was not always fully recognised. Rupert Hart-Davis, one of the young men who came to the Cape firm and who, like others such as Hamish Hamilton and Hamish Miles, developed an affection for Edward and his often eccentric ways and definite opinions, thought that it was Edward's advice that had given the company its strong start, but as time passed both Jonathan Cape and 'Bob' Howard began to think it was their own doing. Hart-Davis remembered Edward's astonishing ability to read a whole lot of manuscripts and, without referring back to them, write up reports that were penetrating and crisp – and used the 'royal we', much to Cape's irritation. Another remarkable characteristic, he thought, was that Edward's enthusiasm and readiness to find new writing seemed to be unaffected by advancing years.[1]

Malcolm Elwin, who was to become a literary adviser himself to Macdonald in 1946, was of the opinion that Edward and Cape were rather guarded in each other's presence and Edward seemed freer in the company of younger members of the firm such as Hamish Miles. Nevertheless the trust that Cape put in Edward's judgment was shown in Elwin's own case, as he recalled:

I owed to Garnett my launching by Cape, who published my first book, *The Playgoer's Handbook to Restoration Drama* in 1928. I then wrote a biography of Congreve, never published because Peter Davies announced a biography of Congreve by Prof. J. Isaacs ... However, Garnett thought so well of my unpublished life of Congreve that, when I proposed to write a biography of Charles Reade, Jonathan Cape asked only that I should submit one specimen chapter, with a synopsis of the book before, on Garnett's recommendation, he gave me a contract, with £100 advance on account of royalties – a useful sum in those days on a book to be published at 12s 6d.

After the success of *Charles Reade* he received a contract for his *Thackeray* and subsequently, 'by Garnett's advice', Cape gave him an advance of £100 for *Victorian Wallflowers*. Elwin was grateful that the publisher's faith in Edward's judgment led Cape to pay him the advance, which helped with his living expenses while the book was being written.[2]

Liam O'Flaherty, Sean O'Faolain and H. E. Bates all benefited in this way from Edward's recommendations and at a time in their careers when there seemed little prospect of a return for such an investment. E. M. Forster made the comment that Edward's tastes in any case were non-commercial and with a trace of irony remarked, 'He sometimes recommended books that do not pay – or rather that do not pay at the time. Which is sad, but scarcely outside the tradition of English Literature: "Paradise Lost", it may be remembered, was anything but a business proposition.'[3]

In following his instinct, Edward not only persuaded Cape to support an author financially with an advance but he was also assiduous in involving others in the fortunes of the writer he was trying to promote. On behalf of H. A. Manhood, Edward enlisted the support of John Wilson as he had for Bates, writing to him on 17 July 1928: 'I want you to pay special attention to a book by a young author of whom I think highly ... It is *Nightseed* by H. A. Manhood ... The stories in "Nightseed" show a rare talent and from the publisher's and bookseller's point of view they should make many friends. They are very strong emotionally; are written with great originality and force and the writer handles words in a most striking manner. He is young and has the faults of youth but he is a new force to be reckoned with . . . '[4] He also used his old friendships to stimulate interest in authors he was encouraging. Galsworthy in reply to his letter said: 'I've only had time to read three of Manhood's stories, "Brotherhood", "The Cough" and "The Unbeliever", but I am mightily impressed. This is authentic talent – genius maybe. The stream of apt images is extraordinary. When I come back at the end of the month I shall read all and would like to meet the young man. He has a career before him – bad word, but will serve. Congratulations on discovering him.'[5] In a letter to Huebsch of The Viking Press, Edward admitted: 'I want Galsworthy to see if he cannot give Manhood a leg up, but Galsworthy is a cautious old bird . . . '[6]

Manhood, like others whose work he thought promising, received from Edward the usual mixture of practical generosity and advice. 'It was very, very handsome of you to send the wine,'[7] Manhood wrote on one occasion, and on another: 'Very many thanks for the loan – I will make good use of the money – it will make things easier for some time to come – give me time to lug something more from my reluctant brain – I will read and return Mark Rutherford soon.'[8] In his writing Manhood had none of Bates's fluency. When he began *Laughter in Pocket*, he wrote to Edward: 'The plan isn't yet apparent but you will be able to say whether it is commonsense stuff . . . I won't go further – I wait for your opinion of the little I send . . . '[9] A few days later on 7 March 1929, he said of it: 'Williamson tells me to write like hell – regardless of style or anything else – but I can't – it isn't my way – I write just as slowly, laboriously now as I did at the beginning – but I don't think he can quite understand that. His last letter put me out of gear for three days – I had to forget it before I could start again.'[10]

Henry Williamson figured in another letter to Edward when Manhood reported his progress:

Glad you've got confidence in me – I should very much like you to see a recent story or so, but the difficulty is that I am writing them (with half an eye to the future) in a most neat MS book – slowly filling it up – will you wait until it is filled?

I have seen Williamson ... [he] wanted to know the hows and whys – where my stuff comes from – origins – I couldn't satisfy him, of course, but it was good to talk a time – to hear him swear – I'm damned if I really know where some of my stuff *does* come from – more than that I manage to sweat it out, I cannot say – Do you think the Hawthornden has done Williamson any good? I'm hoping so. He is certainly unique ... [11]

Despite Edward's encouragement, Manhood's relationship with Cape was less successful than Williamson's for by 1935 he was writing: 'I have suggested to Cape's that they publish another collection of my stories and retain royalties up to the amount of my indebtedness to them under the expired contract ... They've agreed cheerfully enough and I imagine it will leave them freer and more open to discuss another contract when a long book turns up. Don't frown at me too sorrowfully for what must appear to be a misguided gesture for it pleases me to do it and I hope it pleases Cape's too to think that the bad egg wasn't so musty as they'd feared.'[12]

Henry Williamson on the other hand was one of the authors in whom Jonathan Cape took a particular interest. For seven years they exchanged a long intimate correspondence until, inexplicably to Cape who had published four of his books and expected their successful connection to continue, Williamson announced he was going to Faber with *Salar the Salmon* and wished to write another book for Putnam, his old publisher.[13]

Edward had 'captured' Williamson for Cape by following up a letter from Galsworthy, who asked him on 29 November 1926:

Do you know the work of Henry Williamson? It's uneven but at its best extraordinarily good I think. A strange and sensitive nature lover, and worshipper of Jefferies and Hudson. I wish you'd ask him to come and see you. I believe you'd like him, *The Old Stag* is his best book, but he's got one in Press on the life of an otter that he thinks best. He has had a hard struggle to screw enough out of a 'nature-less' public to keep himself, wife and child going. If you like it give him a word of encouragement. He can see and he can write ... [14]

When Edward wrote a letter to Williamson as 'a fly cast into a pool',[15] *Tarka the Otter* had already been sent to Putnam for £50 but, as Williamson remarked, he went 'to Cape with *The Pathway* through Garnett's recommendation'.[16] On holiday at Braunton near where Williamson lived, Edward looked over the manuscript and declared, 'You have brought it off, my dear fellow.'[17] The opinion was confirmed by the author who, when finishing the work, sent a note to Edward: '*Pathway* is now cut and filled out at end. I know it is perfection. If there's no chance of serialisation I want Cape to do it for September. It *is* a masterpiece!!'[18]

In 1927 Williamson was on the high tide of public recognition for he received the Hawthornden Prize that year. It was, as he recalled, presented by Galsworthy at the Aeolian Hall before an audience of a thousand people. Galsworthy's praise was such 'that 30,000 copies were ordered, after an extraordinary press, on the Cinderella theme. One's income was raised 20 times, from near poverty to unparalleled affluence. It was for a period unsettling. There was a fourth leader in the *Daily Telegraph* ... Galsworthy said "A work of tremendous imagination fortified by endless patience and observation" – he had just got the O.M. and his words carried weight.'[19]

In his long autobiographical fictional series *Chronicle of Ancient Sunlight*, Williamson depicted both Edward and Galsworthy in the volume *The Power of the Dead* which deals with this period. It is, perhaps surprisingly, both unflattering and unpleasant in tone. Galsworthy is pictured as the patronising Thomas Morland – 'world famous for his sequence of novels, generally supposed to be based upon the older generation of his family'. Edward is Edward Cornelian – an overbearing literary critic whom Philip Maddison (i.e. Williamson) arranges to meet at a restaurant, where he finds him with Morland. 'Cornelian with a loosening of already loose lips as he smiled at the creator of *The Crouchend Saga*' is pontificating: 'Well, my dear fellow, to sum up, we both agree that Evelyn Crouchend will have to die, but not the way you have *arranged* his death in your first draft.' Philip observes after Cornelian's meandering and parenthetical critical commentary that Thomas Morland suddenly looked tired – 'Morland reflected that Eddie Cornelian had set out, in youth, to be a creative writer, and had never brought it off.'[20]

Williamson uses a pastiche of incidents drawn from Edward's life, character and appearance to portray a self-opinionated boor. When Cornelian arrives 'with an elderly woman friend' to visit Philip he brings another young writer with him, Cabton, who 'in Mr Cornelian's presence gave out a feeling of being slightly superior to all he beheld ...'[21] The same Cabton is depicted in a conversation with Philip, in which after 'merely glancing' at the reports on Philip's early novels written by Edward Cornelian, he says: 'I shouldn't take any notice of what that old fool says. Why, just look at those veins in his legs, obviously signs of gout. I saw bottles and bottles of port in his cupboard when I went to his house in Chelsea, and he used my visit as an excuse to open one as soon as I was inside, although I told him I don't drink ... Anyway, what does he know about writing? He tried to tell me what to write. I told him I never know what I'm going to write. It just comes, once I get an idea. He's all literary, trying to fit in everything.'[22] Similar incidents portray Edward as a domineering, name-dropping critic, quick to take offence and nit-picking in his criticism of the construction of Philip's novel *The Phoenix*. Nevertheless when this was published and nearly all the critics were agreed on the book's weaknesses, Philip, the fictional Williamson, added: 'Edward Cornelian was right.'[23]

This fictional picture was at variance with that of his contemporaries; in the regard they expressed for Edward and in the quality they saw in him which his son David apostrophised, of being someone who was extremely sympathetic and easy to talk to about all personal matters.[24] This filial partiality is confirmed by others and covers a wide range of personalities. Henry Green, in recollection to David Garnett, wrote: 'I loved your father and saw really quite a lot of him. He often came to dinner, but as you say what one remembers most about him is his lying back in his chair, the spectacles up on his forehead and the rug over his knees. I owe far more to him than to anyone else. He had an attitude towards novels and how to write them, from which stems almost any original idea that I have gained, and one day when it would not seem like impertinence to do so I mean to state this publicly.'[25]

Henry Yorke, who used the pseudonym of Green, met Edward through the agency of Guy Pocock of Dent. Green had sent the manuscript of a book he had written to the firm and Pocock wrote to Edward to ask: 'We would be very grateful if you would have a look at a manuscript of a novel called Young and Old, which I am sending to you. It was sent me by a Fellow of Exeter, Oxford, on behalf of a young man of whose ability he thinks very highly indeed. He likes it better than I do; but I should be very glad to have a final opinion from you.'[26]

The youthful Green wrote to Edward on 24 November 1925: 'Mr Pocock has written to tell me that you would be so kind as to see me about my novel ... I should be very grateful if I could have the benefit of your advice, for I am not entirely clear in my own mind as to whether certain things I have done to it on Mr. Pocock's advice will do ... I'm afraid this is the most frightful bore for you, and I only write because it is a thing I can't afford to miss. Don't hesitate to put me off if you are busy as I am sure you are.'[27] This letter with its unassuming tailpiece brought an invitation to Pond Place and in his letter of acceptance Henry Green said of his book, 'It is so nice of you to like the stepmother. Someone said she was a fool, but I don't think she is quite that. Talking the book over with you will be the greatest help ... '[28]

It was at this first meeting that Green experienced what he remembered as Edward's unselfish capacity to help writers without arousing resentment; an ability accompanied by a close analysis of the text and suggestions for improvements in style and expression.[29] This process was evident in the particular problem of bringing *Blindness* (as the novel was now called) to a conclusion. From his home in Tewkesbury on 21 December 1925, Henry Green wrote:

If you remember you were so kind as to say that you would like to see the last chapter of my novel 'Blindness' rewritten after the talk we had about it ... Here it is ... To a certain extent I think that this version escapes the faults of the former one as it is more compact in that it takes place in a room and not, as previously in a walk around London, but somehow I feel that it is not convincing. On the other hand I don't know that I can improve it for the book has begun to nauseate me, and I can only think of the next, which I am sure will be much better. There is this, of course about the last chapter,

that for its position alone, the reader will wade through it
with added courage for he realises that he is in sight of the
end . . . but I wait for your opinion with anxiety . . . [30]

His anxiety was evidently allayed for his next letter thanks
Edward for returning the last chapter and relieving his mind
enormously: 'I was terrified lest you should say that it was all to
be done again. And I will certainly appeal to you if in difficulties
with the proofs . . . '[31] The last chapter was never, Henry Green
thought, resolved to his satisfaction.[32] *Blindness*, nevertheless,
was a remarkable achievement for someone only twenty-one
years of age. It already showed a mastery of manner, poetic and
linguistically original, with which he matched an allusive and
enigmatic treatment of human relationships. When he fell in
love in the late 1920s, he began a second novel called *Mood*,
with the girl he named Catherine Ightam as the central character. The difficulties which he encountered in writing it were
due, he has argued, to the fact that he was still too close to an
adolescence which for him 'was a time of deep depression
shadowed by terror of so much that was unknown, and deep
terror at that'. In his own words, 'As the surge of ideas slowed
down, I lost heart and several times went to see Mr. Garnett for
advice and comfort.'
    Henry Green thought that Edward had 'a genius for encour-
aging the young' and 'would also give up almost any amount of
time if he thought one was any good'. He remembered how
Edward had urged him on as he 'got stuck more and more with
it' and how, faced with Green's increasing hesitation, Edward
had said vehemently: 'Go on, go on and get it finished and then
we can knock the lot into shape afterwards. But you must finish
it first.' The novel *Mood* was never finished; its loss of impetus
Henry Green surmised coincided with the end of his love for the
central character who was the mainspring of the book. He
concurred, however, with Edward's exhortation, remarking
that: 'All I do know is that if Mr. Garnett in the event of my
finishing the book, still liked it then as the greatest book surgeon
of his day, he would have shown me how to cut it open, what to
remove, what to renew and how to sew everything up again
until it was a Novel.'[33]
    Soon after this abortive novel Henry Green began another,

which was to be christened with a characteristically cryptic present participle, *Living* (1929). In sharp contrast to the social milieu of *Blindness* its setting was a factory in the Midlands. Edward wrote to Green on 11 November 1927: 'I heard indirectly today that you are completing a second novel and in case this be so, I am writing to ask you to reserve the "American rights" till I've seen the MS or proofs . . . I am interested in your future as an author and what you may be doing, now or later on, so let me hear any news and give my salaams to your father when you see him.' In a postscript he referred to the first novel: 'Have your Aunts got over the shock of "Blindness" yet? I suppose they are very proud of it.'[34]

A letter dated 27 November indicates the origin of *Living* and Edward's concern that Green should realise his own potential without the pressures that publishers exerted for commercial ends – a constant theme in his relationships with writers:

> Oh, I didn't mean that your 'working class novel' wouldn't be popular. Skilfully presented & paragraphed 'The Moulders' by H.Y. may wreak a sensation unforeseen by you! You may be classed with the Rev. R. H. Shephard, Felix Holt, Vivian Grey, Rupert Brooke and Colonel Lawrence, by the reviewers, if Dent knows his business!
>
> I certainly wouldn't let Pocock hurry you. It depends absolutely on yourself & your own view of the Sketches, as to whether they should be printed. (Between ourselves the critical brains of the Dent firm are not of a prodigious weight.) If it's a question of *your* not being sure, ask the firm to send me the Sketches (when ready) and I will give my opinion. Publishers are always trying to fatten their literary fowls in egg laying competitions. Your second book should be good *enough*. And I expect it is.[35]

In a postscript he added, 'Let me know what you think of "The Ragged Trousered Philanthropists" later on.'

On 1 December, Edward comments on the various ideas they had discussed for future development:

> . . . Yes certainly count those 'Sketches' as one book – & if you get them back send them to me & I'll tell you whether you ought to publish them or not.

I think your novel after the Labour novel must be a *Family* novel – Call it 'The Family' – You've perfectly gorgeous material for it & don't forget the motif of selection of a worthy bride for the young hero who marries an outsider.

If you are not *too* intellectual in your factory ~~attitude~~ [*sic*] you ought to do A.1. work.[36]

This cautionary reminder underlies Edward's reaction to the manuscript of *Living* which he considered at length a year later in a letter of 26 November 1928. He appreciated Green's unorthodox approach and the reasoning behind one of his several attempts to depart from the structure and style of the traditional novel: 'Yes. *Living* is very clever. It gains on me, as one reads and the last third is best. At first I found the style difficult and a trifle affected. But one sees afterwards that you want to keep the tone and atmosphere free from the middle-class manner of writing.' He advised Green to help his readers come to terms with the difficulties which they might find in appreciating his style:

I think you should insert a few descriptive passages, early in the story, so that one may visualise the environment. You have so cleverly rendered the atmosphere of Liverpool that I think you wouldn't find it difficult to give us some snapshots of, say
a) the factory inside
b) „ „ outside
c) the Birmingham streets by day
d) ditto by night
These snapshots would help us to see the men in relation to their work. There is a 'snapshot' somewhere seen from Mr. Craigan's window. I find this both a relief and a help in reading. So perhaps you will look through the first half and see if you can't give us some more snapshots of this kind.

Turning from advice on technique he finished the letter with his usual generosity:

You have accomplished a feat in carrying 'Living' through and so far as it goes it's admirably true. Only just as there is more in upper class life than your 'interludes' express, so there is more in the working class life than the 'conversations' express. But so far as it stretches it's rigorous and exact.

Will you come round some evening for a talk. Would Friday 30th at nine suit you?

P.S. The last third – from the point where the old men are sacked – is damnably good and a fine piece of work.[37]

In his letter from 9 Mansfield Street, W1, accepting the invitation, Henry Green wrote: 'It is very good of you to go to all this trouble over "Living". It was a blow to me that you should think it clever, but at the same time that's a very just description. I'm not a bit satisfied with the book myself but am not sure there is much more to be done to it if I put in descriptions as you suggest. I'm afraid it would hang the whole thing up. However we can have all this out on Friday ... '[38]

Their discussion apparently turned on the probable use of the 'snapshots', but Green found after all that they had no place in his symbolic pattern of images. Edward scolded him in a letter dated 9 January 1929: ' ... I not only told Dutton to take "Living" – but I strongly pointed out that you hadn't written two or three descriptions of the Factory that you *more or less* had agreed to ! I suppose Dent is worrying you about it? I hope so – for a description or two will make all the difference to the comprehensibility of the general *mis-en-scene*.

'Dutton believes in your future! at least I told him that *I* did ... '[39]

Contemporary opinion of *Living* can be gauged by Green's letter to Edward: 'It was extremely kind of you to have written that appreciation of Living I have just seen in the Observer. It is about the first kind word said about it yet except in the Birmingham papers.' He went on to tell Edward of his forthcoming marriage to Dig Biddulph: 'I do hope you will approve, because of after all the manifold ways you have helped me up to now I should feel uneasy if you didn't.'[40]

In his reply, Edward began with mock anxiety at such news: 'I should have been appalled by your grave news had the lady been anybody else but Miss Dig Biddulph ... I felicitate you on the Choice and the Chosen ... ' He went on to discuss the reception given to *Living* and reiterated his opinion of the novel's structure: 'I saw that Gerald Gould was scandalised by "Living" and your little tricks with the definite article. Poor mutt! Well you are punished for not making it easier to start with by inserting those "descriptive" bits. It's your publisher's loss: not yours.'[41] Years later in a *Paris Review* interview Henry Green explained the omission of the definite article: 'I wanted to make the book as taut and spare as possible, to fit the proletarian life I was then leading. So I hit on leaving out the articles. I still think it effective, but would not do it again. It may now seem, I'm afraid, affected.'[42] Green's 'proletarian life' was a consequence of his decision to leave the cerebral and élitist climate of Oxford for work in the family firm, H. Pontifex and Sons manufacturers of bottling machinery and subsidiary products such as sanitary ware. It was this that provided the background for *Living*, for he chose to experience the life of the shop floor and 'lived in lodgings, worked a forty eight hour week first in stores, then in the iron foundry, in the brass foundry and finally as a coppersmith and wrote at night'.[43]

Another ten years were to pass before he published another novel, *Party Going* (1939), but Green and his wife continued their friendship with Edward. His regard for Edward's detection of literary talent he summed up in terms that echoed the 'bird haunted' imagery of his own novels – 'a remarkable ability to spot talent, like a retriever on a bird'.[44] With refreshing directness he commented sympathetically and tersely on Edward's relationship with his employer, observing that Cape was a 'shit' and only 'interested in the money – the bugger'.[45]

A more affectionate view of Jonathan Cape's sharpness is given by Eric Linklater, who described his first meeting with him. Linklater had scarcely finished his first drink 'before he [Cape] presented me with a newly drawn contract, pledging my next three novels to him, and – as he commanded a waiter to bring me more whisky – required me to sign it. I, in the innocence that still surrounded me – gladly obeyed; and not till years later did I realise the mistake I made. Jonathan was a horse-dealer, a cattle-trader, of whom I became oddly fond . . . '[46] But Linklater added that he 'gained much, however, by my unprofitable deal with Cape because it brought me the brief friendship of a very remarkable dedicated man, his literary adviser – that I think was his title – Edward Garnett.

Never have I known anyone more wholeheartedly convinced of the almost sacred importance of well-chosen, well-appointed words ... '47

Edward and Linklater had a long discussion over his *Juan* books. In his report on *Juan in America* Edward thought that 'the 400 odd pages describing Juan's experiences in America are on the whole very picturesque and amusing and though some of the more adventurous episodes are a trifle "tall" there is great inventive fertility shown and they are quite in keeping with what one expects from a modern "Don Juan".' However, Edward found that 'Book I drags too much and should be cut wherever possible' and 'that the American part might also be pruned a little here and there ... '48

Linklater was pleased with Edward's suggestions, writing that they were 'first rate and I've begun to act on them'. He had already 'cut 1600 words in various bits and pieces' and hoped to do more. He was also grateful for two other points which Edward had made – 'one the didactic spot you found, which I shall hurriedly and shamefacedly delete' and the other the 'meeting in the swamp' which was a second coincidence 'too much even in America'. He also noted Edward's encouraging remark that 'if Juan does fairly well in America he might be sent elsewhere'.49 Later Linklater recalled he had argued that the theme of seduction was obsolete 'when girls are as willing to go to bed as you are', but Edward had replied that 'the merit of *Juan* is that you wrote about America, not about seduction, and if you take him to Spain and Italy and Germany, you will write about them, and not about the commonplace – very much the same wherever you go – of tackling a girl on a Spanish, Italian, or German pillow. You've made a good start with a well-written, well-contrived set of adventures for a *picaro* of a sort who can go anywhere he chooses, and I think you should give him his head.'50

Edward's regard for Linklater is evident in his reply to Huebsch of The Viking Press who had enquired about his American rights: 'I know and like Eric Linklater. He is in Scotland, writing a novel on the Viking period in the British Isles. I expect it will have some fine stuff in it ... I will speak to Cape as I think Cape arranges L's American rights ... '51

Linklater for his part found Edward a constructive and sympathetic critic. Replying to his comments on *The Men of Ness*, he said, 'I'm afraid your voice may be a lonely one. I've tried the book out on one or two non-bookish people, who like it, but I doubt you will be alone among the learned. Your retention – in the midst of books – of a non-bookishness is a rare virtue. The weakness you mention – diffusion and anecdotism in the early chapter – I'm ready to admit ... But you're quite right. The first part might have been more smoothly done ... '[52]

A very dissimilar writer of a very different kind of book found in Edward the same capacity for understanding his work. Edward persuaded Cape to publish an immensely long novel by a writer in his mid-fifties. The author J. C. Powys wrote joyfully to his brother Littleton on 29 March 1929: 'The latest bulletin about *Wolf Solent* is very good. Namely a thrilling letter from the great Edward Garnett, the most authoritative of all English critics, and its acceptance by Jonathan Cape. The alterations suggested by Garnett were all "artistic" ones not "moral" ones. He says that "after the first shock" the book will be accepted ... '[53]

The letter which Powys had written in reply to Edward's initial response to the manuscript reflects the incisive nature of Edward's criticism and his understanding of a 'difficult' work in advance of public appreciation. It began:

> I don't think I need tell you how grateful I was to receive your most kind and penetrating criticism of 'Wolf Solent'. Your words of praise did my heart good; and now – ever since your letter reached me – I have been working hard at the proofs, cutting and condensing here and there in accordance with your acute suggestions. I have done something along the lines you indicated, to each of the pages especially noted, by you for the revision and in several other places. I have made cuts and changes following your hints, in particular, reduced in length several of the passages where Wolf's 'mythology' seemed to bulk too large and I have made the 'revelations' in Chapter IX clearer for the reader's benefit.

Powys went into more detail over the alterations he had made to the text and characterisation – 'propping Wolf himself up a bit here and there; where as you say, the reader might get that undesirable sense of "superiority". I've tried to give him the necessary shocks of humiliation without letting him lose too much of his dignity and stoicism.'[54] Edward thought the book 'not far from a great novel'[55] and expressed this conviction in a note he composed for publication purposes: '*Wolf Solent* challenges comparison with Thomas Hardy's great novels. The book is steeped in the human emanations of generations of Dorset country folk.'[56] When he sent a copy of this note to Powys in New York, he complimented him: 'It *is* a feat, you know that you have accomplished, an astonishingly fine feat, and how deeply saturated your being must be in Dorsetshire essences, spiritual and physical that you could conjure up such a mirage as *Wolf Solent* from memory. I can't imagine how you could have preserved this birthright so pure in this alien atmosphere of New York City.'[57]

In a very long letter in reply Powys gave an account of his attitude and feelings about writing and novels which is interesting for its self-revelation and for the indications of Edward's understanding. The publicity comments which Edward had forwarded had 'worked their magic' and the favourable review

> would turn my head if I were not 56 years old! I *am* so grateful to you ... Where therefore – as you cunningly discovered my book tends to ramble, is where this secret self indulgence becomes too much of a pure sensation. The truth is I am weak in the architectonics of a novel just because novel writing to me is a kind of half serious half mystical indulgence like the stories you tell yourself towards the end of a lonely walk when *your* body and brain *are* tired and your imagination has been liberated from all the little teasing things and starts vaguely rambling through the orchards and terraces of dreamy castles in the air! Your criticisms were an immeasurable help to me just because of this weakness and my tendency to drug myself with these semi-pantheistic sensations, and I can see that these conversations *have* made the book a better work of art.

He launched into a dissertation on his pleasure in Dostoevsky: 'Frankly I think I prefer *very* long books with flashes of inspirations here and there to rounded-off works of art – but you will say of course that many of my favourite long books *are* works of art and with more architectonics.' One of the influences on his work which 'not a single critic mentioned', he wrote, was that of Sir Walter Scott, which 'betrays itself on page after page'. In conclusion, apologising for the length of the letter, he remarked, 'You must remember that for 20 years I've earned my living as a lecturer; and have never before had a chance of lecturing on my own work to the best and I'm sure the kindest of English critics.'[58]

It was kindness intermingled with a fearsome charm that endeared Edward to women writers. Mollie Skinner remembered:

> He told me with a roar, that I was so damn damn bad in my work; and, with an angelic smile, so damn good, that he couldn't bear it. He found it hard to believe that so unsophisticated a person had written about three-fourths of the book in question. I marked, at his suggestion, Lawrence's part of *The Boy in the Bush*. And even more he was surprised that 'David' had collaborated with a simplicitas who wept and had to have her tears wiped away with his own handkerchief. He told me to go home and write the best book an Australian has yet achieved. That lion of literature – how I disappointed him.[59]

She wrote to him on 4 November 1924 of the book in question, *The Black Swans*: 'Just to let you know I find your criticism priceless. That the MS is nearly done. That I am dying to return to sunshine and West Australia. That I do nothing else, but tackle this dreadful revision. That I am pleased with it. And to thank you for your excellent advice.'[60] Writing shortly before her departure she recalled their meeting: ' . . . you have been so amazingly understanding, and what is more bothered to make me better. There is no one like you in the world I think. And how you must have disliked it, to be sure, when I began to cry . . . But what I am trying to say is *thank you* and may Cape put on the front-leaf dedicated to you?'[61]

Naomi Mitchison had a similar affection for the person behind the formidable façade and wrote of their meetings when Cape accepted her first book: 'I was 22 and dead scared and wildly excited. I bought a new hat, I remember it plainly, a cloche hat made of little bits of leather sewn together. When I got to the office I think they were surprised that I was such a kid – probably my hair was coming down. Then Garnett asked me if I was Irish, I said no, I was Scots and he smiled at me and said all sorts of nice things, and I left feeling wonderful ... '[62] She put her feelings of this occasion into a poem, which ends:

> And Mr. Garnett terrifying and charming,
> And Mr. Cape ever so polite –
> Only he must have seen
> How I was just dancing out of myself with sheer pleasure![63]

Naomi Mitchison was a great party-giver and Edward, forgetful of his possessions at the best of times, found these gatherings 'so delightful and your guests so brilliant that like a child, I leave my wits and belongings behind me'.[64] Of her work he made direct and encouraging criticisms usually with an eye to the probable reaction of Jonathan Cape, whom Naomi Mitchison 'couldn't bear'.[65] The publisher found the frankness of her novels hard to accept and Edward had to act as a mediator. 'I quite understand your feeling,' he wrote to Naomi Mitchison on 27 August 1925, 'but really I shouldn't worry over the alteration of two or three words. Mr. Cape showed me the passage and asked my advice and I suggested this slight alteration. A great many people are not in our happy position of taking sexual facts simply and naturally and they might raise an outcry which would be annoying. It is impossible for me to pose as arbitrator. I think the passage beautiful myself – but I don't think a little cutting or two or three changes of words would affect its beauty.' He also, he said, liked the story immensely, for 'It is so real *and* imaginative and full of life ... it's the best thing you have done.'[66]

Edward found it more difficult to persuade Cape to accept some of Naomi Mitchison's later books in their entirety. In 1928 he wrote: 'I stuck up for "the bloody tarts" ... but Cape is a Puritan and he said it would cost you and him a couple of hundred readers!! In future you should take a stronger line and tell him that you insist on the inclusion of a piece. Don't bow your neck down in the House of Mammon.'[67] The question arose

again the following year and Edward in this instance told her:
'If Cape worries you about changing passages in "Barbarian
stories" I should simply refuse – except in the matter of two
or three isolated words. I am suspected of being on the side of
License against the Law and Commerce and so I have no
influence to help you, but only to harm you by espousing your
side. I simply advise you to stick to your guns.' The postscript
of the letter indicated why: 'Miss James has been squashed flat
so far by Jix ... '⁶⁸

Norah James, on the staff of Cape, had written a book entitled
Sleeveless Errand, which presented a 'brazen picture of dissolute
Bohemians in London', and it was said that 'a lady of great
political importance who considered herself maligned by the
book used her subterranean influence to have the book
banned'.⁶⁹ But this was the period of 'Jix', the name given by
newspaper columnists to William Joynson-Hicks who was
Home Secretary from 1924 to 1929. He had strong religious
convictions and was a member of the Church Assembly and
President of the Church League in 1921. His period of office was
marked by increased official action against authors and publishers of material alleged to contain obscene libel, such as *The Well
of Loneliness* and *Lady Chatterley's Lover*.

Edward had called on Eric Partridge, who was then running
the Scholartis Press, to ask whether he would care to consider
Sleeveless Errand. Partridge remembered that 'E.G. told me that
Cape didn't want to publish it, for purely domestic reasons; but
he did strongly recommend it. In half an hours talk, he impressed me as a kindly "father figure" and very intelligent, as
one would have surmised. One readily understood why he was
so widely and highly respected.' Partridge published the book
and 'thus contrived for myself a lot of trouble – the book was
banned'.⁷⁰ It was seized by the police and found to be obscene
by a magistrate at Bow Street.

With characteristic promptness Edward marshalled support
against this censorship. He tried to enlist Galsworthy's help, but
Galsworthy replied that he was 'not moved enough to stir in the
matter. I told you it would take a book that got me plumb
centre to make me butt into this State controversy again ... I
admit it has points and passages; but my gosh, if she's skilled in
literary matters she deserves a lesson in thinking she could jam

all that language down the British throat ... The implication is
that a whole decade of women is ungeared. Don't believe it.
Let's meet again soon ... '71 The book, however, was taken up
in another quarter. Jack Kahane, reading the Continental *Daily
Mail* under the trees in his garden in France, saw that a book
published by Eric Partridge, whom he knew slightly, had been
seized by the London police:

> It was by a writer unknown to me, called Norah James, and
> according to the newspaper, it had been recommended to
> Partridge by Edward Garnett. I knew the flawlessness of
> Garnett's discrimination, so I went into the house and, pick-
> ing up the telephone, asked for London ... In little more
> than a month after that decisive conversation the book was
> printed and published and selling like mitigated wildfire at a
> hundred francs a copy ... What passed my comprehension
> was why it had been banned with such terrifying repression.[72]

From this first book an 'exciting and potentially lucrative vocation had emerged'. If, as the law stood, it was illegal to publish
books like *Sleeveless Errand* in England it was not so in France
and Kahane decided to set up a private press.[73] Accordingly he
announced that he was prepared to publish in Paris any
book of literary merit which had been banned in England.

He also wrote to Edward to say that the firm Barbou &
Kahane were anxious that he should do a brief preface to
Sleeveless Errand. Edward agreed and wrote: 'The censoring and
suppression of *Sleeveless Errand* ... is a perfect example of official
blundering. It adds the last link to the chain of the follies
of censorship, which works inevitably to suppress the wrong
books ... ' He commented on the inconsistencies of censorship
whereby *Sleeveless Errand* could be banned while *Fiesta* by Ernest
Hemingway, which dealt in the same way with a similar set of
characters, was not accused of obscenity. He defended the book
against the charge of 'verbal obscenities' and ended his preface
with a sarcastic reference to the taste and hypocrisy of the
reading public: 'How British! in its mixture of moral righteous-
ness and official Pecksniffery.'[74]

As he grew older, however, Edward's impulsiveness gave
way, his son thought, to greater caution and this together with

the climate of the times in book publishing led to a quarrel with Naomi Mitchison over her work. He was very well disposed to her long novel *The Corn King*, writing: 'I've read three parts and after a whole day's solid reading I've had to put the MS aside for a bit. I congratulate you. It's frightfully interesting and audacious and full of human life and high spirits ... Of course its strength is that it is a large hearted feminine view of life – only wise and understanding as well as most womanly.'[75] But when she tackled her first 'modern novel', *We Have Been Warned*, she met resistance not only from Jonathan Cape but also from Edward. As she recalled: 'It is extraordinary now to think how they blenched at what would nowadays be taken very easily. I was prepared to compromise over the words – fuck, bugger and so on, all very mild as they go – but I wasn't going to have all the cuts and re-writing that were demanded of me. So that was that.' The novel was derived from her visit to Russia in 1932 and included 'a seduction, a rape, much intimate marital chat, an abortion scene in the Soviet Union and so on'.[76]

Edward did not like the book, criticising the manuscript in detail for its superfluous passages, its 'smeary, jam-like symbolistic literary stuff' and characterisation which he said was unrealistic, with dialogue 'so thin you could put your finger through the performers'. But the real issue was Naomi Mitchison's outspoken description of contraceptives and sexual episodes. As well as heavily annotating the manuscript with 'cut' and 'tighten up' he referred in a long letter to a passage where, as he put it:

> I don't think this is *possible*. I mean Dione taking off her clothes etc out of that benevolent 'class-equality' motive. *If* she did this she is suffering herself from a complex of sexual obsessions plus Equalitarian Idealism – but you don't diagnose or criticise Dione's case. You seem to regard her action quite natural in the circumstances! I suggest that you re-write this passage – v. simply to make Idris Pritchard try to rape Dione – & then you get rid of the 'rubber' business which I also think is impossible. And I'm not generally squeamish ... [77]

In reply Naomi wrote that 'I'm sorry you don't like the book, but I am afraid it's inevitable. I'll consider your criticisms, but in general I'm afraid I can't accept them. You see, I'm more sure about this book than I've ever been about any of the other books.' She defended the 'rubber business' by explaining that it *'had to be made clear'* that this character was using a 'perfectly efficient contraceptive' and ended her letter with an expression of appreciation for Edward's help but saying that she now had to seek independence: 'But a lot of what you don't like is stuff that I've worked over a lot, read aloud and so on; I know it's not what it ought to be on a lot of grounds, but I *must* finally go my own way. I'm awfully sorry because, as you know, I've taken your criticism before and always believed in it. You are my literary godfather. But I've got to do this on my own. After all, I'm 36, and I must be able to judge for myself.'[78] Looking back at this dispute years afterwards she remembered they had 'quarrelled bitterly ... but [I] had hoped he realised that this wasn't forever – but then he died ... and I still feel badly about it.'[79]

In a letter to Wren Howard at the time of the quarrel Naomi Mitchison had said, 'I take it I shall not be able to write the kind of modern novel, which will strike Edward Garnett as being true to life, such as he knows it ... '[80] Edward had also failed to appreciate the 'modern' approach to the novel in a manuscript which he received on 13 August 1933, entitled *Dream of Fair to Middling Women*. It was by the friend and disciple of James Joyce, Samuel Beckett. Of it Edward reported to Cape: 'I wouldn't touch this with a barge pole. Beckett probably is a clever fellow, but here he has elaborated a slavish, and rather incoherent imitation of Joyce, most eccentric in language and full of disgustingly affected passages – also *indecent*. This school is damned – and you wouldn't sell the book on its title.'[81] Though he developed an admiration for some of Joyce's stories, particularly 'The Dead' which he recommended to young authors to read, he was fundamentally out of sympathy with a style which he dismissed as 'brain-spun'.[82]

In his long experience as reader and critic Edward had seen fashions in literature come and go; he had also kept true to an approach to literature which Middleton Murry in his review of Edward's *Friday Nights*, a collection of critical essays published in 1922, had discerned as one which had as its bedrock the concept of 'veracity' – 'that tense and sinewy word, so much

more rocky and angular than the soft syllable "truth" ... '
Nevertheless, Murry contended, 'he had never conceived it his
mission to say the final word' for Edward had written, 'the
academic critic gathers the honours of the last word ... the task
of marshalling those writers who, by virtue of their qualities,
have survived the censure of the academic critics of their own
day.' A 'beautifully barbed' comment, Murry observed; rather,
he wrote, 'Mr Garnett ... has found his duty elsewhere. It is to
secure a hearing for a Conrad, a Doughty, a W. H. Hudson, a
D. H. Lawrence, to name four of the foremost figures of contemporary English Literature who might still be among the hind-
most but for his exertions.'[83] It was with writers such as these
that Edward resumed his acquaintance while working for Cape.

NINETEEN

Familiar Faces

Busy with a new generation of authors, Edward remembered with affection those of the old. When Hudson died in 1922 he wrote to his friend Cunninghame Graham: 'How wonderfully he wears in his books and in our hearts. I have never been so captured wholly by any man or writer as by Hudson. He had so much frustration, so many difficulties and work in his life, but remained always so strong and gallant in spirit. He was an old eagle with a giant heart.'[1] He congratulated Graham on his diplomatic efforts in persuading the Buenos Aires Committee to do something about a Hudson memorial, and when Hudson's birthplace was declared a national monument, he commented sardonically: 'I suppose someday English people will *read* "El Ombu" but have you noticed that nobody but you and I (and Conrad in a measure) have ever acclaimed it. (We are a herring-gutted race where literature is concerned).'[2]

When Dent asked Conrad for an 'authoritative' paper on Hudson he referred them to Edward as 'the person eminently fitted to write an authoritative article'. He was, Conrad said, 'Hudson's friend for more than twenty years, one of his earliest appreciators long before the public, or for that matter the publishers, recognised the high quality of Hudson's work which he did his utmost to make known to the world. I do not suppose there is another man who has such a profound knowledge of Hudson's work as Edward Garnett.'[3]

Conrad himself was soon to follow Hudson. Cunninghame

Graham wrote to Edward on 13 August 1924: 'It was a sad day at Canterbury. Though poor Conrad was often ill I've always thought he would hang on long, like the proverbial creaking door. He was a great and striking figure, and we shall not see his like again ... genius is a positive handicap in England. I wonder where Jessie will settle ... '[4] Though Edward and Conrad had seen less of each other in later years their mutual friendship and confidence continued in infrequent correspondence and visits. When a de luxe edition of his works was prepared in 1922, Conrad reserved six sets for himself and one of these, which had appreciated to double its price by the publication date, he sent to Edward. One set he kept; the others went to his sons Borys and John, and to Gide and Sir Robert Jones – 'none to Polish relatives or to Graham, Galsworthy, the Colvins, nor to the newer friends such as Jean-Aubry and Walpole'.[5]

It was a gesture eloquent of the regard which he expressed in a letter to Edward in August 1923, shortly before he died. He wrote:

My dear, in your feelings, in your judgments, your enthusiasms and criticisms, in all your fine reactions to that 'best' which not every eye can see, you have been beautifully consistent, both in your subtle and your peremptory moods. It is thirty years now (almost to the day) since I came ashore for good. And the very next year our friendship began! Straight from the sea into your arms, as it were. How much you have done to pull me together intellectually only the Gods that brought us together know. For I myself don't. All I had in my hand was some little creative gift – but not even one single piece of 'cultural' luggage. I am proud after all these years to have understood you from the first.[6]

Edward continued to champion Conrad, convinced that his reputation suffered from misunderstanding and lack of true appreciation. Nevertheless he was not blind to faults which he put into his criticism. Reviewing *Tales of Hearsay* in the *Nation* in 1925 he observed that 'it was Conrad's peculiar strength to establish the relationship between remorseless fact and moral judgment', but at times he 'weakened his art by passages of rhetorical emphasis'.[7] His advocacy of Conrad, however, led

Gerald Gould to question his objectivity, taking him to task in an article entitled, expressively, 'The Danger of Idols' in the *Saturday Review of Literature* in 1925. Edward had, Gould wrote, 'set up an idol in his mind. He has confused the fallible genius of artists such as Conrad or Turgenev with the august infallibility of art itself. He has assumed that to find fault with Conrad is to do wrong to art.' This attack upon someone whom, Gould admitted, 'has done so much for English letters that his lightest, idlest word must be listened to with respect'[8] was occasioned by Edward's criticism of P. C. Kennedy, who had reviewed Conrad's unfinished novel in the *New Statesman*. Kennedy had written: 'I am frankly convinced that if "Suspense" had been the work of an unknown man, it would not have suggested to most people that it was by an author of genius at all ... "Suspense" does not come to life at all.'[9] Edward refuted Gould's comment, pointed to his own severe criticism in manuscript of the first chapter of *Suspense* and answered, 'Why should I deny Mr. P. C. Kennedy or anybody else the right to criticise Conrad's work when I exercised that right myself publicly and privately for thirty years.' He had derided Kennedy's review because it showed 'great insensibility to the artistic qualities of *Suspense*'.[10]

He also took the opportunity to set the record straight when reviewing in the *Weekly Westminster* of 14 February 1925 *Reminiscences of Joseph Conrad* by Ford Madox Ford. 'It is just what I expected from Mr Ford,' Edward wrote, 'and it is also what Conrad would have expected – something between romance and record, fact and fable – an *olla podrida* of memory and imagination – Anything more unlike the style of his conversation than the nebulous, sensational, highly coloured anecdotes, retailed by Mr Ford as droppings from Conrad's lips cannot be imagined.' Nevertheless in tribute to Ford's evocative skill he went on to say, 'At the same time, I can affirm that there is a good deal of true insight and clever description and of genuine atmosphere ... '[11] In a more severe review in the *Nation* he had enlarged on this skill, while at the same time pointedly revealing that quality of Ford's which had caused his friends to query his integrity: 'In the magic name of "impressionism" a man can magnify, distort, or suppress facts and aspects to his own glorification – and then, on being brought to book, he can turn round reprovingly and protest, "But this is a work of art!"'[12] To his sister Olive, who had written to him about this matter, Edward commented: 'I find your remarks on that period very interesting. I wish you would send me a list of what you think are Ford's mis-statements in the book ... You see you never know where you are with Ford ... I used to come down on his gorgeous embroideries in the early days – with the result that he shunned me, and as he never could stand criticism our relations practically ceased before the war.'[13]

Nevertheless in his review Edward thought the book 'quite a clever production ... [it] hits off in a lifelike way many of Conrad's personal ways and mannerisms'. He had to correct quite a few errors, however, one of which was Ford's claim that Conrad was satisfied with their collaboration. The evidence disputing this lay in a letter which Conrad had written to Edward on 26 March 1900.[14] When Edward reproduced this letter in his edition of *Letters from Conrad* it provoked an annoyed reaction from Ford. 'I certainly think that you ought not to have printed this letter which Conrad himself asked you to destroy,' Ford wrote in a long letter to Edward on 5 May 1928. More in sorrow than in anger, Ford intimated, he took exception to its appearance: 'I do ask you to see that the publication of such a letter about myself much discredits the memory of that unfortunate man. At that time he was living in my house and I was letting my own family go short in order to keep him and I was giving my whole time to giving him moral support and to putting his affairs in order – and to writing his books ... and if I resent, as I do with a good deal of sadness, your printing this letter it is entirely for the sake of Conrad and not in the least for my own sake.'

Ford conjured up a picture in his letter of an unselfish concern for Conrad, who despite rumours circulated about 'my relationship with women ... never broke with me, or I with him'. He also had no resentment for the abuse in the reviews by Edward and Galsworthy of his book, for 'As far as I am concerned you and Galsworthy were the only two real intimates of Conrad's that were really of any good to him and because of that whatever you may have done I shall always regard you and speak of you with affection ... both, I mean.' However, Ford went on: 'Conrad told me shortly before his death that you had "got your knife terribly into me" about something I had said or done to you. But my conscience with regard to you is so clean that I have never troubled to investigate the matter. I can only say that I have always felt and expressed the greatest admiration for your achievement and that the feeling is and will be unalterable.' In depicting at length the rapacious market in Conrad memorabilia in New York, Ford piously did not criticise Edward for selling some items, although he asserted: 'For myself I have never sold and never will sell anything of Conrad's, though I have had a great many things stolen.' He had taken steps to ensure that his own letters from Conrad would be burnt and suggested to Edward that he should do the same with the offending letter as a 'beau geste ... for the sake of our generation'.

After references to his own great affection and close ties with Conrad, and to Jessie's abuse of him in public yet requests to him in private regarding Conrad's estate, Ford's letter ended with: 'The reason why I write to you is that we are both of us getting on and I should like one human soul to know something of these matters ... As Conrad said in one of his later letters to me: "Unlike the Serpent which is Wise, you are unchanging". And I think I am and I think you are too, and as we never did agree about anything in literature I see no possibility of our now doing so so there would be little use in our meeting even if you don't cherish the fell serpent's hatred that Conrad said you did for me ... '[15]

Whatever their differences and however much Edward and Ford disagreed over Ford's association with Conrad, it was Jessie Conrad's book on her husband which aroused Edward's anger. It was a book which he thought calculated to damage Conrad's reputation at a time when younger critics were tending to disparage it. When he reviewed *Joseph Conrad and His Circle* in the *London Mercury*, he took pains to make clear the predicament of Conrad as a writer. 'Conrad', he wrote, 'carried a heavy load – gouty constitution, highly neurotic, nervously shattered by blackwater fever, harassed by family demands, constantly struggling with the necessity of producing fresh books of the highest literary merit, of satisfying his own artistic standards ... '[16] The letter which Edward wrote to Jessie Conrad warning her of what he had written in this review reflects

Edward's fierce devotion to Conrad's reputation *and* his opinion of Jessie. It is worth full quotation:

Dear Jessie,

You will see what I think of 'Joseph Conrad & His Circle' by the review that will appear in the August No. of The London Mercury.

I think it is the most detestable book ever written by a wife about her husband. You have exposed Conrad & yourself to ridicule by your petty vindictiveness & treasuring up of all the incidents of his bad temper & outbursts which you suffered in his lifetime; & the complacency & conceit with which you show yourself always superior to him are both amusing & painful.

You have burst [?] up for good & all your claim of loyalty to him. Nobody will believe it in future, for you have damaged his reputation in a way nobody else could ever have done, & you have given opportunity to the younger writers (who are jealous of Conrad's fame) to say, 'So *this* was the great writer! Violent, irritable & petty beneath all his fine words & pretensions.'

Of course there are very interesting things in the book such as your account of your honeymoon & of the war weeks in Galicia – & in addition there are many higher pages: – but your tone is common, that of a woman whose understanding of Conrad – apart from her treatment of him does not extend to the finer shades of his nature, to his essential quality, to his genius – but might be that of a landlady or a manageress of an hotel who had kept house for him for years & is now avenging the slights he put on her by repeating & digging up & exploring the painful episodes in which the dead husband nearly always appears to great disadvantage.

As you have very little critical sense you probably do not & cannot understand what an outrage your book is on good taste & good feeling & how you have shown the world that your 'loyalty' overlay a concealed amount of hate. Your insensitiveness & lack of sympathy are in evidence on nearly every page. However truthful may be your accounts ... you have put, intentionally or not a weapon in the hands of Conrad's detractors that will last for many years. But he will be judged, ultimately, by his work & by dozens of other testimonies.

In publishing this detestable book you have betrayed Conrad's trust in you. I judge that no friend of his will wish to see you again.

Edward Garnett[17]

Jessie's reply demands equally full quotation for its vigour and the light it throws on her attitude to her husband and the help she thought she gave to him:

My dear Edward, As soon as I recovered my breath on receiving your letter I sent a card to Messrs Durrant's Press Cuttings directing them not to include the cutting from 'The London Mercury' (August Number). Forewarned is forearmed and the man who is bitten by the same dog twice etc.

I hope for the sake of your reputation as a cultured man of letters and as a 'gentleman' the tone of your contribution to the 'L.M.' may be a trifle more moderate in tone and expression.

First of all allow me to remind you that I made life for Conrad more possible than in most small households, with small incomes, by my acknowledged ability to cook his food, and keep him happy all the years we were together. I can claim to have been a complete success as *his* wife, a task that many other more intelligent and better educated wives have been unable to accomplish in their married life.

There is not a single word in my book that belittles my husband. I may not be capable – as you say – of appreciating or even understanding his genius, but you may remember one point I make in the 'detestible [*sic*] book' which is that to live in this world one talented partner is enough, the other must be more commonplace and ordinary. I have claimed that distinction for myself.

If I have brought forward his nervous irritability, uncertain temper and irresponsibility, I have but completed, with the addition of his well known generosity, of thought and action, and almost childish waywardness, the whole lovable and complex personality. My picture of him will not detract

in the slightest from anyone's appreciation of his own generation or of those to come. He has made his mark, and made
it my dear Edward with no *inconsiderable* help from me.

I am incapable of concealing my feelings, either of hate or
affection and I have never felt vindictive, never suffered from
more than a pardonable amount of conceit, just sufficient to
enable me to carry on with. One of my critics has said that
Conrad is alive in the book, and the photographs that are
included will dispel the fallacy put forward by both Hueffer
and Wells, that Conrad was a kind of abnormal monster in
appearance.

I have made a typed copy, in fact two, of your letter and
also this. There remains one or two friends of the old days
who knew us both who will, I am sure, find some amusement
out of them when I show them later on. I think this is all.

Jessie Conrad[18]

One of the mutual friends of the old days, Cunninghame Graham,[19] shared Edward's opinion of Jessie and Edward sent him
a copy of his review with a letter saying: 'Jessie ought to have
been the manageress of a fourth-rate hotel or home for Bar-
maids. I knew that from the first & Conrad having no knowledge of the social shades in Englishwomen & wanting a House-
keeper has had to pay at long last, for his experiment.'[20] This
uncharitable comment was at least consistent, for Edward had
'tried to dissuade Conrad from marriage with a woman intellectually beneath him'[21] when he first met Jessie George, the
future Mrs Conrad.

Though the two families developed an amicable and affectionate relationship, Edward's first concern was always for Conrad's
reputation which, in his view, was proof of his conviction
that the public consistently ignored really great writers – or
placed the wrong valuation on their work. Reviewing, with
commendation, a study by Edward Crankshaw entitled *Joseph
Conrad: Some Aspects of the Art of the Novel*, in the *London Mercury*
in 1936, Edward wrote: ' ... personally I think Mr. Crankshaw,
following Henry James has overvalued *Chance*, because it is a
technical *tour de force* ... compared with, say, *The Heart of Darkness*, it falls into the second class of Conrad's creations.'[22] It was
an opinion he had expressed in the *Nation* when *Chance* was

published in 1914[23] and Conrad admitted in a letter to him at the time ' ... as to the exceptions you take I have always had the feeling that your criticism *must* be right'.[24] It was *Chance* which had brought Conrad popular sales, due, Edward thought, not so much to the long review by Colvin in the *Observer*, as to 'the figure of the lady on the jacket' and to the fact that Alfred Knopf, a young energetic member of Double-day's staff, mounted a promotion campaign.[25]

In contrast to what Edward described at Conrad's funeral as 'the crowd's ignorance of even the existence of this great writer', public reaction to Galsworthy's death in 1933 was very differ-ent. At the memorial service in Westminster Abbey 'every sec-tion in British Society was represented ... a national tribute not only to Galsworthy the writer, but to the man who embodied the best English traditions ... '[26] But Galsworthy's reputation fell shortly afterwards and Ada, indignant in defence of her husband's achievements, expressed vituperatively in a letter to Edward her opinion of Leonard Woolf who had attacked it. 'The Woolf one makes me very angry,' she wrote of the reviews she had read:

> That such a pig faced, pink clawed mole of a person should be allowed to do criticism is a scandal – I honestly believe that if I stopped the first person in the street I met and just recounted the bare facts of Jack's various achievements, he would say 'That must have been a great man'. How could 'no personality' or a mere façade produce a revolution in the technique of play writing: a change in the law of his country; write books that are almost as well known as the Bible, write plays that run for a year ... Gosh! Edward, doesn't your soul turn over and over? You *can* write criticism. The little animal even apologizes for his prejudices and blindness. What *is* the use of a critic like that?[27]

Her diatribe was a consequence of the reception given to Marrot's *Life and Letters of John Galsworthy*. When it was first mooted Ben Huebsch had asked Edward: 'Who is responsible for the choice of Marrot as Galsworthy's biographer? Knowing the man only slightly, perhaps I should not pass judgment, but the selection seems quite inept. I hope that you may tell me that I am wrong and that justice will be done Galsworthy.'[28] Edward

replied that he had been surprised by the choice and added
sardonically, 'My experience of the *Great* has taught me that
they need somebody on whom they can rely to be sympathetic
and flattering ... Galsworthy was quite out of touch with the
Younger Generation which derided his work.' In late years,
·Edward said, he had only seen Galsworthy about twice a year
for, although the writer had valued his criticism in the early
stages of his career, he had not felt the need for it later on: 'He
was so consistently successful.' Nevertheless Galsworthy 'never
had his head turned by the showers of attention lavished on him
from all sides'.[29]

A passage in the letter reflects the change in reputations
which the years had made. 'It is curious to reflect', Edward
wrote, 'that D. H. Lawrence who detested J.G.'s ideas & attacked his work is now the *idol* of the young people while J.G.
has no influence whatsoever. An exhibition of D. H. L.'s MSS at
Bumpus's bookshop in 3 weeks had brought 4,000 people ... '

During his headlong career Lawrence had occasional contact
with Edward and wrote rather condescendingly on 17 October
1921: 'I was glad to hear from you again – wonder what you are
doing – still looking after books, pruning them and re-potting
them I know.' But his old affection still remained, for he asked
Edward to write by return to tell him of David's marriage and
wife, and 'do you flirt with your daughter-in-law? If you don't
then seriously something is wrong.' He went on, 'I always think
of you when a hornet hovers around the jam-pots after one has
made jam. Only you're all badger-grey instead of striped. But
a humming wasp all the same.'[30] Perhaps it expressed the nature
of their old association; the memory of which lingered, for on
the publication of *Lady Chatterley's Lover*, he wrote to David
Garnett on 24 August 1928: 'I should like to give your father a
copy, if he'd care for it. Let me know, will you, and if to send to
the Cearne. In my early days your father said to me, "I should
welcome a description of the whole act" – which has stayed in
my mind till I wrote this book. But your mother would disap-
prove ... I always look on the Cearne as my jumping-off point
into the world – and your father as my first backer ... '[31] He sent
Edward a copy of the privately printed edition with the inscription: 'To Edward Garnett who sowed the first seed of this book
years ago at the Cearne – and may not like the full fruit.'[32]

Frieda expressed similar sentiments when, on a visit, she wrote to Edward: 'I am here in England, Lawrence at the last moment could not make up his mind to come with me – how are you and Connie and David? ... I know you will be glad of Lawrence's success, it came so suddenly last year in America ... Could you have tea or lunch with me in town on Tuesday and tell me all your news ... How is the Cearne? Lawrence and I really started our career (was it only 2 years) of crime from there under your blessing!! Well, it's also been great fun, the career I mean among other things.'[33]

When this 'career' came to an end with his death in 1930, Edward's knowledge of Lawrence made him first choice as editor of the posthumous papers, to which he gave the initial title of *The Last Cargo*. The correspondence Edward had with Huebsch of The Viking Press over this proposed collection illustrates his admiration of Lawrence as a writer, the difficulties of such a task, and his prophetic words on future Lawrentian studies. On 15 January 1935, he wrote: 'The bundle of manuscripts ... was in a most unsatisfactory state the typescript copies of the majority of the articles etc. having no indication of place or date of their appearance in the press or whether they *had* appeared or not ... Of course the literary agents have been doing the job in a haphazard fashion & they should have called in some competent man such as E. MacDonald the Bibliographer to advise them ... What an extraordinary fertile creature D. H. Lawrence was! And it is no joke for a critic trying to get round him. There will be labourers in his vineyard for many years to come.'[34]

By August Edward had realised the task required a great deal of bibliographical work and he suggested that the editing and proofing be taken over by E. D. MacDonald 'as the whole field is familiar to him'.[35] When Edward's suggestion was taken up, the bibliographer wrote to thank him, saying: 'I shall be glad to undertake, with your direction and co-operation the task of gathering the material and of preparing it for the press. Indeed the opportunity of working with you is a far greater enticement toward the job than any other consideration ...'[36]

In reply Edward was relieved that MacDonald had agreed to the task, and said: 'You will do more justice to D.H.L. than I have done for your study of his work is that of a specialist and

you are more intimate with it than I am ... '[37] A further letter
from Edward of 2 December 1935, which he began with the
remark that 'D.H. Lawrence would have much liked your letter
of November 1st to me. It is a tribute to him – no mean one –
that your heart "went sort of dead" when you opened his *last*
legacy,' is notable for the comparison he made between Lawrence and Galsworthy. Edward wrote: 'The deep antagonism
that Lawrence felt for Galsworthy was largely a class antagonism: hatred of all that Galsworthy represented by and in his
class – he seized on the lovers. Irene and Bosinney "sniffing like
dogs etc" to wash off his vicious contempt. Galsworthy was a
real "gentleman" incapable of ungentlemanly conduct, this
added to his offence. It is all very natural. Galsworthy of course
lived in his own class all the time and never got outside it.'[38]

After some missing items had been traced eventually in Heinemann's personal safe,[39] the collection took shape under Mac-
Donald's direction, but it became clear that the publishers
wished to exclude the introduction which Edward had prepared
when he took on the task and which he thought would 'give
a clue to D.H.L.'s complex mentality and hold the balance fair
between his contradictory impulses'. Marshall Best of The
Viking Press wrote to him on 5 February 1936 to say that Mr
Frere-Reeves (of Heinemann) and himself had gone over the
matter of Lawrence's *Last Cargo* and ' ... he feels (and I must
say that I see his point) that the introduction which you have
written is an admirable critical essay on Lawrence's work, but
that in its honesty it necessarily belittles a large part of the
contents of this volume: and consequently it seems slightly in-
appropriate for us to publish it in a work which we must present
to the public as an important addition to Lawrencia. In other
words he thinks it would be best not to try to have a critical
preface, but to use instead a brief factual statement of the source
and nature of the material included, which Mr. MacDonald
can easily prepare.' Edward would still appear as joint editor
and the arrangement he had proposed for the contents would
be followed; and in returning the introduction Best suggested
that it would be 'even more effective as an article or review in
one of the periodicals'.[40]

Edward understood the position but asked for his name to be
withdrawn as joint editor for ' ... while I appreciate your

reasons for the change – which you put very nicely in your letter – I am not sure that it would not have been better to let the Introduction canalise the criticisms *pro and con* of the "Contents" and not let reviewers make these discoveries and slop all over in all directions.' Magnanimously he thought his 'share of the fee should be given to Mr. MacDonald', and reassured them: 'I have no "feeling" in the matter of your decision save the natural feeling of a critic who criticised D.H.L. as freely in his lifetime as now after his death . . . '[41] MacDonald, however, was 'astounded and disgusted' for, he told Edward, he had 'welcomed a chance to help on *The Last Cargo* in large part because you were associated with it'.[42] But Edward, who had previously told MacDonald that 'You should have been selected from the first as the Editor and not myself who have neither the special knowledge nor the youthful energy you are bringing to the job,'[43] thanked him for his concern and his suggested plan for a joint preface and said: 'You can easily pay me a compliment if you desire in your Preface by saying "I regret that through untoward circumstances Mr. Edward Garnett etc, etc."'[44]

Later that year when he received a review copy of *The Phoenix*, as it was now entitled, Edward wrote to Ben Huebsch to ask him to congratualte MacDonald 'on the result of his sustained labours & wonderful knowledge. His *Introduction* is very informing & very skilfully written, much better suited to the material than the Preface I sent you . . . '[45] He repeated his opinion to MacDonald himself, assuring him that the triumphant completion of the task would bring him 'the prominent place in the literature of D. H. Lawrence recorders and critical commentators that your Bibliographies should have won long before'. He also thanked MacDonald for the 'graceful and accurate' paragraphs in which he had recorded Edward's own part in the work, adding that 'perhaps you will send me an inscribed copy of the American edition which I will place among my literary possessions since neither the English nor American publishers of "Phoenix" have bestowed on me a copy . . . '[46]

Edward's review copy had come from his friend Scott-James of the *London Mercury* and it was in the *Mercury* that he converted his unpublished Introduction into a review article. In it Edward enlarged on the thesis that in *Phoenix* 'we see Lawrence at his

best and worst', as a poet and artist and moralistic preacher and
teacher. In spite of defects there was 'something magnificent in
this young David's sudden emergence in 1912, and his challenge
to the old British Goliath, the Philistine giant who had maimed
or mutilated so many writers in the nineteenth century'.[47]

Edward was now a regular contributor to the *Mercury*, reviewing works which featured many of the writers he had known
in the past – Yeats, Cunninghame Graham and Doughty. He
helped in the appearance of two studies of his idol Doughty
which arrived for review at the same time. He had persuaded
Cape to publish Anne Treneer's study of Doughty's prose and
verse, and the delighted author wrote to him: 'I knew you were
a magician, but I did not realise that even your magic was as
strong as this. Messrs Cape have not only accepted my Doughty
MS but have offered me £30 in advance ... With very many
thanks to you ... '[48] He advised the other writer, Professor
Barker Fairley, on publishing his selections from *Dawn of
Britain*. His letter indicates a wariness over the reaction of
his old employer Duckworth.

> I think you had better tell Duckworth yourself that you
> have just heard that Cape has accepted Miss Treneer's book
> and that a little time back Mr. Garnett had told you
> that he thought the publication of 'The Extracts' and Miss
> Treneer's 'The Verse and Prose' would be a good thing, if they
> arrived practically together in date of publication and that
> the literary editors would be impressed thereby ... Also I
> don't know how I stand with Duckworth. You see he got
> rid of my 'services' at Xmas 1925 – I became Cape's reader
> 5 or 6 years later – when Cape left Duckworth's employment
> and started on his own, and how Cape's rise to fortune since
> has affected Duckworth's opinion of me I have no means of
> knowing ... [49]

But this successful association was coming to an end; Edward
was beginning to feel his years.

TWENTY

Dew on the Garlic Leaf

AT the end of 1936 Edward ventured to Cape that, 'While I feel quite up to my usual work now, I have reached an age when a yearly agreement gives me no assurance for the future. I feel that my judgment about a manuscript's possibilities is as good as ever, but each added year makes one's anticipations physically more and more grey. The firm of Cape I take it is in a solidly prosperous position, and you might like to show practically your appreciation of my literary advice in the past by adding a clause to the agreement for 1937 guaranteeing me while I am living, and perhaps expanding, my (nominal) share in the business.'[1] Now in his late sixties his eyesight was more troublesome, but his zeal in looking for a promising newcomer remained unabated. He continued the practice which in essence combined flattery and adverse criticism, analysis and suggested remedies to fulfil 'the purpose of the ideal publisher's reader – to discover the author's intention, to make the author himself more aware of it, to call his attention to the various technical means available to him – in short, to make the book the very best the author was capable of writing'.[2]

Geraint Goodwin, his latest acquisition, wrote to him on 3 June 1935: 'Now let me say at once, on the main issue, that your opinion of my stories, qualified as it was, is the most encouraging thing that has happened in my brief career. I did not know whether there was anything in them or not. They were the result of the functioning of an entirely different self. That

seems a strange thing to say but it is perfectly true...' After
discussing his story 'The Auld Earth' he remarked, 'By the way
how well you put your finger on the flaws in the other stories
... I beg of you not to spare me in the least particular ... no-
one can take umbrage at any adjective at all when it is the
outcome of a disinterested kindness on the part of the person
who applies it. Whether I am praised or damned by you I still
feel exactly the same – genuinely and truly grateful for your
interest and kindness ... '[3] His confidence in Edward's opinion
is evident in later letters. In August he sent 'three short stories
which I should be very glad if you would glance at when you
have the time. Two of them are about the Border and the third
one – THE OLD FOLK IN THE DEAD HOUSES – about Wales. I should
like you to read this one last as I am afraid I have hit out at
something and have not brought it off ... '[4] The nature of the
comments he received and his appreciation is evident in his
reply: 'You have no idea what your help means to a young man
not yet sure of himself ... I shall make the necessary alterations
right away. I am glad you like "A Woman in the House". I
ought to get more done in the same style bye and bye. The
others flagged, I realise now.' The old Garnettian advice can be
inferred from a passage in which Goodwin writes: 'I am perfectly sure of one thing now – that "good writing" on its own
account, means nothing. It has taken me a long time to live
down the George Moore influence. All those flowery bits that
you pick out with the eye of a seasoned gardener after weeds,
are a legacy of the past ... So actually I am starting my writing
career now, and the text or rather your text, is like Peer Gynt's –
to be oneself... '[5]

Turning aside from short stories, Goodwin looked for guidance on his first novel:

Here is the MSS of the first part of the novel. I should be
grateful if you would pass judgment on it ... Also I have
sought to keep it in Wales in all particulars. The (perhaps)
bewildering changes of front, the sudden and
unexplained frenzies, might possibly puzzle the English
reader. I can't help that. You told me to write about Wales
and Wales, as you will be the first to admit isn't England with
a few daubs of local colour ... Be ruthless as you like and

don't spare me. I would rather be damned by you than praised by all the pundits ... I send it to you with a great deal of fear and trembling. It is, after all, my first time out in this new venture ... [6]

Like others before him he encountered Edward's decided criticism and he wrote to Edward of his 'two or three days of awful gloom with nothing to lighten it ... But at the same time I felt very happy that you had come down where you had, and still more so that you headed me off where you did. A thing is either real or a fake and I can't endure fakes: yet I was within an ace of perpetrating one! I can't understand how it came about but there is not much doubt about it.'[7]

They continued to discuss the novel and Goodwin reported on its progress, giving on one occasion a detailed commentary on the characterisation and use of language, and on another exclaiming: 'To be quite frank there is very little credit to me in the whole thing. Item – you give me the plot; item – you sketch it out: item – you tell me what to do and what not to do. So you see I can claim to have just as much originality as a performing bear ... And but for you, God only knows what a mess I might have got into. I think that false start I made was one of the best things that could have happened ... If you are in Bedford Square on Wednesday afternoon (which I believe is your day) I should be glad of a few minutes chat over the MSS ... '[8] Near the completion of the novel he sent 'some 58,000 words' for Edward 'to look over', explaining that he had kept to the suggested plan closely, 'except that I have not made the inn-keepers family a large one' and 'if you think the book any good and another inspirational touch comes to you as to the ending, I should be glad to have it. I will write out a synopsis of a suggested ending if you would like to see it. I have it in my mind but I am not sure if it is the right one.'[9]

Edward gave his opinion on the work and on the author's progress to Huebsch who had asked: 'I should like to know what you think of Geraint Goodwin. I have just read his "Heyday in the blood" and it impresses me as being a work of a first rate talent. I see that the book is dedicated to you which means that he is a recent recruit to the army that owes you much for advice and guidance ... '[10] To this Edward replied:

'Cape is just sending to press a vol. of short stories by him *all* good & some very strong and rough & penetrating. He certainly *is* a writer: he has the fitting phrase & real emotional pace and humour . . . He sent me some very strong, racy sketches of Welch life & then started on a novel. But he got on wrong lines & I was happy enough to head him back to the Welsh inn which he knows intimately . . . '[11]

Edward had always considered the short story form to be indicative of a new writer's talent. It was a form of literature not usually regarded as profitable, but he persuaded Cape to publish for a while annual volumes of *Best Short Stories*. In his preface to *Capajon*, a collection of short stories published in 1933, he wrote of Cape as a publisher 'eager to undertake volumes of short stories of original quality'.[12] Nearly all the authors included in what amounted to a tribute to Edward had received some kind of aid from him, usually a combination of advice and hospitality either at Pond Place or The Cearne. In the flat upstairs at Pond Place, Edward – indescribably dishevelled and surrounded by paintings of obscure origin, drinking a peculiar mixture of burgundy and water, and smoking his individual brand of herbal cigarettes – entertained his protégés and acquaintances. Nellie, whose kindly and placid nature complemented Edward's occasional irascibility, was usually there. Sean O'Faolain wrote: 'But will you allow me to say that Miss Heath's cunning concoctions at Pond Place are just as good for my wit as the luxurious Russian restaurant's odiosities – and more suited to these hard times and an Irish household's asceticism.'[13]

At The Cearne, the young writer found equal companionship in Constance, whom H. E. Bates pictured bending in a 'prayerful' position because of her shortsightedness over the flowerbeds of her beloved garden.[14] Though her eyesight had become so poor she still engaged in Russian translations, helped on occasion by Natalie Duddington,[15] the daughter of Alexander Ertel, friend of Tolstoy. She had married Jack Duddington, curator of the Whitechapel Art Gallery and a friend of Edward and Constance from their early days in the East End. Edward respected her opinion and she was one of the people he turned to for advice in his correspondence over a remarkable book which had come out of Russia.

Ben Huebsch had enquired about a Russian novel, 'a triple decker', which had been recommended to him. Its German title was *Der Stille Don* and the author was said to be 'Michail Sholochow'. Huebsch was 'reluctant to undertake the examination of so voluminous an affair on the mere say-so of an outsider, but we can't afford to ignore what may be a good tip'. He therefore wondered if Edward could ask one of his Russian friends who might know the book to 'examine it in the original on our behalf for a fee'.[16] Edward answered that he would ask Mrs Matheson to do the job and remarked that, by coincidence, he had already read about the book that week, commenting:

> It is a novel of Cossack life, beginning before the War & the author conducts his hero into the War with all its horror. It seems to be extremely brutal & my friend complains everybody sweats so much! One episode is the raping of a girl by a whole battalion of Cossacks in barracks, another is a woman being delivered of a child in a pool of blood etc. etc. It is difficult to get Russian books here – there is no good agency in London so if I can borrow the German copy I will have it reported on by Mrs. Matheson – but from what I have said it is probably a book *you* should be in a position to decide on – as we don't know how squeamish *now* the American public is in regard to War novels & the like . . .[17]

In a letter accompanying the report he forwarded from Mrs Matheson, Edward wrote that her view 'puts a fresh face on the matter. It looks as though the book was worth the Viking Press's taking up. Mrs. Matheson is both a good critic & a good translator.' In her report Mrs Matheson gave a succinct account of Sholokhov's theme, justified 'such coarseness as occurs in the book . . . as part of the coarseness of the life described' and concluded, 'The value of the book for foreign readers, apart from it being a well told story, lies in the fact that it conveys the atmosphere of Russia on the eve of the war, and gives an intelligent appreciation of the Russian peasant's mind.'[18] Huebsch, however, was unconvinced and put his doubts into a letter to Edward: 'From this description the book seems to be good, but it does not make me feel that it is so outstandingly good as to demand translation in these times when everything is subjected to unusual scrutiny. I should like to read the book in German if it proves that an option may be had on the man's future work. A novel would have to be of extraordinary quality to warrant accepting it without the chance to recoup for the expense of launching the author by obtaining an option.'[19] In fact this was not the only element of uncertainty. A later commentator has remarked that, 'As a publishing venture, *The Quiet Don* posed serious risks, not only because it was so long but because in 1931 when a typescript became available in England, it was only half finished and also because its frequent references to living persons (Russian émigrés, British and French military personnel) might expose a publisher to libel suits.'[20]

Replying to Huebsch, Edward said: 'Mrs Duddington tells me that she has just been requested by a Russian here to translate two specimen chapters of "The Peaceful Don" for submission to a London publisher, *not specified*, who will bring out a translation . . . ' In the same letter he gave currency to a rumour then in vogue and one which has recently been examined in great detail: 'I am told confidentially by Miss Ertel (Mrs. Duddington's sister) who returned lately from Russia, that the writer who claims to have written the book is *not* in fact the author but that the MS was confided to his care by a "White" officer who was eventually killed but that the Soviet authorities decided to hush up the matter & not have a scandal & explosion.'[21] Later he wrote: ' . . . you might like to know that Mrs. Duddington thinks poorly of "Der Stille Don" – She doesn't want this mentioned for a certain reason – but she finds it too gross & materialistic so I think we may dismiss it from our minds.'[22]

Such comments corroborate the later observation that 'The literary community's first response to Sholokhov was unfriendly. Some critics even accused the writer of "Kulak ideology". Even worse there were rumours, widespread at first, but later published openly in the press that the real author of *The Quiet Don* was not Sholokhov but "some White officer who was killed in the Civil War." '[23] Huebsch, however, thought it desirable to establish relations with the publisher for whom Mrs Duddington was to translate the specimen chapters 'though the fact that the author is no longer living reduces the attractiveness of the venture, for the entire stake would be on a single book . . . '[24] The Viking Press did not publish *The Quiet Don*; it was not until 1934 that Sholokhov's work appeared in the West, in a translation by Stephen Garry.

Edward, meanwhile, continued to interest himself in the Russian approach to the novel. In his introduction to Natalie Duddington's translation of Shchedrin's *Golovlyov Family* he announced that 'the last of the great Russian novels that has been awaiting translation into English is by a writer whose name is scarcely known to the public'.[25]

Great literature and the encouragement of those who wrote it or might write it had been Edward's lifelong devotion. Though this encouragement had been achieved, as Jack Kahane put it, 'by stealth'[26] behind the scenes, the idea that it should be given public recognition was taken up by Hamish Hamilton and Dr Tom Jones. Hamish Hamilton had worked briefly for Cape before setting up his own business. At Cape he had formed a friendship with Edward, staying at his flat in Pond Place.[27] His wife, Jean Forbes-Robertson, had eventually acted the leading part in a performance of Edward's *St Joan*. Edward had kept a paternal eye on them and, as Hamish Hamilton recorded, on 'the disruption of our marriage – dear old Edward Garnett, watching us wisely, wrote a skit upon our menage: "Jimmy's Wreath" or "In at the Death" '.[28]

Dr Tom Jones, Assistant Secretary of the Cabinet, who had a great interest in literature and literary circles, had a high regard for Edward, to whom he had been introduced by Hamish Hamilton. An indirect consequence of their meeting was that the Prime Minister, Stanley Baldwin, was induced to read Mary Webb and his public appreciation of *Precious Bane* swept it into instant celebrity. During their conversation over dinner Edward and Tom Jones had discussed the novel and its location in the Shropshire border area and Jones had spoken of it to Baldwin who came from that part of the country.[29] Jones had contact with Edward in the course of several other literary ventures. As Chairman of the Gregynog Press he published a selection of poems which Edward had edited in memory of his friend Edward Thomas. Occasionally they met at social functions. A diary entry by Jones gives a picture both of Edward's physical presence at the time and the link that then existed between Government circles and the world of letters: 'May 21, 1936: This evening to a party of *Mercury* contributors ... where

I chatted with Edward Garnett, Richard Church, Sean O'Faolain, Austin Clarke and others. Church says there is a young Welsh poet in town Dylan Thomas ... They all praised the work of H. E. Bates. In the crowd Garnett towered physically above the rest, looking like an enormous frog.'[30]

'Jamie' Hamilton and Tom Jones had the idea of making Edward a Companion of Honour but, as David Garnett wrote: 'It did not occur to them that it might be necessary to prepare the ground, though I do not think that any influence would have induced Edward to accept.' Edward was both baffled and annoyed to receive a letter from one of the Prime Minister's secretaries saying that Baldwin 'had it in mind to submit his name to the King for a C.H.' He was adamant in his refusal despite his son's crossness, replying angrily to David that, 'I've always known you were an insider, but I'm an outsider.'[31] It was an attitude more fully explained to Professor Barker Fairley, who had hoped to persuade Edward to accept an academic honour at about the same time. Writing to Fairley on 30 January 1936, Edward said:

> I think I detect your kindly hand in the offer of the University of Manchester to confer the degree of Doctor of Letters on this eccentric person. But I have just written to decline the honour of which I am deeply sensible on the grounds that I regard myself as an outsider, a solitary person, unacademic in essence and unfitted to be Dr. Garnett. I should feel unhappy as a Doctor of Letters, because I am freer as plain Edward Garnett and I may add that a few months ago I refused the Birthday Honour that has I see, been conferred on Dr. Dover Wilson – because for me a writer loses part of his independence, when he is honoured by the Government which expects conformity with the ruling powers, such as the Censorship – at least no opposition.[32]

It was an attitude of mind in sharp contrast to someone like Edward Marsh, who found in Edward a 'tendency to like things because they are right' while he himself was inclined 'to think things right because I like them'.[33] Marsh, the archetypal 'insider' in touch with the leading literary and political figures of the day and patron of the arts, was on a different wavelength to Edward, the convinced 'outsider', out of sympathy with the establishment to the extent of refusing its symbols of recognition. The success which he had sought throughout his working life came in fulfilling what he once defined as the task of the publisher's reader: 'He must be particularly responsive to young writers of promise – while keeping his critical faculty alert. Mentally he lives in a strange kaleidoscope world ... His function is to help the new authors into birth and to discover the rare talent. Withal the "reader" is sure to have his personal prejudices and limitations, his peculiar weaknesses and predilections.'[34]

The task came to an end abruptly in 1937. Rising to dress himself on the morning of 19 February, Edward complained of a severe pain in the head, the symptom of a cerebral haemorrhage that brought about his immediate collapse and a quick death. At his funeral, David, in keeping with beliefs he held appropriate, allowed no religious service, or speeches, or organ music. He thought of the song sung at the burial of kings and princes in China, which it would have seemed an affectation to say aloud:

> How swiftly it dries
> The dew on the garlic leaf
> The dew that dries so fast
> Tomorrow will fall again
> But he whom we carry to the grave
> Will never more return.[35]

Those who attended the cremation at Golders Green included H. A. Manhood, Geraint Goodwin, Hamish Miles, Rupert Hart-Davis and H. E. Bates. Young men, as Bates wrote, who had all delighted in him[36] – a unique personality the like of whom would hardly be seen again in the world of literature and publishing. Middleton Murry, recording Edward's sudden death in his journal, wrote of him: 'A queer old bird, but as disinterested as any literary man I have met ... He utterly disapproved of my forsaking the path of pure literature. He had nobility.'[37] Amongst the letters of sympathy which Constance received was one from Ramsay MacDonald which recollected their early days in the East End. A touch of pathos colours his words: 'The notice of the death of your husband brought into my memory old times which I cherish, and which often return to me when sitting quietly keeping company with myself. May I make

bold to offer you my deep sympathy.'[38] Constance in her reply
to Jonathan Cape's 'kind and understanding letter' was also
evocative of those early days, and of Edward's troubled relationships with publishers: 'As you know Edward began his
career as a "reader" fifty years ago – a boy of 19 – and worked
for many different publishers, but it was only in your firm that
he found himself among friends and in really harmonious surroundings, and I feel that I owe it largely to you that in these
later years he was so happy in his work.'[39]

David enlarged upon his mother's view when he wrote to
Cape a few days after Edward's death:

> I should like to tell you how well I know that my father's work
> with you was the greatest source of happiness and interest to
> him. In the last years this interest in his work and pleasure
> increased steadily, and he valued and enjoyed immensely his
> relations with you all, particularly those luncheons at the
> Etoile of which I caught an outsider's glimpse. His earlier
> years were often embittered by exasperations with the public
> and the publishers. That this passed away latterly was due
> not I think to an increased philosophy, or tolerance of things
> of no value, but very largely to the happy environment he
> found working with all of you.[40]

Jonathan Cape thought David's letter an appropriate conclusion to the tribute he paid to Edward in the house journal, *Now
and Then*. This described, vividly and comprehensively, Edward's approach to his work and his routine over the years
stretching back to his time at Duckworth:

> Edward Garnett, principal reader and keeper of the firm's
> literary conscience, died on February 19th at the age of
> sixty-nine. For 16 years except when absent on short holidays,
> we met on Wednesdays at the Etoile restaurant in Charlotte
> Street for luncheon. His death was sudden. Less than 40
> hours earlier he was with us, apparently well and in good
> spirits. Recently he had considered, and discussed with us,
> the need for someone in the near future to assume the re-
> sponsibility of reading our manuscripts, because he was be-
> ginning to find his eyesight less good. His ability to absorb
> the written word was unimpaired, his judgment as sound as

ever, and his interest in the work in which he had been engaged for nearly fifty years was as keen as always.

During the years that he read for us no scrap of manuscript was sent away without being seen by him. 'I must see *all* the manuscripts' he said. And so it was: every week they were collected together, and he would spend an afternoon going through them. From the pile he would select a batch of a dozen or more for careful reading, and the following week at luncheon he would draw from his pocket a sheaf of reports which he would eagerly read. Usually, he would comment 'One or two quite good things this week', or, 'Several here on the line and will need to be considered carefully', or, 'Rather a poor lot, this week', and more rarely, 'Cape must certainly publish this.' His power to assimilate and assess literary work was amazing. There was never any flagging in his interest, or his search for fresh talent. He was always a keen prospector. A remark of his made to one of our number, deserves to be long remembered. It was in reply to a query as to whether a particular manuscript could find sufficient readers to pay for its printing cost. 'My young friend', he said, 'you must bear in mind that there is still in this country a residuum of educated folk.' The stereotyped, conventional, repetitive work, the slick, inadequate, flashy productions, were summarily dismissed. 'No good for Cape. Tell him to go to So-and-so!' Sometimes, when passing through a second sieve the manuscripts Garnett had glanced at and rejected out of hand, we would find something which we felt required more serious consideration. Manuscripts there were which after careful consideration we finally decided against, but which achieved success when published elsewhere. No one is infallible. No publisher can publish all the good books, and a book may achieve a measure of success under one imprint which it might not have under another. We can count Edward Garnett as one of the main contributors to our present position in the publishing world. May his spirit never be troubled by any sins of commission or omission on the part of those who have to wear his mantle![41]

This mantle fell on William Plomer. He had come to the attention of Edward when Roy Campbell had mentioned in one of his letters: 'My great friend William Plomer, whose book has just been published by the Hogarth Press, is a counter jumper in a native truck store in Zululand.' Campbell regretted that the book had been cut for outspokenness, and his regard for Plomer was such that he said to Edward, ' ... if he has managed to put anything of himself in his novel, it will be certainly worth reading'.[42] In 1933 Edward reported on a collection of Plomer's short stories, giving a perceptive assessment of the author's stature as well as a pessimistic estimate of the public's likely reception of his work. The report on *The Child of Queen Victoria* stated:

> Plomer is certainly about the most original mind of the younger generation, & he comes off in his short stories of Greece & France as he has done with S. Africa & Japan. He is emphatically of the minority – i.e. of the section of writers, the real intelligentsia, the unconventional literary artists whom the British public in general don't like, & therefore only buy in restricted quantities. He is a Left-winger in popularity, i.e. what D. H. Lawrence was to Hugh Walpole, & Cape mustn't expect more than a quiet rise in sales even after Plomer's *The Case is Altered* was chosen by the Book Society. Of course he ought to have gained the 'Book of the Month' years ago – so far as *original* literary excellence goes. But he is too unconventional & keen. Most of these stories are really incisive sketches of manners, or little to titillate vulgar taste. The title story is very good, & the last story is excellent, & the others are well up to Plomer's standard – though one or two such as 'Museum Piece' are a little thin.[43]

On the initiative of Rupert Hart-Davis, William Plomer took over as reader and adviser to Cape. From his own experience over the years he concluded that publishers' readers also have 'their prejudices and passions, their blind spots and little manias'.[44] He had heard for instance that 'Edward Garnett could not bear, let alone enjoy, the writings of Firbank. Not to perceive their technical innovation, skill, and influence seems to me a blind spot; not to be able to enjoy their wit and fancy seems to me a sad deprivation.'[45] Yet Plomer was later to confide: 'It does seem to me that Garnett's activities as a publisher's

reader and as the friend and adviser of writers made him creative in a special sense – far more creative, I consider, than most
writers. Surely for him literature was one of what used to be
called the fine arts, and, from the point of view of 1969 or 1970
when the commercial organisation of publishing has so vastly
developed, he may appear almost prehistoric.'[46]

Such creativity would seem to be at odds with the astringent
views of the doyen of bibliographers, Fredson Bowers, who held
that ' ... as a principle, if we respect our authors, we should
have a passionate concern to see that their words are recovered
and currently transmitted in as close a form to their intention as
we can contrive'.[47] Passages in his *Textual and Literary Criticism*
(1959) are salutary reminders that the author's text is subject to
many vicissitudes from manuscript to final publication. In pursuit of the true text, bibliographers have evolved a number of
techniques to eliminate the variables that arise from the physical
means of production. These techniques have been developed on
the basis of an understanding of the mechanics and routine of
the press: they demand attention to minutiae and exacting
detective work. They focus on the transference of the finished
manuscript to its printed form, and on alterations during that
process.

More subtle and more difficult to determine are those changes
that derive from the ways in which, as Gettman wrote in *A
Victorian Publisher*, the publisher mediates between the readers
and the author, and in so doing influences the text.[48] No greater
influence in this respect exists in publishing than that of the
publisher's reader – who offers not only advice on grammar,
syntax and style, but also suggestions on pacing and changes of
emphasis. Edward did do this kind of work, but in such a way
as to go beyond what D. H. Lawrence referred to as 'still looking
after books – pruning and re-potting them ... '[49] His scrutiny
of theme, motivation and structure, combined with what could
be termed a 'words on the page' kind of criticism, fulfilled
criteria which V. S. Pritchett put forward in the following
terms:

> My ideal publisher is either himself a critic or employs one as
> his literary adviser. One of the greatest of these was the late
> Edward Garnett ... A publisher is often obliged to be tactful

and reticent with an author; but authors can always see through this. They need to find, in their publisher's office, a man who applies disinterested criticism to their work, who helps to provide that warm climate in which their work can grow. One may quarrel with him, as Lawrence quarrelled with Edward Garnett, but the quarrel will be real, an issue of literature, and the kind of thing which writers are used to and by their nature understand. This literary adviser must be a man with a vocation.[50]

A sense of vocation and a profound acumen, experience and knowledge of literature and publishing, explain only in part Edward's success as a reader. It was the contradictory combination of personal qualities which created a close association with writers over three generations and made for the 'warm climate' in which their work could mature. Patient yet quick-tempered, ironic but idealistic, often wrong-headed and holding odd prejudices, he had a tolerance of egotism and vanity in others complemented by a subtlety of mind in conversation usually absent in his written work. Constance and Nellie, who shared the life he devoted to literature, understood in their different ways the contradictions in his character. After his death, Constance – intellectual, shy and sharing many of his literary perceptions – lived on at The Cearne growing more frail and shortsighted with each passing year. Her sympathies had been with the Russian social revolutionaries and she abhorred the Bolshevik dictatorship; her early socialist inclinations were replaced by decided conservative views. When she developed the heart condition which was to lead to her death in December 1946, Nellie came to visit her during the difficult war years, travelling in unheated trains delayed by erratic timetables from Hampshire to Edenbridge.

Immediately after Edward's death Nellie had moved out of Pond Place to a single room in North London, where she lived until the outbreak of the Second World War. Then she settled at Headley Down in Hampshire, next door to an old friend, Dr Elizabeth Wilks. Her social work as prison visitor to the women in Holloway had come to an end with the war. She continued to live alone until her death in November 1962, though she was frequently overwhelmed by visits from the many friends who confided in her. 'It was impossible', said one of these, 'to hide anything from Nellie, but she could not be shocked however bizarre the ideas and behaviour of her confidants because she was always able to penetrate to the human condition beneath.'[51]

Constance, who had called him a bundle of paradoxes in the early days of their marriage,[52] and Nellie, with her sympathetic perceptions, were at one in realising that in Edward Garnett, this most gregarious of men, whose charm and wit could enliven any company, there was a private and profound sense of isolation and impatience with the world and its lack of true values. This never soured him, however irascible or contemptuous his reaction to opinions which he thought were false or meretricious. In the last analysis these were irrelevant; what mattered was that 'he had his own vision and [had] been true to it'.[53]

Abbreviations

The following abbreviations have been used in the notes:

Constance's MSS	Incomplete Autobiography by Constance Garnett. Holograph MSS.
Olive's Diary	Diaries of Olive Garnett 1890–1906. Typewritten MSS.
Nellie Heath's Notes	Reminiscences by Ellen Maurice Heath: 1961 (transcribed by Mrs Caroline White).
Rayne Nickalls (*née* Garnett) Memoir	Extracts from Rayne Nickalls's Memoir: 'The Time is Past and Gone.' Typewritten MSS.
Austin	Humanities Research Center, The University of Texas at Austin.
Beinecke	Collection of American Literature, Beinecke Rare Book and Manuscript Library, Yale University.
Berg	Henry W. and Albert A. Berg Collection, The New York Public Library, Astor, Lenox and Tilden Foundations.
Cape	Archives of Jonathan Cape Ltd (London and Grantham).
Colby	Colby College (Maine).
Columbia	Columbia University Libraries.
Cornell	Cornell University Library.

Hilton Hall	David Garnett's family home.
Urbana	University of Illinois at Urbana-Champaign.
Viking Press	Viking Penguin Inc. (New York).

NOTES: A query has been inserted in cases where dates given in the original documents are difficult to read or otherwise open to question. Where dates are not completely known, only the definite elements are quoted. Total absence of date is shown in the usual way (n.d.).

Notes

Introduction

1 R. A. Scott-James, 'Edward Garnett', *Spectator* CLVIII (1937), 362.
2 H. Miles, 'Edward Garnett', *New Statesman* XIII (1937), 327.
3 H. Green, 'Edward Garnett', *New Statesman* XL (1950), 675.

1: A Touch of the B.M.

1 R. Hoggart, *Speaking to Each Other* (Chatto & Windus 1970), II, 256.
2 E. Miller, *Prince of Librarians: Life and Times of Antonio Panizzi of the B.M.* (Deutsch 1967), 201.
3 Olive's Diary.
4 F. M. Hueffer, *Ancient Lights and Certain New Reflections: Being the Memoirs of a Young Man* (Chapman & Hall 1911), 68.
5 David Garnett, biographical note on Edward Garnett in E. Garnett (ed.), *Conrad's Prefaces to His Works* (Dent 1937), v.
6 'Butleriana: further extracts from the Notebooks of Samuel Butler', *Then and Now, A Selection ... from 'Now and Then' 1921–1935* (Cape 1935), 215.
7 Olive's Diary.
8 V. S. Pritchett to author, 6 Nov. 1969.
9 Constance's MSS (et sqq.).

2: *The Young Garnetts*

1 W. Wallace, review of *The Paradox Club*, *Academy* XXXIV (1888), 132.

2 G. Meredith to Dr Richard Garnett, 30 April 1889, in C. L. Cline (ed.), *Letters of George Meredith* (O.U.P. 1970), II, 955–6.

The novelist and poet acted as a reader for Chapman & Hall for thirty years. As a reader his rejections included one of *the* best-sellers of the nineteenth century, Mrs Humphry Ward's *East Lynne*, Shaw's early efforts as a novelist, and also *Green Mansions* by W. H. Hudson which ultimately achieved publication through the efforts of Edward Garnett. R. A. Gettman, *A Victorian Publisher* (C.U.P. 1960), 182.

3 Review of *Light and Shadow*, *Athenaeum* No. 3243 (1889), 851–2.

4 G. E. Woodberry to Dr Richard Garnett, 3 Feb. 1890, in C. Heilbrun, *The Garnett Family* (Allen & Unwin 1961), 81.

5 Constance Garnett to Dr Richard Garnett, n.d. (Hilton Hall).

6 EG to Dr Richard Garnett, March 1891 (Hilton Hall).

7 Constance Garnett to Dr Richard Garnett, 28 Sept. 1891 (Hilton Hall).

8 Constance Garnett to Dr Richard Garnett, n.d. (Hilton Hall).

9 W. B. Yeats to Olivia Shakespear, 28 Nov. 1894, in A. Wade (ed.), *Letters of W. B. Yeats* (Hart-Davis 1954), 241.

10 A. Norman Jeffares and K. G. W. Cross (eds), *In Excited Reverie: A Centenary Tribute to William Butler Yeats 1865–1939* (Macmillan 1965), 1.

11 W. B. Yeats to Katharine Tynan, June 1891, in R. McHugh (ed.), *Letters to Katharine Tynan* (Burns 1953), 125.

12 EG to Dr Richard Garnett, June 1891 (Hilton Hall).

13 J. B. Townsend, *John Davidson* (Yale University Press 1961), 142.

14 E. Rhys, *Everyman Remembers* (Dent 1931), 237.

15 E. Rhys, Foreword to F. Nietzsche, *Thus Spake Zarathusa* (Dent 1933), xvi.

A major difficulty in making known the ideas of Nietzsche in England was the obstructionist behaviour of his sister Elizabeth Forster-Nietzsche, who jealously guarded her brother's copyrights. Edward had made representations to both Fisher Unwin and Duckworth and 'both firms were keen to exploit the latent public demand for Nietzsche' and had been hampered by 'the pythoness of Weimar'. D. S. Thatcher, *Nietzsche in England 1890–1914* (University of Toronto Press 1970), 44–8.

16 Constance's MSS.
17 Olive's Diary.
18 Ibid.
19 Constance's MSS.
20 Olive's Diary.
21 Ibid.
22 Ibid.
23 Ibid.
24 Ibid.
25 Constance's MSS.
26 David Garnett to author, 21 March 1980.
27 Constance's MSS.
28 Constance Garnett to EG, 7 Jan. 1894 (Hilton Hall).
29 Constance Garnett to EG, n.d. (Hilton Hall).
30 Constance Garnett to EG, n.d. (Hilton Hall).
31 Constance Garnett to EG, n.d. (Hilton Hall).
32 Constance Garnett to EG, n.d. (Hilton Hall).
   Later Tolstoy, in reply to a letter from Edward, wrote on 16 July 1900: ' ... my kind regards to your wife, and I take this opportunity of once more thanking her for her excellent translation of "The Kingdom of God is within you" ' (Austin).
33 Olive's Diary.
34 Constance Garnett to EG, n.d. (Hilton Hall).
35 Olive's Diary.
36 E. V. Lucas, *Reading, Writing and Remembering: A Literary Record* (Methuen 1932), 155.
37 W. B. Yeats to EG, Oct. 1892, in Wade (ed.), *Letters of W. B. Yeats*, 214.
38 J. M. Dent to EG, 30 Oct. 1893 (Hilton Hall).
39 *Speaker*, 8 Sept. 1894, attributed to Yeats in W. B. Yeats,

Uncollected Prose: First Reviews and Articles 1868–1896 collected and edited by J. D. Frayne (Macmillan 1970), I, 341.

40 Olive's Diary.

41 D. Garnett, *The Golden Echo* (Chatto & Windus 1953), 16–17.

42 Constance Garnett to Dr Richard Garnett, Nov. 1895 (Hilton Hall).

43 Olive's Diary.

44 D. Garnett, *Golden Echo*, 20.

3: *The Cearne*

1 Olive's Diary.

2 D. H. Lawrence to Louie Burrows, 16 Oct. 1911, in J. T. Boulton (ed.), *Lawrence in Love: Letters to Louie Burrows* (University of Nottingham 1968), 141.

3 Constance's MSS.

4 Constance Garnett to Dr Richard Garnett, Easter Monday 1896 (Hilton Hall).

5 D. Garnett, *The Golden Echo* (Chatto & Windus 1953), 21.

6 EG to H. G. Wells, 22 May 1907 (Urbana).

7 F. M. Ford, *Return to Yesterday* (Gollancz 1931), 78.

8 EG to R. B. Cunninghame Graham, 9 Feb. 1901 (National Library of Scotland).

9 D. Garnett, *Golden Echo*, 73.

10 *The Times Literary Supplement*, 10 Oct. 1935.

11 William Hedgecock to EG, 13 June 1903 and 5 April 1904 (Hilton Hall).

12 D. Garnett, *Golden Echo*, 69.

13 Ibid., 22.

14 David Garnett to author, 21 March 1980.

15 EG to Richard Curle, 16 Dec. 1933 (Austin).

16 Constance Garnett to Dr Richard Garnett, 23 Nov. 1898 (Hilton Hall).

17 Prince Peter Kropotkin to EG, 23 Nov. 1898 (Hilton Hall).

18 Charles Longman to EG, n.d. (Austin).

19 EG to Charles Longman, 5 Jan. 1899 (Austin).

20 Prince Peter Kropotkin to EG, 8 June 1899 (Hilton Hall).

21 Prince Peter Kropotkin to EG, 22 Nov. 1899 (Hilton Hall).

22 D. Garnett, *Golden Echo*, 36–7.

23 Harold Frederic to Stephen Crane, 1898, in R. W. Stallman and L. Gilkes (eds), *Stephen Crane: Letters* (Peter Owen 1960), 173.
24 EG to Cora Crane, 13 March 1898 (Columbia).
25 Cora Crane to EG, 19 Jan. 1899 (Beinecke).
26 E. Solomon, *Stephen Crane in England: A Portrait of the Artist* (Ohio State University Press 1964), 36.
27 Cora Crane to EG, n.d. (Beinecke).
28 EG to H. G. Wells, Jan. 1903 (Urbana).
29 EG to Dr Richard Garnett, 19 July 1890 (Hilton Hall).

4: Reader's Task

1 Guinevere L. Griest, *Mudie's Circulating Library and the Victorian Novel* (Indiana University Press 1970), 120.
2 Ibid., 174.
3 R. A. Gettman, *A Victorian Publisher: A Study of the Bentley Papers* (C.U.P. 1960), 263.
4 F. Mumby, *Publishing and Bookselling* (Cape 1954), 274.
5 Griest, *Mudie's Circulating Library*, 222.
6 Mumby, *Publishing and Bookselling*, 274.
7 F. M. Ford, 'Travel Notes: I Return to Olivet', *Saturday Review of Literature* XX (1939), 13–14.
8 M. Ward, *Return to Chesterton* (Sheed & Ward 1952), 22.
9 Sir Stanley Unwin, *The Truth about a Publisher* (Allen & Unwin 1960), 80.
10 R. H. Horne, *Exposition of the False Medium and Barriers Excluding Men of Genius from the Public* (1833), 135, quoted in Gettman, *A Victorian Publisher*, 187.
11 Sir Stanley Unwin, *The Truth about Publishing* (Allen & Unwin 1960), 29.
12 David Garnett, biographical note on Edward Garnett in E. Garnett (ed.), *Conrad's Prefaces to His Works* (Dent 1937), vi.
13 Reader's Report (Berg).
14 Reader's Report (Berg).
15 Reader's Report (Berg).
16 Reader's Report (Berg).
17 Reader's Report (Berg).
18 Reader's Report (Berg).

19 Reader's Report (Berg).

20 Reader's Report (Berg).

21 Reader's Report (Berg).

22 Reader's Report (Berg).

23 Reader's Report (Berg).

24 Reader's Report (Berg).

25 W. B. Yeats to Katharine Tynan, 6 Oct. 1890, in R. McHugh (ed.), *Letters to Katharine Tynan* (Burns 1953), 125.

26 W. B. Yeats to EG, Oct. 1892, in A. Wade (ed.), *Letters of W. B. Yeats* (Hart-Davis 1954), 214.

27 W. B. Yeats to EG, 1893, ibid., 227.

28 EG to W. B. Yeats, in J. Hone, *W. B. Yeats 1865–1939* (Macmillan 1942), 98.

29 Ibid., 100.

30 EG to T. F. Unwin, memo (Berg).

31 EG to T. F. Unwin, prospectus (Berg).
Garnett's condemnation of imperialism coloured his assessment of Kipling of whom he wrote to his friend Cunninghame Graham at this time: ' ... Kipling is *the* enemy – He is a creator; and he is the *genius of all we detest.*' EG to R. B. Cunninghame Graham, 26 Jan. 1899, in C. T. Watts (ed.), *Joseph Conrad's Letters to Cunninghame Graham* (C.U.P. 1969), 20.

Nevertheless he was to write later: 'To deplore the popular influence of a writer is, of course most natural, but it is, in fact equivalent to the attitude of those Eastern monarchs who decapitate the bearers of unwelcome tidings. The value of any representative writer is precisely that he is a mouthpiece of his generation, and that his spirit is the working expression of a special drift or tendency ... Mr. Kipling's feats in literature are in truth only to be minimised by prejudiced opponents ... ' E. Garnett, 'Mr. Kipling's Progress', *Speaker* IX (1903), 69–70.

32 EG to R. B. Cunninghame Graham, 16 May 1898 (Austin).

33 Reader's Report (Berg).

34 EG to R. B. Cunninghame Graham, 9 July 1898 (Austin).

35 R. B. Cunninghame Graham to EG, n.d. (Austin).

36 Reader's Report (Berg).

37 EG to T. F. Unwin, memo (Berg).

38 Ford Madox Brown to Watts Dunton, 22 Sept. 1891, in

A. Mizener, *The Saddest Story: A Biography of Ford Madox Ford* (Bodley Head 1972), 17.

Ford Madox Brown contributed to Edward's only venture into publishing. This was a book by his sister-in-law Grace Black entitled *A Beggar and Other Fantasies*. Ford Madox Brown designed a bookplate for this small book of 93 pages. David Rice, writing nostalgically to Edward of their days together at Unwin in a letter of 16 May 1929, referred to it: ' ... I also opened "A Beggar" and found some data there that may be of interest to you ... The separate illustration by Madox Brown seemed curious and I thought at first it was the original but it looks like one specially pulled on japan paper. I remember how pleased you were with the original drawing ... ' (Austin).

39 Reader's Report (Berg).
40 Reader's Report (Berg).
41 Reader's Report (Berg).
42 Reader's Report (Berg).
43 Reader's Report (Berg).
44 Reader's Report (Berg).
45 Reader's Report (Berg).
46 Reader's Report (Berg).
    W. E. Henley (1849–1903) was influential as editor of the *National Observer* (1889–94) and the *New Review* (1898–1903). He earned a reputation as a revolutionary force in English literature, defending the early works of Barrie, Hardy, Kipling, Wells, Shaw and Conrad.
47 Reader's Report (Berg).
48 Reader's Report (Berg).
49 Reader's Report (Berg).
50 Reader's Report (Berg).
51 Reader's Report (Berg).
52 Reader's Report (Berg).
53 F. M. Hueffer, *Ancient Lights and Certain New Reflections: Being the Memoirs of a Young Man* (Chapman & Hall 1911), 226–7. David Garnett to author, 21 March 1980: 'Ford's account is pure invention. Constance's story is that Edward handed her the MS of Almayer saying "Look at this and see if the English is good enough for it to be published". Almayer was published in 1894. Gracie's cottage was not built until 1897

when Ford started wearing smock frocks etc. The MS must have been shown Constance at Henhurst Cross.'

5: Conrad

1 U. Mursia, 'The True "Discoverer" of Joseph Conrad's Literary Talent and Other Notes on Conradian Biography', *Conradiana* IV (1972), 5–22.

2 Joseph Conrad to Mme Poradowska, 12 July 1894, in J. A. Gee and P. S. Storm (eds), *Letters of Joseph Conrad to Marguerite Poradowska 1890–1920* (Yale University Press 1940), 71.

3 Joseph Conrad to Mme Poradowska, Aug. 1894, ibid., 75.

4 Joseph Conrad to Mme Poradowska, 8 Sept. 1894, ibid., 75.

5 U. Mursia, 'True "Discoverer" of Conrad's Talent', 8.

6 Joseph Conrad to Mme Poradowska, 4 Oct. 1894, in Gee and Storm (eds), *Letters of Conrad to Marguerite Poradowska*, 80.

7 R. Curle, *Joseph Conrad: A Study* (Kegan Paul 1914), 5.

8 Joseph Conrad to Mme Poradowska, 4 Oct. 1894, in Gee and Storm (eds), *Letters of Conrad to Marguerite Poradowska*, 80.

9 Joseph Conrad to Mme Poradowska, 10 Oct. 1894, ibid., 81.

10 Gertrude Bone MSS (Austin).

11 J. D. Gordan, *Joseph Conrad: Making of a Novelist* (Harvard University Press 1941), 306–7.

12 Joseph Conrad to EG, 19 June 1896, in E. Garnett (ed.), *Letters from Joseph Conrad 1895–1924* (Bobbs-Merrill 1928), 60.

13 Joseph Conrad to EG, 16 Oct. 1896, ibid., 70.

14 Gordan, *Joseph Conrad*, xiii–xiv.

15 Joseph Conrad to EG, 15 March 1895, in E. Garnett (ed.), *Letters from Joseph Conrad*, 34.

16 Joseph Conrad to EG, 8 March 1895, ibid., 33.

17 Joseph Conrad to EG, 24 Sept. 1895, ibid., 42.

18 Introduction to U. Mursia (ed.), *The Sisters: An Unfinished Story* (U. Mursia, Milan, 1968), 25.

19 Joseph Conrad to EG, 23 March 1896, in E. Garnett (ed.), *Letters from Joseph Conrad*, 46.

20 EG to Joseph Conrad, 26 May 1896 (Austin).

21 Joseph Conrad to EG, 24 May 1896, in E. Garnett (ed.), *Letters from Joseph Conrad*, 53–4.

22 Ibid., 54.

23 Joseph Conrad to T. F. Unwin, 28 May 1896, in Gordan, *Joseph Conrad*, 220.

24 Joseph Conrad to EG, 2 June 1896, in E. Garnett (ed.), *Letters from Joseph Conrad*, 55.

25 Joseph Conrad to EG, 6 June 1896, ibid., 56.

26 Joseph Conrad to EG, 2 June 1896, ibid., 54–5.

27 Review of E. Garnett (ed.), *Letters from Joseph Conrad*, in *The Times Literary Supplement*, No. 1378, 28 June 1928, 483.

28 Joseph Conrad to EG, 19 June 1896, in E. Garnett (ed.), *Letters from Joseph Conrad*, 58–60.

29 Joseph Conrad to T. F. Unwin, in Gordan, *Joseph Conrad*, 241.

30 Joseph Conrad to EG, 14 Aug. 1896, in E. Garnett (ed.), *Letters from Joseph Conrad*, 66–8.

31 Joseph Conrad to EG, 21 Nov. 1896, ibid., 79.

32 Gordan, *Joseph Conrad*, 235–6.

33 Joseph Conrad to EG, 29 Nov. 1896, in E. Garnett (ed.), *Letters from Joseph Conrad*, 79–80.

34 Joseph Conrad to EG, 2 Dec. 1896, ibid., 80–1.

35 Joseph Conrad to EG, 19 Dec. 1896, ibid., 82.

36 Gordan, *Joseph Conrad*, 144–5.

37 Joseph Conrad to EG, 24 Aug. 1897, in E. Garnett (ed.), *Letters from Joseph Conrad*, 101.

38 A. Symons, review of *Triumph of Death* by d'Annunzio, *Saturday Review of Literature* LXXXV (1898), 1456.

39 Joseph Conrad to EG, 2 Feb. 1898, in E. Garnett (ed.), *Letters from Joseph Conrad*, 131.

40 Joseph Conrad to EG, 19 Feb. 1897, ibid., 91.

41 Joseph Conrad to EG, 28 Feb. 1897, ibid., 91.

42 Joseph Conrad to EG, 10 March 1897, ibid., 92.

43 Joseph Conrad to EG, 14 April 1897, ibid., 95.

44 Joseph Conrad to EG, 12 March 1897, ibid., 94.

45 Joseph Conrad to EG, 24 Sept. 1897, ibid., 103.

46 Joseph Conrad to EG, 27 Sept. 1897, ibid., 106.
    Ford Madox Ford put forward the theory that *The Return* and *The Sisters* signified Conrad's deep ambition to be what

Ford termed: 'A straight writer, treating of usual human activities in cities and countrysides normal to the users of Anglo-Saxon or Latin speech. He desired in short to be a Dostoevsky who should also be a conscious artist writing in English or preferably in French.' In Ford's opinion Conrad was extremely dejected at the prospect of becoming a sea writer and bowed to the pressure of 'his friends and the inevitable'. Of these friends the two most persuasive were 'Henley who impressed upon Conrad that his only chance of making a living lay in writing about the sea ... Mr. Edward Garnett also, who at that time was – as I am sure he still is – the literary dictator of London, used very strong pressure upon Conrad not to write in the spirit of *The Return*.' Introduction to U. Mursia (ed.), *The Sisters*, 13–16.

47 Joseph Conrad to EG, 29 Sept. 1897, in E. Garnett (ed.), *Letters from Joseph Conrad*, 107.

48 Joseph Conrad to EG, 11 Oct. 1897, ibid., 111.

49 Ibid., 108n. Footnote quoting Conrad's note to *Tales of Unrest*, collected edition, 1919.

50 Ibid., 7.

51 Sean O'Faolain, *Vive Moi!* (Hart-Davis 1965), 257.

52 Joseph Conrad to EG, 25 Nov. 1896, in E. Garnett (ed.), *Letters from Joseph Conrad*, 21–2.

53 Joseph Conrad to EG, 2 June 1897, ibid., 98.

54 Joseph Conrad to EG, 5 Nov. 1897, ibid., 116.

55 Ibid., 23–4.

56 Joseph Conrad to EG, 29 July 1911, ibid., 231.

57 Introduction to W. M. Blackburn (ed.), *Joseph Conrad: Letters to William Blackwood and D. S. Meldrum* (Duke University Press 1958), xxxii.

58 Joseph Conrad to EG, 29 July 1911, in E. Garnett (ed.), *Letters from Joseph Conrad*, 230.

59 Joseph Conrad to EG, 28 Aug. 1897, ibid., 103.

60 Ibid., 24.

61 Ibid., 27.

62 Constance Garnett to Joseph Conrad, 30 Dec. 1897 (Austin).

63 Joseph Conrad to EG, 26 Oct. 1899, in E. Garnett (ed.), *Letters from Joseph Conrad*, 157.

6: *Leaving Unwin*

1 J. Conrad and F. M. Hueffer, *The Inheritors* (Gresham edn 1925), 18–19.

2 J. A. Meixner, *Ford Madox Ford's Novels* (O.U.P. 1962), 104.

3 R. B. Cunninghame Graham to EG, 8 July 1898, quoted as footnote in C. T. Watts (ed.), *Joseph Conrad's Letters to R. B. Cunninghame Graham* (C.U.P. 1969), 96n.

4 P. Unwin, *The Publishing Unwins* (Heinemann 1972), 46.

5 Quoted in W. H. Hudson to EG, 19 June 1902, in E. Garnett (ed.), *Letters from W. H. Hudson to Edward Garnett* (Dent 1925), 21.

6 EG to R. B. Cunninghame Graham, 4 July 1898 (National Library of Scotland).

7 Constance Garnett to Dr Richard Garnett, 26 Dec. 1899 (Hilton Hall).

8 Footnote in E. Garnett (ed.), *Letters from Joseph Conrad*, 157.

9 EG to Dr Richard Garnett, 15 Feb. 1900 (Hilton Hall).

10 Dr Richard Garnett to EG, n.d. (Hilton Hall).

11 Constance Garnett to Dr Richard Garnett, 2 March 1900 (Hilton Hall).

12 Constance Garnett to Dr Richard Garnett, 2 Aug. 1900 (Hilton Hall).
A note in Olive's Diary described the Huts as 'a collection of holiday homes made by the Blacks from railway carriages, in some meadows near Holmbush, Sussex. Three generations of Garnetts and Blacks used them with infinite delight.'

13 EG to Mrs Olivia Narney Garnett, 5 July 1901 (Hilton Hall).

14 EG to Dr Richard Garnett, 5 July 1901 (Hilton Hall).

15 W. Heinemann to EG, 2 July 1901 (Hilton Hall).

16 Constance Garnett to Dr Richard Garnett, 15 July 1901 (Hilton Hall).

17 EG to Dr Richard Garnett, 4 Oct. 1901 (Hilton Hall).

18 Constance Garnett to Dr Richard Garnett, 4 Oct. 1901 (Hilton Hall).

19 Constance Garnett to Dr Richard Garnett, 12 Nov. 1901 (Hilton Hall).

20 Constance Garnett to Dr Richard Garnett, n.d. (Hilton Hall).

21 Reader's Report (Berg).

22 E. Garnett (ed.), *Letters from W. H. Hudson*, xiii.

23 EG to R. B. Cunninghame Graham, 18 July 1901 (National Library of Scotland).

24 EG to R. B. Cunninghame Graham, 15 April 1902 (Austin).

25 May Sinclair to EG, 14 March (Austin).

26 May Sinclair to EG, 20 March 1902 (Austin).

27 Ford Madox Ford to EG, 1901, in R. M. Ludwig (ed.), *Letters from Ford Madox Ford* (Princeton University Press 1965), 15.

28 Ford Madox Ford to EG, n.d., ibid., 9.

29 Olive's Diary.

30 Ford Madox Ford to EG, in A. Mizener, *The Saddest Story: A Biography of Ford Madox Ford* (Bodley Head 1972), 76.

31 Mizener, *Saddest Story*, 466, 543 n. 16.

32 Ford Madox Ford to EG, 1903 (Cornell).

33 May Morris to EG, 6 June 1905 (Austin).

34 E. Garnett, *Hogarth* (Duckworth 1911), 7.

35 Reader's Report (Hilton Hall).

36 Reader's Report (Hilton Hall).

37 Reader's Report (Hilton Hall).

38 R. Church, *Speaking Aloud* (Heinemann 1968), 258.

39 Quoted in D. G. Hogarth, *The Life of Charles M. Doughty* (O.U.P. 1928), 146.

40 Ibid., 159.

41 Edward Thomas to Gordon Bottomley, 30 March 1908, in R. George Thomas (ed.), *Letters from Edward Thomas to Gordon Bottomley* (O.U.P. 1968), 161.

42 J. Hepburn (ed.), *Letters of Arnold Bennett*, 3 vols (O.U.P. 1966-70), II, 167.

43 Reader's Report (Hilton Hall).

7: *Reader as Critic*

1 Joseph Conrad to D. S. Meldrum, 1 Sept. 1900, in W. M. Blackburn (ed.), *Joseph Conrad: Letters to William Blackwood and D. S. Meldrum* (Duke University Press 1958), 108-9.

2 Ibid., xvi.

3 Joseph Conrad to D. S. Meldrum, 3 Aug. 1901, ibid., 130-1.

4 Joseph Conrad to W. Blackwood, 26 Aug. 1901, ibid., 133.

5 W. Blackwood to Joseph Conrad, 17 Sept. 1901, ibid., 134.

6 Dr Richard Garnett to EG, 1901 (Hilton Hall).

7 Constance Garnett to Dr Richard Garnett, 12 Nov. 1901 (Hilton Hall).

8 E. Garnett, 'The Difficulties of Contemporary Criticism', *Monthly Review* V (1901), 92, reprinted in E. Garnett, *Friday Nights* (Cape 1922), 349–75.

9 M. Elwin, *Old Gods Falling* (Collins 1939), 195.

10 F. Swinnerton, *Background with Chorus* (Hutchinson 1956), 80–2.

11 J. B. Townsend, *John Davidson* (Yale University Press 1961), 140.

12 J. Gross, *The Rise and Fall of the Man of Letters: Aspects of English Literary Life since 1800* (Weidenfeld & Nicolson 1969), 136.

13 Ibid., 137.

14 Elwin, *Old Gods Falling*, 202.

15 R. Wellek, *History of Modern Criticism 1750–1950: The Late Nineteenth Century* (Cape 1966), 416–28.

16 E. M. W. Tillyard, *The Muse Unchained* (1958), in B. Bergonzi (ed.), *The Twentieth Century: History of Literature in the English Language* Vol. 7 (Barrie & Jenkins 1970), 368.

17 Bergonzi, *Twentieth Century*, 370.

18 T. S. Eliot, *Selected Essays* 3rd edn (Faber 1951), 24.

19 F. R. Leavis, *The Common Pursuit* (Chatto & Windus 1965), 212.

20 E. Garnett, 'W. H. Hudson: An Appreciation', *Academy* LXII (1902), 632–4.

21 W. H. Hudson to EG, 16 June 1902, in E. Garnett (ed.), *Letters from W. H. Hudson to Edward Garnett* (Dent 1925), 21.

22 E. Garnett, 'C. M. Doughty's "Arabia Deserta"', *Academy* LXIV (1903), 86–7.

23 E. Garnett, '"Amaryllis at the Fair" and "After London"', *Academy* LXIV (1903), 345–6.

24 EG to R. B. Cunninghame Graham, 25 Nov. 1904 (National Library of Scotland).

25 Henry Lawson to EG, 18 Feb. 1901 (Austin).

26 Henry Lawson to EG, n.d. (Austin).

27 J. Barnes, 'Henry Lawson in London', *Quadrant* (July 1979), 33.

28 Henry Lawson to EG, 29 Jan. 1902 (Austin).

29 Henry Lawson to EG, 1 June 1902 (Austin).

30 E. Garnett, 'An Appreciation', *Academy* LXII (1902), 250–1.

31 Henry Lawson to EG, 27/8 Feb. 1902 (Austin).

32 D. Prout, *Henry Lawson: The Grey Dreamer* (Angus & Robertson 1963), 193.

33 Barnes, 'Henry Lawson', 34.

34 H. M. Green, *History of Australian Literature* (Angus & Robertson 1961), 528; and Prout, *Henry Lawson*, 193.

35 E. Garnett, 'Sarah Orne Jewett', *Academy* LXIV (1903).

36 EG to S. O. Jewett, 9 Sept. 1903 (Colby).

37 S. O. Jewett to EG, 10 March 1904 (Austin).

38 EG to S. O. Jewett, 9 Sept. 1903 (Colby).

39 W. H. Hudson to EG, 12 Nov. 1911, in E. Garnett (ed.), *Letters from Hudson*, 118.

40 E. C. Bentley, *These Days* (Constable 1940), 257.
Edward submitted a report to Duckworth on *Humorous Essays* by E. C. Bentley dated 20 March 1907: 'We have advised the author (an acquaintance) to try Chatto & Windus. The Papers are very clever, with a distinct vein of humour – but all of them are a little too journalistic to suit Duckworth's book. We have also advised him to try his hand at a novel in the "Pettridge (!)" style. His humour is *original* and perhaps he has in him elements necessary for a *popular success*. We may hear of him later.' (Hilton Hall.)

41 F. Swinnerton, *Georgian Literary Scene* 8th edn (Hutchinson 1969), 186–7.

42 F. Swinnerton, *Background with Chorus*, 117.

8: Reader as Reviewer

1 E. Garnett, 'Joseph Conrad', *Academy* LIV (1898), 82–3.

2 E. Garnett, 'Mr Conrad's New Book', *Academy* LXIII (1902), 606–7.

3 F. R. Leavis, *The Great Tradition* (Chatto & Windus 1948), 248.

4 E. Garnett, 'Mr Conrad's New Book', 606–7.

5 N. Sherry (ed.), *Conrad: The Critical Heritage* (Routledge & Kegan Paul 1973), 131.

6 Joseph Conrad to EG, 22 Dec. 1902, in E. Garnett (ed.), *Letters from Joseph Conrad 1895–1924* (Bobbs-Merrill 1928), 184.

7 E. Garnett, 'Mr Conrad's Art' (review of *Nostromo*), *Speaker* XI (1904), 138–9.

8 EG to R. B. Cunninghame Graham, Oct. 1904, quoted in C. T. Watts (ed.), *Joseph Conrad's Letters to Cunninghame Graham* (C.U.P. 1969), 159.

9 EG to Richard Curle, 5 June 1934 (Austin).

10 E. Garnett, 'Mr Stephen Crane: An Appreciation', *Academy* LV (1898), 483–4.

11 EG to Cora Crane, 20 Dec. 1898 (Columbia).

12 Cora Crane to EG, n.d. (Beinecke).

13 Introduction to T. Beer, *Stephen Crane: A Study in American Letters* (Knopf 1923), 23.

14 J. B. Calvert, 'Style and Meaning in Stephen Crane', *Texas Studies in English* XXXVII (1958), 39–40.

15 E. Garnett, 'Two Americans' (review of *The Crossing* by Winston Churchill; *The O'Ruddy* by Stephen Crane), *Speaker* X (1904), 436–7.

16 E. Garnett, *Friday Nights* (Cape 1922), 244.

17 E. Garnett, 'Mrs Humphry Ward's Art', *Speaker* XI (1905), 594–6.

18 W. H. Hudson to EG, 29 March 1908, in E. Garnett (ed.), *Letters from W. H. Hudson to Edward Garnett* (Dent 1925), 104.

19 E. Garnett, *Friday Nights*, 149.

20 E. Garnett, 'Mark Rutherford and Others', *Speaker* X (1904), 361–3.

21 E. Garnett, 'The Novel of the Week' (review of *The Grim Smile of the Five Towns*), *Nation* I (1907), 642.

22 E. Garnett, 'A Provincial Novel' (review of *The Old Wives' Tale*), *Nation* IV (1908), 314–16.

23 Arnold Bennett to EG, 23 Nov. 1908, in J. Hepburn (ed.), *Letters of Arnold Bennett*, 3 vols (O.U.P. 1966–70), II, 232–3.

24 EG to Arnold Bennett, ibid., 233.

25 Arnold Bennett to EG, 29 Sept. 1911 (Austin).

26 E. Garnett, review of *Where Angels Fear to Tread, Spectator* XCV (1905), 1089–90.

27 E. M. Forster, 'The Man behind the Scenes', *News Chronicle*, 30 Nov. 1931, 4.

28 Reader's Report (Hilton Hall).

29 E. Garnett, 'Novel of the Week' (review of *The Longest Journey* by E. M. Forster), *Nation* I (1907), 357–8.

30 E. M. Forster to EG, 5 May 1907 (Austin).

31 E. M. Forster to EG, 22 Nov. 1908 (Austin).

32 E. Garnett, 'English Novels and English Life', *Nation* LXXXVIII (1909), 272–5.

33 E. M. Forster to EG, 10 Nov. 1910 (Austin).

34 E. Garnett, 'Villadom' (review of *Howards End*), *Nation* VIII (1910), 282–4.

35 E. M. Forster to EG, 12 Nov. 1910 (Austin).

36 E. M. Forster to EG, 11 Dec. 1910 (Austin).

37 EG to H. G. Wells, 21 June 1900 (Urbana).

38 H. G. Wells to EG, 26 June 1900 (Austin).

39 EG to H. G. Wells, 19 April 1905 (Urbana).

40 H. G. Wells to EG, 20 April 1905 (Austin).

41 EG to H. G. Wells, 22 Sept. 1906 (Urbana).

42 EG to H. G. Wells, 9 Feb. 1909 (Urbana).

43 EG to H. G. Wells, 19 Jan. 1911 (Urbana).

44 H. W. Massingham to EG, 18 Feb. 1907 (Austin).

45 H. W. Massingham to EG, 5 June (Austin).

46 H. W. Massingham to EG, n.d. (Austin).

47 S. Hynes, *The Edwardian Turn of Mind* (O.U.P. 1968), 201–2.

48 E. Garnett, review of *A Dark Lantern* by E. Robins, *Speaker* XII (1905), 215–16.

49 E. Garnett, 'The Sex Novel', preface to M. C. Braby, *Downward: A Slice of Life* (T. Werner Laurie 1910), unpaged.

50 H. W. Massingham to EG, n.d. (Austin).

9: Galsworthy

1 Reader's Report (Berg).
   Conrad had written to Edward on 19 Feb. 1897: 'I wrote to my literary! friend [i.e. Galsworthy] saying that you promised to give quick attention to his stories. Their title is:

"From the Four Corners", his pseudonym I do not know, and he is going to send them (probably early tomorrow) in the usual way . . . ' E. Garnett (ed.), *Letters from Joseph Conrad 1895–1924* (Bobbs-Merrill 1928), 90–1.

2 Reader's Report (Berg).

3 David Garnett to author, 21 March 1980. Galsworthy dedicated *The Island Pharisees* to Constance, in appreciation of her Turgenev translations.

4 EG to John Galsworthy, 25 Sept. 1900, in E. Garnett (ed.), *Letters from John Galsworthy 1900–1932* (Cape 1932), 17–20.

5 John Galsworthy to EG, 12 Feb. 1902, ibid., 32.

6 EG to John Galsworthy, 10 May 1902, ibid., 38.

7 EG to John Galsworthy, 3 Nov. 1902, ibid., 41–3.

8 John Galsworthy to EG, 5 Nov. 1902, ibid., 44.

9 R. A. Gettman, *A Victorian Publisher: A Study of the Bentley Papers* (O.U.P. 1960), 209.

10 John Galsworthy, 'If I Only Knew', in H. V. Marrot, *Life and Letters of John Galsworthy* (Heinemann 1935), 135.

11 Reader's Report (Hilton Hall).

12 EG to John Galsworthy, 20 May 1903, in E. Garnett (ed.), *Letters from Galsworthy*, 49.

13 EG to John Galsworthy, 12 June 1904, ibid., 53.

14 Ibid., 10–11. Inscription by Galsworthy in TS of *West Country and Other Stories*, 11 Dec. 1929.

15 John Galsworthy to EG, 1 Feb. 1905, ibid., 57.

16 EG to John Galsworthy, 27 May 1905, ibid., 68–72.

17 John Galsworthy to EG, n.d., ibid., 84.

18 John Galsworthy to EG, 14 June 1905, ibid., 91.

19 John Galsworthy to EG, 26 June 1905, ibid., 92.

20 EG to John Galsworthy, 26 June 1905, ibid., 99.

21 John Galsworthy to EG, 6 Jan. 1906, ibid., 103.

22 EG to John Galsworthy, 4 Nov. 1906, ibid., 127–9.

23 EG to John Galsworthy, 13 Jan 1910, ibid., 175.

24 EG to John Galsworthy, Sept. 1910, in Marrot, *Life and Letters of Galsworthy*, 288.

25 John Galsworthy to EG, 1 Sept. 1910, in E. Garnett (ed.), *Letters from Galsworthy*, 181.

26 John Galsworthy to EG, 18 Sept. 1910, ibid., 191.

27 John Galsworthy to EG, 5 Nov. 1910, ibid., 197.

28 John Galsworthy to EG, 13 Nov. 1910, ibid., 199.

29 EG to John Galsworthy, 8 March 1906, ibid., 112–13.

30 John Galsworthy to EG, 10 March 1906, ibid., 114.

31 Ada Galsworthy to R. H. Mottram, 28 Sept. 1906, in C. Dupré, *John Galsworthy, a Biography* (Collins 1976), 120.

32 John Galsworthy to EG, 3 May 1907, in E. Garnett (ed.), *Letters from Galsworthy*, 140.

33 EG to John Galsworthy, 6 May 1907, ibid., 141.

10: Playwright

1 E. Garnett, *The Trial of Jeanne d'Arc and Other Plays* (Cape 1931), 9.
    Edward expressed his interest in the repertory movement in 'The Repertory Theatre in England', *Nation* LXXXIX (1909), 125–6. David Garnett describes how as a boy he took part in Edward's plays for children and praises his father's ability as a producer, in *The Golden Echo* (Chatto & Windus 1953), 72–3.

2 Quoted in Introduction to E. Garnett, *The Breaking Point* (Duckworth 1907), ix.

3 G. A. Redford to EG, 5 July 1907 (Austin).

4 E. Garnett, *Breaking Point*, xxvii.

5 H. V. Marrot, *Life and Letters of John Galsworthy* (Heinemann 1935), 219.

6 William Archer to Lady Mary Murray, 1 Nov. 1907, in C. Archer, *William Archer: Life, Work and Friendships* (Allen & Unwin 1931), 321.

7 F. Vernon, *The Twentieth Century Theatre* (Harrap 1924), 111–12.

8 G. B. Shaw to EG, 14 March 1908 (Hilton Hall).

9 Joseph Conrad to EG, 17 Nov. 1906, in E. Garnett (ed.), *Letters from Joseph Conrad 1895–1924* (Bobbs-Merrill 1928), 195–6.
    Curiously *The Breaking Point* which to modern ears seems innocuous stayed banned long after other plays of this period were reprieved; as late as 1925 a licence was still refused.

10 C. Heilbrun, *The Garnett Family* (Allen & Unwin 1961), 88.

11 Quoted in E. Garnett, *Trial of Jeanne d'Arc*, 12.

12 Edward Thomas to Gordon Bottomley, 12 June 1909, in

R. George Thomas (ed.), *Letters from Edward Thomas to Gordon Bottomley* (O.U.P. 1968), 186.

13 John Galsworthy to EG, 22 Feb. 1906, in E. Garnett (ed.), *Letters from John Galsworthy 1900–1932* (Cape 1932), 109.

14 D. Garnett, *Golden Echo*, 134–5.

15 John Galsworthy to EG, 11 Feb. 1909, in E. Garnett (ed.), *Letters from Galsworthy*, 169.

16 Joseph Conrad to EG, Dec. 1911, in E. Garnett (ed.), *Letters from Conrad*, 235–6.

17 D. Garnett, *Golden Echo*, 135.

18 Review of *The Spanish Lovers*, *Athenaeum* No. 4413 (1912), 603.

19 Joseph Conrad to EG, [March] 1911, in E. Garnett (ed.), *Letters from Conrad*, 202.

20 John Galsworthy to EG, 15 Aug. 1907, in E. Garnett (ed.), *Letters from Galsworthy*, 152–3.

21 EG to Joseph Conrad, 17 Dec. 1921, in C. Heilbrun, *Garnett Family*, 124.

22 John Galsworthy to EG, 14 Sept. 1910, in E. Garnett (ed.), *Letters from Galsworthy*, 188.

23 H. Trench to EG, 29 March 1911 (Hilton Hall).

24 W. Archer to EG, 8 Dec. 1910 (Hilton Hall).

25 R. Speaight, *William Poel and the Elizabethan Revival* (Heinemann 1954), 222. Edward contributed an article entitled 'Mr Poel and the Theatre' to the *English Review* XIV (1913), 589–95.

26 S. Weintraub, *Private Shaw and Public Shaw* (Cape 1963), 67. Jean Forbes-Robertson, daughter of Sir Johnston Forbes-Robertson, had a distinguished stage career and is remembered for her performances as Peter Pan. She married the publisher Hamish Hamilton, a friend of Edward, and he sent them a parody of 'what it was like to be married to Jean'. Hamish Hamilton to author, 7 March 1977.

27 G. B. Shaw to T. E. Lawrence, 8 Nov. 1931, in A. W. Lawrence (ed.), *Letters to T. E. Lawrence* (Cape 1962), 180.

28 E. Garnett, *Trial of Jeanne d'Arc*, vii–viii.

29 D. Garnett, *Golden Echo*, 135.

30 Edward Thomas to Gordon Bottomley, 1 Sept. 1909, in R. George Thomas (ed.), *Letters to Bottomley*, 190.

11: *The Mont Blanc*

1 R. H. Mottram, *John Galsworthy*, Writers and Their Work No. 38 (N.B.L. 1953), 8.

2 Introduction to E. Garnett (ed.), *Letters from W. H. Hudson to Edward Garnett* (Dent 1925), 2.

3 EG to H. G. Wells, 22 Feb. 1910 (Urbana).

4 E. Garnett (ed.), *Letters from Hudson*, 2.

5 Quoted in C. Dupré, *John Galsworthy, a Biography* (Collins 1976), 80.

6 Quoted in R. H. Mottram, *For Some We Have Loved: An Intimate Portrait of Ada and John Galsworthy* (Hutchinson 1956), 22–4.
Galsworthy penned a eulogistic essay on Edward as a critic in his review of Edward's *Tolstoy*, a study which he contributed to Constable's Modern Biographies Series. After a brief reference to the item reviewed he wrote: 'But I am not reviewing a book by Tolstoy, I am reviewing a critical study of him by Edward Garnett, and I am going frankly to take this opportunity of saying what I think of Edward Garnett as a critic; because I feel too few people have an adequate idea of how deeply Mr. Garnett has affected the currents and trend of imaginative work in our time.' There followed a long assessment in which Galsworthy made reference to his friend as one who 'has "discovered" more talent, helped more aspiration, and fought more battles for the cause of good literature than anyone who can be named: and he has done it nearly all in the dark, and all for the love of the real thing . . . ' This long piece reflects Galsworthy's admiration and his own generous mind. J. Galsworthy, 'Edward Garnett: An Appreciation' (review of *Tolstoy* by E. Garnett), *Westminster Gazette*, 28 March 1914.

7 Joseph Conrad to E. Noble, 28 Oct. 1895, in C. Jean-Aubry, *Joseph Conrad: Life and Letters*, 2 vols (Heinemann 1927), I, 183.

8 S. Reynolds to EG, 17 Sept. 1906, in H. Wright (ed.), *Letters from Stephen Reynolds* (Hogarth Press 1933), 32.

9 S. Reynolds to EG, 7 Jan. 1907, ibid., 69.

10 S. Reynolds to EG, 7 Sept. 1908, ibid., 106.

11 S. Reynolds to EG, 27 March 1908, ibid., 101–2.

12 Reader's Report (Hilton Hall).

13 Reader's Report (Hilton Hall).

14 Reader's Report (Hilton Hall).
Edward continued to follow the fortunes of Tomlinson, writing to the author on 29 Aug. 1929: 'I took away the copy of "Galleon's Reach" to Cornwall on my holiday, and am writing a line to congratulate you. I never expected you to bring off a story so successfully. It is remarkable in its deftness, in its craftsmanship, and in its completeness of the illusion ... ' (Austin).

15 Edward Thomas to Gordon Bottomley, 13 Feb. 1909, in R. George Thomas (ed.), *Letters from Edward Thomas to Gordon Bottomley* (O.U.P. 1968), 178.

16 Edward Thomas to EG, 10 Nov. 1909 (Austin).

17 Edward Thomas to EG, 11 Nov. 1909 (Austin).

18 Edward Garnett, 'Some Letters of Edward Thomas', *Athenaeum* Nos 4694, 4695 (1920), 501–3, 533–6.

19 Edward Thomas to EG, n.d., ibid., 503.

20 R. P. Eckert, *Edward Thomas* (Dent 1937), 114.

21 R. J. Stonesifer, *W. H. Davies: A Critical Biography* (Cape 1963), 68.

22 Ibid., 69.

23 Ibid., 69.

24 Reader's Report (Hilton Hall).

25 Stonesifer, *W. H. Davies*, 74.

26 Edward Thomas to EG, 29 Aug. 1907, in E. Garnett, 'Some Letters of Edward Thomas', *Athenaeum* No. 4694, 502.

27 Ibid., 64.
Davies published his first book of verse, *The Soul's Destroyer*, by having 250 copies printed by Watts of Fleet Street then sending a copy accompanied by a begging letter to recipients drawn from a list he had made from a library copy of *Who's Who*. The romantic image of the beggar poet as much as the freshness of his poetry aroused the interest of those who received them.

28 W. H. Davies to EG, 14 June 1907 (Austin).

29 Edward Thomas to EG, in Stonesifer, *W. H. Davies*, 87.

30 Circular letter by Edward Garnett and Edward Thomas, Feb. 1911 (Austin).

31 W. H. Hudson re W. H. Davies, n.d. (Austin).

32 Joseph Conrad re W. H. Davies, n.d. (Austin).

33 W. H. Davies to EG, 26 Feb. 1911 (Austin).

34 Edmund Gosse to EG, 12 April 1911 (Austin).

35 Llewellyn Roberts to EG, 12 April 1911 (Austin).

36 W. H. Davies to EG, 15 April 1911 (Austin).

37 W. H. Davies to EG, 11 Nov. 1911 (Austin).

38 W. H. Davies to EG, 17 Nov. 1911 (Austin).

39 Quoted in Stonesifer, *W. H. Davies*, 86.

40 W. H. Davies, *Later Days* (Cape 1925), 37.

41 Ibid., 48–9.

42 F. M. Hueffer to EG, 1909, in R. M. Ludwig (ed.), *Letters of Ford Madox Ford* (Princeton University Press 1965), 30–1.

43 F. M. Hueffer to EG, 17 Oct. 1908, ibid., 27–8.

44 R. A. Scott-James, Preface to Penguin edition of Ford's Tietjens novels, 1948, quoted in *F. M. Ford: The Critical Heritage* (Routledge & Kegan Paul 1972), 241.

45 E. Jepson, *Memories of an Edwardian and Neo-Georgian* (Richards 1937), 149.

46 Quoted in A. Mizener, *The Saddest Story: A Biography of Ford Madox Ford* (Bodley Head 1972), 165.

47 Ibid., 107.

48 F. H. Hueffer to E. Jepson, 28 Oct. 1910, in Ludwig (ed.), *Letters of F. M. Ford*, 45.

49 Mizener, *Saddest Story*, 212–13.

50 D. Goldring, *South Lodge: Reminiscences of Violet Hunt, Ford Madox Ford and The English Review Circle* (Constable 1943), 169–71.

51 E. Crankshaw, review of *The Last Pre-Raphaelite*, *Saturday Review of Literature* CXXXI (1948), 160–7.

52 F. M. Ford, 'Literary Portraits: XII. Mr. Edward Garnett', *Tribune* 2, 12 Oct. 1907, quoted in D. D. Harvey, *Ford Madox Ford: A Bibliography of Works and Criticism* (Princeton University Press 1962), D68–81 No. 80.

53 EG to John Galsworthy, 8 May 1905, in E. Garnett (ed.), *Letters from John Galsworthy* (Cape 1932), 59.

54 M. Holloway, *Norman Douglas: A Biography* (Secker & Warburg 1976), 153.

55 Ibid., 173.

56 Ibid., 191.

57 D. Garnett, 'The Bolter' (review of M. Holloway, *Norman Douglas*), *New Statesman*, 10 Dec. 1976, 841.
58 N. Cunard, *Grand Man: Memories of Norman Douglas* (Secker & Warburg 1954), 269.
59 Quoted in Holloway, *Norman Douglas*, 226.
60 Ibid., 237.
61 Ibid., 154.
62 D. Garnett, 'The Bolter', 841.
63 Reader's Report (Hilton Hall).
64 Quoted in D. Farr, *Gilbert Cannan: A Georgian Prodigy* (Chatto & Windus 1978), 37–8.
65 Ibid., 38.
66 Ibid., 49.
67 Ibid., 54.
68 Ibid., 56.
69 Ibid., 57.
70 Henry James, 'The Younger Generation', *The Times Literary Supplement* No. 635, 19 March 1914, 132.

12: *The Young Lorenzo*

1 E. Garnett, Introduction to D. H. Lawrence, *A Collier's Friday Night* (Secker 1934), vii.
2 E. Nehls (ed.), *D. H. Lawrence: A Composite Biography* (University of Wisconsin Press 1958), I, 82.
3 EG to J. B. Pinker, 13 July 1911 (Austin).
4 D. H. Lawrence to EG, 25 Aug. 1911, in Harry T. Moore (ed.), *Collected Letters of D. H. Lawrence*, 2 vols (Heinemann 1962), I, 80.
5 D. H. Lawrence to EG, 10 Sept. 1911, ibid., 80.
6 D. H. Lawrence to EG, 25 Sept. 1911, ibid., 80.
7 D. H. Lawrence to EG, 2 Oct. 1911, ibid., 81.
8 D. H. Lawrence to EG, 20 Oct. 1911, ibid., 83.
9 D. H. Lawrence to Louie Burrows, 10 Oct. 1911, in J. T. Boulton (ed.), *Lawrence in Love: Letters to Louie Burrows* (University of Nottingham 1968), 140.
10 D. H. Lawrence to EG, 7 Nov. 1911, in Moore (ed.), *Collected Letters of D. H. Lawrence*, I, 85.
11 Lettice Lawrence to EG, 26 Nov. 1911 (Austin).
12 Lettice Lawrence to EG, 2 Dec. 1911 (Austin).

13 Lettice Lawrence to EG, 17 Dec. 1911 (Austin).

14 D. H. Lawrence to EG, 17 Dec. 1911, in Moore (ed.), *Collected Letters of D. H. Lawrence*, I, 87–8.

15 D. H. Lawrence to EG, 18 Dec. 1911, ibid., 88–9.

16 D. H. Lawrence to Ernest Collings, 14 Nov. 1912, ibid., 158.

17 D. H. Lawrence to EG, 19 Jan. 1912, ibid., 93.

18 D. H. Lawrence to EG, 21 Jan. 1912, ibid., 94.

19 Quoted in E. W. Tedlock, *The Frieda Lawrence Collection of D. H. Lawrence Manuscripts* (University of Mexico Press 1948), 8.

20 D. H. Lawrence to EG, 29 Jan. 1912, in Moore (ed.), *Collected Letters of D. H. Lawrence*, I, 96–7.

21 E. W. Tedlock, *D. H. Lawrence and Sons and Lovers: Sources and Criticisms* (University of London Press 1966), 7.

22 D. H. Lawrence to EG, (?) 22 July 1912, in Moore (ed.), *Collected Letters of D. H. Lawrence*, I, 135.

23 D. H. Lawrence to EG, 14 Nov. 1912, ibid., 160–2.

24 R. A. Gettman, *A Victorian Publisher: A Study of the Bentley Papers* (C.U.P. 1960), 214.

25 D. H. Lawrence to EG, 14 Nov. 1912, in Moore (ed.), *Collected Letters of D. H. Lawrence*, I, 160–2.

26 D. H. Lawrence to EG, 18 Dec. 1911, ibid., 88–9.

27 D. H. Lawrence to EG, postcard, 1 Dec. 1912, in A. Huxley (ed.), *Letters of D. H. Lawrence* (Heinemann 1932), 81.

28 D. H. Lawrence to EG, 19 Dec. 1912, in Moore (ed.), *Collected Letters of D. H. Lawrence*, I, 169.

29 D. H. Lawrence to EG, 29 Dec. 1912, ibid., 173–4.

30 Tedlock, *D. H. Lawrence and Sons and Lovers*, 86–9.
    David Garnett felt that the original text of *Sons and Lovers* should be published in full to clear away any misconceptions (David Garnett to author, 7 Dec. 1969). It is now available: *Sons and Lovers: A Facsimile of a Manuscript*, edited with an introduction by Mark Schorer (University of California Press 1981, price £56), consists of the complete hand-written version of Lawrence's novel, together with six fragments from 'Paul Morel', the penultimate version. Edward Garnett's and Lawrence's deletions are all legible, as are both versions of many of Lawrence's rewritten passages.

31 D. H. Lawrence to EG, 12 Jan. 1913, in Moore (ed.), *Collected Letters of D. H. Lawrence*, I, 175–6.

32 D. H. Lawrence to EG, 18 Feb. 1913, ibid., 186.

33 D. H. Lawrence to EG, 1 Feb. 1913, ibid., 183.

34 D. H. Lawrence to EG, (?) 18 April 1913, ibid., 200.

35 D. H. Lawrence to EG, 19 May 1913, ibid., 204.
Lawrence dedicated *Sons and Lovers* to Edward, and in the presentation copy which he sent to him he wrote the inscription: – 'To my friend and protector in love and literature. Edward Garnett from the author'.

36 D. H. Lawrence and Frieda Weekley to EG, (late May or early June) 1913, ibid., 207–8.

37 D. H. Lawrence to EG, 4 Sept. 1913, ibid., 223.

38 D. H. Lawrence to EG, (?) 15 Sept. 1913, ibid., 224.

39 D. H. Lawrence to EG, 30 Dec. 1913, ibid., 259.

40 D. H. Lawrence to EG, 29 Jan. 1914, ibid., 263.

41 D. H. Lawrence to EG, 22 April 1914, ibid., 272–4.

42 D. H. Lawrence to EG, 5 June 1914, ibid., 282.
The passage reads: 'You mustn't look in my novel for the old stable *ego* of the character. There is another *ego*, according to whose action the individual is unrecognisable, and passes through, as it were, allotropic states which it needs a deeper sense than any we've been used to exercise, to discover are states of the same single radically unchanged element. (Like as diamond and coal are the same pure single element of carbon. The ordinary novel would trace the history of the diamond – but I say, "Diamond, what! This is carbon." And my diamond might be coal or soot, and my theme is carbon.)'

43 D. H. Lawrence to EG, 5 June 1914, ibid., 281–2.

44 R. A. Scott-James, 'Edward Garnett', *Spectator* CLVIII (1937), 362.

45 D. H. Lawrence to EG, 10 Nov. 1921, in Moore (ed.), *Collected Letters of D. H. Lawrence*, II, 674.

46 D. H. Lawrence to EG, 1 Feb. 1913, ibid., 182.

47 W. H. Hudson to EG, 7 Nov. 1913, in E. Garnett (ed.), *Letters from W. H. Hudson to Edward Garnett* (Dent 1925), 130.

48 John Galsworthy to EG, 13 April 1914, in E. Garnett (ed.), *Letters from John Galsworthy 1900–1932* (Cape 1932), 218.

49 Quoted in H. V. Marrot, *Life and Letters of John Galsworthy* (Heinemann 1935), 433.

50 Walter de la Mare to EG, 14 Aug. 1914 (Austin).
51 Robert Lynd to EG, 5 Nov. 1915 (Austin).
52 EG to J. B. Pinker, 23 July 1913 (Austin).
53 E. Garnett, 'Mr. D. H. Lawrence and the Moralists', *Dial* LXI (1916), 377–81.
54 D. H. Lawrence to EG, 17 April 1912, in Moore (ed.), *Collected Letters of D. H. Lawrence*, I, 107–8.
55 D. H. Lawrence to EG, 23 April 1912, ibid., 109.
56 D. H. Lawrence to EG, 29 April 1912, ibid., 110.
57 D. H. Lawrence to EG, (?) 28 July 1913, ibid., 216–17.
58 D. H. Lawrence to EG, (?) 16 May 1914, ibid., 277.
59 Nehls (ed.), *D. H. Lawrence: A Composite Biography*, II, 413.

13: Dostoevsky Corner

1 G. Phelps, *The Russian Novel in English Fiction* (Hutchinson 1956), 12.
2 W. van O'Connor, *Forms of Modern Fiction* (University of Minnesota 1948), 1.
3 Joseph Conrad to EG, May 1917, in E. Garnett (ed.), *Letters from Joseph Conrad 1895–1924* (Bobbs-Merrill 1928), 248–9.
4 E. Garnett, Introduction to I. Turgenev, *The Jew and Other Stories*, trans. Constance Garnett (Heinemann 1899), ix.
5 E. Garnett, Introduction to I. Turgenev, *A Lear of the Steppes and Other Stories*, trans. Constance Garnett (Heinemann 1898), v.
6 T. S. Eliot, 'Turgenev', *Egoist* IV (1917), 167.
7 H. Howarth, *Notes on Some Figures behind T. S. Eliot* (Chatto & Windus 1965), 290.
8 Frank Swinnerton to author, 12 July 1970.
9 Arnold Bennett to EG, 14 Feb. 1897, in J. Hepburn (ed.), *Letters of Arnold Bennett*, 3 vols (O.U.P. 1966–70), II, 80–1.
10 Quoted in W. Martin, *The 'New Age' under Orage* (Manchester University Press 1967), 84.
11 H. G. Wells to Arnold Bennett, 5 July 1900, in W. Harris (ed.), *Arnold Bennett and H. G. Wells: A Record of a Personal and Literary Friendship* (Hart-Davis 1960), 46–7.
12 H. G. Wells to Arnold Bennett, 19 Aug. 1901, ibid., 60.
13 E. Garnett, 'Tolstoy and Turgenieff', *Anglo-Saxon Review* VI (1900), 150.

14 E. Garnett, '"Facts" and "Fiction"', *Speaker* XIV (1906), 339–40.

15 E. Garnett, 'Tolstoy's Place in European Literature', in G. K. Chesterton, *Leo Tolstoy* (Hodder & Stoughton 1903), 36.

16 E. Garnett, 'Maxim Gorky', *Academy* LX (1901), 497–8.

17 E. Garnett, 'Maxim Gorky', *Speaker* XI (1905), 570–1.

18 E. Garnett, Introduction to M. Gorky, *Twenty-six Men and a Girl*, trans. E. Jakowleff and D. B. Montefiore (Duckworth 1902), xiii.

19 Arnold Bennett to EG, 10 March 1902, in Hepburn (ed.), *Letters of Arnold Bennett*, 167.

20 'Gorky in Little' (review of M. Gorky, *Twenty-six Men and a Girl*), *Academy* LXII (1902), 245–6.

21 E. Garnett, 'Dostoevsky', *Academy* LXXI (1906), 202–3.

22 Jacob Tonson [A. Bennett], 'Books and Persons', *New Age* VII (1910), 519.

23 Jacob Tonson [A. Bennett], 'Books and Persons', *New Age* VIII (1911), 349.

24 William Heinemann to Constance Garnett, 19 July 1911 (Hilton Hall).

25 Phelps, *Russian Novel in English Fiction*, 11.

26 F. Swinnerton, *The Georgian Literary Scene* (Hutchinson 1935), 296.

Samuel Hynes in *The Edwardian Turn of Mind* (O.U.P. 1968), 337, wrote: 'Mrs. Garnett's translation of Dostoevsky's *The Brothers Karamazov* became a kind of holy book for the younger generation. Writers like Middleton Murry, Katherine Mansfield and Frank Swinnerton made Dostoevsky their idol and declared *The Brothers Karamazov* the greatest novel ever written.'

The older writers had other opinions over the rival merits of Turgenev and Dostoevsky. To Henry James, Turgenev was 'in a peculiar degree the novelist's novelist, an artistic influence extraordinarily valuable and ineradicably established', for as he wrote to Hugh Walpole in 1912: 'Form alone *takes*, and holds and preserves, substance – saves it from the welter of helpless verbiage that we swim in as in a sea of tasteless tepid pudding ... Tolstoi and Dostoevski are fluid puddings, though not tasteless, because the amount of their own minds and souls in solution in them both gives it savour and flavour, thanks to the strong, rank quality of their genius and experience.'

In the foreword which he contributed to Edward's *Turgenev*, Conrad, with contempt, contrasted Turgenev with the 'convulsed and terror haunted Dostoevsky' whose characters were 'strange beasts in a menagerie or damned souls knocking themselves about in the stuffy darkness of mystical contradictions'.

27 Phelps, *Russian Novel in English Fiction*, 171.
28 V. Woolf, 'Mr. Bennett and Mrs. Brown', *Nation* XXXIV (1923), 342.
29 J. C. Powys, *Autobiography* (Macdonald 1967), 524.
Constance herself said of the comparative value of her translations: 'I should like to be judged by my translation of *War and Peace*. But Tolstoy's simple style goes straight into English without any trouble. There's no difficulty. Dostoievsky is so obscure and so careless a writer that one can scarcely help clarifying him – sometimes it needs some penetration to see what he is trying to say. Turgenev is much the most difficult of the Russians to translate because his style is the most beautiful.' 'The Art of Translation', *Listener* XXXVII (1947), 195. In the same issue of the *Listener* (195-6), Edward Crankshaw summed up Constance's skills and contribution as a translator, calling her 'a providence and a legend', in a short article entitled 'The Work of Constance Garnett'.
30 Olive's Diary.
31 Prince Peter Kropotkin to EG, 4 May 1903 (Austin).
H. G. Wells also incorporated his concern in his letter to Edward of 19 Nov. 1903: 'How is Mrs Garnett now? We think very often of her and her threatened sight and hope against threat.' (Austin.)
32 See D. Garnett, *The Golden Echo* (Chatto & Windus 1953), 74-93.
33 John Galsworthy to EG, Jan. 1910 (Hilton Hall).
34 John Galsworthy to Constance Garnett, 5 Jan. 1910 (Hilton Hall).
35 Constance Garnett to EG, n.d. (Hilton Hall).
36 Ernest Radford to EG, 5 Jan. 1910 (Austin).

37 David Garnett to EG, n.d. (Hilton Hall).

38 William Heinemann to EG, 23 Dec. 1915 (Hilton Hall).

39 EG to William Heinemann, draft (Hilton Hall).

40 *The Times*, 30 May 1911, 13, in S. Hynes, *The Edwardian Turn of Mind* (O.U.P. 1968), 338–9.

41 Jacob Tonson [A. Bennett], 'Books and Persons', *New Age* IX (1911), 132.
   It may be of this production that John Gielgud wrote in a letter to Constance: 'Your generous and appreciative letter delighted us all as you can imagine . . . and of course, without your wonderful work we should never have had a chance of knowing Tchechov in England at all . . . ' 13 Feb. (?) (Hilton Hall).

42 G. B. Shaw, *Heartbreak House* (Brentano 1919), x.

43 Phelps, *Russian Novel in English Fiction*, 187.

44 F. Swinnerton, *Background with Chorus* (Hutchinson 1956), 173–4.

45 E. Garnett, 'Tchehov and His Art', in E. Garnett, *Friday Nights* (Cape 1922), 61.

46 S. O'Faolain, *Vive Moi!* (Hart-Davis 1965), 249.

47 Joseph Conrad to EG, Oct. 1907, in E. Garnett (ed.), *Letters from Joseph Conrad*, 209.

48 Joseph Conrad to EG, 2 Oct. 1911, ibid., 232–3.

49 F. M. Ford, *Return to Yesterday: Reminiscences 1894–1914* (Gollancz 1931), 129.

14: Pond Place

1 D. H. Lawrence to Louie Burrows, 16 Oct. 1911, in J. T. Boulton (ed.), *Lawrence in Love: Letters to Louie Burrows* (University of Nottingham 1968), 141.

2 Constance Garnett to EG, 6 July (Hilton Hall).

3 Nellie Heath's Notes.

4 Constance Garnett to EG, Jan. 1899 (Hilton Hall).

5 Constance Garnett to EG, March 1909 (Hilton Hall).

6 Constance Garnett to EG, n.d. (Austin).

7 Constance Garnett to EG, Sunday n.d. (Austin).

8 EG to Constance Garnett, 5 Sept. 1928 (Austin).

9 Rayne Nickalls (*née* Garnett) Memoir MS (unpaged).
   G. B. Shaw's letter to Henry Salt (13 Dec. 1912) in reply to

Salt's enquiry on behalf of Nellie indicates the spirited stance that she could take *and* typical Shavian appreciation: 'I'm afraid I can't do anything for Nellie: portrait commissions don't come my way; but I've noted her address. The little wretch painted a portrait of me once: and when I wanted her to keep it she wouldn't – just flung it in my face and told me to take my rubbish away. I never saw it again; and it will be sold by somebody presently for £50,000. She should take to Post Impressionism; it's the only live art now going. You can't look at ordinary stuff after it.' (Austin.)

10 EG to J. B. Pinker, 30 Dec. 1915 (Austin).

11 EG to J. B. Pinker, Dec. 1915 (Austin).

12 E. Garnett, review of *Lost Girl*, *Manchester Guardian*, 10 Dec. 1920, 5.

13 E. Garnett, *Papa's War and Other Satires* (Allen & Unwin 1919), 2–3.

14 C. E. Montague to EG, 9 March 1920 (Austin).

15 W. S. Blunt to EG, 9 July 1920 (Austin).

16 Louis Raemaekers, *The Great War: A Neutral's Indictment*, one hundred cartoons by Louis Raemaekers with an appreciation by H. Perry Robinson and descriptive notes by Edward Garnett (Fine Art Society 1916).

17 E. Garnett, Introduction to M. Houghton, *In the Enemy's Country* (Chatto & Windus 1915), ix.

18 E. Garnett, 'The Battle-fronts on the Isonzo', *Manchester Guardian*, 10 Jan. 1916, 6.

19 Jessie Conrad to EG, 22 May 1915 (?) (Austin).

20 F. B. Young to EG, 5 March 1915 (Austin).

21 Quoted in J. B. Young, *Francis Brett Young* (Heinemann 1962), 52.

22 F. B. Young to EG, 13 March 1916 (Austin).

23 F. B. Young to EG, 18 July 1917 (Austin).

24 F. B. Young to EG, 21 Sept. 1919 (Austin).

25 W. H. Davies to EG, 31 Aug. 1916 (Austin).

26 W. H. Davies to EG, 4 Feb. 1914 (Austin).

27 Reader's Report (Hilton Hall).

28 E. Thomas to EG, 13 Dec. 1913 (Austin).

29 R. G. Thomas, 'Edward Thomas: Poet and Critic', *English Association, Essays and Studies*, 1968 (Murray 1969), 120–1.

30 Edward Thomas to EG, 2 Jan. 1914 (Austin).

31 Edward Thomas to EG, 7 Jan. 1914 (Austin).

32 Edward Thomas to EG, 25 June 1915 (Austin).

33 Quoted in W. Cooke, *Edward Thomas* (Faber 1970), 130.

34 Quoted in E. Garnett, 'Some Letters of Edward Thomas', *Athenaeum* Nos 4694, 4695 (1920), 501–3, 533–6.

35 Ibid., 531.

36 Walter de la Mare to EG, 15 March 1916 (Austin).

37 Walter de la Mare to EG, 6 June 1917 (Austin).

38 Edward Thomas to EG, 19 July 1917 (*sic*) (Austin).
The dating of this letter is inaccurate. Myfanwy Thomas suggests that the date has been rather badly guessed at for her father was in fact killed on 9 April of that year. From the diary kept by Edward Thomas entries indicate that he wrote to Edward amongst others on 19/20 Jan. 1917. Date probably 19 Jan. 1917. Myfanwy Thomas to author, 18 June 1973.

39 Edward Thomas to EG, 24 Oct. 1914 (Austin).

40 Edward Thomas to EG, 2 April 1915 (Austin).

41 Quoted in E. Garnett, 'Some Letters of Edward Thomas', *Athenaeum* Nos 4694, 4695 (1920), 501–3, 533–6.

42 Quoted in L. Thompson (ed.), *Selected Letters of Robert Frost* (Cape 1965), 169.

43 Ibid., 169.

44 Ibid., 176.

45 Robert Frost to EG, 12 June 1915, ibid., 179.

46 E. Garnett, 'Remarks on American Fiction', *Atlantic Monthly* CXIV (1914), 747–56.

47 G. Becker, *Documents of Modern Literary Realism* (Princeton University Press 1963), 17.

48 W. D. Howells, 'Garnett's Recent Remarks on American Fiction', *Harpers Magazine* CXXX (1915), 796–9.

49 Robert Frost to EG, 12 June 1915, in Thompson (ed.), *Selected Letters of Robert Frost*, 179–80.

50 Robert Frost to EG, 29 April 1917, ibid., 217.
An ungracious sequel to this took place when Frost, visiting England in 1928, was taken by his friend, Flint, to meet Edward: 'No other critic in England had written of Frost's poetry more appreciatively or had been a closer friend of Edward Thomas and there was every reason for assuming that Frost would enjoy this first meeting ... Unfortunately

Frost was in a grouchy mood. He took offense at Garnett's frank admission that *North of Boston* was still his favourite and when Flint changed the subject to other poets, Frost immediately fell into disagreement with Garnett over what qualities were best in the "new poetry" ... Although Frost's belligerence spoiled the evening, Garnett made a gracious and tactful gesture when his visitors were leaving. No matter what their differences of opinion might be he said, he felt sure that Frost had written one nearly perfect pastoral poem which discerning people would not soon forget: "The Mountain". This was enough to mollify Frost, and the parting was friendly.' L. Thompson, *Robert Frost: The Years of Triumph 1915–1938* (Cape 1971), 340.

51 Helen Thomas to EG, 1927 (Austin).
52 Helen Thomas to EG, 1927 (Austin).
53 E. Garnett, Introduction to E. Thomas, *Selected Poems* (Gregynog Press 1927), v.
54 L. Woolf, *Downhill All the Way: An Autobiography of the Years 1919–1939* (Hogarth Press 1967), 68.
In her diary for November 1928 Virginia Woolf described a gathering in Mr Williams-Ellis's studio, remarking acidulously: ' ... as for old Garnett, I felt surely someone ought to put that surly shaggy unkempt old monstrosity (certainly his nails want cutting and his coat is matted with wind and burrs) in the lethal chamber. Ditto of his mistress, the top half Esquimaux, the bottom Maytime in Hampstead – sprigged muslin, sandals.' V. Woolf, *Diary of Virginia Woolf* (Hogarth Press 1980), III, 204.
55 E. Garnett (ed.), *Letters from W. H. Hudson* (Dent 1925), 10.
56 Foreword to D. M. Richardson, *Pilgrimage: I Pointed Roofs, Backwater, Honeycomb* (Dent 1967), 10.
57 J. D. Beresford to EG, 22 April 1915 (Austin).
58 Dorothy Richardson to EG, n.d. (Austin).
59 Dorothy Richardson to EG, 7 March 1919 (Austin).
60 Dorothy Richardson to EG, 12 March 1919 (Austin).
61 Dorothy Richardson to EG, 7 Feb. 1920 (Austin).
62 Reader's Report (Hilton Hall).
63 Reader's Report (typewritten copy) (Hilton Hall).
64 R. Ellmann (ed.), *Letters of James Joyce* (Faber 1966), II,

65 M. Magalaner, *Time of Apprenticeship: The Fiction of the Young James Joyce* (Abelard-Schuman 1959), 26.

66 Ezra Pound to J. B. Pinker, 30 Jan. 1916, in Ellman (ed.), *Letters of James Joyce*, II, 372–3.

15: Cape

1 Thomas Seccombe to EG, 8 March 1919 (Hilton Hall).

2 Jonathan Cape to EG, 10 Jan. 1921 (Cape).

3 EG to Jonathan Cape, 12 Jan. 1921 (Cape).

4 EG to Jonathan Cape, 18 Jan. 1921 (Cape).

5 Jonathan Cape to EG, 20 Jan. 1921 (Cape).

6 EG to Jonathan Cape, 10 July 1922 (Cape).

7 Michael Howard, *Jonathan Cape Publisher* (Cape 1971), 58-9.

8 EG to Jonathan Cape, 14 July 1921 (Cape).

9 EG to Jonathan Cape, 19 July 1921 (Cape).

10 David Garnett to author, 21 March 1980.

11 David Garnett, biographical note on Edward Garnett in E. Garnett (ed.), *Conrad's Prefaces to His Work* (Dent 1937), vi.

12 S. O'Faolain, *Vive Moi!* (Hart-Davis 1965), 250-1.

13 Howard, *Jonathan Cape Publisher*, 82.

14 J. M. Murry to EG, 12 Nov. 1921 (Austin).

15 The first manuscript of *Seven Pillars of Wisdom* (except for nine chapters) was lost at Reading Station in 1919. Urged by Hogarth, Lawrence immediately began a second version, which was finished in 1920. It was to be published in the U.S.A. by F. N. Doubleday and kept off the English market. This version Lawrence realised was unsatisfactory and he burnt it in 1922. The third version, written in London and Jidda in 1921, was finished in 1922: the manuscript is in the Bodleian Library, Oxford, and eight copies were printed by the Oxford Times Press between Jan. and July 1922 at a cost of £175. The text of this Oxford version was extensively amended in 1923, 1924, 1925 and 1926 at Clouds Hill and Cranwell.

16 EG to T. E. Lawrence, 23 Nov. 1922, in A. W. Lawrence (ed.), *Letters to T. E. Lawrence* (Cape 1962), 93.

17 T. E. Lawrence to G. B. Shaw, 27 Dec. 1922, in D. Garnett (ed.), *The Letters of T. E. Lawrence* (Cape 1938), 391.

18 T. E. Lawrence to EG, 1 Dec. 1922, ibid., 385.
19 T. E. Lawrence to G. B. Shaw, 30 Jan. 1923, ibid., 397.
20 T. E. Lawrence to Jonathan Cape, 23 March 1923, ibid., 404.
21 T. E. Lawrence to Gertrude Bell, 18 Aug. 1923, and T. E. Lawrence to D. G. Hogarth, 23 Aug. 1923, ibid., 427–8.
22 T. E. Lawrence to R. V. Buxton, 26 March 1925, ibid., 472.
23 T. E. Lawrence to EG, 1 March 1927, ibid., 511.
24 Howard, *Jonathan Cape Publisher*, 94.
25 T. E. Lawrence to EG, 28 May 1924 (Austin).
26 G. B. Shaw to EG, 18 June 1925, in S. Weintraub, *Private Shaw and Public Shaw* (Cape 1963), 96.
27 T. E. Lawrence to EG, 15 March 1928 (Austin).
28 T. E. Lawrence to G. B. Shaw, 17 March 1928 (Austin).
29 T. E. Lawrence to EG, 23 April 1928, in D. Garnett (ed.), *Letters of T. E. Lawrence*, 598.
30 T. E. Lawrence to Jonathan Cape, 10 July 1928, in Howard, *Jonathan Cape Publisher*, 148.
31 Ibid., 82.
32 Ibid., 88.
33 Jonathan Cape to Professor W. H. Gardner, 29 April 1959 (Cape).
34 Roy Campbell to EG, n.d. (Austin).
35 E. Garnett, review of *The Flaming Terrapin*, *Nation* XXXV (1924), 323–4.
36 Mary Campbell to EG, n.d. (Austin).
37 Roy Campbell to EG, n.d. (Austin).
38 Roy Campbell to EG, n.d. (Austin).
39 Roy Campbell to EG, n.d. (Austin).
40 Roy Campbell to EG, n.d. (Austin).
41 Jonathan Cape to Professor W. H. Gardner, 29 April 1959 (Cape).
42 Jonathan Cape to EG, 2 Nov. 1925 (Cape).
43 EG to J. B. Pinker, 14 April 1925 (Austin).

16: Literary Conscience of the Firm

1 William Plomer to author, 26 Nov. 1969.
2 Liam O'Flaherty, *Shame the Devil* (Grayson 1934), 42.
3 Ibid., 44.

4 Liam O'Flaherty to EG, 14 May 1923 (Austin).

5 Liam O'Flaherty to EG, May 1923 (Austin).

6 Liam O'Flaherty to EG, 29 May 1923 (Austin).

7 Liam O'Flaherty to EG, 6 June 1923 (Austin).

8 Liam O'Flaherty to EG, 23 June 1923 (Austin).

9 J. Zneimer, *The Literary Vision of Liam O'Flaherty* (Syracuse University Press 1970), 65.

10 Liam O'Flaherty to EG, 19 June 1923 (Austin).

11 Liam O'Flaherty to EG, Aug. 1923 (Austin).

12 Liam O'Flaherty to EG, 17 Aug. 1923 (Austin).

13 Liam O'Flaherty to EG, 23 Aug. 1923 (Austin).

14 Typewritten résumé of when and where Liam O'Flaherty wrote his novels and stories, undated and unsigned, in King's College Library, Aberdeen University.

15 Liam O'Flaherty to EG, 6 May 1924 (Austin).

16 Liam O'Flaherty to EG, April 1924 (Austin).

17 Liam O'Flaherty to EG, 28 June 1924 (Austin).

18 Liam O'Flaherty to EG, 7 July 1924 (Austin).

19 Liam O'Flaherty to EG, 18 Sept. 1924 (Austin).

20 Liam O'Flaherty to EG, April 1923 (Austin).

21 Liam O'Flaherty to EG, 5 May 1923 (Austin).

22 Liam O'Flaherty to EG, 25 May 1923 (Austin).

23 Liam O'Flaherty to EG, 28 Nov. 1923 (Austin).

24 Liam O'Flaherty to EG, 24 Jan. 1924 (Austin).

25 Liam O'Flaherty to EG, 26 Jan. 1924 (Austin).

26 Liam O'Flaherty to EG, 12 March 1924 (Austin).

27 Liam O'Flaherty to EG, 30 March 1924 (Austin).

28 Liam O'Flaherty to EG, 3 April 1924 (Austin).

29 Liam O'Flaherty to EG, 11 April 1924 (Austin).

30 Liam O'Flaherty to EG, 24 April 1924 (Austin).

31 Liam O'Flaherty to EG, July 1925 (Austin).

32 Liam O'Flaherty to EG, 14 July 1925 (Austin).

33 Liam O'Flaherty to EG, 31 July 1925 (Austin).

34 Liam O'Flaherty to EG, 25 July 1923 (Austin).

35 Liam O'Flaherty to EG, May 1924 (Austin).

36 Liam O'Flaherty to EG, 7 Feb. 1924 (Austin).

37 Liam O'Flaherty to EG, 11 Oct. 1927 (Austin).

38 J. M. Murry to EG, 1 July 1923 (Austin).

39 J. M. Murry to EG, n.d. (Austin).

40 L. Woolf to EG, 14 May 1923 (Austin).

41 Liam O'Flaherty to EG, 23 Jan. 1924 (Austin).

42 Liam O'Flaherty to EG, 14 March 1924 (Austin).

43 Liam O'Flaherty to EG, April 1924 (Austin).

44 Liam O'Flaherty to EG, 8 Jan. 1925 (Austin).

45 J. M. Barrie to EG, 12 Jan. 1925 (Austin).

46 E. V. Lucas to EG, 15 Jan. 1925 (Austin).

47 J. Galsworthy to EG, 19 Jan. 1925 (Austin).

48 L. Woolf to EG, 29 Jan. 1925 (Austin).

49 Liam O'Flaherty to EG, 29 Jan. 1925 (Austin).

50 Liam O'Flaherty to EG, 12 Feb. 1925 (Austin).

51 Liam O'Flaherty to EG, 18 Jan. 1926 (Austin).

52 Jonathan Cape to EG, 21 Jan. 1926 (Austin).

53 Liam O'Flaherty to EG, 24 Jan. 1926 (Austin).

54 Liam O'Flaherty to EG, 7 Nov. 1926 (Austin).

55 Topsy O'Flaherty to EG, 14 June 1927 (Austin).

56 Liam O'Flaherty to EG, 28 Nov. 1927 (Austin).

57 Liam O'Flaherty to EG, 6 May 1928 (Austin).

58 Liam O'Flaherty to EG, 29 Feb. 1932 (Austin).

59 Liam O'Flaherty to EG, 3 March 1932 (Austin).

60 Sean O'Faolain to EG, 15 Aug. 1926 (Austin).

61 Sean O'Faolain to EG, 13 Nov. 1928 (Austin).

62 Sean O'Faolain, *Vive Moi!* (Hart-Davis 1965), 244–5.

63 Sean O'Faolain to EG, 4 Nov. 1930 (Austin).

64 Sean O'Faolain to EG (unsigned typewritten letter), (?) 1930 (Austin).

65 Sean O'Faolain to EG, n.d. (Austin).

66 Sean O'Faolain to EG, n.d. (Austin).

67 Sean O'Faolain to EG, n.d. (Austin).

68 EG to Jonathan Cape, 24 June 1931 (Cape).

69 Sean O'Faolain to EG, 27 July 1931 (Austin).

70 Edward Garnett, Introduction to Sean O'Faolain, *Midsummer Night's Madness* (Cape 1932), 12.

71 Sean O'Faolain to EG, 1 Dec. 1931 (Austin).

72 O'Faolain, *Vive Moi!* 262.

73 Sean O'Faolain to EG, 27 July 1931 (Austin).
    A surprising request in view of Edward's book on Turgenev.

74 Sean O'Faolain to EG, Feb. 1933 (Austin).

75 Sean O'Faolain to EG, May 1933 (Austin).

76 Sean O'Faolain to EG, May 1933 (Austin).

77 Sean O'Faolain to EG, 1933 (Austin).

78 EG to T.E. Lawrence, mid-August 1933, in A. W. Lawrence (ed.), *Letters to T. E. Lawrence* (Cape 1962), 103–4.

79 Sean O'Faolain to EG, 1935 (Austin).

80 Sean O'Faolain to EG, n.d. (Austin).

81 O'Faolain, *Vive Moi!* 254–5.

82 B. W. Huebsch to EG, 3 April 1936 (Viking Press).

83 EG to B. W. Huebsch, 17 April 1936 (Viking Press).

84 John Galsworthy to EG, 18 Aug. 1913, in E. Garnett (ed.), *Letters from John Galsworthy 1900–1932* (Cape 1932), 210–11.

85 Introduction to E. Garnett (ed.), *Letters from Galsworthy*, 9.

17: 'Miss Bates'

1 Richard Church to author, 13 Dec. 1970.

2 Introduction to E. Garnett (ed.), *Letters from Joseph Conrad 1895–1924* (Bobbs-Merrill 1928), 4.

3 Introduction to H. E. Bates, *The Two Sisters* (Cape 1926), 11.

4 H. E. Bates, *Edward Garnett* (Max Parrish 1950), 84–6.

5 EG to Joseph Conrad, 17 Dec. 1921, in C. Heilbrun, *The Garnett Family* (Allen & Unwin 1961), 124.

6 Sean O'Faolain, *Vive Moi!* (Hart-Davis 1965), 269.

7 Michael Howard, *Jonathan Cape Publisher* (Cape 1971), 75.

8 Bates, *Edward Garnett*, 12–13.

9 H. E. Bates, *Blossoming World* (Michael Joseph 1971), 16.

10 H. E. Bates to EG, 31 Dec. 1925 (Austin).

11 Bates, *Edward Garnett*, 16–17.

12 H. E. Bates to EG, 11 Jan. 1926 (Austin).

13 EG to H. E. Bates, 14 Jan. 1926 (Austin).

14 EG to H. E. Bates, 15 Jan. 1926 (Austin).

15 H. E. Bates to EG, 19 Jan. 1926 (Austin).

16 EG to H. E. Bates, 4 Feb. 1926 (Austin).

17 Introduction to Bates, *The Two Sisters*, 21.

18 EG to H. E. Bates, 2 Jan. (Austin).

19 EG to H. E. Bates, 16 June 1926 (Austin).

20 EG to H. E. Bates, 19 July 1926 (Austin).

21 EG to H. E. Bates, 21 July 1926 (Austin).

22 EG to H. E. Bates, 14 Feb. 1927 (Austin).

23 EG to H. E. Bates, 16 Feb. 1927 (Austin).
24 EG to H. E. Bates, 20 Feb. 1927 (Austin).
25 H. E. Bates to EG, 7 July (Austin).
26 Quoted in Bates, *Edward Garnett*, 53–9.
27 Quoted, ibid., 60.
28 EG to H. E. Bates, 21 Sept. 1927 (Austin).
29 EG to H. E. Bates, 22 Sept. 1927 (Austin).
30 EG to H. E. Bates, 27 Sept. 1927 (Austin).
31 EG to H. E. Bates, 6 Oct. 1927 (Austin).
32 EG to H. E. Bates, 11 Oct. 1927 (Austin).
33 EG to H. E. Bates, 29 May 1928 (Austin).
34 EG to H. E. Bates, 30 Jan. 1928 (Austin).
35 EG to H. E. Bates, 20 March 1928 (Austin).
36 EG to H. E. Bates, 5 July 1928 (Austin).
37 EG to H. E. Bates, 11 Nov. 1928 (Austin).
38 H. E. Bates to EG, 27 Nov. 1928 (Austin).
39 EG to H. E. Bates, 5 Dec. 1928 (Austin).
40 EG to J. Wilson, 9 Jan. 1929 (Austin).
41 Bates, *Blossoming World*, 39.
42 EG to J. Wilson, 25 Aug. 1926 (Austin).
43 EG to J. Wilson, 6 Oct. 1926 (Austin).
44 EG to H. E. Bates, 16 July 1926 (Austin).
45 EG to H. E. Bates, 26 Sept. (Austin).
46 EG to H. E. Bates, 26 July 1929 (Austin).
47 H. E. Bates to EG, 28 July 1929 (Austin).
48 EG to B. W. Huebsch, 3 Jan. 1930 (Columbia).
49 EG to H. E. Bates, 5 July 1929 (Austin).
50 EG to H. E. Bates, 29 Nov. 1929 (Austin).
51 H. E. Bates to EG, 2 Dec. 1929 (Austin).
52 H. E. Bates to EG, 4 Dec. 1929 (Austin).
53 H. E. Bates to EG, 24 Oct. 1929 (Austin).
54 H. E. Bates to EG, 24 Oct. 1929 (Austin).
55 Bates, *Blossoming World*, 35.
56 Bates, *Edward Garnett*, 72–3.
57 H. E. Bates to EG, 19 June 1931 (Austin).
58 H. E. Bates to EG, 29 Sept. 1931 (Austin).
59 H. E. Bates to EG, 31 May 1933 (Hilton Hall).
60 H. E. Bates to EG, 5 Nov. 1932 (Austin).

18: New Generation

1 Sir Rupert Hart-Davis in conversation with author, 25 Feb. 1977.

2 Malcolm Elwin to author, 26 March 1973.

3 E. M. Forster, *News Chronicle*, 30 Nov. 1931, 4.

4 EG to J. Wilson, 17 July 1928 (Austin).

5 John Galsworthy to EG, 8 Aug. 1928, in E. Garnett (ed.), *Letters from John Galsworthy 1900–1932* (Cape 1932), 246.

6 EG to B. W. Huebsch, 9 July 1930 (Viking Press).
Edward's kindness to young authors and shrewdness in placing books with publishers is reflected in the letter he wrote to Richard Church on 29 April 1929. 'It is a very sincere piece of work', Edward said of Church's first novel, *Oliver's Daughter*, 'but I don't think that it is a novel for Cape on account of its quiet note. I advise you to try Messrs Dent, & *should* they send me the MS & ask my advice I would say – "Publish it" (Dent occasionally asks my decision in doubtful cases). Don't mention my name however, as they would naturally ask why has Cape rejected it? The fact is that from one publisher one expects one sort of book and from another publisher another. And one publisher may be grateful for books which do not suit his rival's list. Longmans, Harrap and Benn are also firms to try if Dent rejects "Oliver's Daughter".'

7 H. A. Manhood to EG, n.d. (Austin).

8 H. A. Manhood to EG, 3 Dec. 1932 (Austin).

9 H. A. Manhood to EG, n.d. (Austin).

10 H. A. Manhood to EG, 7 March 1929 (Austin).

11 H. A. Manhood to EG, n.d. (Austin).

12 H. A. Manhood to EG, 24 May 1935 (Austin).

13 Michael Howard, *Jonathan Cape Publisher* (Cape 1971), 97.

14 John Galsworthy to EG, 29 Nov. 1926, in E. Garnett (ed.), *Letters from Galsworthy*, 243.

15 Howard, *Jonathan Cape Publisher*, 96.

16 Henry Williamson to author, 14 Nov. 1969.

17 Ibid.

18 Henry Williamson to EG, n.d. (Austin).

19 Henry Williamson to author, 14 Nov. 1969.

20 H. Williamson, *The Power of the Dead* (Macdonald 1963), 198–201.

21 Ibid., 304.

22 Ibid., 307.

23 Ibid., 339.
Henry Williamson expressed himself differently in a letter to Edward of 20 March 1936: 'It was so kind of you years ago to send my book to Lawrence, and thereby give me the friendship and advice of one who has helped me immeasurably to absorb and pass away many faults in myself and my work' (Austin).

24 David Garnett, biographical note on Edward Garnett in E. Garnett (ed.), *Conrad's Prefaces to His Work* (Dent 1937), vii–viii.

25 Henry Green to David Garnett, 21 June 1953 (Austin).

26 Guy Pocock to EG, 20 Oct. (Austin).

27 Henry Green to EG, 24 Nov. (Austin).

28 Henry Green to EG, Friday n.d. (Austin).

29 Henry Green in conversation with author, 18 June 1970.

30 Henry Green to EG, 21 Dec. 1925 (Austin).

31 Henry Green to EG, n.d. (Austin).

32 Henry Green in conversation with author, 18 June 1970.

33 Henry Green, 'An Unfinished Novel', *London Magazine* 6(4), 1959, 11–17.

34 EG to Henry Green, 11 Nov. 1927 (letter borrowed from Henry Green).

35 EG to Henry Green, 27 Nov. 1927 (Henry Green).

36 EG to Henry Green, 1 Dec. 1927 (Henry Green).

37 EG to Henry Green, 26 Nov. 1928 (Henry Green).

38 Henry Green to EG, n.d. (Austin).

39 EG to Henry Green, 9 Jan. 1929 (Henry Green).

40 Henry Green to EG, n.d. (Austin).

41 EG to Henry Green, 7 May 1929 (Henry Green).

42 *Writers at Work: The Paris Review Interviews:* 2nd series (Secker & Warburg 1967), 211–12.

43 Henry Green, *Pack My Bag* (Hogarth Press 1940), 236.

44 Henry Green in conversation with author, 18 June 1970.

45 Henry Green in conversation with author, 18 June 1970.

46 E. Linklater, *Fanfare for a Tin Hat* (Macmillan 1970), 124.

47 Ibid., 126.

48 Quoted in Jonathan Cape to EG, 31 Oct. 1930 (Cape).

49 Eric Linklater to EG, 10 Nov. (Austin).

50 Quoted in Linklater, *Fanfare for a Tin Hat*, 125.

51 EG to B. W. Huebsch, 3 June 1932 (Viking Press).

52 Eric Linklater to EG, 20 Sept. (Austin).

53 John Cowper Powys to Littleton Powys, Good Friday (29 March) 1929, in B. Humfrey (ed.), *Essays on John Cowper Powys* (University of Wales Press 1972), 324.

54 John Cowper Powys to EG, 26 Feb. 1929 (Austin).

55 Howard, *Jonathan Cape Publisher*, 132.

56 E. Garnett, 'Wolf Solent', 16 April 1929 (Austin).

57 EG to John Cowper Powys, 3 May 1929 (Austin).

58 John Cowper Powys to EG, 22 May 1929 (Austin).

59 Quoted in E. Nehls (ed.), *D. H. Lawrence: A Composite Biography* (University of Wisconsin Press 1958), II, 273.
Lawrence gave his version of this conversation, dramatising it with glee. 'Old Edward Garnett tackled her. He saw her *Black Swans* floundering and flapping about and went for them tooth and nail like a rough haired Yorkshire terrier. Poor old Mollie Skinner she saw the feathers of her birds flying like black snow, and the swans squawked as if they were at their last gasp. But old Edward twisted at them till they knew what's what.' D. H. Lawrence, *Phoenix II: Uncollected, Unpublished and Other Prose Works*, collected and edited with an introduction and notes by W. Roberts and H. T. Moore (Heinemann 1968), 296.

60 Mollie Skinner to EG, 4 Nov. 1924 (Austin).

61 Mollie Skinner to EG, 21 Dec. 1924 (Austin).

62 Naomi Mitchison to author, 16 Jan. 1972.

63 N. Mitchison, *The Laburnum Branch: Poems* (Cape 1926), 49.

64 EG to Naomi Mitchison, 16 April 1926 (National Library of Scotland).

65 Naomi Mitchison to author, 6 Jan. 1972.

66 EG to Naomi Mitchison, 27 Aug. 1925 (National Library of Scotland).

67 EG to Naomi Mitchison, 12 March 1928 (National Library of Scotland).

68 EG to Naomi Mitchison, 21 March 1929 (National Library of Scotland).

69 H. Ford, *Published in Paris: American and British Writers, Printers and Publishers in Paris 1920–1939* (Garnstone Press 1975), 350.

70 Eric Partridge to author, 14 Feb. 1977.

71 John Galsworthy to EG, 23 March 1929 (Austin).

72 Jack Kahane, *Memoirs of a Booklegger* (Michael Joseph 1939), 223.

73 Ford, *Published in Paris*, 351.

74 E. Garnett, Preface to N. James, *Sleeveless Errand* (Barbou & Kahane, Paris, 1929).

75 EG to Naomi Mitchison, n.d. (National Library of Scotland).

76 Naomi Mitchison to author, 6 Jan. 1972.

77 EG to Naomi Mitchison, 1 June 1933 (Cape).

78 Naomi Mitchison to EG, Friday 1933 (letter borrowed from Lady Mitchison).

79 Naomi Mitchison to author, 6 Jan. 1972.

80 Naomi Mitchison to Wren Howard, 1933 (Cape).

81 EG to Jonathan Cape, 13 Aug. 1933 (Cape).

82 E. Garnett, *Friday Nights* (Cape 1922), 297.

83 J. M. Murry, 'Edward Garnett' (review of *Friday Nights*), *Nation* XXXI (1922), 568–9.

19: Familiar Faces

1 EG to R. B. Cunninghame Graham, 28 Aug. 1928 (letter borrowed from Admiral Sir Angus Cunninghame Graham).

2 EG to R. B. Cunninghame Graham, 23 April (Austin).

3 Quoted in J. Conrad to EG, 12 Sept. 1922, in E. Garnett (ed.), *Letters from Joseph Conrad 1895–1924* (Bobbs-Merrill 1928), 286.

4 R. B. Cunninghame Graham to EG, 13 Aug. 1924 (Austin).

5 F. R. Karl, *Joseph Conrad: The Three Lives: A Biography* (Faber 1979), 866.

6 Joseph Conrad to EG, Aug. 1923, in E. Garnett (ed.), *Letters from Joseph Conrad*, 294.

7 E. Garnett, 'Conrad's Last Tales' (review of *Tales of Hearsay*), *Nation* XXXVI (1925), 718.

8 G. Gould, 'The Danger of Idols', *Saturday Review of Literature* CXL (1925), 471–2.

9 P. C. Kennedy, review of *Suspense*, *New Statesman* 25:666 (26 Sept. 1925).

10 E. Garnett, 'Reply to Gerald Gould', *Saturday Review of Literature* CXL (1925), 505.

11 E. Garnett, review of *Joseph Conrad*, *Weekly Westminster*, 14 Feb. 1925, 473.

12 E. Garnett, review of *Joseph Conrad*, *Nation* XXXVI (1924), 366, 368.

13 EG to Olive Garnett, 9 Dec. 1924 (Mrs A. L. Michell).

14 E. Garnett, review of *Joseph Conrad*, 366, 368.

15 F. M. Ford to EG, 5 May 1928 (Cornell).

16 E. Garnett, 'Joseph Conrad and His Wife', *London Mercury* XXXII (1935), 385–6.

17 EG to Jessie Conrad, 11 July 1935 (Hilton Hall).

18 Jessie Conrad to EG, 14 July 1935 (Hilton Hall).

19 Jean-Aubry dedicated his *Joseph Conrad: Life & Letters*, 2 vols (Heinemann 1927), to Edward Garnett and Robert Cunninghame Graham 'because you two were the first friends Conrad's writings won for him, and because your friendship, which he valued greatly, lasted till the day he died'.

20 EG to R. B. Cunninghame Graham, 20 Aug. 1935 (letter borrowed from Admiral Sir Angus Cunninghame Graham).

21 Karl, *Joseph Conrad*, 346.

22 E. Garnett, 'A New Study of Conrad' (review of *Joseph Conrad* by Edward Crankshaw), *London Mercury* XXXIV (1936), 67–9.

23 E. Garnett, review, *Nation* XIV (1914), 720, 722.

24 J. Conrad to EG, 28 Jan. 1914, in E. Garnett (ed.), *Letters from Conrad*, 243.

25 N. Sherry, *Conrad and His World* (Thames & Hudson 1972), 99.

26 Introduction to E. Garnett (ed.), *Letters from John Galsworthy 1900–1932* (Cape 1932), 14–15.

27 Ada Galsworthy to EG, 13 Feb. 1936 (Austin).

28 B. W. Huebsch to EG, 5 April 1933 (Viking Press).

29 EG to B. W. Huebsch, 14 April 1933 (Viking Press).

30 D. H. Lawrence to EG, 17 Oct. 1921, in Harry T. Moore (ed.), *Collected Letters of D. H. Lawrence*, 2 vols (Heinemann 1962), II, 664.

31 D. H. Lawrence to David Garnett, 24 Aug. 1928, ibid., II, 1079.

32 D. H. Lawrence, *Lady Chatterley's Lover* (1st edn, Florence, 1928, no. 479 of 1000 copies signed by author) (Austin).

33 Frieda Lawrence to EG, Sunday n.d. (Austin).

34 EG to B. W. Huebsch, 15 Jan. 1935 (Viking Press).

35 EG to B. W. Huebsch, 6 Aug. 1935 (Viking Press).

36 E. D. MacDonald to EG, 10 Oct. 1935 (Austin).

37 EG to E. D. MacDonald, 25 Oct. 1935 (Austin).

38 EG to E. D. MacDonald, 2 Dec. 1935 (Austin).

39 EG to E. D. MacDonald, n.d. (Austin).

40 Marshall A. Best to EG, 5 Feb. 1936 (Austin).

41 EG to Viking Press, 13 Feb. 1936 (Viking Press).

42 E. D. MacDonald to EG, 24 Feb. 1936 (Austin).

43 EG to E. D. MacDonald, 13 Feb. 1936 (Austin).

44 EG to E. D. MacDonald, 6 April 1936 (Austin).

45 EG to B. W. Huebsch, 31 Oct. 1936 (Viking Press).

46 EG to E. D. MacDonald, 8 Nov. 1936 (Austin).

47 E. Garnett, 'D. H. Lawrence: His Posthumous Papers' (review of *Phoenix* edited by E. D. MacDonald), *London Mercury* XXXV (1936), 152–60.

48 EG to A. Treneer, 20 April (Austin).

49 EG to Professor Barker Fairley, 24 April 1935 (letter borrowed from Ruth M. Robbins).

20: Dew on the Garlic Leaf

1 Michael Howard, *Jonathan Cape Publisher* (Cape 1971), 167.

2 R. A. Gettman, *A Victorian Publisher: A Study of the Bentley Papers* (C.U.P. 1960), 208.

3 Geraint Goodwin to EG, 3 June 1935 (Austin).

4 Geraint Goodwin to EG, 14 Aug. 1935 (Austin).

5 Geraint Goodwin to EG, 8 Sept. 1935 (Austin).

6 Geraint Goodwin to EG, 22 Oct. 1935 (Austin).

7 Geraint Goodwin to EG, 7 Nov. 1935 (Austin).

8 Geraint Goodwin to EG, 27 Jan. 1936 (Austin).

9 Geraint Goodwin to EG, 3 Feb. 1936 (Austin).

10 B. W. Huebsch to EG, 28 Oct. 1936 (Viking Press).

11 EG to B. W. Huebsch, 5 Nov. 1936 (Viking Press).

12 E. Garnett, Introduction to *Capajon* (Cape 1933), 19.

13 Sean O'Faolain to EG, 16 Sept. 1931 (Austin).

14 H. E. Bates, *The Blossoming World* (Michael Joseph 1971), 33.

15 Stephen Graham, *Part of the Wonderful Scene: An Autobiography* (Collins 1964), 129.
Stephen Graham claimed that Natalie Duddington became one of the best translators from the Russian.

16 B. W. Huebsch to EG, 12 Jan. 1932 (Viking Press).

17 EG to B. W. Huebsch, 20 Jan. 1932 (Viking Press).

18 Mrs Matheson, report on *The Still Don*, in EG to B. W. Huebsch, Jan. 1932 (Viking Press).

19 B. W. Huebsch to EG, 15 Feb. 1932 (Viking Press).

20 D. H. Stewart, *Mikhail Sholokov: A Critical Introduction* (University of Michigan Press 1967), 204–5.

21 EG to B. W. Huebsch, Feb. 1932 (Viking Press).

22 EG to B. W. Huebsch, 11 March 1932 (Viking Press).

23 Vera Alexandrova, *A History of Soviet Literature 1917–1964* (Bell & Sons 1963), 252.

24 B. W. Huebsch to EG, 17 March 1932 (Viking Press).

25 E. Garnett, Introduction to (M. E. Saltykov) Shchedrin, *The Golovlyov Family*, trans. Natalie Duddington (Dent 1934), v–viii.

26 J. Kahane, *Memoirs of a Booklegger* (Michael Joseph 1939), 206.

27 Howard, *Jonathan Cape Publisher*, 71.

28 Hamish Hamilton to author, 7 March 1977.

29 Howard, *Jonathan Cape Publisher*, 100.

30 T. Jones, *A Diary with Letters 1931–1950* (O.U.P. 1954), 202.

31 D. Garnett, *The Familiar Faces* (Chatto & Windus 1962), 157.

32 EG to Professor Barker Fairley, 30 Jan. 1936 (letter borrowed from Ruth M. Robbins).

33 C. Hassall, *Edward Marsh: Patron of the Arts* (Longmans 1959), 282.

34 E. Garnett, 'On Publishing', *Now and Then* (1931; 10th anniversary of the Cape firm).

35 D. Garnett, *Familiar Faces*, 178.

36 Bates, *Blossoming World*, 122.

37 Entry in J. M. Murry's Journal, Tuesday, 23 Feb. 1937 (supplied by Colin Middleton Murry).

Middleton Murry had a long connection with Edward, who sent him stories by his protégés when Murry was an editor. Murry greatly respected Edward's criticism and wrote of it in glowing terms in his review of *Friday Nights* (*Nation* XXXI (1922), 568–9). He also remembered with gratitude Edward's support of his attempt as a novelist. As he wrote at that time on 2 May 1922: 'I read you reviewed my novel in the M.G. As was to be expected it was one of the only *criticisms* I had. I think (or hope) that the next one, which I may finish this year, is a better thing altogether. But I can't talk about it without saying how much I owe you personally. It was your review in the *Nation* of "Still Life" which convinced me that I hadn't made a fool of myself – completely. It's not so much encouragement that matters, you know, as understanding. I felt that you – I didn't know it was you at the time – had divined what I was driving at. And then its utter failure didn't matter ... ' (Austin).

38 J. Ramsay MacDonald to Constance Garnett, 22 Feb. 1937 (Hilton Hall).

39 Constance Garnett to Jonathan Cape, 25 Feb. 1937 (Cape).

40 David Garnett to Jonathan Cape, in *Now and Then* (autumn 1937).

41 *Now and Then* (autumn 1937).

42 Roy Campbell to EG, Nov. n.d. (Austin).

43 Reader's Report (copy sent to author by William Plomer, 26 Nov. 1969).

44 W. Plomer, *At Home* (Cape 1958), 170.

45 Ibid., 175.

46 William Plomer to author, 26 Nov. 1969.

47 Fredson Bowers, *Textual and Literary Criticism* (C.U.P. 1959), 18–19.

48 Gettman, *A Victorian Publisher*, ix.

49 D. H. Lawrence to EG, 17 Oct. 1921, in Harry T. Moore (ed.), *Collected Letters of D. H. Lawrence*, 2 vols (Heinemann 1962), II, 664.

50 V. S. Pritchett, 'V. S. Pritchett on Publishing', *Saturday Review of Literature* XXVIII (1945), 20.

51 Stella Stebbing, 'Notes on Nellie Heath' (Typewritten MSS 1977).

Ada Galsworthy had expressed similar sentiments to Edward: ' ... of course Nelly Heath sees right through me and so she does through everything, I think. I can't imagine her failing in anything unless perhaps in something mathematical and then I should care for her the more...' Ada Galsworthy to EG, 24 Feb. (Austin).

52 Olive's Diary.
53 J. Galsworthy, 'Edward Garnett: An Appreciation', *Westminster Gazette*, 28 March 1914.

Index

Adventure Series (Unwin), 45
Archer, William: and censorship agitation, 119–20; comments on *The Trial of Jeanne d'Arc*, 125–126

Baldwin, Stanley, public appreciation of *Precious Bane* by Mary Webb, 281
Bates, H. E.: meeting with EG, 226–7; EG advises on short stories, 227–8; EG's preface to *Two Sisters*, 229; EG's criticism of 'The Fair Day', 'The Sinners', 'The Baker's Wife', 230–1; EG on O'Flaherty, 231; EG condemns *The Voyagers*, 232; EG advises on stories and sketches, 232–3; EG on *Catherine Foster, Day's End*, 233; EG to John Wilson on Bates, 233–4; EG to Huebsch on Bates, 235; asks EG about *Hessian Prisoner*, 235–6, *Black Boxer*, 237; regard for Constance, 237; acknowledges criticism of *The Fallow Land*, 237; tribute to EG, 238; at EG's funeral, 283
Beckett, Samuel, EG reports on *Dream of Fair to Middling Women*, 259

Bennett, Arnold: EG reports on *Truth about an Author*, 84; EG reviews *The Grim Smile of the Five Towns, Old Wives' Tale, Anna of the Five Towns*, 100–1; correspondence with EG over novels, 101; enquiry to EG about Turgenev, 162; attacked by Wells over the novel, 163; writes as 'Jacob Tonson' in *New Age* on Dostoevsky, 165, on performance of *The Cherry Orchard*, 171
Bentley, E.C., on EG and fiction, *Philip Gaskell's Last Case* (later entitled *Trent's Last Case*), 94–5
Beresford, J. D., to EG on Dorothy Richardson, 187
Black, Clementina: introduces her sister Constance to Garnett family, 11; attitude to marriage of EG and Constance, 13
Black, Grace: comments on EG's attraction for Constance, 12; has Gracie's Cottage built, 36
Bodley Head, EG as reader, 192
Bone, Gertrude, record of Conrad meeting EG, 57
Bowers, Fredson, *Textual and Literary Criticism*, 287
Breaking Point, The: accepted by

Breaking Point—cont.
Frederick Harrison of Haymarket Theatre, 118; banned by Lord Chamberlain's Office, 118–19; sparks off anti-censorship agitation, 119–21; Frank Vernon on, 120; Shaw's criticism and advice to EG, 121–2; performance by Stage Society, 121; Conrad's opinion, 122; David Garnett on performance, 123

Brown, Ford Madox: friend of Dr Richard Garnett, 9; on publication of *Brown Owl* by grandson F. M. Ford, 48; bookplate for EG, 299n

Buchan, John, EG reports on to Unwin, 44

Builders of Britain Series (Unwin), 46

Butler, Samuel, on Dr Richard Garnett, 9

Byrne, James, pseudonym for EG, 123

Cameo Series (Unwin), 45

Campbell, Roy: brought to Cape's notice by T. E. Lawrence, 201; discusses *Flaming Terrapin* with EG, 201–2; on South Africa to EG, 202–3; *Wayzgoose, Adamastor,* 203; on William Plomer to EG, 286

Cannan, Gilbert: EG reports on *Watchman of the Night,* 140–1; corresponds with EG, 141–2; later career, 142

Capajon, collection of short stories, 278

Cape, Jonathan: traveller for Duckworth, 106; establishes firm, 192; invites EG to join firm, 192–5; reputation as hard bargainer, 195; EG's opinion of, as a publisher, 196; relationship with T.E. Lawrence, 197–9; dispute with EG as reader (1925), 203–5; William Plomer on, 206; on

O'Flaherty, 216–17; on H. E. Bates, 226; relationship with Naomi Mitchison, 254–5; tribute to EG, 284–5

Cearne, The: architecture, 29–30; choice of site, 29, 32; situation, 31; description by D. H. Lawrence, 31

Censorship: attitude of EG as a reviewer, 107; EG and the 'sex question', 107; and the banning of *The Breaking Point,* 118–19; Galsworthy and anti-censorship agitation, 119; William Archer describes agitation 119–20; EG support against suppression of *The Rainbow,* 178; banning of *Sleeveless Errand* and EG, Jack Kahane and Paris publishing, 256–7; Naomi Mitchison and dispute with EG, 258–9

'Chapple', maid to Garnett family, 9

Chekhov, I.: translations by Constance, 171–2; EG prefaces to translations, 172; performance of *The Cherry Orchard* (1911), 171

Chesson, W. H.: friend and colleague of EG at Unwin, 40–1; and *Almayer's Folly,* 55, 56

Chesterton, G. K.: at Unwin, 40; EG reports on *The Babe Unborn,* 42

Children's Library Series (Unwin), 47

Church, Richard: on EG, 225; EG's advice on *Oliver's Daughter,* 331n

Conrad, Jessie: to EG about war service, 180; EG on Jessie Conrad, 265–7; Jessie Conrad's reply to EG, 267–8; Cunninghame Graham's opinion of, 268

Conrad, Joseph: F. M. Ford on EG receiving *Almayer's Folly,* 54; receipt of *Almayer's Folly* by Unwin publishing house, 55–6; pseudonym 'Kamudi', 55; corresponds with aunt, Mme Poradowska, 55-6; EG and *Almayer's Folly*, 56; meeting EG, 57; EG and *Two Vagabonds*, 57, *Outcast of the Islands*, 59, *The Sisters*, 59,60, *The Rescuer*, 60, 61-2; his dislike of Unwin, 61, 71; EG and *Idiots*, 61, *Outpost of Progress*, 62-3, *The Lagoon*, 62, 63, *The Nigger of the Narcissus*, 63-5, 69, 'Karain', 66, 68, *Lord Jim*, 66, *Nostromo*, 67, *The Return*, 67; on Constance as translator of Turgenev, 69-70, 161; depicts EG as Lea in *The Inheritors*, 71; recommends EG to Blackwood as a critic, 85; critical appreciation by EG in *Academy*, 96; EG reviews *Youth, End of the Tether* and *Heart of Darkness*, 96-7, *Nostromo*, 97-8; introduces Galsworthy to EG, 110, 308-9n; opinion of *The Breaking Point*, 122, *Lords and Masters*, 123; to Edward Noble on EG as critic, 129; to EG on Russian writers, 172-3; opinion of Dostoevsky, 320n; on his friendship with EG, 262; death and funeral, 262; his reputation defended by EG, 262-8; EG on *Chance*, 268-9

Cowlishaw, H., architect of The Cearne, 29

Crane, Cora: to EG on Brede, 37; to EG on Stephen Crane, 98

Crane, Stephen, EG on, 37, 98-9

Crankshaw, Edward: on Goldring's *The Last Pre-Raphaelite*, 138; EG comments on his *Joseph Conrad*, 268; on Constance as translator, 320n

Crockett, S. R., reports on by EG, 43-4

Cunninghame Graham, R. B.: beginning of friendship with EG, 47; in Overseas Series, 46-7; on T. F. Unwin, 71; in Greenback Series, 79; on Conrad's death and funeral, 262

Davies, W. H.: and the Mont Blanc, 131, 181; introduced to EG by Edward Thomas, 132; EG on *Poet Tramp's Life* and *Autobiography of a Super-Tramp*, 132-4, *Nature Poems*, 134, *Weak Woman*, 134; EG and the Civil List pension, 134, Royal Literary Fund, 134-5; *The True Traveller*, 135, *Songs of Joy*, 135; on EG's character, 135-6; his concern for Edward Thomas, 182

de la Mare, Walter: and *Sons and Lovers*, 157; and Civil List pension for Edward Thomas, 183

Dell, E. M.: EG on *Bristles*, 81-2; her connection with Unwin, 81-2

Dent, J. M.: EG introduces to Ernest Rhys, 18-19; publishes *Imaged World*, 29

Dostoevsky Corner: origin of name, 173; F. M. Ford on, 173

Dostoevsky, F.: translations by Constance, 165-7; EG on, 165; reception given to *The Brothers Karamazov* translation, 166, 319n; Conrad on, 320n

Doughty, C. M.: EG reports on *Adam and Eve (Hawwa)*, 82-3, *Dawn of Britain*, 83; EG's abridgement of *Arabia Deserta (Wanderings in Arabia Deserta)*, 83; appreciation by EG, 90; and publication by Cape, 197; EG reviews in *London Mercury*, 274

Douglas, Norman: help of Conrad, Ford and EG, 139; visits to The Cearne, 139-40; EG's regard for as a writer, 140

Duckworth, Gerald: EG as reader for, 77-84; Cape as traveller for, 106

Duddington, Natalie: helps Constance in translating, 278; advises EG on Sholokhov's *The Quiet Don*, 280; EG's introduction to her translation of Shchedrin's *Golovlyov Family*, 281

Eastaway, Edward, pseudonym of Edward Thomas, 183

Eliot, T. S., reviews EG's preface to Turgenev, 162

Elwin, Malcolm: on EG and Lang, 87; on EG and Cape, 239–40

English Review, 136

Fabian Society: and EG and Constance as members, 15; EG to Wells on, 32

Fairley, Professor Barker: and honorary doctorate for EG, 282; review by EG of his book on Doughty, 274

Feud, The: refused by Forbes-Robertson, 122; Edward Thomas on, 122; performed at Manchester, 122; Galsworthy on construction of play, 122–3; David Garnett on performance, 123

Forbes-Robertson, Jean: performance in *The Trial of Jeanne d'Arc*, 126; EG and her marriage to Hamish Hamilton, 281

Forbes-Robertson, Johnston, opinion of *The Feud*, 122

Ford, Ford Madox: as childhood friend of Garnetts, 10; on EG at school, 10; as tenant of Gracie's Cottage, 36–7; introduced to Conrad by EG, 37, 54; *The Brown Owl*, 47; on discovery of Conrad, 54; on Conrad's *The Sisters*, 59, 60; *Holbein, Rossetti*, 80; advice of EG on writing, 81; upset by EG, 136; and *The English Review*, 136; and R. A. Scott-James, 137; *The Simple Life Limited*, 139; EG on *Soul of London*, 139; and D. H. Lawrence, 147; on Dostoevsky Corner, 173; his *Reminiscences of Conrad*, 263–4; on his disagreement with EG and collaboration with Conrad, 263–5; on Conrad's *The Return*, 301n, 302n

Forster, E. M.: EG on *Where Angels Fear to Tread*, 101; gratitude to EG, 101–2; EG reports on short stories, 102; EG reviews *Longest Journey*, 102–3; correspondence with EG over *A Room with a View*, *Howards End*, 103–4; on EG recommending uncommercial books, 240

Frederic, Harold, on EG as reader, 37

Friends' Ambulance Unit, EG service in, 180

Frost, Robert: friendship with Edward Thomas, 184–5; EG on *North of Boston*, 184; visit to EG, 323–4n

Galsworthy, Ada: on EG as critic, 129; to EG on Leonard Woolf, 269

Galsworthy, John: EG reports on *From the Four Corners*, 109, *Jocelyn*, 110; Conrad introduces to EG, 110, 308–9n; EG advises on *Man of Devon*, 110–11; on EG and *The Pagan (The Island Pharisees)*, 111–13; EG reports on, 112; corresponds and discusses *The Man of Property* with EG, 113–14; EG appreciation of *The Country House*, 114; dispute with EG over *The Patrician*, 115–16; EG comments on *The Silver Box*, 116; as successful playwright, 116–17; and censorship agitation, 119; advises EG on *The Feud*, 122, *The Trial of Jeanne d'Arc*, 124; on EG as critic, 129, 312n; comments on *Sons and Lovers*, 156; on D. H. Lawrence, 157; and Civil List pension for Constance, 167–8; help to O'Flaherty, 215; on EG's encouragement to authors, 224; commends Henry Williamson to EG, 242; praises Williamson on Hawthornden award, 243; depicted by Williamson in *The Power and the Dead*, 243; to EG on *Sleeveless Errand* and its suppression, 256–

7; EG on death and funeral, 269; EG on choice of Marrot as biographer, 270; EG compares posthumous reputation with D. H. Lawrence, 270; EG on D. H. Lawrence's antipathy for, 272

Ganconagh, pseudonym of W. B. Yeats, 45

Garnett, Constance: her family, 10–11; at Cambridge, 11; meets Garnett family, 11; courtship of EG, 12; on EG's entry to Unwin firm, 13; approval from Dr Garnett, 13; marriage of, 14; appointed librarian at People's Palace, 14; and Fabian Society, 15; on Whitechapel, 15; and life at Henhurst Cross, 17–18; and birth of David, 20; and Russian exiles, 19–20; learns Russian and begins translations, 20; estrangement from EG, 21, 24–6, 174–5; and Stepniak, 21–2; visits Russia, 23–7; on Tolstoy, 27; on prefaces to Turgenev translations, 27; on life at Froghole, 30; and The Cearne, 30–2; on EG with typhoid, 31–2; to Conrad on *The Nigger of the Narcissus*, 69; on EG leaving Unwin, 72–3; on EG at Heinemann, 74, 76–7; on EG joining Duckworth, 77; on EG and his critical article, 87; and D. H. Lawrence, 158–9; and Russian translations, 160–73; Russian trip (1904), 167; impaired eyesight, 167; and Civil List pension, 168–9; relationship with Nellie Heath, 176–7; and H. E. Bates, 237, 278; to Cape on EG, 284; old age and death, 288; own estimation of her translations, 320n

Garnett, David: birth, 20; on *The Breaking Point, The Feud*, 123; on *Lords and Masters*, 124; on *The Trial of Jeanne d'Arc*, 126–7; trip to Russia with Constance, 167; on Civil List pension for Constance, 169; on EG and *Lady into Fox*, 195; D. H. Lawrence to on *Lady Chatterley's Lover*, 270; on EG's refusal of CH, 282; on death of EG, 283; to Cape on EG, 284

Garnett, Edward, *life*: birth, 8; family background, 9–10; courtship of Constance Black, 12–13; marriage, 14; married life in East End, 15–17; moves to Henhurst Cross, 17; early friendships, 18–19; and Russian exiles, 19; moves to The Cearne, 30; contracts typhoid, 31–2; incident with madman, 33–4; character and characteristics, 34–5; at Unwin, 40; at Heinemann, 73; at Duckworth, 77; liaison with Nellie Heath, 176–8; with Friends' Ambulance Unit in Great War, 180; at Bodley Head, 192; joins Cape firm, 193; death, 283; *publications: The Paradox Club* (novel), 16; *Light and Shadow* (novel), 16; *Imaged World* (prose-poem), 28–9, review by Yeats, 29; *Hogarth* (monograph), 81; *Wanderings in Arabia Deserta* (abridgement of *Arabia Deserta*), 83; *The Breaking Point* (play), *see* individual entry; *The Feud* (play), *see* individual entry; *Jealousy (Lords and Masters)* (play), 123; *The Spanish Lovers* (play), 123–4; *The Trial of Jeanne d'Arc* (play), 124–6; *Papa's War and Other Satires* (essays), 179; *see also* The Cearne, Censorship, and under entries for writers and publishers

Garnett, Jeremiah, 5–6

Garnett, May, sister of EG, comments on EG and marriage to Constance, 13

Garnett, Olive, sister of EG: and Stepniak, 21, 22; on Constance's character, 23; on Constance going to Russia, 23; and Stepniak

Garnett, Olive—*cont.*
on Heinemann, 27; contrasts Garnett and Black family characteristics, 28; description of The Cearne, 31

Garnett, Olivia Narney (née Singleton), mother of EG, 8

Garnett, Rayne, on EG and Nellie Heath, 177–8

Garnett, Dr Richard: father of EG, birth, 6; career at British Museum, 7; character, 7–8; and *Twilight of the Gods*, 8; as A. G. Trent, 8; family life, 8; friendships, 9; to Unwin about EG, 12; approval of Constance, 13; Meredith to about *Paradox Club*, Woodberry to about *Light and Shadow*, 16; Constance to about Froghole, 30; patriotism during Boer war, 33; EG to on Heinemann, 74–6; on EG's article *Contemporary Criticism*, 86

Garnett, Richard (1789–1850): EG's grandfather, 6; at British Museum, 7

Garnett, Thomas, 5

Garnett, William, EG's great-grandfather, 5

Gibbon, Perceval, EG reports on *Salvation*, 130

Goldring, Douglas, opinion of EG and the *English Review*, 137–8

Goodwin, Geraint, EG advises on writing, 275–7

Gordan, J. D.: on Conrad and EG connection, 58, 59; on *The Nigger of the Narcissus* manuscript, 63, 64

Gorky, M., EG on, 164

Gould, Gerald: on EG as critic of Conrad, 263; reply by EG, 263

Granville-Barker, H., *Waste* and censorship, 119

Green, Henry: on EG to David Garnett, 244; EG and *Blindness*, 245; *Mood*, 246; *Living*, 247–50; remarks on Cape, 250

Greenback Series (Duckworth), 79

Hamilton, Hamish ('Jamie'), friendship with EG, 281; EG and his marriage to Jean Forbes-Robertson, 281; on CH for EG, 282

Harrison, Frederick, and *The Breaking Point*, 118–19

Hart-Davis, Rupert: on Cape and EG, 239; and William Plomer, 286

Heath, Nellie: and Heath family, 176; on EG and Stepniak, 176; relationship with EG and Constance, 176–7; character, 177–8; death, 288; G. B. Shaw on, 332n; Ada Galsworthy on, 339n

Heath, Richard: and EG and Constance, 14; his family, 176

Heinemann, William: and first translation by Constance, 22; and Turgenev prefaces, 22–3; and Stepniak, 27; EG as reader, 74–6; and D. H. Lawrence, 144–5; on publishing Russian translations, 166, 169–71; and posthumous papers of D. H. Lawrence, 272

Hobbes, John Oliver, pseudonym Pearl Craigie, reports by EG, 43

Howard, Wren, partner of Cape, on success of Cape firm and T. E. Lawrence, 197

Howells, W. D., on EG's criticism of American novelists, 185

Hudson, W. H.: meets with EG, 78; EG on *Mr. Abel*, *El Ombu*, 78; and critical article by EG in *Academy*, 90; at the Mont Blanc, 128; and *Sons and Lovers*, 156; death, 261

Huebsch, B.: publishes James Joyce, 191; appoints EG adviser for Viking Press, 191; EG recommends O'Faolain to, 220–1; EG on H. E. Bates to, 235; asks EG about Eric Linklater, 251; enquires about Marrot, 269; and posthumous papers of D. H. Lawrence, 271–3; on Geraint

Goodwin and EG, 277–8; and Sholokhov's *The Quiet Don*, 279–81

Hueffer, Ford Madox, *see* Ford, Ford Madox

Hyde, William, illustrator of *Imaged World*, 28

James, Henry: and 'The Younger Generation', 142; on Russian writers, 319–20n

James, Norah, and *Sleeveless Errand*, 256

Jefferies, Richard: EG on, 91; biography by Edward Thomas, 131

Jepson, Edgar, and Ford Madox Ford, 137

Jewett, Sarah Orne: report by EG, 53; EG on, 93–4

'Jix', *see* Joynson-Hicks, William

Jones, Dr Tom: and Baldwin's appreciation of *Precious Bane*, 281; and literary circles, 281; and CH for EG, 282

Joyce, James: EG reports on *Portrait of the Artist as a Young Man*, 188–90; published by Huebsch, 191

Joynson-Hicks, William, and censorship, 256

Kahane, Jack, publishes *Sleeveless Errand* and censorship, 257

'Kamudi', pseudonym of Conrad, 55

Kennedy, P. C., criticism of Conrad's *Suspense*, 263

Kropotkin, Prince Peter: friendship with Garnetts, 19; EG as literary adviser to, 35–6; on Constance's eyesight, 167

Lane, John, and EG at Bodley Head, 192

Lang, Andrew: and EG, 86; as a critic, 88

Lawrence, D. H.: description of The Cearne, 31; friendship with EG and early advice, 143–4; on Heinemann, 144–5; EG and *The Trespasser*, 145–8; on Ford Madox Ford, 147; EG and *Paul Morel*, 149, *Sons and Lovers*, 150–1, *The Sisters*, 151, *The Wedding Ring*, *Women in Love*, *Rainbow*, 153–4, Hudson and Galsworthy on *Sons and Lovers*, 156; EG's critical estimation of, 157–8; EG to Pinker on 'Honour & Arms', 157; on Constance translating, 158–9; EG on *The Rainbow*, 178; sends copy of *Lady Chatterley's Lover* to EG, 270; death, 271; posthumous papers of, 271–3; EG on posthumous reputation, 270; EG on *Phoenix*, 273–4; on EG and Mollie Skinner, 333n

Lawrence, Frieda: and *The Wedding Ring*, 152; on meeting EG, 271

Lawrence, Lettice, on her brother's illness, 145–6

Lawrence, T. E., and beginning of Cape firm, 197; and publishing *Revolt in the Desert* and *Seven Pillars of Wisdom*, 197–9; EG and his suicide threat, 199; Uxbridge Notes, R.A.F. Notes, *The Mint*, 200–1; and Roy Campbell, 201; Oxford edition of *Seven Pillars*, 325n

Lawson, Henry: EG recommends for Overseas Series, 47; critical appreciation by EG, 92; advice of EG, 91–3

Linklater, Eric: on Cape, 250; on EG, 251–2; EG and the *Juan* books, 251; EG and *The Men of Ness*, 252

Longman, Charles, and Kropotkin's *Memoirs*, 35–6

Lucas, E. V.: neighbour of EG, 91; and Henry Lawson, 91, 92; O'Flaherty and the Royal Literary Fund, 215

Lynd, Robert, to EG on *Sons and Lovers*, 157

MacDonald, E. D., relationship

Macdonald, E. D.—*cont.*
with EG in editing posthumous
papers of D. H. Lawrence, 271–3
MacDonald, Ramsay, to Con-
stance on EG's death, 283
Manhood, H. A.: EG recommends
to John Wilson, 240, and Gals-
worthy, 241; to EG on Henry
Williamson, 241–2; and Cape,
242
Marrot, H. V., biographer of Gals-
worthy, 269
Marsh, Edward, opinion of EG, 282
Massingham, H. W., editor of *Na-
tion* and EG as reviewer, 106–8
Maugham, W. Somerset, EG re-
ports on *A Bad Example*, 50, *A
Lambeth Idyll*, 51–2, *The Making
of a Saint*, 52, *Daisy*, 52
Meredith, George: on *The Paradox
Club*, 16; as reader to Chapman
& Hall, 294n
Mermaid Series (Unwin), 45
Mitchison, Naomi: on meeting EG
and Cape, 254–5; frankness on
sex and Cape, 255; *Corn King*,
258; quarrel with EG, 258–9; on
EG and the novel, 259
Mont Blanc, 128
Morris, May, and Popular Library
of Art, 81
Mottram, R. H., on EG at the
Mont Blanc, 128
Mudie, C. E., circulating libraries
and publishing, 39
Murry, J. M.: to EG on Doughty,
197; and O'Flaherty, 213–14; on
EG as a critic, 259–60; on EG's
death, 283; on EG's review of *Still
Life*, 338n

Nesbit, E.: recommended by EG for
Children's Library, 48; EG re-
ports on *The Treasure Seekers*, *The
Seven Dragons*, 49

O'Faolain, Sean: on Yeats recollected by EG, 18; introduces his

work to EG, 218; advisory rela-
tionship with EG, 219; EG re-
commends to Huebsch, 220–1;
EG and *Midsummer Night's Mad-
ness*, 221, *A Nest of Simple Folk*,
221–2, *Bird Alone*, 223; dispute
with EG, 223–4
O'Flaherty, Liam: noticed by EG
for Cape, 206; EG and *The Black
Soul*, 207–9, *The Informer*, 209;
EG advises on short stories, 209–
13; his personal problems and
EG, 212–13; J. M. Murry and L.
Woolf, 214; quarrel with EG over
The Tent, 216–17; to EG on *The
Assassin*, 217–18, *Skerrett*, 218
Overseas Library Series (Unwin),
45

Panizzi, A., and Richard Garnett
(the elder), 6, (the younger), 7
Partridge, Eric, his Scholartis Press
publishes *Sleeveless Errand*, 256
Pawling, S. S.: and Conrad, 68; EG
reading for at Heinemann, 73;
Constance on, 76
Plomer, William: succeeds EG as
reader for Cape, 285; Roy Campbell on, 285–6; on EG as reader,
286–7; EG considers his work,
286
Pocock, Guy, to EG on Henry
Green, 245
Poel, William, produces excerpts
from *The Trial of Jeanne d'Arc*,
126
Poradowska, Mme Marguerite,
and Conrad, 55
Pound, Ezra, on EG's report on *Portrait of the Artist as a Young Man*,
191
Powys, J. C.: on Constance as translator, 166–7; EG and *Wolf
Solent*, 252; to EG on novel writing, 253–4
Pritchett, V. S.: on Garnett family,
10; on the publisher's reader and
EG, 287–8

Pseudonym Library (Unwin), 45
Publisher's reader, role of, 41

Radford, Ernest, and Civil List pension for Constance, 167–9
Raemaekers, Louis, *The Great War: A Neutral's Indictment*, descriptive notes by EG, 179–80
Redford, G. A., censorship of *The Breaking Point*, 118–19
Reynolds, Stephen: at the Mont Blanc, 129; *Poor Man's House* and EG, 129–30
Rhymers Club, 18, 19
Rhys, Ernest: on meeting EG and Dent, 18–19; on Rhymers Club, 18–19
Rice, David: Ford on, 40; to EG on *A Beggar and Other Fantasies*, 299n
Richardson, Dorothy, EG and *Pointed Roofs*, 187
'Rita', EG reports on *Husband of No Importance*, 49
Robins, Elizabeth, EG and *A Dark Lantern*, 107
Rutherford, Mark, *see* White, W. Hale

Sala, EG reports on *Margaret Forster*, 50
Schreiner, Olive: reports by EG, 42–3; Roy Campbell on, 202–3
Scott-James, R. A.: on Ford Madox Ford, 137; on EG, 155
Seccombe, Thomas, to EG on the Mont Blanc, 192
'Sex question', censorship and EG, 107
Shaw, G. B.: asks Constance about EG, 12; advice on *The Breaking Point*, 121–2; on Jean Forbes-Robertson and *The Trial of Jeanne d'Arc*, 126; and W. H. Davies, preface to *Autobiography of a Super-Tramp*, 133; on *The Cherry Orchard* performance, 171; and T. E. Lawrence, *Seven Pillars*, 197–8,

The Mint, 200; portrait by Nellie Heath, 322n
Sholokhov, M., EG to Huebsch on *The Quiet Don*, 279–81
Sickert, Walter, and Nellie Heath, 176
Sinclair, May, replies to advice from EG, and Greenback Library, 79–80
Skinner, Mollie: encounter with EG over *The Black Swans*, 254; D. H. Lawrence on, 333n
Stepniak, Fanny: friendship with Garnett, 35; and Dostoevsky Corner, 173
Stepniak, Sergei: friendship with Garnetts, 19; relationship with Constance, 21–2; and Turgenev prefaces, 23, 27; death, 30
Swinnerton, Frank: EG's report on *The Real Way*, 82; on EG and the novel, 95; on reception given to *The Brothers Karamazov* translation, 166; on publishing Chekhov translations, 171–2
Story of Nations Library (Unwin), 45

Thomas, Edward: on *The Feud*, 122; on EG as literary adviser, 127; meeting and friendship with EG, 131; EG advises on sketches, 131–2; and *Richard Jefferies* biography, 131; and W. H. Davies, 132–5; EG's report on *Four and Twenty Blackbirds*, 182; confides in EG on publishing difficulties, 182; character of, 182; his poems and EG, 182–4; and petition for Civil List pension, 183; joining Army and his death, 183; friendship with Robert Frost, 184–5; preface by EG in *Selected Poems*, 186
Thomas, Helen: to EG on her husband, 185–6; asks EG to write D.N.B. entry, 186
Tolstoy, L.: translations by Constance, 22, 160; described by

Tolstoy, L.—*cont.*
Constance, 26; EG on, 164; to EG on translation by Constance, 294n

Tomlinson, H. M.: EG reports on *London Clay*, *A City on the Sea*, 130-1; EG to on *Galleon's Reach*, 258n

Tonson, Jacob, *see* Bennett, Arnold

Trench, Herbert (of Haymarket Theatre), and *The Trial of Jeanne d'Arc*, 125

Turgenev, I.: translations by Constance, 161; prefaces by EG, 161-3

Unwin, Sir Stanley: on T. F. Unwin, 41; on task of publisher's reader, 41

Unwin, T. F.: publishing firm, 40; character, 41; EG as reader for, 41-54; on accepting *Almayer's Folly*, 56; Conrad's relationship with, 61; depicted as Polehampton in *The Inheritors*, 71; Philip Unwin on, 71; differences with EG, 71-2; EG leaves Unwin firm, 71-2

Vengerov, Zina: friendship with Constance, 22; on Russian visit of Constance, 24

Vernon, Frank, on censorship of *The Breaking Point*, 120-1

Viking Press: EG appointed as adviser, 205; *see also* Huebsch, B.

Volkhovsky, Felix: friendship with Garnetts, 19-20; encourages Constance to learn Russian, 20; contributions to Children's Library, 48

Wallas, Graham: friend of EG, 15; Cape and *The Art of Thought*, 205

Ward, Mrs Humphry, EG on as a novelist, 99

Webb, Mary, Stanley Baldwin and *Precious Bane*, 281

Wells, H. G.: to EG on Fabian Society, 32; and EG's early novel, 38; EG's report on *The Time Machine*, 53; correspondence with EG on *Love and Mr. Lewisham*, 104-5, *Utopia*, 105, *Ann Veronica*, 105-6, *Tono-Bungay*, 106; on EG and Turgenev, 163; to EG on Constance's eyesight, 320n

Weyman, Stanley, EG on as a novelist, 44

White, W. Hale: EG's report on *Clara Hopgood*, 54; EG on as a novelist, 99

Williamson, Henry: and H. A. Manhood, 241; and Cape, 241; Galsworthy recommends to EG, 242; on receiving Hawthornden prize, 243; and depiction of EG and Galsworthy in *The Power and the Dead*, 243-4; and T. E. Lawrence, 332n

Wilson, John, EG to on Bates, 233-4, 235; EG to on Manhood, 240

Woolf, Leonard: on EG and *The Voyage Out*, 186; and O'Flaherty, 214; Ada Galsworthy to EG on, 269

Woolf, Virginia: on Russian translations of Constance, 166; EG and *The Voyage Out*, 186-7; description of EG and Nellie Heath, 324n

Yeats, W. B.: friendship with EG, 18; and *Imaged World*, 28-9; as Ganconagh in Pseudonym Library, 45; poetry in Cameo Series, 45; and Adventure Series, 45; EG and the Irish Literary Society, 45-6

Yershov, Sasha, friend of Constance in Russia, 24, 167

Yorke, Henry, *see* Green, Henry

Young, F. B., and advice from EG, 180-1